CHARLOTTE PERKINS GILMAN

Liverpool Science Fiction Texts and Studies
General Editor
David Seed

Series Advisers
I. F. Clarke   Edward James   Patrick Parrinder
Brian Stableford

Charlotte Perkins Gilman reading, c. 1915.
Photo by Bianca Conti.
Courtesy Schlesinger Library, Radcliffe College.

CHARLOTTE PERKINS GILMAN

Her Progress Toward Utopia
with Selected Writings

Carol Farley Kessler

Liverpool University Press

Published 1995 by
LIVERPOOL UNIVERSITY PRESS
PO Box 147
Liverpool
L69 3BX

British Library Cataloguing-in-Publication Data
A British Library CIP Record is available
ISBN 0-85323-489-2 cased
ISBN 0-85323-499-X paper

Printed and bound in the United States of America

For my mother,
Emily Josephine Puder Farley,

my son,
Jonathan Farley Kessler,

and my daughter,
Melissa Beth Kessler,

with love, appreciation, and grateful thanks

CAROL FARLEY KESSLER is professor of English, American Studies, and Women's Studies at Penn State Delaware County Campus. She is author of *Elizabeth Stuart Phelps,* editor of *Daring to Dream: Utopian Stories by United States Women, 1836–1919* and *The Story of Avis* by Elizabeth Stuart Phelps, and contributor of numerous articles to *Utopian Studies, Legacy, Extrapolation, Journal of General Education,* and *Frontiers: A Journal of Women Studies.*

Contents

Acknowledgments

BOOKS ARE LONG IN THE MAKING and regularly incur more debts than an author can adequately acknowledge. But I shall try. And I hope that anyone whom I miss mentioning will understand that I am nonetheless grateful, as well as embarrassed about the omission.

First I gratefully acknowledge research support for this book from the Arthur and Elizabeth Schlesinger Library on the History of Women in America at Radcliffe College for a grant waiving the usual fees for borrowing microfiche materials; from Penn State for a sabbatical semester and for a semester supported by both a Research Development Grant and a grant from the Institute for Arts and Humanistic Studies; and from the National Endowment for the Humanities for a one-year Research Fellowship for College Teachers and Independent Scholars. I thank Janice A. Radway, Kenneth M. Roemer, and Lyman Tower Sargent for agreeing to recommend me for this fellowship. My campus administrators, Edward S. J. Tomezsko and Madlyn Hanes, have enthusiastically supported my research, as have English Department Head Robert Secor and Associate Head Kenneth Thigpen. To College of Liberal Arts Acting Dean Theodore E. Kiffer, now emeritus, one last time I offer thanks for a decade of reliable support in response to numerous requests.

Always I incur heavy debts to support staff. Librarians Sara Whildin, Susan Ware, and Jean Sphar, at Penn State's Delaware County Campus, cheerily answered questions, researched obscure data, and processed interlibrary loan requests, no matter how many times I asked. Elizabeth Shenton and Susan J. von Salis of the Arthur and Elizabeth Schlesinger Library on the History of Women in America at Radcliffe College maintained an efficient flow of numerous microfiches from the Charlotte Perkins Gilman Collection.

And typist Loretta Catanzaro prepared meticulous diskette files from partially illegible photocopies.

Finally, how could any author manage without scholars' support and readers' responses? Lyman Sargent provided detailed editorial commentary and strong support that expedited the manuscript's acceptance at Syracuse University Press. Elaine Showalter boosted my morale by requesting a reference essay on Gilman, an essay that grew into much of chapter 2 and then into the rest of this book. With respect to individual chapters, endnotes indicate where readers' suggestions have entered my text. Among the readers of chapter 2, I am grateful for the early encouragement of Joan Stevens and for the helpful suggestions of Mary Armfield Hill, Madelyn Gutwirth, Shirley Marchalonis, and Gary Scharnhorst. Chapter 3 benefited from the insightful overviews of Shirley Marchalonis, Ian Marshall, Mimi Mortimer, and Vivian Pollak, as well as from the sage advice of Madelyn Gutwirth. I am especially thankful to Jane Donawerth, Elaine Hedges, and Carol Kolmerten, who each provided essential suggestions for revising portions of this chapter. Chapter 4 is definitely better for having been read by Priscilla Ferguson Clement and Rachel Hare-Mustin, each of whom generously shared with me her particular expertise. Mary Armfield Hill requires a sentence of thanks all her own for so generously sharing, in the manner of utopian communitarian practice, her unpublished research, which exemplifies the best in feminist scholarship. Sandra Eisdorfer provided editing that ably and judiciously guided the book to its current shape, while Cynthia Maude-Gembler effectively shepherded the book that I planned into existence. My mother enthusiastically read early drafts, and Jon and M'liss unreservedly urged me forward.

Without the undergirding of the pyramid of support that I have described, this book could never have come into existence. Whatever I have individually accomplished has been developed only upon the foundations and support of others before or around me. I am grateful for the community of support that I have enjoyed. And I again thank each of the foregoing.

Quirks of interpretation or remaining errors are mine alone.

Merion, Pennsylvania   Carol Farley Kessler

CHARLOTTE PERKINS GILMAN

1

Utopian Writing as "Cultural Work"

How CHARLOTTE PERKINS GILMAN DEVELOPED her capacity to imagine a full-blown utopia for women is the focus of this book. It presents Gilman's utopian writing both in four chapters of scholarly discussion and in a fifth chapter that contains fourteen brief reprinted selections from Gilman's utopian writing. This combination of scholarship and selection of original works is essential for an understanding of Gilman because her work is so expansive, so contradictory, that selection can bias the interpretation of her work. In addition, it permits a contextual reading of utopian writing and the simultaneous practice of utopia as an act of reading. Since most of these selections from Gilman's work are not readily available, the only way to ensure that readers will be able to provide a check on interpretation and a contextual, utopian reading is by including them here. Such a blend of scholarship and texts is in the forefront of a cultural studies approach to literature.

Why Read Utopias

What is the use today of reading turn-of-the-twentieth-century utopian visions by Charlotte Perkins Gilman? In our larger societal lives, as in our individual lives, we continue repeating what we do not understand, what we have not resolved. In her writing, Gilman explored existential issues still problematic for contemporary women, especially in the correspondence with her second-husband-to-be, George Houghton Gilman. Even though she did not fully resolve problems she explicated, she delineated territory that remains for us to continue exploring and thus provides a guide for our further journey. In agreement with current scholars of utopia, myself included, who argue that utopias are guides rather than blueprints,

1

Gilman expected her writing to guide readers: she believed readers —when presented with alternatives—able to make intelligent choices to achieve changes they might desire. She advocated through the medium of her fiction numerous social changes, especially focused upon women and gender arrangements. And she embodied these ideas in character and plot.[1] She expected writing to affect readers' lives substantially.

Contemporary cultural theorists concur. Cathy N. Davidson, in *Revolution and the Word,* argues for a view of the novel that acknowledges the power of its "mimetic properties" to inspire readers (262). And Janice A. Radway, in the analysis of her study of romance reading, "Identifying Ideological Seams," observes what may also be true for any reading by women, including the reading of utopias. It is, she claims, an activity addressing the failure of patriarchy

> to provide women with the emotional care and attention it engenders them to need precisely because it asymmetrically engenders men in such a way that they cannot adequately provide that care. When looked at in this way, . . . reading can be viewed as an activity centered about an essential and potentially fatal contradiction within patriarchy[—] . . . the contradiction between its validation and sanctioning of heterosexuality and its asymmetrical engendering practices which virtually ensure that the psychological "fits" between men and women in that relationship will not be perfect, at least from the woman's point of view (113–14).

This study of Gilman reveals how one woman and man overcame at least some of this contradiction and how her fiction written after this resolution can offer alternatives to readers today.

Radway exhorts academics to "abandon the activity of writing only for academic audiences" and to make such writing "fully available and comprehensible to any woman who wanted to engage it," a reason to include Gilman's utopias in this volume (115). I agree with Radway that "a great deal is at stake here and therefore believe it essential that we begin to think of practical and political ways to *use* the information we generate analytically about the connections between forms of mass culture, real people, and consciousness" (114–15). Radway quotes Valerie Walkerdine's belief: "If wish-fulfillment through fantasy is an important device for working through conflict, then resolutions will have to be engaged with, to create possible paths for action" (118; Walkerdine 183).[2] Gilman's utopias "envision a larger pattern that [c]ould truly transform the whole" (114).[3]

Utopian fiction such as Gilman's *Herland* performs such "cultural work" as the demonstration of alternative kinds of community, a feature linking utopian communitarian fiction to what Sandra A. Zagarell has delineated as a "narrative of community."[4] She claims that the narrative of community "embrac[es] increasingly heterogeneous visions of the collective life" and "expand[s] the story of human connection and continuity" (527). More recently, Zagarell concluded that narratives of community by nineteenth-century women "might become genuine alternatives to corrosive individualism, social disintegration, opportunistic alliances, and other threats to contemporary life—become, that is, the broadly sustaining form of group life which many of our writers, as well as many social thinkers thought—and still think—community to be" (10).[5] In my view, Zagarell also states the purpose of many feminist utopian writers, including, of course, Gilman.

The statement of alternatives, whether of forms of community or of the position of gender within community, itself creates the possibility for the existence of alternatives. Erving Goffman (1974) argues that one need break or imagine breaking a frame, or social limit, only once to eradicate the prohibition against the behavior so contained.[6] This is both the power and the danger of utopian writing, of the human imagination functioning in society. This is why in Plato's *Republic* the poet was feared as a dangerous person, why twentieth-century dictators control all communications media. It is also why feminist thought is rightly feared by members of an established status quo, for, as Catharine Stimpson makes eminently clear, "even for utopian thinking, feminism is ambitious" (2).

Although readers may be tempted to discount as unrealistic many of Gilman's suggestions for social transformation, those in her more realistic stories and novels, as well as those in articles, represent astute and realizable visions of change that people could begin to approach. For Gilman, utopian writing was her "sensational design" (to use Jane Tompkins' words) for the transformation of women's condition in the United States, if not the world. If Ursula Le Guin, in *Always Coming Home* (1985), teaches us, in the words of Lee Cullen Khanna, "not to dedicate [ourselves] to some absolute utopian vision, but rather to make and unmake multiple worlds, to learn to experiment with alternative realities" (133), we as readers can approach Gilman's writing with a comparable awareness of possible changes always in process.[7] We are readers of the late twentieth century, influenced as much as Gilman by the intellectual climate of our times, a social chaos offering possibilites for new directions, tempered by a knowledge that ideology both limits and enables.[8] I hope to suggest that Gilman's living and writing surely deserve our consideration as available sets of realizable possibilities.

This study recasts Charlotte Perkins Gilman: it presents the *literary woman* as social activist, a foregrounding of her literary action, making her writing a center for her living.[9] *Herland,* after all, is a "no place" of the imagination; short fiction from Gilman's magazine *The Forerunner* is just that—short, not yet conceptualized to the extent of novelistic worlds. But in the 1897–1900 correspondence between Charlotte Perkins Gilman and George Houghton Gilman, Charlotte told the truth about her life in a way that she had previously been unable to do, so that at last in the texts of these letters she could "herself become a mentor," as Carolyn Heilbrun insightfully notes Gilman could not be in her autobiography, *The Living of Charlotte Perkins Gilman.*[10] As Gilman matured, her writing, like her living, was an ongoing activity, the two inseparably intertwined.[11] To grasp this blend, readers require access to her texts themselves. In Gilman's living and utopian writing, she becomes—in what she recommends, and even more in her persisting effort to find ways to reframe and rearrange living—a potential model for readers today. To ask perfection of her or of her utopias, any more than of ourselves, is I hope an understood impossibility.

What "Cultural Work" Is

Charlotte Perkins Gilman wrote both to explicate problems of human existence and to gain relief from her own experience of them. Such writing can empower both author and reader. In particular, Gilman's utopian writing, both fiction and nonfiction, is especially instructive, since this didactic genre can illuminate Gilman's practice as well as reveal transformational possibilities of writing and reading. Gilman might even be said to carry on a dialogic relationship with her readers, whom she invites to join in the dialogue both verbally and behaviorally, with the end of enacting possibilities she illuminates. Thus the possibilities under consideration here are both the *techne* of writing and the *praxis* of living. As Gilman writes, she constructs her life and offers readers alternative models for human lives.

We can construe the articulation of these alternative models as the "cultural work" of Gilman's utopian writing—culture being understood as a system of beliefs, values, and ideas about a society's people and objects that provides meaning and organization for a way of life (Geertz 1973). Jane Tompkins suggests that we can speak of the "cultural work" of texts as an "attempt to redefine the social order" (1985, xi), that literary texts do work in the sense of explaining and shaping the social context that produces them (200). Tompkins further argues that we should study novels and stories "because they offer powerful examples of the way a culture thinks about itself, articulating and proposing solutions for the problems that shape a particular historical moment" (xi).[12] Like her great-aunt Harriet Beecher Stowe, included in Tompkins' study, Gilman wrote "to win the belief and influence the behavior of the widest possible audience": she had "designs upon her audiences, in the sense of wanting to make people think and act in a particular way" (xi).

Thus a complex communication process ensues when fiction emerges from an author's life and moves into that of a reader. It includes five components: the world that the author experiences, the author, her text, the reader, and the world that the reader experiences. This study includes the first three components, with the focus equally divided between author and text.[13] Although in our society gender relationships are unequal and connection is devalued compared to individuation, the cultural work of texts such as Gilman's is to recode such connection as valued. Including a selection of her texts permits the communication process to move full circle to encompass the remaining two components of the process, readers and their worlds. These last two are the site of cultural work, the utopian change that Gilman hoped her writing would effect.

This study of utopian writing simulates an ethnography in its investigation of Gilman's writing as a social process, which investigation then becomes available to a set of readers as their social process. Gilman through her texts—public and personal, published and handwritten—thus functions as my informant. I have "quot[ed] her] often" and tried to "be as conscious and as open as possible about the context and the purposes that are guiding [my] observations and constructions" (Radway 1986, 105).[14] Equally in my mind are readers for whom this text then becomes an informant and whose lives the text may have the potential for changing. Instead of abstract ideas, fiction presents to our imaginations concrete possibilities that we may not have realized. It can incite us to actualize these ideas in our real lives; thus the fiction functions as a model.[15]

In her 1910 study called *Our Androcentric Culture; or, The Man-Made World,* Gilman devoted one chapter to discussing what she labeled "Masculine Literature." Here Gilman explains her understanding that readers would more readily accept nontraditional views if they were presented as stories illustrating possibilities for future action. In her fiction, Gilman "re-presented" her ideas clothed as characters. She explains this view of the social function of literature thus:

> The thought of the world is made and handed out to us in the main. The makers of books are the makers of thoughts and feelings for people in general. Fiction is the most popular form in which this world-food is taken. If it were true, it would teach us life easily, swiftly, truly; teach not by preaching but by truly *re-presenting* [my italics]; and we should grow up becoming acquainted with a far wider range of life in books than could even be ours in person. Then meeting life in reality we should be wise [be utopian or "bee-wise," the title of a 1913 short story]—and not be disappointed (21).

Gilman subscribes to a literature that can be called cultural work, can enact social changes, can function as social action, can convey alternative versions or visions of human action—a position of clear self-consciousness regarding literary didacticism.[16]

In her utopian fiction, Gilman advocated changes in gender. The Russian cultural critic M[ikhail] M[ikhailovitch] Bakhtin (1895–1975) reminds us that

> in our enthusiasm for specification we have ignored questions of interconnection and interdependence of various areas of culture; we have frequently forgotten that the boundaries of these areas are not absolute, that in various epochs they have been drawn in various ways; and we have not taken into account that *the most intense and productive life of culture takes place on the boundaries of its individual areas* and not in places where these areas have become enclosed in their own specificity (1986, 2).[17]

This productivity of culture then occurs exactly along such boundaries as gender, and utopia becomes a primary locus for culture-creation or cultural work. By refusing to accept definitions of traditional male (dominant) and female (subordinate) roles and instead offering clear alternatives to such mainstream notions, Gilman forces readers to question boundaries defining behavior assumed acceptable on the basis of gender; many of her views are still in the 1990s ahead of much social practice. The cultural work, then, of the utopian fiction of Charlotte Perkins Gilman is proclaiming the belief that the female half of humanity not be confined to one traditional mode of being—wife/motherhood, but fill as varied social roles as male counterparts, that the female work of society be valued equally with that of the male.

How "Utopia" Is Now Defined

And what of this term *utopia* or *eutopia?* Never in this book is *utopia* used to mean "unrealistic," "fantastic," or "impractical." *Utopia* is the generic term for an imagined society, after the 1516 eponymous work by Sir Thomas More. The word is a pun on *ou* (after the Greek for "no") and *eu* (after the Greek for "good"); *topus* means "place" in Greek. Thus *eutopia* is the ideal "no place" of the imagination, the possible "good place," better than the author's current society; *dystopia* is the "bad place," a deterioration of the author's current society.[18] Scholarship also defines *utopia* as a fictionalized society in the process of becoming better, though not perfect; such fictions are guides toward, not blueprints for, utopia. In keeping with a feminist viewpoint, process, not product—with an emphasis upon means more than ends or goals—is the focus. The book's subtitle, "progress toward utopia," foregrounds this focus.

A useful new concept in utopian studies is that of the realizable, possible, or achievable utopia, called "pragmatopia" by Riane Eisler and defined as a "realizable scenario for a partnership future" (198).[19] Eisler uses the term *partnership* to name a principle of organization that lacks the domination hierarchy of male over female that is typical of patriarchal societies (105).[20] In fact the concept of power, in partnership as opposed to hierarchical organizations, undergoes change. Barbara Bellow Watson, in "On Power and the Literary Text," defines three types of power. In addition to (1) power as dominance, she adds (2) power as ability or competence and (3) power as energy (113). Eisler offers yet another category, (4) power as affiliation, partnership, or cooperation (193).[21] And Elise Boulding, discussing the "heritage of utopianism" residing in "images from Antiquity," describes what I will call (5) power as imagination,

the power emanating from utopian imagery (1988, 7–11). She finds
that even "well-known warrior societies" in their images of an "idealized social order" "have in commmon an idea of human togeth-
erness and sharing" (7). The warriors come to embody "both
nurturant and assertive traits of humanity" (7). They become nonsexist partners in society. Boulding finds that the common images
are "the world as a family" and as "the peaceable garden" (10, 11).
Humanity has dreamed of and realized arriving on the moon; we
have also dreamed of peaceable families and gardens, and we can
realize these if we will, our utopian thinkers tell us.

The achievable partnership society that Boulding and Eisler
define was already present in Gilman's imagination as revealed in
her turn-of-the-century novels and short stories: the alternative or
partner-oriented gender roles she depicts *could be* realized or
achieved then or in the present-day society that we know. To convey
her view, Gilman relies not upon fantasy in the *Forerunner* short
stories, but upon realism. But she uses realism subversively, her
"design" for effecting the cultural work of her utopian fiction. Most
often, as Anne Cranny-Francis reminds us, realism is the narrative
mode employed to naturalize ideology into the lives of readers
(137).[22] In what I suggest are additional versions of cultural work,
Cranny-Francis claims that texts may (1) encourage the mainte-
nance of a status quo—that is, may make what is ideology appear
as if derived from natural order—as well as (2) encourage the social
transformation that is the goal of utopian writers. Thus Gilman, in
a realistic mode, seeks to dislodge traditional gender ideology by
presenting alternative, realizable possibilities for more egalitarian
gender roles: critics of utopias typically decry their alternative pos-
siblities by alleging how unrealistic they are.[23] What critics may
mean is that they are afraid of the implications of these possibilities:
they would lose power, feel too guilty, have to accept responsibility,
have to give up comfortable habits, have to learn new roles as nur-
turers, have to become the servants they wish to be served by, and
so forth.[24]

In Gilman's utopianism, a discourse of possibility (or realizability) collides with a discourse of realism, completely changing the
latter. It is this quality of realizability that I wish to examine in
Gilman's utopian writing, both as a strategic process, cultural
work, and as an imagined product, "realizable utopia," all the while
remembering that utopian writing is today conceptualized not as
blueprint, but as alternative or future possibility; that what we

imagine today does move us toward how we act tomorrow; that through our choices in the present we voluntarily shape our future history.[25]

What This Study Discusses

Short utopian texts collected at the end of this volume are especially useful for demonstrating Gilman's writing strategies. However, to understand any examples of writing, all of which are cultural artifacts, we need as good ethnographers to understand the cultural context from which these artifacts emerged. In particular, we need as background two kinds of information: first, a knowledge of the writer's life, work, and era; and second, a general overview of the category of her writing under consideration, in this case, her utopian writing. What follows, therefore, are three chapters, each a journey of exploration: first, an overview of Gilman's life; second, a survey of her utopian writing; and third, a review of the first two, illuminating connections between them. These three journeys contextualize Gilman's feminist utopia, *Herland,* with biography and lesser-known utopian writing.

The first journey, in chapter 2, "Making Herself: A Biographical Exploration," delineates four problematic areas of Gilman's life that the fourth chapter will demonstrate to have influenced her utopian writing, all problems concerning her connections to others: a compelling legacy of ancestral expectations; her relationships to father, mother, and daughter; the experience of two marriages and a divorce; and her friendships with women. In her fiction, Gilman offers possible solutions for psychological malaise emanating from gender relationships, as the fourth chapter will clarify. Thus chapter 2 provides needed biographical context.

Charting Charlotte Perkins Gilman's progress from her first overtly utopian essay, "The Beauty of the Block" in 1904, to her full-blown utopia for women, the 1915 *Herland,* is the subject of the second journey, in chapter 3, " 'This Prancing Young Utopia.' " This chapter contextualizes *Herland* in terms of Gilman's utopian writing. It focuses upon her writings between 1904 and 1921, her most prolific period, which is contemporaneous with a presumably supportive second marriage and includes her single-handed editing of her magazine, the *Forerunner,* from 1910 through 1916. It delineates three stages in the development of her utopian imagination. First, she imagined small social units up to the level of neighborhoods, writing alternately fiction and nonfiction. Second, she tested in fiction, especially in *Forerunner* short stories, the expression of utopian principles explained in her nonfiction, including ideas expanded in other writings. Finally, she created the whole society, the 1915 *Herland.* The earlier writing represents Gilman's presentation in realistic fiction of solutions that she had recommended in her 1898 feminist treatise, *Women and Economics: The Economic Factor Between Men and Women as a Factor in Social Evolution.*

The third journey through Gilman's life, in chapter 4, "Writing to Empower Living," examines the fit between Gilman's living and her utopian writing. Although her insights regarding social realities are impressive, even more so is her experience in living them out. Her biography reveals numerous possible stumbling blocks to creativity in work and life. In her writing, from her ten-year-old "Literary and Artistic Vurks [*sic*] of the Princess Charlotte" through her 75-year-old *The Living of Charlotte Perkins Gilman,* she created herself. Her dialogue with readers continues, reestablished by current reprinting of her work. Especially in the realm of relations between the sexes, her critique of social life remains cogent. As significant is her legacy of living, itself a model for women's experimentation in social possibilities.

As readers, we need to be aware of the experiential conditions of Gilman's life in order to avoid inadvertent misreading of her work. For example, *Women and Economics* is not inspired primarily by anger toward patriarchy, although it does express such anger. Nor can *Herland* be read solely as a paean to a female separatist society, however much it is exactly this. This third chapter suggests connections among "The Yellow Wallpaper," *Women and Economics,* the *Forerunner* short stories, *Herland, With Her in Ourland,* and *The Living of Charlotte Perkins Gilman.* "The Yellow Wallpaper," a reversal of the positive *Herland,* reveals part of the context to which *Herland* responds. *Women and Economics* states in the abstract what *Herland,* along with *With Her in Ourland* and the *Forerunner* short stories, make concrete in plot and character. And *The Living of Charlotte Perkins Gilman* offers in heroic proportion an autobiographical self expected to save readers from experiencing the anguish conveyed in "The Yellow Wallpaper." In fact, Mary A. Hill's forthcoming selection of correspondence between Charlotte Perkins Gilman and George Houghton Gilman provides a real-life model of one courageous woman's conflicted effort to actualize possibilities for women that she would later imagine in her utopian writing:

chapter 4 provides a detailed discussion of these letters as background.

Following these three interpretative chapters is a final chapter, " 'Making Better People': Experiencing Gilman's Legacy." A brief introduction is followed by fourteen selections from Gilman's utopian writing, each prefaced by a headnote, thirteen representing utopian fiction that is currently out of print (eleven titles from the *Forerunner* plus two earlier) as well as one chapter from *Herland*. (Selections retain the vagaries of Gilman's usage.) Cross-referenced to chapter three as each selection is discussed, they enable readers to experience for themselves otherwise difficult-to-locate works by Gilman. This combination of scholarship and selections of original works is, I believe, essential for an understanding of Gilman, because her work is so expansive, so contradictory, that scholarly selection risks biasing the interpretation of her work. The blend of scholarship and selections seems to me more valid than a text of scholarship alone, and better exemplifies an awareness of the tentative nature of interpreting cultural documents. What's more, ending with Gilman's writing places theorizing in the background: the focus is upon her life and work, theoretical concepts introduced by way of explication.[26]

How This Book Evolved

Charlotte Perkins Gilman: Her Progress Toward Utopia, with Selected Writings grew from what was to have been a one-chapter case study of Gilman in a survey of utopian writing by women in the United States. But treating Gilman adequately required a book devoted solely to her. The book's direction changed as it evolved. I began with the hypothesis that the published utopian writing itself had functioned as a primary healing process for Gilman. Ann J. Lane, in discussing Gilman's correspondence with her second husband in *To "Herland" and Beyond,* suggests that Gilman's healing began while writing these letters (chap. 8). But Mary Armfield Hill's interpretation of private letters written to Houghton Gilman by Charlotte Perkins Gilman actually convinced me that this correspondence is in fact the primary locus of much of the enabling inner healing that underlies Gilman's capacity to envision women less as victims (as in "The Yellow Wallpaper") than as potentially victorious agents of social reform (as in *Herland* and other utopian fiction).[27] Therefore, I quote these letters sufficiently to demonstrate the process of healing that Hill maps and to document Gilman's changed vision, which I present as a foundation for the utopian writing I discuss. The utopian writing, then, did not initiate the process of Gilman's healing as I had supposed, but is more the outcome—perhaps also the continuation—of such healing.

Whether Gilman's utopian writing continued or instigated her healing, it has the potential to initiate ours. For us, reading at the turn of the twenty-first century, Gilman's utopian fiction might guide us into transitional spaces that could encourage our passages to other worlds. We, too, can progress toward utopia in reading fiction that asks us as readers to imagine other possibilities for the conduct of our lives. Contemporary scholars of utopia stress the concept that utopias are not finished, perfect places, but rather open-ended sets of possibilities in the process of becoming, alternatives about to be realized, which are beginning to emerge even as we read such utopian texts. A change of mental framework or standpoint can lead in time to comparable behavioral change. This view emphasizes the political potential of reading. We readers can participate in the process that utopian writing, such as Gilman's, initiates. The inclusion of fourteen selections permits readers both to appreciate Gilman's achievement and to participate in their own progress toward utopia.

For so important a person, Gilman has been grossly under-studied. Although numerous articles discuss *Herland,* none focuses upon placing this work within the context of Gilman's life and utopian writing as a whole. Thus this book addresses what has been a scholarly void. Gilman is beginning to receive the acclaim she deserves. Ann Lane has completed a biography (1990) and has written a new introduction for *The Living of Charlotte Perkins Gilman* (1990). A nonfiction reader, a collection of critical essays, and two collections of readings on "The Yellow Wallpaper" are available. Two mass-circulation collections exist. Mary Hill has selected and interpreted key letters from Gilman's 1897–1900 courtship correspondence with her second husband, George Houghton Gilman (forthcoming). The current volume joins an incoming tide of overdue recognition for the achievement of Charlotte Perkins Gilman.[28]

2

Making Herself
A Biographical Exploration

IN A 1903 POEM, "TWO CALLINGS," Charlotte Perkins Gilman suc-
cinctly joined for women the Home and the World, two spheres then
separately allocated by gender to women and men, respectively:
"Home was the World—the World was Home to me!" (*The Home,*
xi).[1] In her utopian writing, she sought to join into one sphere what
for the majority of nineteenth-century, middle-class women in the
United States were ideologically separate. Gilman managed such
integration in her own life with less ease than her words suggest,
as this chapter's discussion will demonstrate. Nevertheless, she left
a prodigious seventy-five year accomplishment of writing and living: by her death in 1935, she had to her credit twelve books of
verse, fiction, and polemic—as well as a nine-volume serial, written
entirely by herself (this last, also including drama): in total, she
produced, by her calculation, the equivalent of thirty books (SLR
Folder 16).[2] In this writing, she strove to join home and world both
for herself and for women in general.

Well recognized during her lifetime, Gilman was named on lists
of the ten or twelve greatest United States women. Gilman stood at
the intellectual, as opposed to the activist, helm of the broader
women's rights movement during the first two decades of the twentieth century.[3] She was an evolutionary (Fabian) rather than a revolutionary (Marxist) socialist and feminist: although she herself
preferred the labels "humanist" or "sociologist" to "feminist" (Degler in *Women and Economics,* vi–vii), in 1932 she apparently permitted an advertising circular to label one course of six lectures
"The Larger Feminism" (DLC, Benjamin Huebsch Papers, Container 10). By her death in 1935, she had delivered so many lectures

on ethics, economics, and sociology that she had lost count. Lecture-tours during which she gave sermons and stump speeches, spoke at conventions, and made club appearances took her to nearly every state in the Union and to many western European countries as well. She met numerous notables of the Western world. Yet even with such impressive achievement and recognition, as late in her life as 1917, when she was fifty-eight and after her major writing was complete, Gilman nonetheless wondered whether she had accomplished enough to justify her existence and thought she needed "a few more books" (SLR Folder 16).

Although Gilman most often concluded with self-justification, again and again in her private writing she queried herself concerning the sufficiency of her achievement. Underlying her marked public success ran a darker current of private self-doubt. This would ground her soaring mind, once with a depression of several years; thereafter her depression was an intermittent though less severe tax on her energy. A residue of nineteenth-century self-righteous perfectionism, a legacy from her New England ancestors, left her unable to mitigate the excessive emotional demands that she felt compelled to set upon herself, with a substantial expense of energy. Though we may marvel at her lifework, we must recognize a harshly relentless and unreasonable pattern of self-criticism, apparent even as she records the facts of her birth in her autobiography *The Living of Charlotte Perkins Gilman* (1935).

Early Years, 1860–1882

Gilman was born Charlotte Anna Perkins in Hartford, Connecticut, on the afternoon of 3 July 1860.[4] Of this birthdate, she bemoaned, "If only I'd been a little bit slower and made it the glorious Fourth! This may be called the first misplay in a long game that is full of them" (*Living*, 8), but the humorous tone of her negatives does not eliminate her self-denigration. At birth, Gilman inherited an illustrious and notorious lineage, but also one that bequeathed her conflicting models for womanhood. Her parents were Frederick Beecher Perkins (1826–1899), scion of the noted Beecher family, and Mary A. Fitch Westcott (1828–1893), a descendant of one of Rhode Island's founders—a New England heritage which made her feel proud, but also responsible. From the paternal Beecher-Perkins side of her lineage, she received a relentlessly demanding legacy: to take pride in her womanhood (although opposing models existed), to courageously assert her own viewpoint, to be fearless in the face of censure, and to achieve through serving society at large. In contrast, her mother, Mary A. Fitch Westcott, brought a heritage more traditionally feminine, though comparably independent-minded.

A survey of Gilman's relatives from both parents' family trees indicates secure social standing within a white, Anglo-Saxon, protestant middle class, with ministers, lawyers, and educators predominating: hers was a legacy from the New England region's cultural arbiters, a genteel position, albeit with very restricted financial means. Heading Gilman's paternal ancestry was the Congregational pastor Lyman Beecher (1775–1863), her great grandfather. His only child not in public life, daughter Mary Foote Beecher (1805–1900), was Gilman's grandmother: with some irony in view of Gilman's "carr[ying] the Beecher sisters' legacy into the twentieth century," Mary's life closely approximated the domestic ideal of true womanhood; she even refused entrance to her sister Isabella Beecher Hooker because of the latter's association with suffragists (Boydston, 357).[5] In 1827, she had married Hartford lawyer Thomas C. Perkins, who later took as law partner his second son, Charles. Mary's first son was Gilman's father, Frederick. Frederick's sister Emily (Gilman's favorite aunt and one of Lyman Beecher's granddaughters) married Edward Everett Hale (1822–1909), Unitarian minister and author of such utopias as *Sybaris and Other Homes* (1869), a book that gave Gilman an early model of utopian writing, as did his household a model of "how lovely family life could be" (*Living*, 31).[6] Later, he helped Gilman by introducing her to wealthy and cultured Rhode Island families.[7] Another sister of Gilman's father, her Aunt Katherine, married William C. Gilman; they were the parents of Gilman's second husband, George Houghton Gilman (1867–1934), who was thus a first cousin.

These relatives were important to Gilman's future life, as were past legacies from several Beecher notables (of whom her father was a nephew): Catharine Beecher (1800–1878), Harriet Beecher Stowe (1811–1896), Isabella Beecher Hooker (1822–1907), and Henry Ward Beecher (1813–1887). Catharine wrote *Treatise on Domestic Economy, For the Use of Young Ladies at Home and at School* (1841), and with her sister Harriet wrote the even more popular *The American Woman's Home* (1869), an advice book expanding the home economics *Treatise*. Harriet morally galvanized a nation in 1852 by writing *Uncle Tom's Cabin,* and later scandalized genteel society on both sides of the Atlantic with an exposé of Lord Byron's incest, *Lady Byron Vindicated* (1870). Isabella, also outspoken, crusaded for women's emancipation and sided openly with radical feminists against her brother Henry, an eminent New York preacher, who gained notoriety for a sex scandal involving a female parishioner.[8] Such was Gilman's diverse paternal legacy, one offering her challenging, albeit conflicting, models for being a woman.

In contrast, her mother, Mary Westcott, was more traditional in her conception of woman as mother and homemaker. But the fact of single motherhood would require her to live out the concept differently from the tradition and with considerable independence. She was the frail child of a June-December marriage, a descendant of Stukely Westcott, settler with Roger Williams of the Providence Plantations, populated by dissenters from the Puritan religious orthodoxy in Massachusetts. Her elderly father, Henry Westcott, a courageous and pacifist Unitarian, practiced incorrigible benevolence at the expense of his family, a pattern of nonsupport that her own husband would follow. As a widower, he took a fifteen-year-old second wife, Mary's spoiled and petted mother, Clarissa Fitch Perkins, who was eighteen when Mary was born. Mary became her father's darling, and since her mother permitted her to accept the attentions of a succession of admiring beaux, Mary grew to expect others to dote upon her.

In 1857, when Mary Westcott was twenty-nine, she married a second cousin, Frederick Beecher Perkins, a linguist, scholar, and professional librarian, who was an intellectual model for their daughter Charlotte. (On the rebound from a broken engagement, he apparently was attracted by Mary's resemblance to this former beloved.) But, with the birth of Gilman in July 1860 and, fourteen months later, her brother Thomas Adie Perkins on 9 May 1859—and with the deaths in infancy of two additional children (Hill 1980, 22)—Frederick left his family, perhaps in response to a physician's warning that Mary could not survive another pregnancy. Since he did not return, Mary divorced her husband in 1873 expressly so that he might remarry if he wished. That same year, he became assistant director of the Boston Public Library, and from 1880 to 1894 he headed the San Francisco Public Library. But not until 1894, after Mary's 1893 death, did Frederick return East to marry his cousin and first love, the widow Frankie Johnson Beecher, whose engagement to him had years before been broken by her family (Hill 1980, 21).

The facts of Gilman's precarious childhood can only increase our appreciation for her achievement. She grew up in a fatherless, itinerant household, only sporadically financed by Frederick. Money was constantly in short supply. Although she came of a socially prominent family, her mother, as a divorced woman with two children to support, lived close to poverty much of the time. Gilman records in her autobiography that the family moved "nineteen times in eighteen years, fourteen of them from one city to another" (*Living*, 8). Though Mary had "a natural genius for teaching little ones" (SLR Folder 234), she was able to find only intermittent employment. As a "poor relation" in a prominent family, Mary and her children resided in one household, then another. But after the divorce, considered a disgrace by the family, she was no longer welcome. In 1873, she went to Providence to care first for her dying grandmother and then for her dying mother. A single mother with no income, she next lived for a year and one-half with a Swedenborgian cooperative housekeeping group that disbanded in 1876. A rebellious sixteen-year-old at the time, Gilman intensely disliked this residence, and throughout her adult life, she continually voiced her dislike of cooperative ventures.[9]

Perhaps even harder than these moves for a growing child was Mary's ill-conceived effort to save her daughter from the emotional deprivation she had known: by withholding physical expressions of affection, Mary hoped to suppress the need for it. Gilman reported that "her caresses were not given unless [Thomas and I] were asleep, or she thought us so" (*Living*, 23). Gilman knew little tenderness—"Never [any] from anyone, and I did want it" (*Living*, 31). In addition, her mother feared the rich and active fantasy life that Gilman had developed as a successful coping strategy. Gilman early felt a utopian impulse toward creating within what might be lacking without. But her mother, apprehensive about "what she was led [by a friend with a pre-Freudian mind] to suppose this inner life might become," forbad Gilman the fantasy world she "industriously construct[ed]" in her imagination (*Living*, 23). This world is visible in "The Literary and Artistic Vurks [*sic*] of the Princess Charlotte," an unpublished manuscript written in 1870 when Gilman was ten. These early unfulfilled yearnings emerge as a child's utopia, especially in the character Elmondine, heroine of "A Fairy Story," who befriends other women. The tale suggests that female peers are good, older males good but helpless, and older females bad or useless (SLR Volume 12).

Mary also deluged Gilman with "ceaseless criticism" and withheld permissions—for instance, to go out with friends, especially if male (C. W. Stetson, quoted by Hill *Endure* 113); in sum, Mary wanted Gilman well within her control. To protect herself against being disappointed by her mother's refusals, Gilman developed a tactic of self-denial. As a result, she required years of adult living before she could easily accept invitations, so persistent were these emotional scars. On the one hand, Gilman's diary entries indicate a high-spirited individual who does not appear to be unduly burdened. Her energy and intelligence seem to have sustained her as a young-ster, but the tendency to depression as an adult may well have had one source in these emotional deficits in her maternal relationship. On the other hand, the dissatisfaction that Gilman must have felt, given the emotional deficits she experienced, also provided fertile ground for an adult growth of utopian fantasy and social activism.

A bright child, Gilman was better able to compensate for her intermittent education—"four years, among seven different institu-tions, ending when I was fifteen" (*Living,* 18). Although she never shone as a student, she impressed teachers with the fund of knowl-edge she had gleaned from the wide reading her father sometimes guided. (Throughout her childhood, Gilman tried to garner her fa-ther's attention through correspondence: very occasional letters and reading lists were the extent of his response; she knew him person-ally only during the 1890s.) Gilman attests in her autobiography to regularly reading the children's magazine *Our Young Folks* (1865–1873), which was edited by poet and author Lucy Larcom (1824–1893), as well as novels by antisuffragist Mrs. Adeline Dutton Train Whitney (1824–1906) and prosuffragist Louisa May Alcott (1832–1888), all three creators of heroines who triumph (*Living,* 19, 35, 64). Such moral stories, though soon out of fashion, Gilman believed "immensely useful in forming ethical standards" (SLR Folder 234).

Gilman and her mother together read and wept over sentimen-tal novels, bonding them to each other and affirming of their female-ness (Hill 1980, 60). Although sentimental heroines often enacted self-defeating female roles, Nina Baym has demonstrated that these novels could empower women readers through the heroine's final triumph, albeit over her many trials.[10] Gilman's youthful reading, often with her mother, early revealed to her the power of words to shape action, even the power of words as a form of action in the world—Burkean "equipment for living."[11] This reading with her mother was a positively formative influence upon her later utopian writing, one of which Gilman seems to have been unaware. Her

1915 utopia *Herland* would elevate motherhood to be the most revered national occupation, with nurturance (not competition) the ruling stance toward others, vindicating her mother's, as well as her own much later, maternal experience. But instead of the positive, Gilman stressed the negative in her autobiography, noting her mother's "painfully thwarted" life, a condition that she herself would not completely surmount (*Living*, 8).[12]

During her late teens, Gilman pursued a blend of formal training, self-directed improvements, and gainful employment. In 1878, she attended the Rhode Island School of Design, with her mother's reluctant approval and her father's willingness "to pay the fees" (*Living*, 45).[13] While there she gained sufficient skill that in 1883, one of her watercolors was accepted for a juried exhibit. At about this time, Gilman also followed self-directed programs of physical culture and spiritual development. She instituted for herself five rules of health, which she conscientiously observed: plenty of good air, exercise, food, and sleep, but as little clothing as possible— this last representing a stand for dress reform and against weighty Victorian garments. She found several ways of earning money: giving drawing lessons, selling floral watercolors, and painting advertising cards for a soap company. A ten-week position as a governess in Maine during the summer of 1883 pleased her less: caring for a spoiled little boy and performing duties of a maid left too little time for her own pursuits.

Gilman's attachments were varied. Although she enjoyed the attentions of numerous young swains, her closest friends came from a circle of young women: some were fellow participants at a women's gymnasium in Providence that she had established, some were associated with Brown University, and some were affiliated with Beecher relatives. The deepest emotional tie of these years was to Martha Luther (1862–1948). During the summer of 1881, Gilman wrote almost daily letters to Martha, an intensely affectionate correspondence—"friendly *(not intimate)*,"—that has survived (italics hers, quoted in Langley 58). She asked Martha, "Why in the name of heaven have we so confounded love with passion that it sounds to our century tutored ears either wicked or absurd to name it between women?" (quoted in Langley 59). Gilman experienced a profound sense of loss upon Martha's engagement in 1881 and subsequent marriage in 1882 to Charles A. Lane (1851–1894).[14] A letter to Martha in January 1890 indicates how hurt Gilman had felt by Martha's marriage. She wrote, "I loved you better than anyone" and admitted to harboring "only audacious fancies" (quoted in Langley, 63). Nevertheless, the friendship endured throughout Gilman's lifetime. Her relationships with women provide additional instances of the positive feelings women felt free to express to each other (see Smith-Rosenberg).Gilman's utopian *Herland* expands upon these positive, loving experiences between women.

First Marriage, 1882–1891

On 12 January 1882, Gilman met Charles Walter Stetson (1858–1911), a budding artist, whom, she confided to her diary, she found "an original: eccentric because unconventional, and well versed in almost everything, I guess!" (SLR Volume 18). However, in a February 20 letter to Walter, Gilman acknowledged her resistance: she did not desire to follow the "precedent of centuries" of women in choosing marriage over a profession, but intended to pursue her goal of sacrificing personal pleasure to doing good and serving the world (Hill 1980, 97). Her journal entry for September 10 indicates that she was continuing the fiction-writing begun when ten: she notes reading to Walter her novel when he visits, but no known trace remains today of this early work (SLR Volume 18).

Given her aspirations, Gilman vacillated for two years between desire for marriage and fear of it. Ironically, as she debated Walter, she was not able to imagine for herself what we now call a dual-career marriage. In this respect, her thinking at this time was bound to nineteenth-century notions of "true womanhood," however astutely she would in the future critique the inequities of women's narrowly restricted social place. Gilman also complained that Walter was not "such a friend as I have already"—presumably Martha Luther Lane, who accepted Gilman just as she was (Langley 66). By March 6, Gilman wanted him to wait a year or so, to give her back to herself (SLR Folder 39); by August 30, she had come to feel herself his property (SLR Volume 18). By New Year's Eve, she was determined not to marry: she saw herself as willful, solitary, and self-reliant, and she felt strong and powerful enough to pursue her goal of sacrificing personal pleasure to doing good and serving the world (SLR Volume 18).

By mid-March 1883, Walter noted how "improved" Gilman was: he delighted to find her "not the strongly independent creature she was a year ago"! (Hill 1985, 139). He felt he must stop her from her goal of fame and freedom, that she must become less selfish (Hill

1985, 147, 157ff). Yet his own arrogance astounds, especially as he made her refuse a gift copy of Walt Whitman's *The Leaves of Grass* because he judged it too coarse for her (Hill 1985, xxx, 201–2). (It would become one of the two books, along with Olive Schreiner's *Dreams,* that Gilman always carried on her travels.)[15] By mid-May 1883, when Walter's self-esteem was damaged by learning from a respected reader that his sonnets were no better than "slight," Gilman's sympathy decided her in his favor, though she required him to delay marriage for one year (SLR Volume 18; Hill 1985, 187). She feared she could not give her whole self to Walter, as she stereotypically believed a woman should, because she felt the Beecher call to a larger world service: she was just then determining that for her this would be reform of women's condition in society.

Walter seemed to pursue Gilman under the assumption that, because he loved her, she must of course return the feeling, that his love gave him a right to her. Like so many men of his era, he fondly expected that a wife would support and inspire him to do his best work.[16] Stetson's diaries for this period, published as *Endure,* reveal in yet greater detail how, even in loving a woman, a man could thus compromise her life. These diaries provide us today with a record of the social context out of which Gilman would in 1890 construct her literary masterpiece, "The Yellow Wallpaper," a gem among short stories by United States women. And the experience of her first marriage, as expressed in "The Yellow Wallpaper," can be understood as a negative reversal of the positively utopian *Herland.*

Gilman married Walter on 2 May 1884. One week later, she suggested that he pay her for her housekeeping services; he was offended, she then tearful. (Housekeeping would be a central consideration both as she contemplated a second marriage during the late 1890s and in her utopian writing contained in the *Forerunner.*) Another cause for her 1884 tears was his view that she was "too affectionately expressive": she was to await his initiatives. And so the friction between them continued, though she was to claim that he was "a devoted husband" (*Living,* 109). Before long, pregnancy consumed her energy: after 13 October 1884, her journal is blank until New Year's Day 1885, and that year's diary is more blank than written (SLR Volume 19). Her entries from 1 September 1884 through 4 October 1884 indicate that she was reading Elizabeth Stuart Phelps' *Dr. Zay* (1882), a novel about a heroine pursuing her medical mission to serve women and children: exactly at the point when Gilman became unable any longer to focus upon keeping her diary, she encountered a model both for her own later life and for later utopian characters she would create.

On 23 March 1885, Katharine Beecher Stetson was born. Kate, a "heavenly baby" (*Living*, 89), was named for Gilman's great-aunt Catharine Beecher and friend Kate Bucknell, to whom Gilman had paid summer visits in Ogunquit, Maine, before her marriage. Depressed for the last half of her pregnancy, Gilman lapsed into an even more serious condition after Kate's birth—now recognized as postpartum depression, a condition not surprising, since for many women, motherhood ends their unhampered pursuit of intellectual or creative goals, a restriction of possibilities unlike the expanding experiences that fatherhood can bring to men. With relief, Gilman welcomed the arrival of her mother to take over the care of two-month-old Kate. As an antidote to depression, she decided to winter in California.

Thus in the fall of 1885, Gilman left to visit a girlhood friend, poet and fiction writer Grace Ellery Channing (1862–1937), then living in Pasadena, California, and found that the change of scene led to her complete recuperation. A return to Walter and Kate the following March, however, brought back her former symptoms. Her 1886 verse "Nature's Answer" expresses her anger at both inequality in the marriage relation and the emotional pain a woman experiences as a result, which "had no limit but her power to feel" (*In This Our World*, 4). She developed a pattern of controlled public expression, which masked her inability to make others aware of her privately intense emotional needs. In January 1887, Walter participated in Gilman's "course of reading about women," including Margaret Fuller's *Woman in the Nineteenth Century*, which he read to her but with no apparent increase in his comprehension of Gilman's plight (SLR Volume 20). Later in 1887, she tried the rest cure of Philadelphia nerve specialist Dr. S. Weir Mitchell, but his prescription—to "never touch pen, brush, or pencil" as long as she lived—only exacerbated her condition (*Forerunner* 1913, 217). She soon refused to pursue his regimen.

With a formal separation from Walter mutually agreed upon, in September 1888 Gilman set out for Pasadena with Kate and settled near the Channings. Gilman continued to collaborate with Grace Channing on writing and acting in drawing room comedies that exposed the illogic of relations between the sexes, particularly in "A Pretty Idiot" and "Changing Hands" (c. 1890).[17] She credited Grace with "sav[ing] what there is of me"; they were to be close friends for over fifty years (RIHS, 20 Jan. 1890). Gilman then proceeded to make a living from what by 1896 she would see as her vocation: public speaking, organizing, and writing for a purpose (SLR Folder 16).

Gilman caught the 1890s popular fever for Nationalism, a country-wide network of clubs, a veritable political party, founded to support principles advocated by Edward Bellamy in his 1888 non-Marxist, socialist utopia, *Looking Backward, 2000–1887*.[18] Her Boston uncle Edward Everett Hale was also a Nationalist supporter. Another of Gilman's early supporters in Nationalist circles was feminist activist Harriet Howe (1865?–1948), thereafter a lifelong friend. With Howe's backing, Gilman quickly became a frequent lecturer before Nationalist Club audiences and a writer in support of Nationalist reforms: her Nationalist activity predominated between 1890 and 1895. Club speakers typically addressed such issues as government ownership of transportation and utilities, civil service reform, and public aid to education. Bellamy's key ideas were cooperation and community, which were to be achieved through evolutionary change as opposed to then-accepted Darwinian competition or Marxist revolution. Enthusiasts, including Gilman, did not question the paternalistic and racist tone of some Nationalist thinking; its intended idealism was what caught their attention.

In April 1890, the *Nationalist* published Gilman's satiric poem "Similar Cases," which has been reprinted numerous times, including in Zona Gale's Introduction to Gilman's autobiography (*Living*, xxxiv–xxxvii). A refrain, "You would have to change your nature," satirizes the unthinking ease with which conservatives offer nature as an argument against social change. With the publication and subsequent favorable critical notice of this poem, Gilman began her career as an author. William Dean Howells was among those congratulating her: he claimed that the poem was the best of its kind since *The Biglow Papers,* satiric verse published in 1848 and 1867 by the Massachusetts poet James Russell Lowell.[19] Gilman's uncle Edward Everett Hale believed that the poem was "a great campaign document," and on an 1891 visit to her in Pasadena, he attended and critiqued one of her lectures (*Living*, 129). Of the past year 1890, Gilman wrote on New Year's Eve 1891, "My whole literary reputation dates within it—mainly from 'Similar Cases.' Also the dawn of my work as a lecturer" (SLR Volume 29).

In August 1890, Gilman wrote a letter to the world, her masterpiece "The Yellow Wallpaper." She would struggle for two years to locate a publisher. In 1890 Horace Scudder, the *Atlantic Monthly* editor rejecting the story for publication, wrote to Gilman, "I could not forgive myself if I made others as miserable as I have made myself [in reading your story]!" (*Living,* 119) And William Dean Howells, who later included it in his 1920 *Great Modern American Stories,* called it "terrible and too wholly dire," "too terribly good to be printed."[20] Not until 1892 was Gilman to find in the *New England Magazine* a publisher for the tale.[21]

"The Yellow Wallpaper"—a brilliant exposé not only of Mitchell's rest-cure treatment, but also of patriarchal marriage—provides a rending depiction of a woman driven mad by her environment, this madness her revenge upon, and rebellion against, patriarchal confinement. The structure of the story is deceptively simple: ten diary entries by a wife-narrator (perhaps the "Jane" of the next-to-last paragraph) recording a summer stay at an "ancestral hall," under the care of her husband-physician John and his sister-nurse Jennie, apparently for her recuperation from "temporary nervous depression—a slight hysterical tendency" (Hedges 1973, 36, 63 n. 18, 9, 10).[22] But the heroine-narrator finds herself confined to a third-floor nursery-playroom with barred windows. Gradually she identifies with the figure of a woman she thinks she sees caught in the wallpaper design.

The short story has received acclaim for its powerful imagery of wallpaper as prison and release, and also for its heroine, who perceives herself as having both an authentic self and a male-constructed self, two selves she learns to read as if texts. Recent critics interpret it variously: some consider it a gothic portrayal of a doomed heroine; others see in it a realistic statement about the experience of women in patriarchy.[23] Some stress biographical antecedents; others stress literary merit. In the context of studying Gilman's utopian writing, "The Yellow Wallpaper" articulates the conditions for women against which she wrote her utopias, the experiential deficits that utopia will counter. If we think of "sunshine and shadow" quilts, those Amish designs that mirror each other in lighter and darker tones, then we can see a similar array of experiential issues informing on the one hand Gilman's utopian writing, and on the other such later polemical works as *Women and Economics* (1898) or *Human Work* (1904), *The Man-Made World* (1911) or *His Religion and Hers* (1923).

Never again would Gilman achieve so aesthetically forceful a work; this once she was able to join her public and private expression in a work of devastating impact. Perhaps because no person in her life was meeting her insistent emotional needs, she had no alternative outlet for her feelings, save to harness them to public expression in art. Later, after her second marriage to Houghton Gilman, she split her emotions from her written work, published or personal: apparently they emerged solely in private living since, after her second marriage, she kept only a datebook, no longer a journal. Her emotional energy would go not into personal self-expression, but into social amelioration and private experience. During the 1890s, however, she was still struggling to make herself into the person capable of homemaking activities on a global scale.

Years of Seeking, 1891–1897

In the spring of 1891, Gilman met Adeline E. Knapp (1860–1909), called Dora in her autobiography but Delle in her diaries, a friend with whom she had "sincerely hoped to live continually" and for whom she felt "really passionate love," she wrote in 1899.[24] She later explained in writing to Houghton Gilman that letters existed documenting "that I loved her that way" (SLR Folder 66; quoted in Hill 1980, 190): "that way" recalls the "audacious fancies" of Gilman's earlier letters to Martha Luther Lane. Delle was a reporter for the San Francisco *Call* and Gilman's co-worker in the Pacific Coast Women's Press Association. That September, along with Kate, they set up housekeeping in Oakland, then were joined by Gilman's mother, who was dying of cancer. This household placed considerable strain upon Gilman. Determined, however, not to have "failed in every relation in life," she cared for her mother until she died in 1893 (SLR Volume 32). She then vowed she would not force daughter Kate ever to endure such "needless" misery as extended nursing of a terminally ill parent. Her father angered her by refusing to visit his dying wife one last time, even though he then lived nearby.

Through all this, Gilman continued writing, and for once could pride herself that "Nothing seems to seriously affect my power to write" (SLR Volume 32, 3 March 1893). As her mother died, she was working out her thoughts for a speech on the immorality of women's dependence upon men for a living, perhaps her earliest written attempt to state the central insight of her masterwork, *Women and Economics: A Study of the Economic Relation Between Men and Women as a Factor in Social Evolution,* to appear in 1898. (Lectures delivered in California during the year and one-half before her mother's 1893 death provide additional sources.)[25]

By early 1893, Knapp, too, was gone, after she and Gilman found they were unsuited; Gilman was angry and disappointed for what she experienced as perfidy and disloyalty on Knapp's part (*Living*, 133–44). Lane suggests that they were too different in class and personality for a relationship to have been workable (1990, chap. 7; see also Hill 1980, chap. 9).

In 1893, Gilman's first book appeared—*In This Our World*,[26] a collection of predominantly satiric verse with a decidedly radical intent; it was enlarged and reprinted in 1895 and 1898. *In This Our World* was written during the interval between her marriages, the period of her most creative thinking when she experienced the least emotional support. Reviews of her verse were positive. William Dean Howells in 1894 wrote Gilman a letter praising her book as the "wittiest and wisest" in a long time and commending her for a "tongue like a two-edged sword"; however, he noted that her frankness might limit her popularity (SLR Folder 120, 11 Feb.). In the 1899 *North American Review*, he wrote that "her civic satire is of a form which she has herself invented": her "humor and sarcasm . . . teach by parable" (589). For example, in "Six Hours a Day," Gilman explodes the reverence accorded homemaking by cavalierly observing that "each living man, / Strive as he may" must acknowledge that " 'His mother was a cook!' ": few women, no matter their professional callings, escape frequently menial domestic activity and thus correctly can be identified as cooks (136–137).

The public view of Gilman's personal life was another matter. Indeed, the press considered it scandalous, both for her continued friendship with Stetson and for giving up her daughter to him and his second wife. In 1894, when Gilman's divorce became final, newspapers printed expressions of horror (SLR Folder 282, Volume 7). Journalists found enraging the fact that she had remained on good terms with Stetson throughout: apparently divorcing or remarrying couples were expected to be totally estranged from each other. His marrying Gilman's best friend, Grace Channing, "before the year was over" (*Living*, 167), and with Gilman's blessing, further confounded assumptions.[27] Even more outrageous, however, was a mother's giving up her daughter to the man she had divorced. Because of the time and energy required to make a living, because Gilman did not wish her daughter to grow up as she had in a fatherless household, and because Kate already knew well Stetson's new wife, Grace Channing, Gilman decided to send Kate with her grand-father (Gilman's father) to join the Stetsons in New York City. (A record of the Stetsons' preferences seems not to be extant.) This decision never ceased to pain Gilman: thirty years later, as she wrote about it in her autobiography, she noted, "I have to stop typing and cry as I tell about it" (*Living,* 163). Nonetheless, the press scalded her severely for this act.

Gilman's own claims of devotion notwithstanding, her correspondence with Kate through the years is, however, strangely formal: letters typically open "Dear Child." Apparently Kate always resented having been sent away by her mother (SLR Folders 87–106). And perhaps Gilman fundamentally did prefer other roles to that of mothering: her actions suggest this to have been true. However, the nineteenth-century ideology dictating that "true women" must be cheerfully dedicated mothers could undermine the self-confidence and increase the guilt of those like Gilman who might make other choices, and also increase the sense of desertion experienced by a child like Kate living in such a climate.

Also during the 1890s, Gilman was in touch with such literary notables as poets Ina Coolbrith, Edwin Markham, and Joaquin Miller. She felt that she "took a queer turn and became 'attractive' " to men. She exclaimed in her diary, "Within two days I receive two declarations of love!!!"—presumably from Markham and Eugene Hough, a radical reformer. She found these "hopeless," but "gratifying" (SLR Volume 34). Her residence became the location of a salon frequented by a cross-section of literary and political people interested in a wide range of issues, including the exposure of flagrant railroad monopolies. She was living experimentally, with personal and intellectual freedom that she had never before known as daughter, wife, or mother—an experience that could be modulated into later utopian fiction.

During the summer of 1894, Gilman moved to San Francisco for work and companionship. She edited the *Impress* (1893–1895), originally called the *Bulletin* (1893), a publication of the Pacific Coast Women's Press Association. She shared this work with Helen Campbell (1839–1918), author of *The Ainslee Stories,* popular juvenile fiction that had been a Gilman favorite.[28] A pioneer muckraking journalist, Campbell exposed the economic conditions of lower-class women in *Prisoners of Poverty* (1887). Possibly through her, Gilman met the Stanford University socio-economist Edward Alsworth Ross (1866–1951), like Campbell a Populist and a Progressive: his academic career would prosper at the University of Wisconsin from 1900, although Campbell, with comparable credentials, would have to move on after offering two courses in 1895.

Until about 1912, when poor health curtailed Campbell's activities, she was for Gilman an "adopted mother." Campbell, her "adopted son" Paul Tyner (d. 1925), and Gilman shared living quarters. Tyner managed the *Impress,* which would become a family weekly paper. Campbell contributed a "Household Affairs" column to it. And for her part, Gilman contributed two series: fictional imitations, a literary guessing-game called "Studies in Style," and puzzles called "Everyday Ethical Problems," solutions to each provided in subsequent issues.[29] Under this editorial triad, the *Impress* espoused an ever-stronger Populist viewpoint, admired by local intelligentsia. Always her advocate, Edward Everett Hale claimed in 1894, "I think the Impress [*sic*] is brilliantly written, and full of good things" (quoted in Hill 1980, 254). But, owing to the reputation that Gilman gained from her notorious divorce from Stetson, the *Impress* lasted only twenty weeks: "Nothing that Mrs. Stetson does can succeed here," Campbell was told. Although the *Impress* was short lived, it provided an apprenticeship in journalism that would bear fruit from 1909 to 1916 as Gilman's own magazine, the *Forerunner.*

Gilman was also active in annual California Women's Congresses. Although these congresses were advertised to arouse women's interest in improving moral and social conditions, some discussions had clearly feminist and reform intentions as well. For instance, in 1894 Gilman, Adeline Knapp, and Helen Campbell spoke on socialism, unemployed women, and working women, respectively. In 1895, Gilman met congress speakers Anna Howard Shaw (1847–1919), feminist minister; Susan B. Anthony (1820–1906), leader in the movement for woman suffrage; and Jane Addams (1860–1935), founder of Hull House in Chicago, which Gilman soon visited. These congresses appear to have been the catalyst that precipitated Gilman into a wider arena. With the support of a nation-wide suffrage network, Gilman began to contemplate the possibility of lecture-tours. That she enjoyed an already established reputation as an author surely must have encouraged her.

In 1896, Gilman launched herself as a personage on the national and international stage. She would both earn her way as she traveled and spread ideas to which she was committed; here was utopia in action. Her itinerary for this year included the National American Woman's Suffrage Association Convention (commonly referred to as the Woman's Suffrage Convention) in Washington, D.C.; Hull House in Chicago; and the International Socialist and Labor Congress in London. In Washington, Gilman herself spoke, but she was especially engaged by the debate over Elizabeth Cady Stanton's *Woman's Bible,* a collection of those passages from the Old and New Testaments of the Bible concerning women, supplemented by feminist interpretations. (Gilman would pen her own religious analysis in the 1923 *His Religion and Hers.*) Stanton (1815–1902) argued that woman-affirming religion is essential to women's welfare. Gilman was dismayed that the convention did not vote to endorse Stanton's Bible. Also at this convention, Gilman met the social evolutionist and "father of sociology," Lester Frank Ward (1841–1913), who advocated a "Gynaecocentric Theory" in an 1888 *Forum* article entitled "Our Better Halves." He posited that "the grandest fact in nature is woman"; she, not man, is central to civilization's advance.[30] (Some sixty years later, Ashley Montagu argued similarly: see his *The Natural Superiority of Women,* 1952.)

Heady with new contacts and ideas, Gilman returned to Hull House, which she had set as her base while "at large" (*Living,* 181). Letters to daughter Kate detail her experience of this visit. She met the accomplished group of women surrounding Jane Addams: Alice Hamilton (1867–1963), physician and scientist; Florence Kelley (1854–1932), lawyer and factory inspector; Julia Clifford Lathrop (1858–1932), social researcher and children's advocate; and Ellen Gates Starr (1859–1940), organizer and activist for women workers. Here, in fact, was a group of talented women who were improving the quality of life in poor Chicago neighborhoods: before Gilman's eyes functioned a model woman-centered utopia. Gilman was impressed by Addams' work, and with Helen Campbell she would have headed another settlement house on Chicago's North Side, "Little Hell," had her poor mental health not determined otherwise. Mary A. Hill astutely suggests that the relapse into depression that Gilman experienced while at Hull House may have been triggered by her being confronted by several idealizations of motherhood—namely, Stanton's "Heavenly Mother," Ward's "Mother of the Race," and Addams' "Mother of Civilization" (1980, 280–82). Each of these idealizations empowered women on the basis of maternal capacity and influence, but Gilman had recently sent her own child from her. Another causative factor may have been Gilman's apparent need for solitude, a room of her own, to maintain a steady sense of self

(Hill 1980, 281). So she tried to escape the impending siege of depression by moving on.

From spring into midsummer of 1896, Gilman lectured in eastern and midwestern cities. Still depressed yet restless, she nonetheless embarked for the International Socialist and Labor Congress in London. She spoke in drenching rain on a Hyde Park platform that included German social democrat leader August Bebel and British Fabian socialist and dramatist George Bernard Shaw. Though fascinated by a radical Anarchist like Pëtr Kropotkin, she was more in agreement with gradualist Fabians. She also met the utopian author and artisan William Morris; the feminist daughter of Elizabeth Cady Stanton, Harriot Stanton Blatch (1856–1940); and the "distinguished Fabians" Beatrice and Sidney Webb. But depression hit once more, and she left England discouraged. Once home, she went directly to the boarding house kept by her stepmother, Frankie Johnson Beecher, only to find that her father had recently been committed to the Delaware Water Gap Sanitorium because of a complete mental breakdown. The welcome reconciliation with him that had occurred during the years after her mother's death had ended. Gilman could no longer look to Frederick for support. He would die in 1899. She was, however, encouraged by a subsequent invitation from editor Prestonia Mann to become a contributing editor of the *American Fabian,* which she did for Volumes 3 and 4 from January 1897 through August 1898.[31] A welcoming tribute therein from former suitor Eugene Hough especially moved her.[32] Her own lead essay, called "Working Love" (12 Dec. 1897), defines the society that her 1915 *Herland* would depict: "A fully civilized community is one wherein the feelings of the social heart are fully and freely expressed through the activity of the social body, where human love can work itself out in orderly channels, as it is so painfully striving to do today."

This period until 1900 Gilman labeled the "wander years" (*Living,* 215). She traveled constantly as a lecturer, delivering such speeches as "Our Brains and What Ails Them," "Women and Politics," "The New Motherhood," and "Home: Past, Present, and Future."[33] Her audiences varied from club members to church parishioners to political reformers. She did not, however, gain more than a small income from this lecturing. Nonetheless, her daughter, Katharine Stetson Chamberlin, later noted her mother's generosity to her relatives in spite of these meagre earnings (SLR Folder 88, June 1972). And she wrote as she wandered. In the late summer of

1897, while visiting five different households, she completed the first draft of her masterwork *Women and Economics*. She noted in her journal that she needed a total of only seventeen days, and on one day wrote thirty-six hundred words! In less than six months, by early 1898, the book was in an admiring public's hands: "A masterpiece," said Jane Addams; "the first real, substantial contribution made by a woman to the science of economics," claimed Florence Kelley.[34] The work joins an eminent tradition of polemical writing on behalf of women's rights: the British Mary Wollstonecraft, in her 1792 *A Vindication of the Rights of Woman*, argued from women's common humanity, reflecting Enlightenment rationalism, while the American Margaret Fuller, in her 1845 *Woman in the Nineteenth Century*, claimed women's individualistic difference, couched in romantic transcendental idealism.

In *Women and Economics*, Gilman mustered arguments depending upon both women's commonalities with and differences from men.[35] She showed that economic dependence made women slaves of men and thereby hindered social evolution. She believed women central to social progress. In the book, she delineated numerous ills and explained their possible cures. First, she insisted that men had subjected women to their control. She decried women's meaningless work, largely limited to domestic servitude in exchange for food and shelter, an arrangement sanctioned by an androcentric Church and State. Second, Gilman claimed that women's narrowness of character and atrophied public capacities derived from this condition. To obtain a mercenary marriage, nearly a woman's sole respectable means of livelihood, she must exaggerate sexual and maternal traits. Third, a mother so ignorant could not adequately perform the child-care and homemaking to which she was limited. Home and Family thereby suffered. Fourth, so excessive was the sex distinction between women and men that two divergent worldviews had evolved. Two such individuals could hardly function as equal partners in marriage; hence, a double standard existed. Gilman recommended that women seek economic independence through specialized work. The required training would thus diversify women's capacities, enable women to perform public service, and lead to general social progress. Improved child care and improved marriages would result.

In *Women and Economics*, Gilman demonstrated the relationship between women's status and historical conditions. Thus she made apparent the social construction of womanhood and denied that anatomy is destiny, yet affirmed differences between the sexes. This book undergirds most of her subsequent writing, in particular her utopian essays and fiction, which expand and explicate various themes (see chaps. 3 and 4). Though a radical reform tract, it was nonetheless immensely popular and was translated into seven languages. The study demonstrated Gilman's knowledgeable command of the main intellectual currents of the time—Social Darwinism, progress, democracy, Fabian socialism, and the Social Gospel—although she herself, in *The Living of Charlotte Perkins Gilman*, credited the influence of only two works, "Our Better Halves" by Lester Ward (1842–1913) and *The Evolution of Sex* (1889) by Sir Patrick Geddes (1854–1932).[36] Ward's Gynaecocentric Theory of human evolution posited that the female, not the male, selects a mate; that the male exists solely to impregnate the female; and that the female is "primary in point both of origin and of importance in the history and economy of organic life" (275). He concluded his article: "True science teaches that the elevation of woman is the only sure road to the evolution of man [*sic*]" (275). In her 1915 utopia *Herland,* Gilman would embody Ward's theory in fiction by creating an all-female society.

Years of Fruition, 1897–1917

About this time, Gilman consulted her cousin George Houghton Gilman (called Ho) regarding a legal matter. From this unlikely circumstance, a passionate correspondence ensued: from March 1897 through May 1900, she wrote Ho multipage letters at least twice a week, occasionally even twice a day, reviewing her whole life—works, acts, and feelings, as well as her judgments upon them. In these letters, Gilman laid bare conflicts and insecurities that had not abated, contrary to the impression conveyed in her autobiography. She continued to fear the pull of tradition: on 15 September 1898, she implored Houghton to "work out such a plan of living as shall leave me free to move. . . . *I must not* focus on 'home duties'; and entangle myself in them" (SLR Folder 55).[37]

In the spring of 1899, Gilman sailed for Europe, this time to attend the Quinquennial Congress of the International Council of Women, again in London. Houghton joined her for a portion of this trip. Gilman was much lionized both as the author of *Women and Economics* and as the leading intellectual in the United States' women's movement. Here, she again met Edward A. Ross, Stanford

University sociologist and former colleague of Helen Campbell. The warm reception she received throughout England and Scotland gratified her immensely, and she returned home much encouraged. Immediately she set off on a lecture tour of the eastern and midwestern states before settling in California to write for the winter. In Oakland, she was relieved finally to pay off long-overdue debts. Then, in a Pasadena boarding house near her daughter Katharine, she wrote a first of four drafts of *Human Work,* a book that never satisfied her and of which she remarked, "Later thinkers must make it plainer" (*Living,* 286). In the spring of 1900, Gilman made her way eastward, lecturing as she traveled.

On 11 June 1900, Charlotte married Houghton Gilman very quietly in Detroit. Her subsequent productivity suggests that, in spite of her ambivalence, this marriage created the safe place for her to do her work that Stetson had earlier wanted from her for his work (see chap. 3). Joined by daughter Katharine, the couple moved into a New York City apartment hotel, but, in keeping with Gilman's beliefs about women's larger social work, they arranged to take their meals at a nearby boardinghouse.[38] Remaining in the city until 1922, they relocated three times. Secured by husband, daughter, and home, Gilman felt content. Though she argued for innovation, she required a modicum of traditional stasis for her productivity. Finally receiving in Houghton the support and collaboration of a caring companion, she entered the most active phase of her writing career, which also included becoming her own publisher.

Three nonfiction works appeared before Gilman established her monthly magazine, the *Forerunner,* in 1909. In *Concerning Children* (1900), she argued for a social motherhood characterized by trained experts providing child care, with mothers taking as their domain the whole of society. Next, in *The Home: Its Work and Influence* (1903), she attacked the single-family home as wasteful and isolated; instead she advocated socialized house care and kitchenless houses, with public kitchens and food delivery services. As Ann Lane stresses, these two books expand upon segments of *Women and Economics* (1990, chap. 9): *Herland* would correct the numerous ills that they delineate. In *Human Work* (1904), Gilman argued for an organic, sociocentric (communitarian)—as opposed to an egocentric (individualistic)—theory of society. She believed that labor has two facets, mutualism (labor serving the common good of all) and specialization (division of labor whereby individuals perform work for which they are specially suited). She argued that paid specialized work would emancipate women. She saw work as essential to human happiness, both as a form of social service and as a form of personal enjoyment. In her emphasis upon work as central to a human life, she was in accord with Freud, however much she decried his emphasis upon sex. She did not accept economic Want Theory, namely, that people work "to gratify wants, and that if [their] wants are otherwise gratified [they] will not work" (65). She was never satisfied, however, with her development of these ideas.[39] Like the earlier "The Yellow Wallpaper," *Women and Economics* provided a view of the underside of society that Gilman would later attempt to right in *Herland*.

In addition to a prodigious annual amount of writing, including a contributing editorship at the weekly newspaper the *Woman's Journal* throughout 1904 and into 1905, Gilman also made several trips abroad.[40] She attended the 1904 International Congress of Women in Berlin, where her reception exceeded even that in London in 1899. After a ten-day sojourn in Italy with Katharine and the Stetsons, Gilman returned home with plans to make a lecture tour the next year that would take her to England, the Netherlands, Germany, Austria, and Hungary. Throughout the decade 1900–1910, Gilman regularly published essays in such magazines as *Appleton's, Harper's Bazar,* the *Independent,* the *Saturday Evening Post, Scribner's, Success,* and *Woman's Home Companion.* These essays, along with her lectures, often provided themes for the *Forerunner's* longer works.

In 1905, Gilman first considered publishing her own magazine as a way to relieve her conscience that she was not doing everything possible to promote socialism and advocate causes in which she believed (SLR Folder 16, 9 October). She found that she was producing far more than she was able to place with publishers. Later, when told to consider more what editors wanted, she retorted, "If the editors and publishers will not bring out my work, I will!" (*Living,* 304) And so in 1909, the first twenty-eight-page issue of the *Forerunner* appeared. *Charlo*tte and Hough*ton* formed the Charlton Company (with offices at 67 Wall Street·in New York) to publish both this monthly magazine and four of its serializations as separate books in 1910 and 1911; Charlotte benefited from Houghton's training as an attorney in the conduct of her publishing business. But the writing was hers alone: she calculated each annual volume to be the equivalent of four books of thirty-six thousand words each.

Some of the pieces in the *Forerunner* had first appeared in the *Impress* or another magazine, but, for the most part, each issue consisted of new works.[41] The magazine was distributed in America and abroad by the National American Woman Suffrage Association, the Women's Political Union, and the Socialist Literature Company. Paid subscriptions, however, totaled only about fifteen hundred a year at one dollar a subscription. Since the magazine accepted no advertising that editor Gilman disliked, publishing costs were met by her lecturing and "extra work in writing" (*Living,* 305). The magazine includes—in addition to serializations of works separately discussed—poems, short stories, fables, essays, editorials, plays, one serialized novel and typically one serialized work of nonfiction per volume. The *Forerunner,* in the view of its contemporary editor, Madeleine Stern, is Gilman's "greatest single achievement," unique in combining "a crusade for women's rights and a plea for socialism." It received little critical notice, however, and was a financial drain upon the Gilmans' resources.[42] Through it, however, she committed herself to a utopian *praxis.*

With the possible exception of *The Man-Made World, or Our Androcentric Culture* (1911), which several have found comparable to *Women and Economics* in importance, none of the nonfiction serialized in the *Forerunner* repeated the independence of mind exhibited in Gilman's 1898 classic.[43] In *The Man-Made World,* Gilman expounded her gynaecocentric theory of sexual differentiation, for which she noted her debt to Lester Ward: men enjoy both fatherhood and productive work, while women must choose either motherhood or such work. Society is thus deprived of the traits relegated to women—cooperation, peacefulness, and life-orientation, while male domination maintains a society centered upon competition, war, and death-orientation, the traits admired in men. The study presented a social constructivist view of gender difference and provided encyclopedic coverage of family, health, dress, the arts and literature, leisure, ethics and religion, education, law and government, crime and punishment, war and politics, industry and economics.

Subsequent *Forerunner* nonfiction either rehashed former material or joined what had been shorter pieces. "Our Brains and What Ails Them" (1912, a frequent lecture topic), "Humanness" (1913), and "Social Ethics" (1914) are all revising *Human Work.* "The Dress of Women" (1915) expanded an 1891 essay from the Nationalist *Pacific Rural Press* called "The Dress and the Body." Gilman had antedated Thorstein Veblen's 1899 notion, developed in *The Theory of the Leisure Class,* of women's dress as a display of conspicuous consumption. "Growth and Combat" (1916) connected editorials on current issues.

Ironically, the *Forerunner*'s short stories and serialized fiction, given Gilman's estimate that she was better at expository writing, hold greater interest for readers today. Particularly noteworthy are four utopian works. *What Diantha Did* (1909–1910) fictionalizes a solution to problems analyzed in *Women and Economics* and further discussed in *The Home* and *Human Work.* The heroine, Diantha Bell, demonstrates how a cooked food delivery service and cafeteria can, through specialized labor, relieve women of individual domestic drudgery. Gilman declares her belief in the superiority of professionalizing housework over cooperative schemes of reform. The novel extends the tradition of early nineteenth-century communitarian (Owenite) socialism to the late nineteenth-century "grand domestic revolution" of the United States' "material feminists," who wished to professionalize domestic science. As Dolores Hayden explains in *The Grand Domestic Revolution,* they "concentrated on economic and spatial issues as the basis of material life" (3).

Moving the Mountain (1911) expands what Gilman had begun to envision in a 1907 fragment, "A Woman's Utopia," here seen through the eyes of a male narrator lost for thirty years. He reports changed lives for urban women, accomplished not by technological, but by social and socialist, innovations. Gilman reveals a flaw, however, in her willingness to let the ends of an ideal society override the questionable means of violating individual rights.

Gilman's "lost feminist utopia," *Herland* (1915), joins a tradition in the United States extending from 1836, the date of the first known utopian fiction by a woman, to 1880, when a first all-female society was imagined by a compatriot.[44] *Herland* is the liveliest and most feminist of these three works. It wittily recounts the adventure of three men from the United States, in search of an all-female country, which they name Herland. They are astonished both to find the women indifferent to their charms as males and to view the sophisticated environment these women have built. Gilman validates motherhood by making it the nation's highest office. Her reverence for mothers is both personally compensatory and socially reformist. The influence of Lester Ward is apparent here. In reviewing Ward's *Pure Sociology* (1893) in 1910, Gilman especially recommended to women chapter 14 and paraphrased its central argument: "The female sex is the present form of the original type of life, once capable in itself of the primary process of reproduction; while the male sex is a later addition, introduced as an assistant to the original organism, in the secondary process of fertilization" (*Forerunner* 1, no. 10: 26c).[45] She noted Ward's finding that woman is the "race-type," man the "sex-type," a reversal of the premises of Western thought since Adam and Eve in the Garden of Eden (26d). *Herland,* therefore, is a thought-experiment extrapolated from Ward's theory. A sequel, *With Her in Ourland* (1916), plods by comparison as one of the male adventurers and his Herland bride fly over our globe, viewing with shock the devastation of World War I.

Four additional novels were serialized in the *Forerunner.* The reform tract *The Crux* (1911) argues against marriage between a syphilis-infected man and an uninfected woman, the crux of the matter being to avoid committing a biological sin. "Mag-Marjorie" (1912), using the plot from her unpublished play, "The Balsam Fir," written between 1906 and 1910, presents the tale of a fallen woman whose reputation is restored by a protective benefactress who cares for her child and educates her. This once-fallen woman is rewarded by a successful medical career and marriage. "Won Over" (1913), also enlarged from a play, "Interrupted," written in 1909, depicts a husband won over, with perhaps unrealistic ease, by his wife's professional success. Finally, in "Benigna Machiavelli" (1914), the heroine firmly rejects the upbringing that a "girl of the period" received from her family; instead the heroine arranges her household to her own and others' needs, but not without Gilman's ease of subverting ends to means, the benign manipulation suggested by the heroine's name.

During the *Forerunner* years, the pace of Gilman's life continued unabated. Her first husband, Walter Stetson, died in Italy in 1911; Gilman then consoled his widow, her own dear friend Grace Channing Stetson. That year she also made a ten-week lecture tour of the United States to raise money for the *Forerunner.* In 1913, she attended the International Woman's Suffrage Congress in Budapest, lecturing as well in England, Germany, and Scandinavia. The Great War and Gilman's outspoken condemnation of Germany astonished those who had admired her sermons on the need for human unity and growth. Socialist friends found her position narrow. Gilman decided to cease publication of the *Forerunner* at the end of 1916, not long before the United States declared war. She claimed she had printed what she was compelled to say. Reviewing her life's work in 1917, she acknowledged that "yes, I have a shelf of books now," but, less satisfied the next year, noted that "at 58, a few more books should do" (SLR Folder 16).

Final Years, 1917–1935

Gilman continued to find ways to make her views known. In 1919, she tried two popular ventures, writing articles for the *New York Tribune* syndicate and lecturing on the Chautauqua circuit, giving the same talk on successive nights (SLR Folder 294). Although she pronounced herself a failure at both, she continued to give occasional talks to women's club audiences. She participated for a while in the Heterodoxy Club, located in New York's Village, but wearied of their turn to pacifism and sex-psychology. (One of her frequent lectures during the 1920s was "The Falsity of Freud.") She preferred the subjects of the professional women at the Query Club, but she did "not like the smell of tobacco" (*Living*, 314). That suffrage was won in 1920 goes unmarked in *The Living of Charlotte Perkins Gilman*, but then Gilman held no illusions about the power of the ballot in the hands of economically dependent women.

By 1922, their nativism evident, the Gilmans left New York's ethnic mix "with measureless relief" for Norwich Town, Connecticut, the site of Houghton's recently inherited homestead (*Living*, 324).[46] During the years that followed, the Gilmans socialized with other progressive couples—Prestonia Mann and her husband, John Martin, as well as Martha and Robert Bruère.[47] There Gilman wrote *His Religion and Hers: A Study in the Faith of Our Fathers and the Work of Our Mothers* (1923), a corollary to *The Man-Made World* in stressing nature more equally with nurture as a basis for sex differences. She showed that men's control of religion, because of their propensity for war and competition, had led to an overemphasis upon death; women, experiencing childbirth and nurturing life, would as ministers bring a more life-affirming orientation to religion. Gilman saw religion as an ethical and social force, not as a theology. A mid-1920s brochure advertising her lectures includes as "typical lectures in courses" such topics as "The Larger Feminism" and "Studies in Masculism," as well as "His Religion and Hers."[48]

By 1925, Gilman had completed all but the final chapter of *The Living of Charlotte Perkins Gilman*. Though immensely revealing, this autobiography must be read cautiously: discrepancies exist between it and other extant documents. Gilman's purpose in writing it, however, was not only to write her own life, but also to inspire young women to fuller lives as women. Thus she occasionally adjusts information that would reduce her stature as a model. Gilman's diaries reveal far more frequent episodes of internal angst and uncertainty than her autobiography indicates. The attitudes toward herself in both diaries and autobiography attest to poor mental health practices—an excess of self-criticism, superhuman expectations, and a tendency to devalue herself. She concealed anger behind her devotion to social service. The autobiography is a monument to the public persona of Charlotte Perkins Gilman, very much a social construction authored by herself; although she intended to offer an inspirational model to readers and justify to herself a life productively lived, she has left the impression that women can expect to live as superwomen and that those who fail in this impossible endeavor can blame themselves for living inadequately.[49] In fact, she had done just this to herself throughout her life.

Because Gilman missed living up to her grandiose expectations for herself, she claimed a lifelong legacy of mental ill health as a result of the postpartum depression that she had experienced after Kate's birth. Had she permitted herself a more reasonable goal than undoing in her lifetime the sex imbalance between women and men, she might have felt more satisfied with the very substantial accomplishments that she did attain. Her autobiography, then, cannot be read as fully accurate. As Ann J. Lane notes in her introduction to the most recent reprint of *The Living of Charlotte Perkins Gilman,* "Gilman was trying to carve from her unrepresentative life insights about how any woman might live in a world in which such an unrepresentative life as hers could become accessible to all women. . . . She herself struggled for, and her work spoke to, a vision of a structurally equitable society in which ordinary women—and that meant unaffluent wives and mothers—could live and develop their gifts and interests" (*Life,* xxi).

By the end of the 1920s, uneasy about the influx of immigrants, who she felt were somehow lesser peoples, Gilman hit upon a new topic in "Progress Through Birth Control" (1927) and "Sex and Race Progress" (1929): careful selection of partners and limitation of births would lead to peace and progressive race evolution. (Although this stance is xenophobic, during the 1890s, Gilman had been one of the few feminists who had not sanctioned a literacy test to stem the tide of largely Jewish, Eastern European immigrants.) Then, like Candide, she retired to her garden, where with Houghton she grew thirty kinds of vegetables.

Around 1929, Gilman wrote a never-published detective novel, "Unpunished." An angry work, it presents her most villainous male character, who, like the villain in Agatha Christie's *Murder on the Orient Express* (1934), meets murder at the hands of those he has mistreated (SLR Folder 231). With it, Gilman's fiction writing came full circle; for, like her earliest stories, this, too, contains elements of the gothic. By 1930, all of her work was out of print.

In 1932, Gilman learned that she had inoperable breast cancer. Houghton died suddenly in May 1934; thereafter, she made her home in Pasadena, near daughter Katharine and her family—her husband, artist F[rank] Tolles Chamberlin, and their children, Dorothy and Walter. On 17 August 1935, determining that her work was finished, she bathed, went to bed, placed chloroform-soaked cloths over her face, and died peacefully—almost exactly a decade after her prediction in July 1925 that she had ten years left (*New York Times,* 20 August 1935, SLR Folders 284, 16). Gilman's suicide resembles one that she had described in 1912 in the *Forerunner:* she approved the "good taste . . . in suicide" of "a well-bred New England woman" who was found dead of chloroform in her bed, "no trouble to anyone" (3, no. 5:130). Gilman herself left a note asserting, "I have preferred chloroform to cancer" (*Living,* 334).

The death of Charlotte Perkins Gilman was thoroughly consistent with the values by which she had lived. Her act to control her own body and her own life stirred much controversy in newspapers, but those who knew and loved her applauded what they saw as her courage. Praise arrived from diverse quarters. Carrie Chapman Catt (1859–1947), former head of the National American Woman Suffrage Association and mobilizer of the finally successful (though racially compromised) campaign for suffrage, expressed her shock, but remarked, "A woman of her vigor would do exactly that thing to avoid trouble to her daughter . . . and pain to herself. I think she was quite right." The novelist Fannie Hurst (1889–1968) believed that Gilman "died as wisely as she lived." Activist Ida Tarbell (1857–1944), while disagreeing with the solution of suicide, noted that she could "see how Mrs. Gilman might have been driven to an extremity" (*New York World Telegram,* 20 August 1935, SLR Folder 284). *The Living of Charlotte Perkins Gilman* appeared posthumously in October 1935.

In the September 1936 *Equal Rights,* Hattie Howe wrote of her good friend Charlotte, "Indomitable, valiant, she was never vanquished, she even conquered death. . . . She went resolutely to meet it" (216). Although Gilman in her autobiography does build a case for herself, which Howe has accepted, as the consistently conquering heroine that she was not, her desire was thereby to inspire younger women to follow her in responding to "two callings"—living fully and forcefully as long as possible in a wide arena joining both Home and World. Ann Lane agrees that Gilman wrote her autobiography with the goal of influencing women's behavior. In *To "Herland" and Beyond,* Lane quotes Gilman as hoping the book would "stir some women," even change "one girl . . . into a mover of others" (346). No less did Gilman hope would result from her utopian writing, as the next chapter will demonstrate.

3

"This Prancing Young Utopia"

ALTHOUGH CHARLOTTE PERKINS GILMAN dismissed her capacity
to create literature—"I have never made any pretense of being literary" (*Living*, 284); "I have definitely proved that I am not a novelist"
(*Living*, 306)—she nonetheless understood well its social function:
through it, "we know the past, govern the present, and influence the
future," she remarked (*Forerunner* 1.5: 18).[1] She would have agreed
with socialist playwright Bertolt Brecht (1898–1956) that art is a
hammer for creating society, rather than a mirror for reflecting it.[2]
As a crafter of words for presenting social possibilities, she underes-
timated her rhetorical skill.[3] Her purpose in fiction writing was not
so much aesthetic or belletristic—the accepted (and elitist) goals of
post-Victorian imaginative writing—but rather rhetorical, the goal
we have come to expect of nonfiction writing. If her work happened
also to exhibit aesthetic merit, as critics unanimously agree is the
case with her 1892 short story, "The Yellow Wallpaper," so much
the better.[4]

In Gilman's view, her fiction was eminently "realistic," since
she fondly expected her views and depictions to lead readers to effect
massive changes in the social environment, thereby to alter reality.
During the first two decades of this century, she was the leading
feminist theorist in the United States. This status largely derived
from the publication in 1898 of her internationally acclaimed treatise *Women and Economics*. At the end of her life, she was dismayed
to find that so little in fact had changed, that in the early 1930s so
little interest in her and her work existed that she received no calls
to speak, even from the local Connecticut chapter of the League of

Chapter title is taken from "Aunt Mary's Pie Plant" (June 1908) 48; also reprinted
in chapter 5: 117–28.

Women Voters. What seems to have happened in the decade following World War I and the passage of the women's suffrage amendment in 1920 was a constriction of a nearly ubiquitous Protestant
work ethic before a proliferating Freudian pleasure principle. Literature need no longer carry a message, rather might primarily entertain.

But of course, cultural myths do not erase cultural verities: literature always carries a cultural message, however covertly. What
cultural work Jane Tompkins claims for Stowe's novel holds also for
Gilman's lesser-known utopian writing: Gilman, too, "reconceives
the role of men in human history" with "import" that is "world-
shaking" (*Designs,* 146). But where Stowe relegated men to "groom-
[ing] themselves contentedly in a corner" (146), Gilman requires
more active participation, although she stops far short of a current
feminist ideal, shared domestic responsibility. Like Stowe's novel,
the mission of Gilman's utopian writing is "global and its interests
identical with the interests of the [human] race" (146): Gilman's
utopian texts also do "a certain kind of cultural work within a specific historical situation, . . . expressing and shaping the social context that produced them" (200). Specifically, the cultural work of
this writing is the demonstration that women are not confined to
one traditional mode of being, wife/motherhood, but can fill as varied social roles as can male counterparts. Such cultural work
amounts to an "attempt to redefine the social order" (xi).

Gilman's 1910 study, *Our Androcentric Culture; or, The Man-
Made World,* discusses her view of the social function of literature,
a view analogous to Tompkins' concept of cultural work. Gilman
believes that literature can enact social changes, can function as
social action, can convey alternative versions or visions of human
action—a position of clear self-consciousness regarding literary didacticism. The cultural work central to Gilman's utopian fiction is a
"re-presentation" of alternative possibilities for being female or
male. By refusing to accept definitions of traditional male and female roles and instead offering alternatives to mainstream expectations, Gilman forces readers to question boundaries defining
behavior assumed acceptable on the basis of gender—in the 1990s
her views being still ahead of widespread social practice. Gilman's
utopian fiction, taken as a whole, offers challenges in social transformation. Although she directs her concern to expanding women's
possibilities, she also suggests changes in men that would enable
women to change even more. I wish now to examine this quality of

"realizability" in Gilman's utopian fiction, as it presents relocations (or is it dislocations?) of the individual with respect to gender in the structuring of families, neighborhoods, occupations, and societies as a whole, an order of increasing social complexity that also informs the following discussion.

How Charlotte Perkins Gilman developed from her first overtly utopian essay the capacity to imagine a full-blown utopia for women is the focus of this chapter. Gilman's utopian writing, published from 1904 to 1921, progressed by stages. At first, she imagined social units the size of neighborhoods and smaller, alternately composing fiction and nonfiction. Next, she experimented in fiction—especially in *Forerunner* short stories—with the neighborhood practice of social reforms presented in her nonfiction, including ideas expanded in earlier, concurrent, or later book-length work. Occasionally, she sustained for the length of a short story innovations that never appear in the longer structure of novel narratives. These first two stages constituted almost a decade's foreground of utopian writing in advance of her most fully realized utopian society. Finally, she created this whole society—her 1915 satire *Herland*—where she infused fiction with the often biting wit evident in her 1895 collection of verse, *In This Our World*.

All of the foregoing writing represents Gilman's effort to actualize in realistic fiction solutions that she had recommended in her 1898 feminist treatise, *Women and Economics*. The weight of her life, of course, shapes this writing. These stages in her conceptualization of a women's utopia reveal the impact of her lifetime, as the next chapter will illuminate. Gilman's resolution of psychological problems in living intertwines with the development of fictional solutions in her writing. That literary realism was in fashion during her historical moment offered her a serendipitous coincidence, even though she wrote at the very end of that era. Perhaps one reason why all of her work had gone out of print by 1930 was that she had held to a literary fashion beyond its passing. The fact of a Great War did not dampen her expectation of human progress, nor did the furor over Freud temper her belief in the human capacity to choose rationally. Her life offers hints suggesting why she was indomitable.

Beautiful Blocks: The Initiating Foundations, 1904–1910

A prolific writer, Charlotte Perkins Gilman overwhelms students of her life and work. To make her at all manageable, one must impose categories that the complexity of her ideas, in fact, defies fitting into. Because my aim in this chapter is to demonstrate how in her utopian fiction she actualized the recommendations of her polemical writing, I shall consider first her nonfictional exposition, then the fictional actualization of that exposition. This study shows the complementary viewpoints Gilman presented in *Women and Economics* and her utopian fiction, including *Herland.*

During what I label the first stage in the development of Gilman's utopian imagination, from 1904 to 1910, she alternated between essay and fiction as she honed her notion of utopia by imagining social units up to the level of neighborhoods. The earliest are two 1904 essays, "The Beauty of the Block" and "The Passing of the Home in Great American Cities." The last three essays were sandwiched in among fiction, realistically depicting the reforms recommended. The first is the 1907 "Why Cooperative Housekeeping Fails," which followed within months the never-completed "A Woman's Utopia." Utopian communities are more fully envisioned in the 1908 "Aunt Mary's Pie Plant" and in the 1910 novel, *What Diantha Did.* The 1908 "A Suggestion on the Negro Problem" reveals Gilman's racism and elitism, features that are clearly part of her thinking; these unintentionally dystopian attitudes qualify her utopian vision. Finally, the 1909 "How Home Conditions React upon the Family" appeared three months before "A Garden of Babies."

Four years of living in New York City with Houghton gave Charlotte experience in urban living that she turned to print in several early utopian essays. In "The Beauty of the Block" (*Independent* 57, 14 July 1904) a tongue-in-cheek title, Gilman scorned a "solid cubical honeycomb (without the honey!)" (67). She noted then-current irrationality in allocating precious outdoor space to laundry use—though needed only one day out of the week; of consigning a whole cellar level to heating and a basement level to cooking, thereby crowding the many remaining activities of a family onto three levels. In contrast, apartment houses and hotels might provide attractive courtyards, common recreation and service facilities, all the while retaining family privacy. The common city block might incorporate for each family member "all the club comforts" found in the multiple-dwelling edifice (71). This arrangement would combine the advantages of both individual and multiple residences.[5] In "The Passing of the Home in Great American Cities" (*Cosmopolitan* 38 [December 1904]: 137–47), Gilman demonstrates the replacement of the individual family home by apartments, approves the "expansion of the home life into 'society life' " (145), but pleads for attention to the needs of children: roofs might become child-gardens, other spaces might be furnished as nurseries, playrooms, and gymnasia. Thus should a woman "serve society as does her human mate, and they, together, should go home to rest. It is this change in the heart of the world which is changing the house of the world; and its ultimate meaning is good," Gilman proclaimed (147). These essays particularize the implementation of a new public role for women equal to that of men, as suggested in *Women and Economics* (chaps. 12, 13). They also offer solutions to the difficulties of motherhood, whether as a single mother trying to support and care for children (an experience shared by Gilman and her mother), as a mother with a nonparticipating partner, or as a mother whose nurture of her children their father shares.

Many at this time advocated or were experimenting with cooperative housekeeping as a solution to the ills leading to the "passing of the home." But in "Why Cooperative Housekeeping Fails" (*Harper's Bazar* 41 [July 1907]: 625–29), Gilman placed the blame for home failure on families' being isolated and self-centered units, lacking experts trained in housework. Failing individually, they could not succeed joined. Though love, marriage, home, and family belong together, we do not sing, "Housework, sweet housework, there's nothing like housework!" Gilman noted (627). Thus she recommended assigning housework skills to specialists, who would execute the work far better and more efficiently than untrained family members.[6] Contemporary fast food chains, frozen prepared food companies, take-out windows in restaurants, and catering services testify to the efficacy of Gilman's reform, if not to the quality available, often falling far short of the healthful nutrition Gilman required. Her insight that housework performed by experts would be "good business" has been vindicated by the market of the 1980s and 1990s (629): housekeeping services of varied quality and frequency are currently available in suburban regions. Corporations begin to see the wisdom of making child-care services available to employees. And such governmental bodies as legislatures and school boards are also responding to the needs of children and their caretakers.

"How Home Conditions React upon the Family" (*American Journal of Sociology* 14, March 1909) expands Gilman's argument, only hinted in "Cooperative Housekeeping" (628), that the economic dependence of women, entailing a man's ownership of a woman and her service to him, constitute "conditions" so detrimental to the well-being of the family as to require the removal of housework from the home: "'That an entire sex should be the domestic servants of the other sex is abhorrent and incredible" (598). "Six Hours a Day," a poem from her 1898 *In This Our World,* decries this circumstance:

> Six mortal hours a day the woman spends on food!
> Six mortal hours . . .
> . . . while the slow finger of Heredity
> Writes on the forehead of each living man,
> Strive as he may, "His mother was a cook!" (136–137)

Of course, this complaint regarding women's dependence is also central to *Women and Economics:* in this essay, Gilman reiterates a segment of that treatise. She explains how this material condition affects marriage, maternity, child-culture (rearing), the individual, and society. Women delay marrying because they dislike the status of servant, and men, because unable to afford the cost of a wife. Instead of recognizing the realities of the situation, society blames women for refusing their "natural" marital role. Maternity suffers because women's duty is construed to be first to her spouse and only then to her child. In addition, women lack the power either to select the best mate or to control maternity itself. Child-culture stands second to kitchen service; neither time nor space is consciously set aside for the needs and interests of children. Finally, Gilman finds that individual men, in maintaining a traditional home, impede social change by keeping individual women irresponsible to greater society. Untrained women cannot raise children effectively: this circumstance restrains social progress.

However acute Gilman's thinking was on women's issues, her views on race contrast strikingly and reveal ethnocentrism. On this issue, she was unable to think beyond her era. Much of her better-known work places into the background this flaw in her thinking. Contemporary critics, however, reveal racism that today embarrasses whites and insults peoples of color.[7] Gilman believed in racial evolution, a feature of social Darwinism. In "A Suggestion on the Negro Problem" (*American Journal of Sociology* 14 [July 1908]: 78–85), she baldly refers to "[negroes'] inferiority" as what makes racial exploitation possible (78): she missed understanding that belief in such inferiority, far more than verifiable evidence of it, fuels such exploitation. Her very notion of a "Negro Problem" is racist: solely the prejudicial behavior of whites creates a "Negro problem." That

Gilman nowhere draws the analogy between gender and race as twin sources of subordinate status, that she claims as genetic inferiority what are cultural or environmental differences reveals the ethnocentric limits of her analysis. The question is not, as Gilman asks (80), "What can we do to improve [the negro]," but rather, How can those with power learn to accept difference? Gilman's unacceptable recommendation of compulsory enlistment in an army of "all negroes [men, women, and children] below a certain standard of citizenship" (80) would exacerbate rather than solve any "problem." She expects part of this army's program to be educational, with training on model farms, "as a large percentage of the negro population is best suited to agricultural labor" (81). She construes this army as little other than labor enlisted on behalf of "southern" society as a whole: since "applied labor is wealth" (82), no additional cost would accrue to society. On two points she was right: educational opportunity would lead to acculturation (though many today question whether such implied Eurocentric education in the absence of Afrocentric culture would only further deracinate, and whites who could not manage to accommodate to Africans themselves needed "a scheme of racial betterment" (84), one view eliciting an unqualified "Amen."

Nowhere does Gilman suggest, nor would she have, that a comparable enlisted army might upgrade the "retarded," "restricted" womanhood of which she complains in Women and Economics (336). She could see that men, but not whites, needed reeducation to understand that a subordinated group deserves a fuller life. Though otherwise intelligent and creative, Gilman's social Darwinist views blinded her to her own racism and permitted her to displace upon marginalized peoples the malaise she was beginning to experience as immigrants flooded into New York City.[8]

Regarding women's issues, however, Gilman did stand ahead of her time and is still ahead of ours. Wisely understanding that readers would better accept her heretical views if they were presented as stories enacting alternative choices for action, Gilman "represented" her ideas clothed as characters. Her view of the social function of literature, as explained in the introduction, bears repeating here. In "Masculine Literature" (quoted in chap. 1; from Our Androcentric Culture), Gilman explained how she understood fiction to be "world-food" that "re-presents" rather than "preaches" ideas (1910, 21). Hence, her ideas from these five essays reappear as fiction: one 1907 fragmented serialization, "A Woman's Utopia"; two stories, "A Garden of Babies" in 1909 and "Aunt Mary's Pie Plant" in 1908; and one 1910 novel, *What Diantha Did.* "A Woman's Utopia" develops several utopian reforms, while each short story focuses upon one. "A Garden of Babies" expands the child-care and motherhood theme presented in the last chapter of "A Woman's Utopia," while "Aunt Mary's Pie Plant" provides a foundation for *What Diantha Did,* both treating problems of housekeeping service.

The 1907 "A Woman's Utopia" represents the reforms in improved physical, social, and residential environments that the elevation of women would effect.[9] Gilman set this five-chapter fragment, her first consciously utopian fiction, in New York only two decades into the future. (She would further estrange time or place in her later completed utopias, the more convincingly to permit readers' suspension of disbelief.) In "A Woman's Utopia," narrator Morgan G. Street challenges his beloved cousin Hope Cartwright and her R. G. U. [Argue] Club to improve the United States: while he travels for twenty years, the club, heretofore devoted to arguing about reforms, will demonstrate the difference that his donation of twenty million dollars could make (chap. 1).

Gilman envisioned Morgan, upon his return to New York harbor in May 1927, gradually converted by Hope from masculism to feminism—a partial reprise of Gilman's own recent courtship from 1897 to 1900 with Houghton Gilman, to whom she had written numerous lengthy letters explicating her worldview. Morton is initially dismayed to find women politically influential enough to have instituted free trade and done away with customs, but he is impressed with clear harbor water, smokeless air, and a gilded Statue of Liberty. He notes more greenery between buildings than he had recalled (chap. 2). Hope plans a one-week tour to show Morgan the changed lives of women, but the fragment stops after the second day.

What Gilman did write covers the beginning of this proposed tour. First Morgan learns from Dale Edwards, of the Upgrade Publication Company, that religion has become the study of ethics, "the science of conduct" (372). A central ethical issue is the elevation of women from a dependent condition; such elevation has improved not only women, but men and children also. A "science of child-culture" leads to greatly improved, though not perfect, results: a humanity far advanced along the path "from egoism to socioism" (373). "Love in Action" is the central religious tenet, one's duty being to serve humanity beyond the family (375). Religious worship occurs in performing social services (chap. 3).

Next, Hope explains "some beginnings" in the social and physi-

cal conditions of living. "City mothers" are active in effecting reforms; they study Domestic Economy and Child Culture, topics of
two 1904 *Independent* essays by Gilman (499; see note 5 above).
Women see the whole world as their province, as they work alongside men. Urban residential areas have now been renovated with
the result that courtyards, electric heating and ventilation, roof
gardens for children's play, tree-lined streets, as well as clean air
and water are now the rule. Morgan mentions that the effect reminds him of a book which he has read, Henry Olerich's 1893 utopia, *A Cityless and Countryless World*.[10] Hope points out that the
services provided have been good business: model establishments
bring in good income, which, when invested, generates more capital
for investment.

Essential to these changes have been the decentralization of
business and the institution of a social service, akin to the "army"
proposed in "A Suggestion on the Negro Problem." Hope explains,
"[Social service] took up the overplus of immigration in a most convenient way; and it settled the negro problem" (504). Reading these
words today, we flinch at best. They prefigure the impending, mis-
guided capitulation of the majority of white women to racism in
order to effect the 1920 passage of a women's suffrage Constitutional Amendment, as well as a national xenophobic reaction to
immigrants that closed the doors to "huddled masses" also in 1920.[11]

Finally, Hope takes Morgan to view residential facilities. First
they visit a typical worker's family, the Whitebergs of Russian-
German peasant ancestry.[12] Hope observes that "now we allow a
certain number [of immigrants] each year, from each country—and
take care of them" (593) (further evidence of Gilman's occasional
patronizing and xenophobic stance). Both parents are gainfully employed, Nina as a garment worker and Morris as an electrician.
Their children receive rooftop day care at an infant garden or at a
playground for toddlers through children aged five years or so. Together the parents bring their children home for meals. A food service provides these in the Whitebergs' private, kitchenless
apartment of four rooms. Nina finds herself less cross with her children because she does not care for them all day long, as she had
once done. Children are far healthier, Morris points out: they do not
die during their first three years as before. Hope then takes Morgan
on a tour of the block's facilities. The upper levels house residences.
Public dining rooms are on the roof or ground levels, clothing workshops employing many mothers are on the second, while recreation

areas are on the rooftop, for running and promenading, or on the basement level, for activities from dancing and bowling to swimming and reading, some in spaces under sidewalks.

This narrative emphasizes a new "civilized motherhood," in Hope's words, "the mainstay of our whole system of living": "the voting mother . . . has made these brilliant happy cities—this world of education . . . these homes that are really built for children" (596). Only women who enjoy child care actually rear children; the rest develop other specialties. And women do not marry inferior men so that the human species will improve. Hope notes, "The mass of the population is less specialized than the more highly organized racial savants—naturally. But we have no longer as low a grade of people as we used to have" (596). Again, "A Woman's Utopia" provides evidence of Gilman's elitism and racism, as well as of her readiness to level—to be sure, attitudes of her times, but also lapses of humanity on her part.[13] More constructively, Gilman realistically imagined such improvements as specialization of domestic labor, provision of remunerative work for both parents, and construction of residential blocks incorporating workplace and child care in close physical proximity. These concerns anticipate Gilman's later utopias, the 1911 *Moving the Mountain* as well as the 1915 *Herland*.

Gilman believed maternal nurturing to be learned rather than innate (at a time when the latter was accepted as truth) and particularly appropriate for women (a view more traditional than others she held regarding women's place in the world). With respect to mothering, Gilman's thought was simultaneously conservative—in her belief that child care is an activity appropriate to women, though not every woman—and innovative. That she recognized the need both for careful nurturing of small infants and children and for the specialized training of their caretakers contradicts the prevailing assumption that every mother naturally knew how to care for her baby. Gilman's fiction demonstrates her agreement, however, with the view that primarily women should perform child care. Her short story "A Garden of Babies" (see selection 2; *Success* 12, June 1909) particularizes this role of the female child-nurturer, while at the same time showing that not all women have either the desire or the ability to function effectively as child-care givers. In this story, adults of both sexes work together to establish a baby garden for the health and welfare of mothers and children. Two sisters, each a mother, have different capacities: Jessie, trained as a pediatrics nurse and kindergarten teacher, is a genius with very young children; the other sister, the unnamed narrator, innovates an intensive gardening business. Jessie's life seems a utopian revision of Gilman's mother's life; the narrator's, of her own.

Jessie, widowed and bereft of a baby son, nearly mad with grief, is healed by her father's idea that she assume the care of the narrator's twins. She will have the use of a sunny, spacious home with extensive lawns, along with the support of her parents and brother. Her mother will eventually give classes in child care to crêche mothers, who trust her as a grandmother rather than as a "mere theorist" (371). The crêche becomes known in the neighborhood as "The Babies University" (371)! The sister-narrator had initially suffered from a physical breakdown; however, her husband, Huntley, accompanied her to California to restore her strength.

Had the solutions envisioned here existed in reality, Gilman herself would have enjoyed a different childhood and the experience generating "The Yellow Wallpaper" would not have occurred.[14] The story also demonstrates how men as physicians—here a father and son, brother of the sisters—participate in the changed behavior necessary for women's lives to expand. Their provision of daily medical examinations of the children does not, however, include shared child care or parenting. But Gilman's utopian solution is again marred by her bias: Jessie snaps her criticism of mothers who will hire as a nanny "any kind of an ignorant young thing—a low-class foreigner" (410). Gilman does not escape her era's cult of the mother as the savior of her home: again, she seems to worship mothering, especially as a business for some women in order to free other women. But she does begin to question the necessity for all women to practice mothering and for all mothering to be done in private homes. And although she edges toward requiring participation of men and fathers in this essential social activity, she never equals Nancy Chodorow in the belief that children require nurturance from adults of both sexes.[15] The story exemplifies Gilman's two-part labor theory: "mutualism" (labor service for the common good of all) and "specialization" (division of labor whereby individuals perform work in which they are particularly interested or for which they are specially suited).[16]

"Aunt Mary's Pie Plant" (see selection 1; *Woman's Home Companion* 6, June 1908) further develops the theme of specialization and points toward Gilman's first novel, *What Diantha Did,* a study in alternative housekeeping methods. An editorial headnote proclaims that "Mrs. Gilman's characters show in a convincing way how her beliefs and remedies would work out in practice. [This story] will be found a realistic miniature [of Edward Bellamy's] 'Looking Backward' " (14).[17] Gilman likely benefited from her own lecturing before the Nationalist Clubs in imagining this story, which demonstrates how the evolution toward cooperation and community advocated by Nationalists might occur through club activity.

The club organizer here is Mary Gardiner, whose niece, reporter Maria Potter, returns after a twelve-year absence, with the assignment to write a newspaper story about the sleepy town she expects to find. Instead of sleepiness, Maria finds bustling activity: her aunt now practices her pie-making skill in a thriving factory—M. GARDINER, PIES. Other women of rural New Newton have likewise established businesses offering various household services. Active businesswomen, they are now individually richer, and their town collectively more prosperous, than previously. At the Woman's Farm and Garden Club meeting, women deliver knowledgeable papers on asparagus culture, beekeeping, and fruit jellies. Their competence surprises Maria. Ever in touch with her times, Gilman has "re-presented" both Nationalist and women's club activity of the era: not welcome officially in the business world, women had banded together to effect change, to socialize, to learn, and to earn.[18]

Through this Club, the New Newton women have bolstered each other's business projects. Overall town prosperity has led to the construction in a park-like setting of a New Central School, equipped to serve luncheon to students and to offer a crèche and kindergarten facilities to mothers. The instigator behind all the innovation is the minister: Gilman is typically unbiased in attributing to characters of either sex the capacity to innovate.[19] He has led the women to see the cash value of their domestic skills. Their husbands respect them more now that they see women's work converted into pay. The women want cash, but not cooperation, as they prefer not to mix up families. A cooked food service, run by the best cooks, delivers hot fare that is better and cheaper than the fare individual homes earlier provided.[20]

Maria despairs of writing the required article about "this prancing young Utopia" (317). Then she capitulates entirely by accepting the marriage proposal of her aunt's plant manager. He convinces Maria that she can continue to write because housekeeping need take none of her time and rural free delivery will post her articles anywhere they are required to be sent. Here Gilman retrospectively meets the dual needs unmet in her first unsuccessful marriage: both to perform domestic work for a household and to accomplish her own work for the world. Although Gilman's mother experienced a disastrous marriage, and although her own first marriage led to a severe psychic breakdown, the biographical precedent of her second happy marriage in 1900 likely encouraged her to make satisfactory marriages one of the elements possible in her utopian terrain—even though, in her own projection of new plots for heroines, she downplays the traditional endings for women of marriage or death.[21]

In *What Diantha Did* (*Forerunner* 1, Nov. 1909–Dec. 1910), Gilman expands her consideration of the fit between a woman's professional and personal roles, as well as continuing her "re-presentation" of housekeeping improvements. She dedicated this novel to "The Housewife." The heroine, Diantha Bell, demonstrates that this role has numerous possibilities for energetic professional action. First, to learn directly of the problems at issue, she works as a professional household manager for the Porne family. She frees mother and architect I. H. Wright (Mrs. Edgar Porne, Ellie to her family) to pursue her profession. Not skilled in housework, Ellie has been distressed because marriage and motherhood have required her to change her work: "I'd rather plan a dozen houses! Yes—I'd rather build 'em—than keep one clean!" she growls (chap. 4). Diantha sets the terms of her own six-month contract, then so improves the home atmosphere that Edgar finds her essential to the family's well-being, whatever her price.

Next, Diantha becomes a social activist. She establishes a Study and Amusement Club for local working women as an educational effort, both to learn herself about women's working conditions and to offer support to club members. As a result of the club work, Diantha receives an invitation to deliver a lecture on "The True Nature of Industry" at the Orchardina [California] Home and Culture Club, a group of employers whose employees belong to the Study and Amusement Club (see selection 3). Diantha's lecture encapsulates ideas from Gilman's *Human Work,* as well as from essays discussed previously, and draws upon Gilman's experiences presenting lectures on radically controversial social issues. Gilman cleverly inserts exposition of theory later to be realized in the action of the novel.

Diantha makes five points. First, she defines "domestic industry" as a stage, not a kind, of labor, since all labor originally was domestic, though much is now becoming social—that is, performed in specialized factories away from the home. Second, she explains that domestic workers are a survival of slave labor, of the ancient household of a man and his female servants, that the problem is the demand for celibate workers. A constantly changing series of untrained, unmarried girls cannot master the skills of household management. Third, she argues that "house service [is] exacting and responsible, involving a high degree of skill as well as moral character," that pay for such service is less than for unskilled labor and includes primitive barter (chap. 7, 14). (Gilman does not question capitalism and does not support cooperative ventures, such as bartering services. She assumes that a work ethic functions to control abusive behavior.) Fourth, Diantha turns to the notion of "domestic economy" and enumerates all the wastes that private housekeeping can entail. She explains, "If one hundred men undertake some common business, they do not divide into two halves, each man having another man to serve him—fifty productive laborers, and fifty cooks. Two or three cooks could provide for the whole group; to use fifty is to waste 47 per cent. of the labor" (chap. 7, 14). Fifth, she notes that we waste even more money than labor.

Finally, Diantha turns to solutions. She proclaims that cooperative housekeeping will not work (and repeats ideas from Gilman's article on the subject): collecting unskilled workers will not help, and families need the privacy of separate homes. Instead the kitchen (and other domestic labor, such as the laundry) will go the way of the cow to a common source of supply, the local dairy in this case, and "we shall order our food cooked instead of raw" (chap. 7, 15). Diantha concludes:

> This will give to the employees a respectable well-paid profession, with their own homes and families; and to the employers a saving of about two-thirds of the expense of living, as well as an end of all our difficulties with the servant question. That is the way to elevate—to enoble domestic service. It must cease to be domestic service—and become world service (chap. 7, 15).[22]

A melee of discussion breaks out, with the minister commending Miss Bell for her "rational" and "hopeful" words, and her supporters within the audience seceding to form a New Women's Club. Gilman expanded upon these five sources of waste in an essay based upon Diantha's lecture and called "The Waste of Private Housekeeping," so that in 1913 life followed fiction.

As a result of this lecture, Diantha can move to the next stage of her plan, staffing the old Union Hotel as a model of housekeeping reform. A club member and wealthy widow, Viva Weatherstone, will hire the staff that Diantha selects. Thus in the fall, a cafeteria and a lunch-pail service begin. Diantha innovates a Business Men's Lunch and supports a House Worker's Union. Then Viva returns from Europe with a wagon for providing a cooked food delivery service. Diantha's mother arrives to handle the bookkeeping. And New Union Home, the household employees' club and residence, becomes a famous Orchardina institution. Former servants escape the economic and sexual exploitation often experienced when living within the households that they served.

Finally, in concert with architect Isabel and financier Viva, Diantha builds and opens the Hotel del las Casas [*sic*], a Centre of Housekeeping. The complex has a central building surrounded by kitchenless cottages. So successful is her management that, within a year, she has bought out the company. Diantha proves that a cooked food delivery service and cafeteria can, through specialized labor, relieve women of individual domestic drudgery or difficulty with domestic service. In addition, women are freed to pursue independent careers and to enjoy family life, whether as employers of or employees in domestic specialized service.[23]

Too often, however, Gilman notes the ethnic identity of such servants or workers, occasionally even those of foreign nobility, not to include but to exclude and distance them from equality with typically Anglo-European central characters. As in other selections discussed, *What Diantha Did,* too, shows Gilman's ethnic insensitivity through the depiction of the only "blacks" as servants (chap. 1); the slur "Chinks," in the mouth of an ignorant speaker (chap. 13); and references to Asians (Gilman uses "Oriental" or "Chinaman," chap. 14), Danes (chap. 10), and Swedes (chap. 11) as agricultural or domestic laborers only.[24] Throughout *What Diantha Did,* Gilman typically uses ethnic epithets to devalue or elevate, to marginalize the person so named—in contrast to what happens in a utopia such as Piercy's *Women on the Edge of Time,* where differences are causes for celebration.

Although Gilman slips problematically into ethnocentricity, she remains brilliant on gender issues. Her heroine Diantha triumphs personally as she does professionally: Ross Warden, her fiancé, then spouse, gradually learns to accept and value her work. At first, Ross baffles Diantha by assuming for himself career freedom that he does not extend to her. She refuses to leave her business to join him, and assures herself that, in not wanting her to keep her work as he expects to do himself, he has in fact refused her. She speaks a little bitterly of men who *are* "willing to let their wives grow" (chap. 11). Ross at last learns on his professional travels that Diantha's now-famous innovations have contributed greatly to the improvement of daily life. The novel concludes upon her reading a letter from him acknowledging his newly found pride in her achievement. Gilman refuses the more typical endings of marriage or death, and instead highlights in closure the man's acceptance of his wife as a complete human being, having the same rights and needs as himself—in stark contrast to Charles Walter Stetson. Gilman shows that Diantha is at least as moved by this acceptance of her work and her full humanness as by Ross's earlier marriage proposal. Marriage without growth-enhancing work stifles and depresses a married woman as much as it would a man.

The novel closes with a demonstration that a husband can fully understand his wife's need to attain professional achievement. This couple is both more convincing and more advanced in their capacity to cooperate and extend mutual respect to each other than are two other couples in Gilman's early narratives: at the conclusion of "Aunt Mary's Pie Plant," readers are simply led to expect that such understanding can be achieved; concluding "A Woman's Utopia," Gilman sketches a quickly converted man without revealing the process of his change.

The ideas of *What Diantha Did* belong to the tradition of early nineteenth-century Owenite socialism, part of a "grand domestic revolution" of "material feminists" in the late nineteenth-century United States. Dolores Hayden discusses Gilman's contribution in *The Grand Domestic Revolution,* a study of women's thought and reform regarding changed domestic arrangements as a means of improving women's status.[25] Hayden believes that Gilman supported a "benevolent capitalism" that challenged neither social nor economic class, nor women's responsibility for domestic work. Hayden believes that Gilman was concerned primarily with professional wife-mothers, who were a very small demographic group during Gilman's lifetime: most professional women chose not to marry. Finally, Hayden criticizes Gilman for not supporting producers' cooperatives as a means for women to gain control over their labor. But she extols Gilman for making clear a connection between "feminist ideals" and "improved motherhood," for contributing the perception that improving women's condition would promote the evolution of humanity, rather than evolution promoting women's emancipation (184, 197, 203–5).

Polly Wynn Allen, in *Building Domestic Liberty,* expands the analysis of Gilman's thought and practice by considering how she embodies principles of "architectural feminism" in utopian fiction. Allen finds that Gilman exemplifies her principles of neighborhood design in *What Diantha Did* (114–15). In short stories, Gilman presents four more specific models: apartment hotels and boardinghouses (146), housing clustered around a common labor center (151), clubhouses especially for women's improvement and support (155), and spaces designed for women's recovery from excessive demands upon her energy (158). And in her utopian novels, Gilman develops a complete "nonsexist landscape," a fully imagined society, though the lesser-known *Moving the Mountain,* not the nostalgic *Herland,* provides the more panoramic view of specific urban and suburban developments (100). Allen stresses the integral position that Gilman's fiction holds in her utopian imagination (especially chaps. 4 and 7).[26]

In addition to exemplifying "a grand domestic revolution" expressed in terms of architectural feminism, *What Diantha Did* also sums up the first stage in the development of Gilman's utopian thinking. It expands and concretizes ideas central to *Women and Economics,* namely, women's need to be economically self-supporting as well as the crucial economic value of domestic work. And it, too, glosses Gilman's biography, with Diantha an alter ego for Gilman as lecturer, radical innovator, and seeker after social betterment, and Ross blending traits of both Gilman's husbands in showing how a self-oriented Walter Stetson might grow into an other-supporting Houghton Gilman.

Published in the *Forerunner* during the serialization of *What Diantha Did* and one-half year after "A Garden of Babies," "Her Housekeeper," by contrast, does anticipate Chodorow (see selection 4; *Forerunner* 1.4, January 1910). A male realtor and manager of boardinghouses provides the environment in which the woman he loves, also mother of a son not his own, can pursue her career: he finds for her live-in help—a governess to provide child care and a maid to housekeep, a cook to her taste, and friends as co-tenants. The woman finds him a "real comfort" because he can "leave off being a man" and "just be a human creature" (4). The "plot" consists of his refutation of her list of six reasons why she will not "remarry."

Gilman has placed at the center of this story radical reform of the institution of marriage: a wife may retain her freedom, keep her profession, take lovers—so long as she does not love them—and need never housekeep (6–8)! In this story, the woman's son would figure as "an added attraction" to this successful suitor (6): if she wanted to take a foreign tour, he would with delight care for her son (7).[27] What appears is a model feminist partner, caring for a woman as much as for her child. Dare we call him, by analogy to Joanna Russ's *Female Man* (1975), a "male woman"? The transformative redrawing of male gender boundaries enacted in these two family stories is realizably utopian.

Moving the Mountain: Previews of Herland, 1911–1913

The lowest level of social organization, the family—the usual institution in Western or European cultures for child care—engaged Gilman's attention during the first stage of her progress toward *Herland*. She began to adjust the male gender role so that a man could provide greater autonomy and support for a woman, or, at the least, not get in the way of her work. Gilman also considered how families might be part a next-higher level of social organization, the neighborhood, as she questioned the inefficient insularity of private families.

Then Gilman moved on to tackle a second stage of development in her utopian imaginative writing: she enlarged her view beyond the immediate family and neighborhood to society as a whole. As earlier, she continued to test in *Forerunner* fiction from 1911 to 1913 the utopian principles explained in previous or concurrent nonfiction. One novel, one essay, and six short stories constitute this group. Gilman wrote her first novel, the 1911 *Moving the Mountain,* to construct a whole society. The stories, three from 1912 and from 1913, develop some facet of society: three stories, along with a 1913 essay—"Her Memories," "Maidstone Comfort," "Mrs. Hines' Money," and the essay "The Waste of Private Housekeeping"—continue to consider issues from *What Diantha Did*; one, "A Strange Land," anticipates the 1915 *Herland,* while being two-sexed; and two—"Bee Wise" and "A Council of War"—anticipate the woman-centered feature of *Herland.*

A futuristic romance, *Moving the Mountain (Forerunner* 2, 1911), amplifies the society that Gilman had begun to sketch in the 1907 "A Woman's Utopia." As in that text, a male narrator returning to the United States finds substantial social improvement, much of it attributable to an expansion of women's roles. Here John Robertson, lost in Tibet for thirty years, finds that, by 1940, women are filling positions formerly allotted only to men. His younger sister Nellie, a physician, now heads a coeducational college. He is shocked to find that women now perform whatever work was formerly relegated to men alone, from store management to civil engineering. Nellie proudly explains that a new religion has changed people's minds: since society has effected conditions beyond those formerly believed to constitute heaven, the religious emphasis now rests upon Life and Living (chap. 2). As their steamer passes Ellis Island, Nellie observes that a process of Compulsory Socialization for immigrants electing to enter the country has melted them into the national pot. On the one hand, Gilman clearly believed that newcomers could participate equally in the democratic process; on the other, her patronizing imposition of training, carrying with it the assumption that our ways are superior to any other ways, provides additional evidence of Gilman's ethnocentrism and increasing xenophobia (chap. 3).[28]

Upon their arrival in New York City, Nellie introduces John to her husband, son, and daughter. All are eager to explain the numerous reforms that have occurred. Repeating the domestic practices Gilman had depicted in *What Diantha Did,* housekeeping and child care are managed by experts so that women may enjoy remunerative labor; poverty has therefore disappeared (chap. 4)—an indication of Gilman's accurate recognition of the extent to which poverty is predominantly female. Gilman incorporates the innovative theory of sociologist Lester F. Ward that, as Nellie's husband, Owen, puts it, " 'The female *is* the race type; the male *is* her assistant' " (136). (In his 1888 *Forum* article, "Our Better Halves," Ward had posited that the apparently superior strength and intellect of the male exists to win as his mate the female, she being the evolutionarily prior, stable sex, who is usually sole defender of her young.) Married women no longer provide domestic service to their spouses or families, but function as fully human individuals instead of "over-sexed female animals" (138), an epithet recalling Gilman's argument in *Women and Economics.* Owen assures John that the changed practices benefit both sexes: women consider men less overbearing nuisances than formerly, while men now find the fully human women more attractive (chap. 5).

Overwhelmed by new information, John writes himself a digest of it, which he asks the others to critique. First, he considers material prosperity and social progress—labor, residence, transit, and agriculture. Foremost on his mind is the disappearance of poverty, behind which lies a changed understanding of labor, including women's labor. "Work is social service—social service is religion," he is told (166). Not work itself, but bad working conditions, caused people's previous dislike of it. Controlled reproduction, along with improved education, and environment also contributed. Now work in the form of world service benefits all (chap. 6).

Next, John investigates one of the earliest rural "residence groups," Westholm Park. It seems to him like a great summer resort. Recreation facilities for adults and children abound. All is strikingly beautiful: to ensure that residents maintain such beauty, a board of judges is elected, who can be changed or recalled. A central kitchen furnishes food to private dining rooms in homes or to public dining areas. Food bought and prepared in bulk is cheaper and better. Organized housekeeping has improved conditions for all women—those who specialize either in it or in some other line of labor. And children receive far more parental time than "on a Sunday in the suburbs" (195; chap. 7). On another day, John experiences transportation as efficient, clean (completely electrified), and beautiful. Productive trees line transitways, their insect diseases controlled by natural predators. Hydroculture flourishes. Local Town Houses provide rooms for numerous activities, though social drinking has diminished in popularity. Constructive civilization, not destructive war, predominates. Women receive credit for these last changes (chap. 8), an essentialism we today may wish to question, although Gilman is more typically nonsexist in her estimates that human possibility not be tied to sex identity.

Finally, John examines cultural changes in education, the arts, and religion (see selection 5, chap. 9 on education). The education of children began with changed mothers—whole persons, economically independent, with specialized child care available. Veritable "Infant Paradises" now exist as child-gardens where all is arranged for the pleasure and welfare of the child. With children the first priority of society, the best artists—half of whom are mothers—create work to beautify and educate them. Children are protected from fear and discomfort. Factories provide "mother time" for the nursing of infants in neighboring child-gardens, where mothers can go after the two-hour shifts men as well as women work to prevent bodily harm from assembly-line specialization (252). Ample suitable equipment permits infants to develop physically into able toddlers (chap. 9). Varied activities and materials allow children always to be doing what they like. Children receive the interested attention of parents, nurses, and teachers, all of whom work short shifts to prevent their tiring. Learning comes predominantly from experience, rather than from books; girls and boys do not exhibit gender-specific behavior (chap. 9).

Arts and theatre flourish; age does not limit activities. John learns that "real human living requires a larger group than one family" (277); many participate in artistic creativity, thanks to abundant leisure and a university extension movement. The Press has improved under a socialist reorganization of business that forbids advertising (chap. 10)! The extent of human growth possible under the new conditions most impresses John with respect to the rehabilitation of his friend Frank Borderson from petty criminal to ethics professor. In place of religion, Frank argues for ethics, a science of human relation, or applied sociology, that is developed and spread by many individuals working in concert. Love, with its power, is central as duty and service to others. Frank explains the view that human life is now understood as a continuous stream, made up of temporary individuals. Some incorrigible misfits were killed, but many improved with changed social conditions. Socialism spread peacefully: with war and graft curtailed, the economic base could provide the increased capital needed to support social change (chap. 11). Travel demonstrates to John the efficacy of new ways in country towns: employment and life's necessities are assured to all.

But John is homesick. He quietly sets off for the private mountain residence of his father's brother, Uncle Jake, and his family, where former conditions persist. However, John finds that the new ways are better, and leaves with his cousin Drusilla as his wife. They find that the new world of 1940 fulfills their vision of heaven (chap. 12), a witty and optimistic reversal of the nineteenth-century "Gates" books by Elizabeth Stuart Phelps, in which she presented a heavenly afterlife as the utopia missed on earth.

The barely disguised rhetorical argumentation of *Moving the Mountain* is clumsier than the more realistic treatment of *What Diantha Did* or the cleverly satiric wit of *Herland*. Nonetheless, in it Gilman hoped to validate a society changed to suit women's needs by presenting it through the initially doubting male eyes of John Robertson. This tactic she would multiply by three in *Herland* in order to puncture three types of male attitudes toward women. Robertson's thorough conversion by the end of *Moving the Mountain,* which is counterpointed by his visit back to the earlier social stage represented by Uncle Jake, carries formal narrative conviction. The social changes depicted include those portrayed earlier in *What Diantha Did* and amplify the innovations of "A Woman's Utopia."

What is new in *Moving the Mountain* is its broader scope: a whole society changes. Gilman attempts to indicate how the practice of ideas explained in *Women and Economics, Concerning Children, The Home,* and *Human Work* could effect a better world. In the 1898 *Women and Economics,* she demonstrated that women's inferior status with respect to men derives from economic dependence upon them. In the 1900 *Concerning Children,* she argued for a social motherhood characterized by trained experts providing child care. Next, in the 1903 *The Home: Its Work and Influence,* she attacked the single-family home as wasteful and isolated; instead she advocated socialized house care and kitchenless houses, with public kitchens and food delivery services. In the 1904 *Human Work,* Gilman argued for an organic, sociocentric (communitarian), as opposed to an egocentric (individualistic), theory of society. Although she never satisfactorily worked out the ideas of this book, chapter 11 of *Moving the Mountain* demonstrates its notion of work as communal service.

In *Moving the Mountain,* Gilman sketches social changes that she would present more fully in *Herland.* In short stories that appear in the *Forerunner* during 1912 and 1913, she particularizes how some of the improvements in *Moving the Mountain* might come about. In four short stories as well as a 1913 essay, she continues to consider issues central to *What Diantha Did,* while in three other stories she looks ahead to *Herland.* In the first group are "Her Memories," "Maidstone Comfort," "Mrs. Hines' Money," and "Forsythe & Forsythe": in each Gilman shows the potential effect of women's reforms upon society. The essay, "The Waste of Private Housekeeping," is a revision for separate publication of Diantha's lecture to the Orchardina club women. The second group reveals features more estranged from Gilman's present than the first: "A Strange Land" anticipates communal traits of the 1915 *Herland,* while being two-sexed; "Bee Wise" and "A Council of War" anticipate the woman-centered society that *Herland* would later feature. In the earlier three stories, Gilman bases innovations upon reform within current society, whereas in the later three she depicts a more radically evolved society.

The Diantha-related stories provide greater fictional detail regarding the working out of Gilman's beliefs about what women will need in order to contribute effectively to society as a whole, according to Gilman's experience of society—that is, one based upon monogamous, nuclear family units supported by a capitalistic economy. In 1912, two years after *What Diantha Did,* "Her Memories" appeared (see selection 6; *Forerunner* 3, August 1912). In it, an unnamed male narrator recounts his female companion's memories of her life at Home Court, recalled as the two drift down the Hudson River past its location. This utopian community, situated in four high-rise buildings, provided child care and baby culture in covered, connected rooftop playgrounds; its adult amenities included a quiet central courtyard with fountains, surrounded by cool arcades. Individual families resided in kitchenless apartments, their meals coming up from a common basement kitchen on a service elevator— an innovation not original with Gilman, as Dolores Hayden makes clear.[29] Again Gilman stresses the varied capacities that different women have for mothering; some are suited to the very young, some to the school-aged, and some utterly out of tune with any children, including their own. And Gilman forces us today to rethink commonplace daily activities and recognize their relatedness to larger social goals. Although not limited to gender adjustments, "Her Memories" restructures the domestic environment to permit more equitable relations between the sexes. In this story, Gilman transfers to urban New York City the semirural solutions of "A Garden of Babies" and *What Diantha Did;* she fictionalizes "The Beauty of the Block."

The month after "Her Memories," Gilman published "Maidstone Comfort," in which she imagines utopia as a summer resort community of the same name, featuring kitchenless cottages (see selection 8; *Forerunner* 3, September 1912).[30] The female narrator is a friend of both the manager-owner, Sarah Maidstone Pellett, and the funding instigator of this enterprise, Mrs. Benigna McAvelly,[31] who connected Sarah with Molly Bellew, inheritor of Maidstone Comfort: a women's network lies behind the establishment of the resort, as an inheritance of seashore land by one woman is joined by a second to the developmental and managerial skills of a third. The grounds are tastefully landscaped, the placement of a "casino" and cottages intertwined with winding paths, the accommodations including private bathrooms. "Motor-wagons" deliver meals to guests wherever in the resort they choose to dine. No servants exist, but skilled employees make the resort run smoothly. As in "A Woman's Utopia," the capitalistic basis of this tale may seem at odds with Gilman's Fabian socialist beliefs: rather than continuing her earlier more radical innovations, after her 1900 marriage, she appears more willing to depict bourgeois, middle-class solutions, but she makes women the primary actors on her stage.

Seven months later, Gilman again depended upon an inheritance, rather than behavioral and structural change—the basis she credits for social improvement in *Moving the Mountain*. In "Mrs. Hines' Money," Eva Hines independently creates social innovations that improve the quality of life in her town. Widowed as the result of an accident, she retains her own legal counsel, rather than depending upon that of her brother (see selection 10; *Forerunner* 4, April 1913). With careful planning derived from ideas she has gained through her own travels and from the social service–oriented magazine the *Survey*,[32] she uses the money of her husband, Jason, to build in his memory The Hines Building. She expects this utopian project to raise the consciousness and knowledge of the town by housing within this building a library, an auditorium or theatre, men's and women's lounges, a swimming pool and a gymnasium, a roof tea garden, and meeting rooms for clubs with memberships of all ages. Although these last two tales may be less convincing to us today as social change than the earlier narratives discussed, we must recall that, in Gilman's time, family summer "resorts" were commonplace and a women's club movement was strong and influential. What is, nonetheless, transformative about them is the broad social agency attributed to individual, capable neighborhood-women, a theme broached earlier in "Aunt Mary's Pie Plant."

A facet of society as a whole that is central to Gilman's concern is occupational structure, especially with respect to gender. In the 1913 "Forsythe & Forsythe" (see selection 9; *Forerunner* 4, January 1913), she continues to consider this issue, as presented in two previously discussed stories, the 1908 "Aunt Mary's Pie Plant" and the 1910 "Her Housekeeper." "Aunt Mary's Pie Plant" suggests—both through Aunt Mary, the expert pie-maker, and through her niece, the reporter who will marry and mail articles to her publishers—that women can pursue the world's work in a domestic setting, an early version of flextime. And "Her Housekeeper," in which a real estate broker arranges the life support for an actress, stresses that men's sharing of domestic responsibilities could enable women to experience career success.

Continuing to consider the mesh between domestic relationships and occupations, "Forsythe & Forsythe" stars wife-and-husband law partners, Georgiana Forsythe and her cousin and husband, George Forsythe, whose firm is located in Seattle, Washington. They resolve the problem of housekeeping by living in a residence hotel. A former best friend from college days, businessman James R. "Jimmy-Jack" Jackson, renews his friendship with George. Jimmy-Jack finds that his wife, Susie, a self-centered pleasure seeker, pales in contrast to his first love, George's sister Clare Forsythe, now a sanitary engineer who lives in the same residence hotel. With the arrival of Susie's divorce decree, he proposes marriage to Clare, whose independent competence he admires. Gilman undermines popular wisdom by showing a nondomestic career woman as more attractive to a suitor than a woman for whom marriage is the "crowning event of her life" (2). She also suggests that men might find female competence not a threat, but a boon. This story counters what Gilman claims, in a chapter called "The Effects of the Position of Women on the Race Mind" from "Our Brains and What Ails Them" (serialized, *Forerunner* 3, 1912), is an accepted attitude, namely, that the "wider-experienced, more-socially developed man seeks woman as a female—and avoids her as a friend and companion" (251). In both this tale and "Her Housekeeper," gender adjustments erase the separation of private and public in the occupational structure, and thereby permit the equal participation of both sexes.

As if to underline the need for the solutions fictionalized in the previous stories, Gilman reiterated the problems with housekeeping that underlay them in the same month, July 1913, in which her *Forerunner* story would look ahead to *Herland*. She looked back to Diantha's lecture before the Orchardina club women in *What Diantha Did*, revising it for separate publication as the essay "The Waste of Private Housekeeping" (*American Academy of Political and Social Science Annals* 48, July 1913). Gilman amplifies supporting statistics, and she still enumerates five problems, though a somewhat different five. She retains her concept of "domestic industry" as a relic stage of labor and argues that this stage insures permanently inefficient household labor (91). Household labor is wasted, as all women, whether suited to that type of labor or not, replicate each others' activities in as many households (92). The household plant is likewise wastefully replicated (93): the resulting retail purchasing of individual items occurs without the advantage of wholesale prices available for purchasing larger units (93). And finally, human life is wasted in lost health, energy, and potential growth

(95). Whereas Diantha's lecture also discussed solutions, Gilman's essay focuses solely upon problems: additional solutions would emerge in subsequent stories and in *Herland.*

Finally, during 1912 and 1913, Gilman published three visionary stories, prefiguring the all-female, communitarian society of *Herland*—"A Strange Land," "Bee Wise," and "A Council of War." They depict utopia exhibiting behavioral change that is more in accord with current feminist-socialist theory than that in foregoing stories. In 1912, Gilman imagined an allegorical country, "A Strange Land," where people "governed themselves" (see selection 6; *Forerunner* 3, August 1912). Although she called this a "Democracy," her description suggests autarchy (individual or self-government) or anarchy (no government or no common structure, a society having great diversity).[33] The society has two sexes, but is gynaecocentric. "How to Make Better People" is its root goal. Work toward this end becomes the "Chief Exercise and Basic Condition of Life." "The Beauty of People"—clearly differentiated from "Sex-Attraction," "Fashion," and "Conspicuous Waste"—is studied and appears nearly a religion. The land becomes a "Blooming Garden." Long before "green politics" emerged in the last quarter of the twentieth century, Gilman espoused an ethic of "greening."[34]

The following year, Gilman wrote two more visionary stories, one a month after the other, each featuring the centrality of women in society. "Bee Wise" (see selection 11; *Forerunner* 4, July 1913) takes its title from the statement, "Go to the ant, thou sluggard; consider her ways and be wise" (173).[35] In "Bee Wise," as in "Mrs. Hines' Money," an inheritance makes possible the establishment of a utopian experiment: a ten-million-dollar gift permits a group of friends at a women's college to form a "combination" to create "a little Eden" in California (171). Women establish two model communities. The inheritance combines a California property—in the form Beewise, an upland valley, and Herways, a small coastal port—along with the capital to develop the property. They envision each as "a perfectly natural little town, planned, built, and managed—by women—for women—and *children!*" (171)

Gilman repeats her strategy of "Aunt Mary's Pie Plant": a utopian visitor in the guise of a woman reporter arrives to write an article about these burgeoning little towns, populated largely by women and children, though men live happily in them, too. Discovering that the "Mayor of Herways" is a former college classmate, the reporter agrees to remain as a public relations specialist who

prepares pamphlets to explain to other towns how they can dupli-
cate this experiment. As readers, we are then let in on the winning
practices of Beewise and Herways. Herways, a beach town, boasts
industries such as power generated by reservoir, tide, and wind;
preserved fruits; wool products from Angora goats; cotton and silk
fabrics and garments; wood and leather products; honey; and perfumes. The women agree, "We want to show what a bunch of women
can do successfully. Men can help, but this time we will manage"
(172).

In Beewise, the women establish numerous residential enterprises—a guest house especially for women and children, a sanitarium, a baby-garden, a kindergarten, and a school. The town is run
as a Residence Club; every new arrival has to be approved. (Gilman's ease with exclusionary practices—whether relating to gender, race, or class—is troublesome.) Men are accepted as husbands,
but they are "carefully selected" to preserve a "high grade of motherhood" (172).[36] All are workers; no servants exist. Highly paid nutritional experts prepare the community's food in laboratories.
Child-culture experts extend the practices of Friedrich Froebel and
Maria Montessori. A cap on growth ensures that urban blight would
not develop.

Gilman concludes by proclaiming that "a group of human beings
could live together in such wise as to decrease the hours of labor,
increase the value of the product, ensure health, peace and prosperity, and multiply human happiness beyond measure" (173). This
short story has two major functions: it fictionalizes the values of
Women and Economics and clearly provides a preliminary sketch
for *Herland*. Gilman's intent is neither to exclude men from utopia,
nor to express general hostility toward men, but rather to demonstrate that women's capacity for world service and society building
equals men's. As the fictional social structure has become more complex, Gilman has correspondingly expanded women's social roles.
What a woman can imagine, women can do, she insists: a whole
town's social structure is now transformed.

The next month, Gilman published another woman-centered
story, again focused upon a whole society—"A Council of War" (see
selection 12; *Forerunner* 4, August 1913). Here, in the face of the
apparent imminence of war, twenty to thirty "true and tried" (197)
London women attend a "council" meeting at which women plan "a
government within a government," ambiguously named "an Extension Committee" (199). One councilor reads to the assembled group

her indictment of male rule or domination, the longer "war" of the title. This indictment includes an enumeration of evil consequences and a call "to remove this devastating error in relation and to establish a free and conscious womanhood for the right service of the world" (198).

Although the women know that "the ballot is the best weapon," they determine that "there are others," notably their vision of cooperative action (199).[37] They will tell nothing and begin small—with a "series of businesses," including schools and nurseries, after the manner of "Aunt Mary's Pie Plant," but set up as a "league of interconnected businesses, with the economic advantages of such large union" (199). They envision owning paper mills and printing offices as a second stage, training women in economic organization as a third, and establishing *"right conditions"* in all the foregoing as a fourth. At the prospect of a "woman's world, clean and kind and safe and serviceable [including "the right kind" of man as "needed"], . . . the women looked at one another with the light of a new hope in their eyes" (199, 201): an apt description of *Herland,* to begin appearing in about one year. In this story, Gilman prefigures the Outsiders' Society, populated by the daughters of "educated" men, imagined by Virginia Woolf in her 1938 *Three Guineas* on the eve of yet another world war.[38] "A Council of War" also suggests the antiwar stance of *With Her in Ourland,* a 1916 sequel to *Herland.* Unfortunately, by the end of 1916, Gilman would renounce her antiwar stance. But she continued to prefer reason to violence as a mode of resolving difference.

From *Herland* to *Ourland,* 1915–1921

These last three tales by Gilman point directly toward *Herland* in sketching the outlines of a whole society. The viewpoints they express indicate that Gilman's design for *Herland* was to reveal a world of possibilities and potentials available to women as a sex, rather than to present a sex-separatist society as a final utopian solution.[39] By controlling the factor of sex, Gilman demonstrated the full, adult humanity of women, shared in common with adult men. In this, she simply emulated scientific method: remove one variable to discover how another will function on its own, a veritable thought-experiment.[40] She was clear that women need each other's support to prosper. The previous three stories show Gilman's preference for monogamous family units. *Herland* is more communitarian than her previous writing. In it Gilman extends the family unit over a whole community of women, who responsibly perform the public world-service Gilman advocated, in place of personal service to a nuclear family's domestic unit.[41] This emphasis contradicts the apparently more traditional social structure of her short stories. However, women's communities have existed through history. What we may now enjoy less of, since leaving hunting and gathering societies evolutionarily behind us, are the often more gender-egalitarian practice of these so-called primitive groups.[42] Gilman set as utopia a society in which both sexes developed with equal diversity and strength. But, to bring convincingly before the eyes of her readers the possibility that women and men are, in fact, equally capable, in 1915 she presented in the *Forerunner* a society of women only, seen through the amazed eyes of three male visitors. She had declared in *Our Brains and What Ails Them* (*Forerunner* 3, 1912), "After a few centuries of full human usefulness on the part of women, we shall have not only new achievements to measure but new standards of measurement" (249). In *Herland*, she imagines women having had the previously lacking experience and responsibility to provide these new standards (1912, 250).

This satiric *Herland* incorporates narrative tactics from "A Woman's Utopia" and *Moving the Mountain,* as well as the reform realism of Gilman's short stories and the achievable utopia of *What Diantha Did.* The innovation of *Herland,* in contrast to much of her other didactic fiction, is her use of the often biting wit evident in her 1895 collection of verse, *In This Our World.* Parody in *Herland* is an effective strategy for subverting gender assumptions and practices. In addition, *Herland* society disengages women from the sex parasitism that Gilman deplored in *Women and Economics* and demonstrates that women hold with men a common human potential for world-service.

Herland (*Forerunner* 6, 1915) wittily recounts the adventure of three men from the United States, searching for an all-female country, which they name Herland. They learn that travel to Herland is dangerous: no one has ever returned. Gilman here acknowledges male phobic projection: men's fear of and awe at the power of women —the residual little boy's fear of a seemingly all-powerful mother; this Amazonian myth is a universal male nightmare according to psychologist Phyllis Chesler (3, 5). Chesler notes that feared mythic female power has justified male self-protective aggression against women. Gilman's adventurers claim to know "the stuff that savage dreams are made of"; Gilman provides the reader much fun in her revelation that the adventurers are as susceptible to such dreams as the "savages" to whom they feel superior (3). Her inversion of male phobia is ironic: *Herland* and *With Her in Ourland* together reveal to readers that the male, not the female, is the dangerous sex of the species. In *Herland,* Gilman turns the tables so that the three men by their behavior require women to restrain them. As her frame for a gynaecocentric society, Gilman deliberately invokes misogynist mythology so that she can demonstrate its false nature as unverified assumption.

As for the fact that men "never came back" from this "strange and terrible Woman Land" (3, 2), we find Gilman performing another reversal: although one of the adventurers is an incorrigible masculinist, the other two male visitors (who by contrast appear far more reasonable) undergo a rite of passage, a conversion, to Herland's culture. As visitors to utopian Herland, they confront reversals of their previous sense of everyday life. This confrontation throws them into a liminal state, one of ambiguity and transition. And they function as enticing models for Gilman's readers, who also may enter liminal time by reading *Herland.* So, in this sense, the same men who arrived can "never come back" because they have become different men.[43]

As in "A Woman's Utopia" and *Moving the Mountain,* Gilman exploited the tactic of using naïve male viewpoints: these male visitors to utopia are informed by knowledgeable female guides, who thereby model for the reading audience competent women converting ignorant men to new ways that benefit all. Male acceptance of new information presumably validates it for androcentric readers. Unlike those two utopias, Gilman includes three different male types among the *Herland* adventurers: wealthy macho womanizer Terry O. Nicholson; romantic botanist and physician Jeff Margrave; and rational sociologist and egalitarian Vandyck Jennings. Only the most extreme male type, Terry, dislikes Herland and will be unable to adapt to Herlander ways. The three viewpoints permit Gilman much fun in exposing miscellaneous male misinformation regarding women's ways. For each adventurer, women exist for a different purpose: to be conquered for his pleasure and use, to be idealized and protected by him, or to be objects of scientific inquiry, understood in terms of their biological limitations. Terry tosses off three names for this country—Feminisia, Ladyland, and finally Herland. We never learn the women's own name for their country!

At last arriving in Herland, the three assume that "there must be men," because from their airplane they see that "this is a *civilized* country" (11).⁴⁴ Some years before, writing the lead essay called "Working Love" for the *American Fabian,* Gilman had explained, "A fully civilized community is one wherein the feelings of the social heart are fully and freely expressed through the activity of the social body, where human love can work itself out in orderly channels, as it is so painfully striving to do today." But the visitors have yet to understand this Herlander view of civilization. Deplaning, they enter woods where voices in the trees attract their attention—the voices of three "girls." The initial interaction between the men and the "girls" reveals, in the men's dehumanizing and objectifying manner of address, the extent of their bias against women; to them, women are not human as they themselves are, but rather mere game to be chased or pets to be enjoyed, incapable of the "civilized" heights they consider natural to themselves. They are already exposing the shallowness of their humanity, the thin veneer of their civilization, in their sexist words and manipulative or violent acts (chap. 2).

The three adventurers then experience a "peculiar imprisonment," a variation of the so-called therapeutic confinement of a neurasthenic woman in Gilman's 1892 "The Yellow Wallpaper": they "have been . . . put to bed like so many yearling babies" (25). But this confinement is more than gender-role reversal: Gilman demonstrates what kind of behavior such nursery confinement does suit—immature outbursts in adult men—a more rational use of this treatment than further confinement of an already constricted woman so as to enmadden her completely. Discussion during confinement reveals that each man's belief about how they will be treated accords once again with his attitude toward women: each projects onto the women his own model of ideal gender interaction —host-guest, deliverer-victim, and social scientist-curious phenomenon (26–27). Only the first does not render women inferior. One admires, another exudes professional competence, another evinces interest (28). They are astonished to find the women indifferent to their charms as males, "as if our being men was a minor incident" (30). Each is provided with a special tutor in the language and culture of the country. After an attempted escape fails (chap. 4), they focus in earnest upon learning Herland's history, which follows (54–57).

They are informed that, about two thousand years ago, a volcanic eruption had sealed this "Aryan" (Germanic white) people's mountainous country from its former outlet to the sea—another instance of Gilman's ease with a position of white racial superiority (54; see selection 13: Chapter 5, "A Unique History"). Many of these men died at their posts of defense at that time. The rest were killed in a slave uprising, quelled by the predominant population of "infuriated virgins" (55). A new race of parthenogenetic women developed, all descendants of one First Mother, Maaia: "Queen-Priestess-Mother of them all" (57). Her daughters all began to bear at age twenty-five the first of five daughters, as she had done. Extreme gender traits disappeared; the women were neither especially feminine nor noticeably masculine. They functioned as a family of mothers and sisters, devoted to "Beauty, Health, Strength, Intelligence, Goodness"—all supported by a religion of Maternal Pantheism (59). Mother Earth and motherhood together yielded life as a "long cycle of motherhood" (59), by which Gilman means nurturance and responsible caring for land and people. Her historical finding of prior Goddess-worship comports with current evidence, as does her depiction of relatively egalitarian prior social structure; however, Gilman is less humanly inclusive than are any current theorists of thealogy [*sic*] (see Culpepper 1987).[45] Education became the Herlanders' solution to making "the best kind of people" (59): recall the 1912 "A Strange Land." War and competition did not exist. Gilman ladens with irony the Herlanders' query, "What is the work of the world, that men do—that we have not here?" (60) (Primarily war and violence, *With Her in Ourland* will suggest.)

Quite deliberately, Gilman sets up numerous "odious" comparisons between Herland and Ourland (Our = the readers' world). The three men learn the high social and cultural level attained by Herlanders and view the sophisticated environment they have built. They hold knowledge in common: "what one knew, all know" (64); no hierarchy of information existed. They practice the "fullest and subtlest coordination," such that they seem to exist in a state of constant unanimity. Since all are Mothers, the welfare of children is central to all planning. They function "like an enormous anthill" in their capacity to cooperate for the general welfare: " 'Go to the ant, thou sluggard,' " Jeff sings out to Terry (67).[46] They decided as "Conscious Makers of People" to limit their population, usually to one child per mother if she is deemed fit; a second is permitted only to Over Mothers as the highest reward of the state. Infanticide is unheard of; all mothers consider all children their care. Children consitute less than one-third of the total population. Hygiene and health care of the highest quality ensure the physical well-being of everyone. Psychological knowledge and practice support an ethic of caring (chap. 6).

The more the three men learn about Herland as they are escorted about, the more modest they become about their land, which appears increasingly less reasonable in comparison. Herlanders credit mutation and education for their genetic diversity (77). But Gilman does not develop individualized female characters; rather, they show a troublesome, dystopian flatness. Does this sameness conceal an anxiety of difference? Although an excluding ethnocentrism appears in Gilman's thought, she does, however, make gestures in the direction of inclusion.[47] If she had not labeled Herlanders as "Aryan" and had not, elsewhere in her writing, expressed racist or ethnocentric views, we might be able to use the words of Elizabeth Spelman—"the many turn out to be one, and the one that they are is me" (1988, 159)—with regard to Herlanders and ourselves. But Gilman is not truly supportive of cultural diversity: much of the time, the other in her writing is accorded lesser fictional status and is not presented as a peer of those like herself.[48]

The men note that Herlanders constantly seek improvement— in themselves, in educational method, in agricultural process, in nutritional yield. They have bred out criminal types by discouraging those showing such inclinations from reproducing, and only the most highly competent educate the children. Gilman is glib about making such judgments of fitness: nowhere does she indicate how such selection proceeds, and nowhere does she question human capacity to make such judgments.

After one-half year of learning about Herland in confinement, the men are permitted "to address general audiences and classes of girls" (84). Gilman then puts each through courtship paces. They reencounter the three young women first heard in the trees, and learn just how far wrong their estimates had been concerning their reception. Because they cannot rely upon gifts as part of courtship, they must depend solely upon their personalities. To their chagrin, previously reliable courting demeanor backfires, because these women have too much self-esteem to be taken in by manipulative tactics. And their patriotism encompasses love of home, family, community, and country with such strength that they are not subject to romantic dependency: they neither yield nor submit.

This remarkable self-esteem derives from Herland's mode of

life: the residents are communally integrated from birth to death. Youngsters learn through carefully devised play and games; formal educational training occurs only to transmit job skills to adolescents. Life is of one piece. Herlanders have no marriage, no homes per se. Nursing infants remain close to their birth mothers, but soon specially trained co-mothers take over. Children experience living in all the regions of the country so that they will feel at home everywhere in it.[49] "Education for citizenship" is what they receive (108).[50] Self-assured adult women result.

Herlanders' religion, too, fosters female confidence. Central is their deification of motherhood, practice of a common motherhood, and consequent orientation toward their children's future.[51] Education and treatment have replaced punishment. The practice of autarchy, or self-government, in place of patriarchal domination, and a theory of a Loving Power have permitted each Herlander to develop a strong and positive sense of self. The ubiquity of little temples providing Temple Service—counsel offered by those with a gift for it, called Temple Mothers—makes immediately available the assuaging of fears, anxieties, uncertainties, or occasional hurts. The Herlanders find immortality in the continuation of the race, rather than of the individual, so that dying becomes an event in the process of the life of the race. Although "Their Religion" clashes with "Our Marriages," to strains of the "Hymn of The Coming Life," at the Altar of Motherhood, the three men exchange marriage vows with three Herland women before the Herland multitude (chap. 10).

Then the "Difficulties" emerge. They are related by the male narrator, sociologist Vandyck Jennings, who suggests many male viewpoints that Gilman had learned from her own experience. *Herland* exposes the absurdity of the men's expected mastery and the reasonableness of Herland women's self-respect. Van explains, "We . . . fondly imagined that we could convince them otherwise. What we imagined, before marriage, did not matter any more than what an average innocent young girl imagines. We found the facts to be different" (122). Gilman draws the analogies of ants in anthills or angels in divine service to suggest the dilemma of these three male innocents. They complain that their partners do not understand "the very nature of the relation" (124)[52]—the meaning of wifehood, the pleasure of sexuality for its own sake beyond its function in fatherhood, according to their male viewpoint. Instead of seeking ultra-maleness or ultra-femaleness, Herlanders wish human comaraderie to exist between spouses. And they expel from Herland the one spouse, macho Terry, who insists upon practicing mastery, but they delay his departure until he has sworn not to reveal the location of Herland: in his former view, a "sublimated summer resort— just Girls," a veritable male Paradise of women (10); further irony occurs in the Herlanders' view that, as a male, he has brought the sin of violation into this female Eden!

In *Herland*, Gilman validates motherhood by making it the nation's highest religious and social office.[53] Herland applauds "The New Motherhood" and awaits to celebrate the first nonvirgin birth in two thousand years, "this new miracle of union," an ironic reversal of Christianity's beginning (140)! But the central couple, Ellador and Vandyck, will delay childbearing until they return from a year of surveying the world beyond Herland.

The 1916 sequel, *With Her in Ourland*, recounts this world survey. Vandyck Jennings and his Herland bride, Ellador, fly eastward over our globe to view the devastation being wrought by World War I (chap. 2), to visit China and Japan (chaps. 3 and 4), but predominantly to inspect and diagnose conditions in the United States (chaps. 5–12). The contrasts between Our ways and Hers astonish Ellador into satiric commentary. Gilman utilizes a traditional antiutopian mode: satiric dialogue and travelogue from the viewpoint of a visitor from utopia. But in comparison with *Herland*, *With Her in Ourland* plods. No adventure or romance plot provides *Herland*'s momentum. Ellador decries war either as an expression of hatred and madness, or as a mode of population control; she views "human life as a thing in the making, with human beings as the makers" (44). Upon arriving in San Francisco, Ellador notes, "The very first thing that strikes me in this great rich lovely land of yours is its *unmotherliness*. We are of course used to seeing everything taken care of" (126). Ellador finds Our country untrained in democracy: she sees appalling inequities of income, egregious wastefulness in individual households, and incomprehensible greed among a corporate elite.[54] She also finds the private sector of marriage and home life inadequate, and public transportation and communication beneath what is needed.

Throughout the novel, Gilman's racism, anti-Semitism, and ethnocentrism unfortunately surface. Especially chapter 6, called "The Diagnosis," with its xenophobic ethnocentrism, and chapter 10, (untitled) with its racial prejudice, exemplify Gilman's problems. In chapter 6, Ellador observes to Van that in the United States "you have stuffed yourself with the most ill-assorted and unassimilable mass of human material that was ever held together by artificial means" (153). From this, the chapter then rushes downhill to "Black —yes, and how about the yellow? Do they 'melt'?" (155) and "New York . . . reverts to the clan system with its Irishmen, and back of that, to the patriarchy, with its Jews" (157). Although the later chapter opens with Ellador defending an African-American against a "Southern sociologist" (263), she quickly resumes a prejudicial stance: "if they are decent, orderly and progressive, there is no problem. It is the degraded negro that is so feared" (264). For the remaining two-thirds of the chapter, she waxes anti-Semitic: "I think the Christian races have helped the Jews to overestimate their religion" (266). Ellador's solution to "the Jewish problem" is for the Jews to "leave off being Jews" (267). The pages of the chapter multiply such biased and dystopian commentary.

Feminism remains Gilman's strongest suit and the important utopian strain to examine in this work, especially in the final two chapters. Whereas Ellador has offered general criticism of Ourland, Van takes over in analyzing the status of women, the cause of which he locates in men's treatment of women (see selection 14, untitled chap. 11 on feminist issues). In a potentially clever ploy, Gilman uses a male voice to name male errors. Van claims, "We men, having all human power in our hands, have used it to warp and check the growth of women. . . . With every conceivable advantage—we have blamed women for the sins of the world!" (292). But Ellador objects, and in her mouth Gilman places astonishingly unsympathetic views: "What ails the women *now*. . . . They have had some education for several generations, numbers of them have time to think, some few have money—I cannot be reconciled to the women" (292). Ellador ridicules women's absurd dress (292–93), and then regrets these comments as "harsh" and proceeds to praise "the woman's movement" (295).[55] She advocates the usual array of Gilman reforms. Van concludes his account of the exchange by noting, "How to make the best kind of people and how to keep them at their best and growing better—surely that is what we are here for" (297), nearly a direct quotation from Gilman's 1912 "A Strange Land."

The couple returns to Herland, and the reader is told, by way of conclusion, that "in due time a son was born to [them]" (325). Does this suggest no innovation, but a stereotypic preference for male offspring? At least two viewpoints are possible. First, a serious view: just as the birth of a female child can be taken as metaphoric of a rebirth of female potential or of a new woman, so here this birth can prefigure the birth of a new man able to shoulder equally with a new woman the stewardship of the world and its society.[56] This view is continuous with Gilman's most innovative *Forerunner* short stories. Second, in a jocular vein, I see a mischievous smirk on Gilman's face: she finds no more convincing place for the male sex in society than the increased genetic diversity permitted by sexual reproduction and fatherhood, just as men have found motherhood the paramount use for the female sex. Once again, she offers us witty gender reversal. Common human capacity and potential accounts for all else: gender might thus become irrelevant. Sexuality for its own sake is beyond Gilman's capacity to consider: that is a topic for another occasion.[57] Like social scientists today, Gilman carefully differentiated between gender—the social roles, in which she found human gender similarity nearly limitless—and sex, the biological functions, to which she found sex difference limited.[58]

Close in time to the Herland books, Gilman wrote three articles on towns: "Standardizing Towns" (1915), "Applepieville" (1920), and "Making Towns Fit to Live In" (1921). "Standardizing Towns" appeared concurrently with the third chapter of *Herland* in the *Forerunner,* as if Gilman were clarifying her own thoughts on utopian towns before the three adventurers could discover the superiority of those in *Herland.* In the article, Gilman recommends a "Better Towns Contest," such as "The Better Babies' Contest," to arouse interest in a standardized scale for measuring "what a Town should be." She suggests as an outline ten "Points," all together providing ample "work for our Women's Clubs!" (54) (In the 1920s and 1930s, women participated very seriously in numerous clubs, as previously noted; Gilman herself belonged to several, including the famous avant-garde Heterodoxy Club in New York City.) Under (1) Health, she includes carefully kept vital statistics, along with technical and social provisions for public hygiene. She includes under (2) Beauty not location, but city planning, such as the Chicago World's Fair of 1893 demonstrated. She would show (3) Virtue by recording public vice and crime. An Honor Record of (4) Public Spirit would demonstrate all instances of charity, correction, and reform. (5) Educational Facilities Gilman finds in general good, if unevenly so; she offers no specifics here. She applauds the school extension movement as a way to provide (6) Social Facilities for gatherings, amusement, and instruction. A standard of (7) Minimum Prosperity would mean "no poverty" would become the accepted standard for town pride. An honor record for (8) Administrative Efficiency and (9)

Administrative Honesty is in order, and (10) Progressiveness might be noted by recognizing courage and advancement: Gilman is vague here. But population and commercial statistics are not, to her mind, adequate measures. *Herland,* in fact, incorporates these ten points as standards for social life.

Five years after *Herland,* Gilman wrote "Applepieville," a discussion of rural development that would make country living more congenial. She envisioned farms radiating from a community center like wedges of pie. The center would include a bandstand, surrounded by a ring of park blocks, along the outer circumference of which would be ranged a church, a town hall, a post office-bank, stores, a school with a playground and pool behind, a community house, and a library. This layout would be a method to stem the flow of farm family members to "crowded cities and uncongenial work," while at the same time making their lives more fulfilling. Village, as opposed to individual, farming has the advantage of being easier to implement: a common creamery, shared farm machinery, and group marketing of produce are among the possibilities. Gilman argues for organized group effort. Central to her concern is women's place: one hundred farms do not need one hundred women to provide domestic service, but maybe twenty-five, so seventy-five can be released for other, productive, work. This is the 1908 story "Aunt Mary's Pie Plant" recast as an essay on the needs of farm residents, with points from the 1913 "The Waste of Private Housekeeping" blended in for good measure.

In 1921, "Making Towns Fit to Live In" (*The Century* 102, July), again recapitulates, this time the *Forerunner's* 1915 "Standardizing Towns." Gilman amplifies the earlier article by creating five sections, three of them new. She begins as before, noting that "boasters" has become "boosters" with respect to town pride, and wondering what standards can be developed for judging towns. She charges club women, even though now "commanding the power of the ballot," to be active in making cities worthy of pride. In a second section, she enumerates the types of cities—factory, mining, and county seat—and suggests that citizens "need a little book on 'What Is a City?' " (362). She expects such a book to explain civilization as being based in cities, farms as part of a city-based culture, and human growth as affected by town quality. Her third section describes the remaining contents of "What Is a City?": the nutritive system, the bases of civic development, and the civic functions of a first-class modern town. Section four enumerates these functions and summarizes the ten points characteristic of "banner towns," already familiar from "Standardizing Towns." In a final section, Gilman suggests developing a "sample town" for demonstrating improvements, establishing minimum requirements, projecting civic activities, and anticipating economic problems. Such efforts will, she believes, permit citizens to boast of their towns "on sure grounds."

A last utopian piece, a one-page typed outline, "A Proclamation of Inter-dependence," dates probably from September 1928. Like other forward-looking citizens, Gilman, too, must have felt dismay that the United States waited until 1921 to ratify the 1915 Treaty of Versailles, which officially concluded World War I, and, in xenophobic and isolationist complacency, never joined the League of Nations. Gilman here enumerates five reasons justifying a call for a conference of all the nations of the earth to draw up a Federated Union of the World: (1) the need for world co-operation; (2) the impossibility of peace without the agreement of all to keep it; (3) the inability of separate nations alone to prevent international disturbances; (4) the numerous interrelationships now providing a basis for such union; and (5) the natural process of national evolution requiring such federation as a next step. More than a decade after writing *With Her in Ourland,* Gilman returned for a moment to a global view, in spite of her personal xenophobic retreat from advocacy of a pluralist society.

This brief piece completes Gilman's journey from home to world —through neighborhood and society toward utopia, in short story, essay, and novel—between 1904 and 1928. Having considered this survey, we may wonder what is the use today of reading utopian visions imagined by Charlotte Perkins Gilman. Can they, in the 1990s, still perform "cultural work"? I think the answer is affirmative. Both individually and collectively, we repeat whatever we do not understand or have not resolved. In her writing, Gilman explored existential issues that are still problematic for contemporary women. Even though problems she explicated remain unsolved, she mapped territory that remains for us to continue exploring. Although current scholars of utopia argue that utopias are guides rather than blueprints, Gilman herself wrote, whether in fiction or nonfiction, to change people's behavior: hers was polemical writing with a clearly rhetorical purpose, far closer to blueprint than guide. She advocates a program of social change. She expects what she writes to move readers to change the conditions of their lives. Her didactic aesthetic permitted her to accept utopia as blueprint, even though we may view her writing more as mapping the territory we must evaluate, the "cultural work" her writing performs now for us, as we imagine our progress toward utopia.

Readers may be tempted to discount many of Gilman's schemes as those of a "mere" dreamer. But particularly those in her more realistic stories, as well as those in her articles, represent astute and realistic visions of change that people could ease into, change that could lead to the attitudinal innovation presented, for example, in *Moving the Mountain*. Psychologists tell us that behavioral change precedes attitudinal change. For instance, one treatment for depression, called cognitive therapy, involves actively confronting and setting aside negative thought patterns in order to alter one's overall attitude—or, to put the insight into other words, our conscious minds actively reprogram unconscious, automatic behavioral responses that have developed through living.[59] Fiction can function in a likewise suggestive mode for the receptive reader. Self-fulfilling prophecies, as "learned optimism," have long been understood to bring about the very event or action believed in. Thus Gilman's presentation of possibilities that currently do not exist simply by naming them begins to generate belief in their realizability: hers might be called a "visionary realism."[60]

Emotional authenticity, rather than logical consistency, is the strength of Gilman's thought: she imagined a wide variety of possible innovations, not necessarily consistent with each other, and not aiming for consistency. In this nonconcern for consistency, she seems to anticipate current theories about chaos and complex systems: the more complex a system, or a society, the more spaces it contains to hold diversity; it can incorporate seemingly antagonistic elements.[61] For, as earlier noted, Gilman's utopian writing was her "sensational design" for the transformation of women's condition in the United States, if not in the world.

The question remains, how did Gilman "design" her own life through her writing? Elaine Hedges noted that my ordering of Gilman's "increasing social complexity and ever broadening social vision might also suggest that the very act of writing helped Gilman progressively discover what it was she wanted and needed to say."[62] Part of the answer to this question lies in the published writing just discussed; another part remains in her personal or unpublished writing, the material of the next chapter.

4

Writing to Empower Living

THIS CHAPTER CONSTITUTES a third journey through the life of
Charlotte Perkins Gilman, this time exploring the interaction between her living and utopian writing. Although Gilman's insights
regarding social realities are impressive, even more so is the way in
which she succeeded in implementing her beliefs in the acts of living, of which her writing is one instance. Her biography reveals
numerous possible stumbling blocks to creativity in work as well as
in life. In her writing, from the juvenile "Vurks" [sic] through the
mature *The Living of Charlotte Perkins Gilman,* she "made herself
again" (Friedman 93).[1] She did so in a process that death only interrupted: the joined corpus of her life and work admirably demonstrate Mikhail Bakhtin's concept of the unfinalizability of any given
human life or work.[2] Her dialogue with readers is renewed with
current scholarly retrieval of women's history and literature, and
continues as her writing is increasingly restored to contemporary
readers. Although many of Gilman's views are culturally bound,
many of her insights still point beyond present social practices in
the realm of relations between the sexes. Her critique of gender
relations remains cogent. But we miss much of her legacy to us if
we fail to notice that her living, of which her writing is but one
facet, itself bequeaths us a model—one individual's experiment in
social possibilities.

Bakhtin (1895–1975), a near-contemporary, cultural critic, insisted that writing be "answerable," responsible, that aesthetics and
ethics be connected, as Gilman also believed.[3] In his 1919 "Art and
Answerability," he argues for connecting living and writing, one
form of "art," of making order, an activity that we can construe as a
trope for human creativity in general. Bakhtin claims, "I have to
answer with my own life for what I have experienced and under-

stood in art, so that everything I have experienced and understood would not remain ineffectual in my life. . . . Art and life are not one, but they must become united in myself—in the unity of my answerability" (1, 3). Also pertinent is Bakhtin's multifaceted approach to culture, his insistence upon its composition of irreducible, individual consciousnesses. Any reader, then, needs knowledge of the informing plural contexts of an author's life. Comprehension of any given text from an author's corpus, for instance Gilman's *Herland*, requires more background than any one scholar can possibly manage to provide; we can only each of us contribute to reducing the gap between our limited knowing and what exists to be known, an "unfinalizable" process.

This third journey, then, will explicate Gilman's intertwined living and writing as if a multifaceted internal conversation or dialogue occurs between her living and writing, and among her writings. Misunderstanding of an author's work can easily develop if readers are unaware of the psychological conditions of her life. Bakhtin warns us that context determines meaning, and that meaning cannot be finalized: new meanings will continue to emerge as readers gain additional understandings of cultural contexts supporting Gilman and her work. *Herland*, for example, cannot be read solely as a paean to a female separatist society, however much it is exactly this. Nor is *Women and Economics* primarily inspired by anger toward patriarchy, although it does express such anger. Here I shall offer possible connections among the multivoiced strands connecting Gilman's personal writings—juvenile fiction and mature correspondence—and her published work—"The Yellow Wallpaper"; *Women and Economics;* the *Forerunner* fiction, including *Herland* and *With Her in Ourland;* and *The Living of Charlotte Perkins Gilman*. This discussion seeks to document the *biographical* foreground and contemporary context of *Herland*, Gilman's major utopian statement.

The title of Ann Lane's 1990 biography *To 'Herland' and Beyond* accurately contains the utopia within the life: Gilman's life "beyond" her writing is also her legacy to us. And to read *Herland* is to experience echoes of Gilman's living. In this chapter, I shall follow the chronology of Gilman's life, rather than the structure of the novel *Herland*, because I wish to make *Herland*'s context the focus, to centralize what literary critics frequently marginalize.

Whereas in chapter 3 the focus was upon writing as "cultural work," here it is upon writing as personal or psychological work.

Gilman's example reveals the extent to which we make ourselves, voluntarily choose our biographies, and harbor within creative seeds that are ours alone to cultivate.

Childhood Fantasies, circa 1870

In 1870, when about ten years old, Gilman already had begun to foreshadow *Herland* in her earliest writing. She records, in *The Living of Charlotte Perkins Gilman*, that

> no one had a richer, more glorious life than I had, inside. It grew into fairy-tales, one I have yet; it spread to limitless ambitions. With "my wishes" I modestly chose to be the most beautiful, the wisest, the best person in the world; the most talented in music, painting, literature, sculpture—why not, when one was wishing?
>
> But no personal wealth or glory satisfied me. Soon there developed a Prince and Princess of magic powers, who went about the world collecting unhappy children and taking them to a guarded Paradise in the South Seas. I had a boundless sympathy for children, feeling them to be suppressed, misunderstood.
>
> It speaks volumes for the lack of happiness in my own actual life that I should so industriously construct it in imagination. I wanted affection, expressed affection. My brother was really fond of me, but his teasing hid it from me entirely. Mother loved us desperately, but her tireless devotion was not the same thing as petting, her caresses were not given unless we were asleep, or she thought us so. (23)

Gilman is not fully accurate regarding the amount of her early writing that survived: in fact, a notebook full of pieces she wrote when she was ten years old survives today. But a tale fitting this description does not appear, though Gilman mentions a similar tale in an 1897 birthday letter to her daughter. Perhaps she simply did not recall or could not be bothered checking. Of greater interest for readers of *Herland* is Gilman's acknowledgement of the compensatory and self-fulfilling function for her of fictional heroines, with whom she strongly identified. They exemplify as well a legacy of Beecher do-goodism: Gilman felt called upon to create heroines who were performers of good works, even when she was engaged in the pleasureable act of writing fantasy.[4]

Among Gilman's earliest extant writing is a substantially illegible and undated twenty-page fantasy called "A Dream" (SLR Folder 159: "Early Writing") and the previously mentioned, dated notebook that the young Gilman kept. The first paragraph of this early fantasy evokes imagery of the meeting in *Herland* between the three arriving adventurers and the three Herlanders observing them from their perches in trees (14–15).

> I had a dream, and I thought that I was wandering alone in a forest, the extent of which I did not know. . . . Strange noises and rustlings were heard on every side, and presently the clouds overhead having united in one black canopy it began to rain; not fiercely, nor gently, but heavily with a dull whispering sound as if the elfish inhabitants of these trees and swamps were talking of me in muffled voices (2),

as indeed the Herlanders were of the intruding men. As a young author, Gilman imagined herself as adventurer, an early (though not precisely dated) demonstration of the agency that *Herland* stresses for women.

The notebook title—"The Literary and Artistic Vurks of the Princess Charlotte" (SLR Volume 12)—suggests that Gilman has early gained a rudimentary sense of the parodic, in her awareness of German language sounds, and perhaps even of nineteenth-century Germanic worldview, in her romantic self-inflation as "the Princess Charlotte," creator of art works. The royal title may also, of course, have been an effort at self-esteem in a first female child with a younger brother in a society valuing males more than females.[5] She shows, in the beginnings of parodic wit and the need to bolster self-esteem, that her progress toward *Herland* has already begun.

In her fifteen-page "A Fairy Story," the child Gilman discovers the pleasures of fantasy—because pleasurable, likely "wrong," but nonetheless confidently pursued (SLR Folder 234, "Autobiography," chap. 2). Central in the story are girls and women exhibiting effective public agency. Setting her tale on another planet before the creation of the earth, Gilman suggests an interest in otherworldly science fiction not to be born out by her adult writing. The heroine, Princess Araphenia, has "no one to talk to but her mother and the servants" (1): apparently mothers are not preferred as conversationalists. Fairy Elmondine, from yet another planet, comes to the rescue of Princess Araphenia, who is worried about helping her besieged father, King Ezephon. Elmondine helps. Araphenia, disguised as a young warrior, leads forces provided by Elmondine against the besiegers; she has a snow-white war-horse "which nothing could hurt" (6), a magic sword, and a lance. She commands "thousands" (6) of knights wearing impenetrable silver armor. In this story, a capable female child rescues her overwhelmed male parent. She demonstrates the efficacy of a daughter in the absence of a son, an omitted pesky brother!

Upon Araphenia's disclosure as her father's victorious savior, the king offers her whatever she wishes. Araphenia's mother will "give her permission to anything [the king, her father] thought fit" (7). How different the actual experience of ten-year-old Gilman![6] In fact, Gilman's mother would eventually forbid the writing of fantasies and place frequent restraints upon Gilman's freedom to socialize. As the always-present parent responsible for the setting and maintaining of behavioral limits, Gilman's mother received more than her due of childhood animosity, whereas her father, the always-absent parent, was imbued with desire and approval unmitigated by daily actions. This tale fantasizes Gilman both undoing her experience of adult domestic female authority in her mother, and nonetheless revealing female authority in the story's youthful heroines: she imagines a character who denies the subordination of being the recipient of female authority, but who gladly assumes this very authority as a model for her own practice. In spite of her claims of childhood "suppression" in *The Living of Charlotte Perkins Gilman,* Gilman imagines considerable self-assertion in her characters: although Araphenia requests a modest one- to two-week visit to Elmondine's planet, as the two depart, Araphenia announces that she will return in one month.

Twenty-four birds of paradise take the girls to Elmondine's planet. After meeting Elmondine's royal parents, they ascend marble stairs to a domed room where "millions" of incense burners fill the air with fragrance. Beds suspended from the ceiling can be swung by attendants. To Elmondine's query regarding sleeping alone or sharing one bed, "Araphenia said she had rather sleep with her" (9).[7]

The next two notebook pages, numbered 10 and 11, are blank: it is possible that the pages simply stuck together as childish hands hastily turned over pages. But why more haste at this particular moment in the text? Might she have intended to complete the pages later? In *The Living of Charlotte Perkins Gilman,* Gilman notes:

My dream world was no secret. I was but too ready to share it, but there were no sympathetic listeners. It was my life, but lived entirely alone. Then, influenced by a friend with a pre-Freudien mind, alarmed at what she was led to suppose this inner life might become, my mother called on me to give it up. This was a command. According to all the ethics I knew I must obey, and I did. . . . [Gilman's ellipsis]

Just thirteen. This had been my chief happiness for five years. It was by far the largest, most active part of my mind. I was called upon to close off the main building as it were and live in the "L." No one could tell if I did it or not, it was an inner fortress, open only to me. . . . [Gilman's ellipsis]

But obedience was Right, the thing had to be done and I did it. Night after night to shut the door on happiness, and hold it shut. Never, when dear, bright, glittering dreams pushed hard, to let them in. Just thirteen . . . [Gilman's ellipsis] (23–24).[8]

To be sure, the notebook in question carries the notation "1870–71," making Gilman nine or ten, so this story was written three years before she was actually forbidden this pleasure. But, for a Beecher, the mere act of pleasure was questionable: Gilman notes in an early autobiographical fragment that, upon discovering the pleasures of the imagination, she surmised that anything so pleasurable must be wrong (SLR Folder 234, "Autobiography," chap. 2). The "female world of love and ritual," delineated by Carroll Smith-Rosenberg, was still holding in the 1870s, though during the next decade it would begin to shrink. Delight—especially in the body, reveled in and encouraged by her mother—was not part of Gilman's recalled childhood experience, though for about a half decade no adult actually proscribed that pleasure which she derived from fantasy.

Subsequently in "A Fairy Story," the young author describes her version of the "Big Rock Candy Mountain" of American folklore, a veritable latter-day "Land of Cockaygne." The girls explore a sensuously appealing Edenic garden, where they enjoy fragrant air, singing birds, and fruit and ice cream brought to them in a "temple made entirely from flowers" (12), where they stop to rest. While they are relaxing together, Araphenia begs Elmondine to tell her story. Here Charlotte freely adapts "Sleeping Beauty": at birth Elmondine had been granted many gifts by the most powerful fairies in the land—including the power to have all her wishes granted. In true Beecher fashion, Elmondine had used this gift to benefit the needy: she had actively searched out those needing rescue. On such an excursion to another planet, she had found Araphenia. To please Araphenia, Elmondine relates one of her other rescues. Elmondine tells of finding "an unprotected female in the hands of twelve ruffians . . . in the act of forcing her into the mouth of a deep dark cavern" (14) of a witch who would kill her. These ruffians were sent by a lover whom the maiden had refused to accept. The final sentence of the story acknowledges that the maiden's father has come "searching for her" (14) as Elmondine is in the process of taking her back to him; the young author's actual desire is gratified in fantasy. Once father and daughter are reunited, no need remains for continuing this story.[9]

Readers might well place *Herland* against this deep desire for a fathered childhood, one in which the daughter receives both her father's approval and his desire. *Herland*'s conclusion with the reconstitution of a two-sexed family, and *With Her in Ourland*'s with the birth of a son, thus hint at the possibility of a future in which growing daughters can enjoy the presence of empathic fathers. Although these outcomes may appear reactionary in terms of roles for adult women, we know from the fiction in the nine volumes of the *Forerunner* that Gilman also could imagine women functioning in families without traditional subordination: she restructured families to meet the needs of both women and children. She herself for a brief period actually mothered a daughter in an Oakland women-only household, a possibility she reimagined in her serialized novel "Mag-Marjorie" (*Forerunner* 1912), as well as in several *Forerunner* short stories.[10] As early, then, as the 1870 "Vurks," Gilman found female peers good; older men, good but helpless; and older women, there but useless.[11]

Young boys—brother surrogates—were "bad," with the partial exception of the hero in "Prince Cherry."[12] Only one "bad" young female exists, the rabbit Bunch from "The Story of Mr. and Mrs. Rabbit," who disobediently gets caught in a snare—one set by "bad boys." Behind Gilman's consistent refusal to see good in boys or very much bad in girls likely lay a persistently teasing younger brother Thomas, who seemed to her youthful eyes vastly more privileged than herself in his freedom to hunt and set snares for animals. In a pre-1900 attempt at composing her autobiography, Gilman noted both the ceaseless teasing of her brother, and the mischief that brother and sister together perpetrated, mischief not acknowledged in *Living* (SLR Folder 234, chap. 2). By denigrating boys and elevating girls—a reversal of the priorities she experienced in real life —Gilman wrote gender-biased fantasies to compensate herself for feeling second-class.

Reading was at this time Gilman's principal joy. She subscribed to *Our Young Folks,* and later commented that especially moral stories, though subsequently scorned, were "immensely useful in forming ethical standards" (SLR Folder 234, "Autobiography" chap. 2).[13] In fact, it was a Beecher truism that readers should learn from their books and that learning should be fun: both her father and her uncle Edward Everett Hale agreed (Hill 1980, 41). Pleasure associated with a social end such as education received emphatic Beecher approval: her fantasy-writing, as noted earlier, was for her mother another matter.

As a young girl, Gilman read Helen Campbell's popular 1868 *The Ainslee Stories:* Campbell's fiction written during the 1880s and 1890s presents models of fictionalized career and domestic experimentation that would reappear in Gilman's *Forerunner* fiction.[14] Given her father's and uncle's view and the model of her great-aunt Harriet's *Uncle Tom's Cabin,* as well as the influence of childhood reading, it is no surprise that Gilman would expect her fiction to have the power to convert readers to her viewpoint, to activate them to foment social changes: readers were supposed to respond strenuously to what they read. This legacy of confident expectation that writing would effect changes in readers and thereby instigate their performance of social reforms was thus grounded for Gilman in the beliefs and texts of both family and friends.

A literary criticism of effects was also part of the era's cultural climate: Howells and James, as well as others, looked upon literature very seriously for its capacity to influence morals and to exemplify outcomes.[15] Although by the 1915 publication of *Herland,* an intrinsic literary criticism was emerging, the literary critical context shaping Gilman was that of the conservative older mode. Her creativity expressed itself less in form or language than in innovative content: *Herland* smashes the prevalent gender system. Gilman alone cannot be credited with the totality of the innovation expressed; however, she placed her life on the cutting edge of social innovation and soaked up intellectual ferment occurring along the boundaries of human experience: recall Bakhtin's belief, quoted earlier, that *"the most intense and productive life of culture takes place on the boundaries of its individual areas"* ("Response" 2).

Letters to Kate, 1895–1897

Considerable boundary adjustment occurred at this time among women, who must be understood not as a monolith but as a plenitude of social subgroups. Women's adjustments intertwined with those of other marginalized people—various groups of immigrants and citizens: mutual needs might be met by such experimentation as that found in settlement houses. Settlements could provide newly college-educated women with meaningful adult occupation in addressing the plight of marginalized groups. One important such social settlement in the United States of the late 1890s was Chicago's Hull House, established in 1889 by Jane Addams and Ellen Gates Starr.[16] Responding to an invitation from Addams, Gilman made Hull House her base from late summer into the winter of 1895. She wrote letters to her daughter, Kate, then living in Pasadena with her father, Walter Stetson, and his second wife, Gilman's good friend, Grace Channing. Letters to Kate required care. Writing to her cousin George Houghton Gilman two years later, Gilman noted, "Kate's letters must be adapted to her—bless her! You wouldn't believe how hard I work at her letters" (SLR Folder 40, 25 April 1897). Two of three letters written to Kate from Hull House suggest that it was an inspiration both for Gilman's *Forerunner* fiction, as well as for *Herland*'s female community of effective social planners —exemplars, like the Hull House residents, of "social motherhood"; a third reveals Gilman's anxiety regarding personal space.

On 20 August 1895, Gilman wrote to Kate of her arrival at Hull House. The last three paragraphs detail both Gilman's quarters, which clearly please her, and the activities of Hull House.

> I am getting along very nicely here. I have a southwest room in the third story, a very comfortable little room indeed, with two windows, a closet, a steam-heater and various other conveniences. This house is a large beautiful one with pictures, busts, and casts of lovely things all about. The inmates are folks who want to come here to study the life of the poor people about them and help them if they can; for the house is in a very poor quarter of the city. It is largely a foreign quarter also, Italians, Hungarians, Polish Jews, all sorts of immigrants.
>
> Hull House furnishes them with clubrooms, kindergartens, a crêche, and many classes in various studies. I enclose a last winter's circular, so that you can see how many things they do. I am

glad to be here for a while and study the [Settlement] movement. Tonight I am to go with a Russian girl, to meet some members of a Socialist Club of Polish Jews. Next Tuesday I speak for the Radical Club (SLR Folder 89, 4–6).

With the exception of the first paragraph, virtually every sentence foreshadows the concerns of utopian fiction that Gilman would publish in the *Forerunner* between 1909 and 1916. She would imagine providing educational or cultural opportunities and meeting space for adult members of a community, as well as care for infants and young children. She would also imagine those who were better off providing for the less fortunate: the social reformer was a frequent inhabitant of her imagined worlds.

About three weeks later, on 15 September 1895, having recently addressed the Mother's Club at the Northwestern Settlement, Gilman explains to Kate what settlements are:

Some people who have money and education and culture, and who feel badly because so many other people have none of these things, come to live among these other people in order to be friends with them and help them live. It is not to help them by giving money, nor by preaching, nor by teaching, but to be friends and help in all sorts of ways as it happens; and to give the poor people a large beautiful place to meet in and do things for themselves. You see people have to get together to do much and poor people have no place to meet in however much they want to. This particular Settlement, Hull House, is the largest and best known in the country, and has spread into many kinds of work. There is a crêche or day nursery where women who have to work out by the day can leave their babies, and feel safe about it. They pay five cents. There is a kindergarten of course, with three teachers. There is a gymnasium which has both male and female classes. There is a men's club, with billiard tables; and the women's and girl's and boy's and mixed clubs all over the place, in various rooms and halls.

It is big and busy and theres [*sic*] lots to do. Each resident— that is what they call the people who live here and help—each resident has some kind of a club or class or department to attend to. I am supposed mostly to hold myself free for lecturing, to all kinds of clubs etc. Then I help about in the house, wait on the door, see visitors and "tote." That is what they call it when there are visitors and we residents take them about—tote them. I make a splendid "toter" for I rejoice to talk in a glib and cheerful manner about the place and its purposes and achievements. We all get our breakfast in the Hull House restaurant—a public eating house they maintain—and lunch and dinner in our capacious dining hall. There is a nice housekeeper, Miss Mary Keyser, who has been with Miss Addams from the beginning. Then there is a chambermaid and waitress. The cooking is done in the big kitchen, the one that feeds the restaurant. . . .

Last night there was a meeting in the gymnasium—which also is theatre and lecture hall, holding five hundred when full— on the "Adulturation of Food." They are having a dreadful time here in the city about milk. The milkmen are being arrested for selling bad milk, and it is making lots of trouble for them. It ought to. A man that will poison babies to make money ought to be arrested—don't you think so? Now if there was a City Dairy open to the public, managed to the highest pitch of scientific perfection, and the workers in it liable to be turned out if they didn't do well —then we could have the best milk there was (SLR Folder 89, 2–6).

Gilman's description, painstakingly detailed for her daughter, stresses the social obligation of those better off, the efficacy of group action, the leadership of a model institution, the various groups whose social needs Hull House serves, her own duties as a guest-resident, the housekeeping arrangements, and an instance of social education leading her to suggest a solution—a nascent utopian kernal. Eight years later, as a New York City resident, Gilman would write a social reform story called "A Personal Motive" (*Forerunner* 4.5, 1913), its plot clearly derived from this Chicago milk disaster of 1895: motivated by the death from unfit milk of their infant son, a New York couple, Mr. and Mrs. Geoffrey Miles, vow to force out bad milk by establishing a model dairy in New Jersey, the Meadow-sweet Milk Company. They create a market for their milk and drive out the milk trusts. Finally, "[t]he baby-killers are exterminated!" (118). The couple work together effectively, the husband showing marked admiration for his wife's political skills, she being the initiator of action. They may well give us a hint of Gilman's second marital partnership.

The last letter to Kate from Hull House is dated 14 October 1895. Gilman is less enthusiastic than formerly. She writes:

Things are happening now quite vigorously—or least I am happening! I happen to be visiting around at present; because I don't like to stay at Hull House and sleep in half a room. They are

so full that three rooms are double bedded and double inhabited
and as I am but a transient guest I was one of these doublers. But
I didn't like it because the other occupant was not accustomed to
as much air as I—only one window open for two people! One of my
possible roommates raised her's [*sic*] about a foot—that didn't suit
me at all. The other opened her's [*sic*] fairly wide, but she read in
bed, by the light of a large lamp, until midnight, and I liked that
still less.

I didn't mind the light so much as I did the greedy lamp eating
up my air! So then I went down and slept in great state on a fine
long wide soft smooth sofa in the drawing room.

That was *fine*. Such a grand big room! (SLR Folder 89, 1–2)

The somewhat carping tone of this passage emphasizes Gilman's
unease with any limit upon her personal freedom. As an adolescent,
she had not enjoyed her initial venture in communal living during
1874, when her mother had joined a "cooperative housekeeping
group" (*Living,* 25–26).[17] However much Gilman advocated group
activism and what we today call "networking," personally she must
be unhindered in her use of time and space—perhaps the legacy of
an overdirected childhood, perhaps of years of independent adult
wandering. She never advocated cooperative housekeeping because
this did not change women's lack of economic independence. Her
answer, instead, was professional specialization of housework activities, a version of her great-aunt Catherine Beecher's valorization
of the American home. This letter provides an instance of how Gilman's impetus toward social reform was tempered by an equally
strong sense of personal comfort and personal liberty.[18]

That these 1895 Hull House letters, prefiguring so many utopian themes from *Herland,* should have been written to her daughter binds living and writing closely together, since *Herland*
delineates a mother-centered society where the highest position is
that of the mother, where the greatest social honor is to be deemed
an Over Mother, one whose mothering is so superior that she may
bear more than one child (69). But Gilman's maternity held both
bitterness and desire. She agonized over ceding her daughter to the
Stetsons, so that Kate might experience life with her father (but,
given Walter's personality, Grace in fact assumed the primary child-
care responsibility). But Gilman also delighted in restoring Kate to
her own household once she was remarried to Houghton Gilman.

These are Gilman's claims in her 1935 autobiography (*Living,*
162–64), but the evidence suggests as at least possible the explana-

tion that Kate's presence impeded Gilman's developing career in public service and, knowing that Grace had strongly supportive personal qualities, Gilman could send Kate off with the knowledge that her daughter would receive loving care—though at the expense of Grace's time and energy rather than her own. Gilman alleged that her act was solely for Kate, rather than to any extent for herself: current views regarding motherhood saw the giving up of a child as monstrous, especially if to meet the developmental (read "selfish") needs of the mother. And Gilman's "five-year plan [covering 1895–1900] did not include Katharine" (Lane 1990, 184).

Biographers agree upon Gilman's ambivalence regarding motherhood.[19] A complex of family ties impinged upon Gilman, her mother, and her daughter, as the two younger generations attempted to sort out their feelings for their mothers. Love and hurt entangled them in an ambivalent oscillation between respect and recrimination. Such experiential ambiguity regarding motherhood is the context for *Herland*'s unqualifiedly confident depiction of what Adrienne Rich labels a premier patriarchal institution.[20]

Upon the occasion of Kate's twelfth birthday, two years later, Gilman, then in New York, on 14 March 1897, wrote to Kate in Pasadena. Gilman refers to one of her childhood tales. It sounds suspiciously reminiscent of those in "The Vurks of the Princess Charlotte" and also recalls her comments, in *The Living of Charlotte Perkins Gilman,* about her fantasy writing. She writes to Kate:

> Twelve years old! When I was twelve I was living in a wonderland of my own mostly. Shall I send you the fairy story I wrote at that time—"The Story of Elmondine and Ferolio"? It is a very philanthropic fairy story. [This tale may not be extant. I have not been able to locate any story featuring Elmondine and Ferolio, though Elmondine functions as the savior-fairy in "A Fairy Story," as previously discussed.]
>
> I used to spend lots of time in the [Rehoboth, Massachusetts] woods, picking flowers, climbing the tall soft-boughed pine trees and swinging in their tops, wading in brooks, swimming in the little river, dreaming always of lovely things beyond [a "beyond" eventually to culminate in the 1915 *Herland*]. The outside world was fair, but I enjoyed the inside the best (SLR Folder 89, 5–6; *Living,* 21–23).

Through a similar woodland scene, the paragraph joins Gilman's childhood experience, her memory and sharing of this experience with her daughter (both as lived and as written), and the *Herland* meeting between three intruding men and three Herland women that initiates the narrative action. This scene evokes Gilman's childhood desire to create a "world in which to find a place to discover a self"; it reveals Gilman returning, as one "among persons of genius, to this landscape of childhood in order to renew the power and impulse to create at its very source" (Fryer, 46).[21] *Herland's* emotional roots exist for Gilman first, in her own childhood's fantasies; next, in her desires both to be with her daughter and for her daughter to enjoy the best possible from life; and finally, in her relationships to her mother and father, as well as to her two husbands and many women friends, although these last are not evident in the foregoing letters to Kate, excepting—in the middle of the 1897 letter—Gilman's account of her delighted rediscovery of George Houghton (Ho) Gilman, a Beecher cousin seven years her junior.

Gilman continues this letter to Kate as if the phrase "dreaming always of lovely things beyond" had also sparked her mind concerning the next topic to be addressed:

> Last week I made a delightful discovery! Found a cousin! Cousins are real nice. They are better than brothers. [She continues to recapitulate themes apparently re/called by "Vurks."] You have one boy cousin on my side, and quite a lot on your father's side—five I believe—no, four. I hope you'll enjoy them as much as I have mine. This cousin is Houghton Gilman [Ho]—George H. Gilman. He is now a grown man—nearly thirty; when I remember him he was just your age (6).

Herself at twelve, Kate at twelve, Ho at twelve, the scene that will later instigate *Herland's* action—past, present, and future, life and fiction Gilman has bound up closely in these three paragraphs! And I mention only several of the strands that weave the pattern of this paragraph; much more remains unarticulated in her memory, in the silences between lines and words.[22]

Correspondence with Ho, 1897–1900

Childhood fantasies and letters to Kate reveal deficits needing repair, indicate coping strategies, and provide early contextualization for Gilman's utopian writing. The letters written from 1897 to

1900 between Charlotte Perkins Gilman and George Houghton (Ho) Gilman provide essential context for the writing of *Herland*. This correspondence demonstrates how Gilman came to be able to imagine a *Herland*, the climax of her utopian fiction—sources for which I have been seeking to illuminate. The correspondence appears to have functioned for her as a form of healing-by-writing—to the point of her spiritual rebirth. The correspondence can also be seen as itself a form of utopian writing, albeit autobiographical in nature —part of her "writing to empower living," the writing in which she remade herself, reconceptualized her past, released her creative powers for the public lecturing and writing that she was doing concurrently and afterwards. In these letters, she would manage to articulate better than previously her deepest convictions, her understanding of her personal past, her doubt, conflict, and ambivalence. She inscribed what elsewhere are her silences, as completely and as honestly as she could: she wanted to be sure that Ho knew exactly whom he was desiring and agreeing to marry. She also wanted to understand her own motives. This coming to terms with herself as human and as female, analogous to a course of therapy, could be seen as freeing her capacity to imagine for women the utopian society that she describes in *Herland*.

Ann J. Lane's chapter entitled "Houghton," in *To "Herland" and Beyond*, while it also suggests Gilman's healing and resolution, does not trace the intricate, spiraling, stage-by-stage psychological growth that Mary Armfield Hill's forthcoming explication of the correpondence delineates. Hill traces in Gilman's letters a spiraling process of healing that, with each return to an existential problem, shows Gilman's clearer sense of self. In the pages that follow, Hill's interpretive selection of letters provides a context for reading Gilman's utopian writing: I discuss Hill's selection of letters looking backward from the vantage points of *Herland*, the utopian fiction I seek to contextualize, and current feminist theory. I also read backward into this correspondence the utopian values that I had previously believed would emerge predominantly from Gilman's twentieth-century utopian writing.

The narrative presented by this correspondence—that of the "heterosexual female lover"—reads, as noted, like a newly recovered autobiographical account by Gilman. Her letters to Ho exemplify "the female lover, [as] an actively desiring female subject" (Holmlund, 294).[23] Although she expresses "her need-desire to be loved" (294), Gilman also pushes herself—with much ambivalence and anguish—to attempt the expression of "her own love," and thereby contradicts Irigaray's claim that "the heterosexual female lover does not yet exist" (294). In what we today can understand retrospectively as a revolutionary political and personally possessive act, Gilman destroyed Ho's letters, alleging that, because she was "at large" during the years of their correspondence, she had no permanent residence where she could store possessions. All that remains today, therefore, is her voice, that of "the heterosexual female lover" struggling to be born. Her subjectivity alone can engage readers' attention: only she ever read Ho's letters.[24]

These love letters are important also in that they provide additional evidence that members of a muted group may prefer noncanonical genres. Mary Crawford and Roger Chaffin, in reviewing the research that supports perceiving women as a muted group, report the finding of Cheris Kramarae that "women seek to express themselves by writing in other than the dominant (public) modes of expression"—that is, in letters or diaries (22). They suggest that letters may be "less constricting to the articulation of [women's] own experience" (22): no [typically male] agents or publishers interfere. In such private expressions, Gilman perseveres in communicating her feelings and experience—of inadequate nurture, hunger for reassurance, struggle toward desire—the foregoing all cries from a "wild zone," a "no man's land," of which, as Elaine Showalter explains, the dominant culture is unaware (262). Women's emotions and agency, because they are not inscribed in the dominant culture, tend to pass unrecognized: in the terms of Crawford and Chaffin, they are not contained by any familiar schemata. Those facets of female experience generally unknown to men are lodged in a "wild zone," outside the dominant culture. Hence the value of Gilman's letters, emanating as they do from muted territory.[25]

These letters admirably exemplify Gilman's "daily experience": they demonstrate Bettina Aptheker's claim, in *Tapestries of Life,* that materials such as these letters "integrate ideas about love and healing, about balance and connection, about beauty and growing, into our everyday ways of being" (254). Aptheker continues, "We [women] have to believe in the value of our own experiences and in the value of our ways of knowing, our ways of doing things." The letters demonstrate Gilman writing to integrate and find value in her own experience; they offer readers a potential model for the "cultural work" of individual self-definition. This correspondence is an important part of Gilman's writing to empower living, a truly healing experience in which she could—at last—unburden her soul before another.

The scrupulous honesty with which Gilman writes these letters indicates the magnitude of her trust in Ho. They freed her creative self: during the writing of this courtship correspondence, she wrote two books—*Women and Economics* (1898) and *Concerning Children* (1900), enlarged her collection of verse with *In This Our World* (1898), and delivered numerous lectures, both on tour and at conventions. Her creative release continued as two more books, *The Home: Its Work and Influence* (1903) and *Human Work* (1904), and numerous articles appeared before she launched the *Forerunner,* a seven-year commitment to writing one complete issue each month. This correspondence reveals the near-daily process whereby Gilman expanded her capacity to imagine women—a process initiated by an 1892 short story depicting an individual victimized woman, "The Yellow Wallpaper," and culminating in a 1915 novel presenting a society of victorious women, *Herland,* the latter, of course, originally appearing in the *Forerunner* (Vol. 6).

This correspondence with Ho, which must be seen as an essential component of Gilman's writing to enlighten living, permitted her to review her life, to remake herself, so that after 1900 she was in fact a person more self-accepting and less self-critical than she had been before. Ho, providing the eyes that mirrored her life, acted as the accepting, nurturant mother Gilman believed that she had never known.[26] She early recognized his functioning in this way for her: "Strange that a young man's eyes should call up a never satisfied longing for mother love!" she wrote on 19 May 1897, only two months after they had reestablished contact (SLR Folder 41).

As Adrienne Rich has observed, in *Of Woman Born* (1976), "The woman who has felt 'unmothered' may seek mothers all her life—may even seek them in men" (242). It is just this deficiency that Ho was apparently able and willing to undertake meeting—and it may have been his behavior that provided Gilman with a model for *Herland*'s Over-Mothers. In November, referring to her mother's deficient love, Gilman commented, "You see[,] all my life I haven't had what I wanted in the way of being loved. I've told you all about that. From mother up. The whole way is lived with—not all gravestones, but some, and some kind of trap-door-stones that keep things down. When the will-strength, or brain-strength, or whatever it is that keeps me happy and steady and brave, gives out, up hop all these buried things, dead and alive" (SLR Folder 47, 3 Nov. 1897).[27]

Ho's unquestioning acceptance—of whatever or whoever Gilman had been, was, or would become—surrounded her with a reflecting mirror of affirmation, a reassurance that began to fill her hunger for affection, for love, both *agape* as well as *eros*. His accepting love empowered her to permit repressed hurts to escape through these letters and leave her largely healed. In an early undated letter, Gilman wrote, "[Y]our presence, real or imagined, gives me the same pleasure that a work of art or the right piece of nature does—it is Beautiful. Of course you must have some weak spots and bad qualities somewhere—but so far that is why you are such a deep comfort to me; because of the rest it is to me to look up to a good man and feel the power of a strong one; . . . to continually realize how beautifully it is love" (SLR Folder 40, Apr. 1897, catalogued between letters dated the twelfth and twenty-first). The tremendous outpouring of writing that followed her 1900 marriage attests to its restorative and empowering effect.

Gilman's letters indicate her assertion, as an active female subject, that Ho could provide what rarely mother or daughter in a "man-made world" has the capacity to offer: acceptance from one who both holds social power and has the capacity to nurture and thereby to heal. Ruth Perry, introducing *Mothering the Mind*, observes that "[a]nother mind . . . takes away the strain of isolation and releases energy for inner exploration" (7). Ho's apparently receptive mental stance enabled Gilman to move within. In the letters, she explains her mother and sees that Ho compensates for her mother's unavoidable lacks. She recovers her "joy" in her daughter Kate and receives "glimpses of what a mother's happiness should be" (SLR Folder 54, 7 Aug. 1898).[28] However, in August 1898 she indicated the more marginalized position Kate held in her affections, a subtext to her ambivalent proclamations regarding the centrality of motherhood: "I was willing to give up, even my child if it was right. But you—I *want* you. And it so hurts and frightens. . . . I admit it, absolutely; and shall undertake to prolong my life by giving myself a thing that I want—namely *You*." (SLR Folder 55, 7 p.m. 14 Sept. 1898). What did she mean by "right" with respect to her child? Right solely according to the needs of Kate? Right according to her moral need as a Beecher to live up to a legacy of service, even if a single parent? Right according to her personal economic need to provide for herself, in a society unsupportive of a working mother? The ambiguity regarding her meaning of *right* must stand as part of the context of *Herland*.

But Gilman's *"want . . . you"* was her assertion as an active sub-ject that Ho could provide what rarely mother or daughter in a "man-made world" has the capacity to offer: acceptance from one who both holds social power and has the capacity to nurture and thereby to heal. History and scholarship have given little space to explicating the heroism of those who have nurtured the achieve-ments of notable women. Nor do we typically construe such behavior as heroic, albeit the *sine qua non* of human creativity. Others in Gilman's life, as well as Ho, nurtured her: Martha Luther Lane, Adeline Knapp, Helen Campbell, and Grace Channing Stetson sub-stantially eased her existence, showed her that, the larger society notwithstanding, women might be each other's best colleagues, friends, or lovers—an understanding that Gilman must gain for *Herland* to be realized. With none of these good women, however, did Gilman live intimately for as long as she did with Ho, although she indicated that she could have.[29] Gilman's healing, instigated by previous friendships in her life, was solidified in her relationship with Ho. These letters to him are the means that established what became, for Charlotte Perkins Gilman, a liberating, empowering relationship, a central part of the context for creating *Herland*.

Additional concerns in this correspondence that I wish to high-light as context for *Herland* include two that undermined Gilman—her ambivalence regarding marriage and her insecurity regarding her own self-worth—and two that affirmed her—her acceptance of commonality with Ho and her success at self-definition. Each of these pairs is interconnected, the one pair the obverse of the other.

Throughout much of Gilman's writing are her excessively high expectations for herself, expectations that, as Karen Horney has explained in *Neurosis and Human Growth,* mask and compensate a person's sense of her own unworthiness. Horney hypothesizes that an ideal self (one holding excessively high expectations) emerges as a self constructed to meet external demands at the expense of an actual self (one sensing personal unworthiness), which is then sub-merged.[30] Because one never achieves an ideal, the construct of an ideal self maintains a person's feeling of inadequacy. Although Gil-man did gain increased self-acceptance, she held grandiose goals for herself, which she never entirely abandoned. She complained that she was unworthy of a person as good as Ho. She cited her neediness, self-deprecation, dependence, and mental instability; the unfairness to Ho of her inadequacies as a wife committed to her own pursuits; the possibility that some feature of her past would haunt the couple, such as her passionate relationship with Adeline Knapp. The insecurity beneath these protests is easy for readers to see; the accumulation of negativism, painful to feel.

Gilman rode an emotional seesaw.[31] Her unreasonable expectations that human life could proceed with no variations and that a relationship could lead to her feeling consistently happy suggest a perilous belief in a perfection that life could not possibly provide. She experienced periodic bouts of depression throughout her adult life; however, it must be acknowledged that a contributing factor was her perceiving as unique to herself what we now understand to be normal variation.

A strategy Gilman used in these letters to bolster her ego in the face of such a continuous struggle to develop a secure sense of self-worth was noting any praise she received—such praise peppering her text far less often than self-doubts. Meticulously she reports to Ho listeners' commendations of various lectures—revels in such praise, which "adds much to [her] always wobbly sense of professional value" (SLR Folder 51, 10:45 a.m., 18 May 1898)—and enumerates invitations to visit embellished with "airy brags" that she claimed "keep my spirits up" (SLR Folder 55, 18 Sept. 1898). If only her "airy brags" had been more frequent than her "wobbly" doubts! The letters suggest that, like many other women—like many of us today—Gilman expended energy fighting an internalized set of undermining constrictions: in spite of her intellectual stress upon women's rights and capacities, she herself found that emotional acceptance of this knowledge frequently evaded her grasp. Somehow, we are astonished to find this sense of self-doubt in a woman with the intellectual stature of Charlotte Perkins Gilman, who was considered a leading feminist theorist at the turn of the century.[32] We must admire Gilman's stoic determination and her refusal to give up a complex challenge—her steadfast pursuit of remaking herself.

Gilman's remade self emerges fleetingly at first, then more firmly toward the end of the correspondence as she becomes able, most of the time, to accept that Ho truly loves and accepts her, just as she is. With her increased belief in his acceptance of her and her continued belief in him as an admirable person, she must begin to accept herself as in some measure worthy of his acceptance. Interspersed with her expressions of unworthiness as a wife for Ho, Gilman also notes, "No one else on earth touches my early life as you do. And when I think of all I have been through, and of what it has cost me to tell even you about it . . . why I just want to bury my face in your neck . . . never *never* to stir away from you. Our friendship, comradeship, cheery intimacy, means so much to me. The games and jokes and fun—that is like my brother and the pleasures of my childhood" (SLR Folder 51, 10:45 a.m., 18 May 1898).[33] Under the influence of Ho, even her brother's previously noted incessant teasing becomes one of "the pleasures of my childhood"! As in Gilman's initial letter to Kate quoted above, exuberance based in childhood experience emerges. A crucial element alluded to here is the Beecher family legacy shared by the cousins, a legacy that likely predisposed Ho to accept and support Charlotte's dedication to "world service."

Gilman continues pensively, "A man might come much nearer my work, my thought, that is true. . . . If I find a co-thinker, man or woman, there is nothing to prevent our co-thinking that I know of! I don't have to marry 'em! My one grave doubt has been deliciously settled; I know now that we are fitted to one another in the most important things. . . . You understand to the full that I am a worldworker and must be" (SLR Folder 51, 10:45 a.m., 18 May 1898). Clearly an important qualification Ho met was his willingness to play the support role for her "world service." In a later letter, she also expresses appreciation for their many-faceted congruence as a couple. Noting Ho's "quiet contented conservative temperament" and her own capacity to "suit lots of people personally— utterly different people," Charlotte worried on Ho's behalf regarding possible "life-long unrest and pain for [him]." Then she revells in the fact that Ho covers her facets "more satisfactorily than any [other] man I ever saw"; still she wonders whether her prominence would injure his male pride (SLR Folder 66, 6 Mar. 1899).

About her role as a "world builder," Gilman became increasingly clear and confident.[34] By September 1898, she articulated a clear goal and responsibility for herself:

Now it may yet appear that I shall develop a new power—a man's power; and learn to detach my personal from my professional life; learn to be the strong free helpful spirit in my work—giving due time to it; and yet come home to you, a happy wife for the rest of the time.

Come now! This is what women have got to learn to do, if my new world is to come true! It may be part of my work to accomplish just this thing! To do world's work and live large and glad in it; to love and wed and be great mothers too—this is before the women of the world; and I must at least try at it. The most hampering circumstance is the mechanical detail of household life (SLR Folder 55, 9:30 a.m., 16 Sept. 1898).

Next she begs Ho to "help me stand against my own sex instinct and life habits. *I must not* focus on 'home duties'; and entangle myself in them" (SLR Folder 55, 9:30 a.m., 16 Sept. 1898). She confuses *instinct,* a biological term, with learned gender socialization; she does not appear here to be discussing "sex instinct" as sexuality, an omission also true of *Herland.* With respect to heterosexual women's truncated capacity to imagine or experience autonomous sexuality as a facet of human totality, Jane Flax notes the apparent repression of self-motivated sexuality, and especially of the possibility of being both a thinking and a sexual woman ("Re-Membering," 101).[35] Gilman's letters reveal precisely this struggle. Even a strenuosly intellectual woman could be subject to ubiquitous gender indoctrination.

With regard to "home duties," Gilman would in later letters assert, "Our problem is . . . the housekeeping. . . . We must try to live like two friendly bachelors in apartments. We must really give much earnest thought to it, and plan carefully." (SLR Folder 66, 5 Mar. 1899). And the next day: "When I think of any call to human service being denied because at that time I had no cook—it simply can not be" (SLR Folder 66, 6 Mar. 1899). "Household machinery" was the "danger" to her marriage, once contracted, that most worried Gilman (SLR Folder 66, 5 Mar. 1899). Housekeeping for most middle-class women of small or moderate means was a problem: many did not wish to incur the bound service of other women, although they themselves did not like the drudgery of household labor. In her later fiction, Gilman sought ways to resolve this dilemma.[36]

In an earlier letter, Gilman had pleaded, "Help me to feel that our love and our life together is but a part of the real human life, which is for the good of all. . . . I must feel and see that our life together is a helpful factor in working for the whole world. It must be to me a means to an end—not an end in itself" (SLR Folder 55, 9:30 a.m., 16 Sept. 1898). Three days later, she attests to her belief that Ho offers her "the best hope for what remains of my life and strength" (SLR Folder 55, "Quarter of eight," 19 Sept. 1898). Continuing to mull over the effect of marriage on her life's work, she claims, "[I]t seemed to me that at bottom I was really a *thinker;* a kind of social philosopher; and that my best expression was and would always be in writing, and in an essentially amateurish and inspirational sort of speaking. Then . . . it seemed to me there was nothing to prevent this work, and much to help it in our being together; that it would probably grow saner, rounder, sounder, more effective" (SLR Folder 55, 21 Sept. 1898).[37]

What Ho provided for Gilman is what Flax (and Irigaray, among others) find yet missing or "forbidden" as a cultural assumption regarding women: the acceptance of women as self-defined, rather than as defined by cultural stereotype or male desire (1987, 104). Discussing Irigaray's views, Flax explains that many a man wants to control female pleasure so as to make it accessible to himself alone and not to a woman at all: a woman may not define herself without his input. George Houghton Gilman was one individual man who, given remaining circumstantial evidence, appears to have been sufficiently secure in himself to permit a woman the freedom "to speak for herself" and "among her/our selves" (104).[38]

In addition to according Gilman such freedom, Houghton apparently was adept in another way. Jessica Benjamin suggests a new psychoanalytic construct, *intersubjectivity,* to name psychological space between individuals, in which they are acutely and interactively aware of each other: the presence of an empathic other permits heightened self-awareness and empowers self-realization as in the release of creativity. The reverse of such intersubjectivity is being "encapsulated in our subjective bubbles, having fantasies about one another" (93). The latter occurred between Gilman and her first husband, Walter Stetson. I suspect, on the basis of reports by herself and others, that Ho may have been more skilled in the intersubjective mode than Charlotte, though I believe that she would have acknowledged this to be her interactional aim, as well. The case of the Gilmans particularizes the construct with possible historical experience; the problem is that only partial evidence remains.[39]

More complete evidence is recorded, however, in the case of George Eliot and George Henry Lewes, and it may suggest what transpired between the Gilmans. Eliot, in a journal entry for 6 December 1857, wrote "How I Came to Write Fiction": this essay describes how Lewes, in his empathic responsiveness over time to her hinted aspiration—"the possibility of my being able to write a novel"—facilitated its realization (vol. 2: 407). As Jean Wyatt explains, "the presence of a loving other later in life can again grant access to unconscious intuitions [the ground of creativity] and enable one to claim them as one's own" (107): Lewes, "like the empathic mother . . . mirrors [Eliot's aspiration] back to her with unqualified enthusiasm[,] . . . smoothing the transition from dream to actuality . . . and mark[ing] out a safe ground for experimentation that is free of the dread of failure (and of success)" (107). Gilman's "search for the self in the mirror of the other's face" (7) had ended: she had found "a lover who remothers her" (126). By providing unconditional nurture, Ho enabled Gilman to exorcise her matriphobia, to cease "denying in [her]self everything associated with the mother, including capacities and needs for fusion, empathy, intimacy" (113).[40]

By fall 1898, the aura of acceptance with which Ho's caring surrounded Gilman was freeing her to take riskier plunges into self-analysis. She explained to Ho that she thought herself "nearer the truth of what ails me than any doctor ever got" (SLR Folder 55, 22 Sept. 1898). The truth she found lay both in the soundness with which she wrote and spoke (that is, pursued her public activities) and in the "disease" residing in her practice of any "personal relation": her public persona, developed in adulthood, remained less tainted than was the private by the deficiencies of her childhood. She claimed, "Now you are bringing me food and drink and blessed blessed comfort where all has been waste so long" (SLR Folder 55, 22 Sept. 1898). By spring 1899, Gilman demonstrated the effect of Ho's presence in her life. In one paragraph, she turned herself from self-doubt to self-affirmation, a feat she could not earlier have accomplished so easily:

> And as to my changeableness—I'm not going to quarrel with it any more. It's me—part of the character which makes me able to reach so many people in so many ways. And of course it brings me with exquisite intensity to the person I love most—and equally of course it swings me away again. I'm not going to blame myself anymore or grieve because I'm not like you. Why should I expect to manifest every virtue? (SLR Folder 67, 16 Mar. 1899).

The letters demonstrate the psychological healing Gilman was accomplishing and show the therapeutic value of her remembering through letter-writing and of her enjoying an accepting reader.

The combination of Gilman's persistence and Ho's acceptance effected a release of her creative powers—here in reforming thought patterns. Although once Charlotte and Ho lived together, no more letters passed between them, and although she herself left minimal evidence about her second marriage with which to form a judgment (*Living,* 281), scholars seem agreed that her expectation that her work would increase in effectiveness probably was accurate: the circumstantial evidence of her impressive productivity exists. In her "Thoughts and Figgerings" entry for 9 May 1900, Gilman expects marriage to be a safe place to do her work (SLR Folder 16). Couples-therapist Polly Young-Eisendrath concludes, "As women and men become more able to shape their relationships through mutuality of trust and respect, they become able to move toward a rejuvenative bond of *communitas* or shared meaning" (154–55). George Houghton Gilman evidently did provide the "mothering [for Charlotte's] mind."[41]

Gilman's courtship correspondence with Houghton appears to have made possible her self-realized state, at least insofar as she considered the needs of women like herself—those white and middle-class. Her goal in writing was not the creation of aesthetic objects, but the communication of alternative human possibilities to readers, with the hoped-for end of changing their behavior to ameliorate human society. The goal is to "make better people," she was to write (*Forerunner* 3.8 (1912): 207). In *Herland,* Gilman would imagine a healthy society, which reveals her intuitive understanding of human verities that humanistic psychologists were developing. Instead of the first two schools in modern psychological theory, Freudian psychoanalysis and behavioristic conditioning, some psychologists believe in a humanistic school, an "evolutionary constructive" force, which urges a person "to realize [her] given potentialities" (Horney 1950, 15).[42] Whereas Gilman's life exemplifies both the self-alienation of childhood deprivation and the potential self-actualization of adult fulfillment, her imagined *Herland* depicts a human growth–enhancing culture, one in which human well-being results from social synergy—that is, integrated interaction at all levels of society.

Published Persona, 1890–1935

In 1891, one-half decade before the empowering letters to Ho, articulating a dystopian underside to the utopian *Herland,* Charlotte Perkins Gilman wrote "The Yellow Wallpaper" (1892), a delineation of postpartum depression, one of the classics of feminist sociocritical fiction. This short story accurately delineates this condition as well as the ill-advised treatment to which its narrator-mother is subjected.[43] Instead of a psychomedical model for analyzing motherhood, Kathryn Allen Rabuzzi, in a recent study, *Motherself,* offers an alternative—two mythic paths for women: the child "heroself" or the adult "motherself." The "way of the hero" includes fear of loss of self in another, while the "way of the mother" requires developing the capacity to acknowledge another outside of and in addition to the self.[44] Rabuzzi sees Gilman's narrator as unable to accept her "motherselfhood" because it is too "overwhelming," preferring instead the way of the child-hero (216). But by 1915, when at fifty-five Gilman published *Herland,* she had achieved the motherselfhood that had eluded her in 1885, when only twenty-five at the time of Kate's birth. Both professional acclaim and personal support wrought this change.

"The Yellow Wallpaper" contrasts with Gilman's utopian writing and provides an essential dystopian vision of female constriction. This view is analogous to that of Marge Piercy's dystopian Rockover State Psychiatric Hospital, which contrasts to utopian Mouth-of-Mattapoisett in *Woman on the Edge of Time* (1976). "The Yellow Wallpaper" provides the dark side that *Herland* looks beyond. Once Gilman had successfully channeled her artistic creative energy into this brief masterpiece exposing the ways of androcratic man toward woman, she turned her creative energies instead toward the practice of living, toward the creation of partnership, whether in her private life or in the larger human community. The correspondence with George Houghton Gilman was essential as part of Charlotte's progress toward developing a healthier self: the initiating writing and energy for accomplishing this development were hers, but the necessary catalysing acceptance was his.

The public counterpart to Gilman's private letters from 1897 to 1900 was her both radical and revolutionary *Women and Economics,* appearing in 1898. We must recognize the conjunction of her letters and this treatise as manifestations of creative personality, antecedents to the sociological creativity of her utopian fiction. We typically associate creativity with art: we need to understand that art artifacts come to symbolize human creative capacity in whatever fields of human endeavor they appear. Otto Rank (1884–1939), for example, in *Art and Artists* (1932), reminds us that *"creativity begins with the individual h[er]self—that is, with the self-making of the personality into the artist. . . . The creative artistic personality is* thus the first work of the productive individual" (28).[45] He explicates the process that Gilman followed in her courtship correspondence with her cousin Ho.

Gilman's creative energy now emerged not as earlier (in such art as "The Yellow Wallpaper"), but instead in letters to Ho that revealed her to be engaged in a process of rethinking the feelings and events of her life to date—of actually bringing her feelings under better understanding and control than she had heretofore enjoyed—with the result that she increased her happiness through placing under more conscious control anxieties originating in childhood deficits. Rather than additional self-expressive, aesthetically elegant writing—such as "The Yellow Wallpaper" or her two Gothic tales, "The Giant Wistaria" and "The Rocking Chair"—all three written during the early 1890s, Gilman preferred after her 1900 marriage to see her writing and speaking as social action for the betterment of life.[46] If Rank's dictum permits writing as a form of social action for a "representative of the new human type," then Gilman in her desire to be a "woman of the world," a "world-builder," or, as she put it, a "world rouser," exemplifies this larger creativity.[47] Her *Women and Economics* is a major creative work, not aesthetic or belletristic to be sure, but sociological and expository in its innovative thought, its creativity, its expectation of fomenting social change. (See also chap. 2.)

In this work, Gilman argues that women need the possibility of being simultaneously successful as both parent and professional, as private and public person—as has typically been possible for men. In 1898, although men had enjoyed a dominant place in Western industrialized society through institutionalizing the assumed domestic and emotional support of a wife in marriage and a salary based on occupational gender preference in the economy, women had only begun to recognize and dislodge male privilege. One century later much has changed, but Charlotte Perkins Gilman's critique of economic bias against women in *Women and Economics* remains provocative today—not for its now-dated evolutionary theory, but for its use of gender as a basic locus of analysis. This work provides the exposition of social values and goals imagined narratively in *Herland*. Central for *Herland* are the ideas that *Women and Economics* present regarding motherhood.

In *Women and Economics*, Gilman claims, "A mother economically free, a world-servant instead of a house-servant; a mother knowing the world and living in it—can be to her children far more than has ever been possible before. Motherhood in the world will make that world a different place for her child" (269). In *Herland,* she will demonstrate how such a world would be different. Here she claims that the new home will retire its myth of privacy to permit the entrance of specialized services and the exit of free women. Specialized professional food and cleaning (requiring "the service of fewer women [but of a lower class] for fewer hours a day," 245), simplicity of decoration and furnishings—these will free [white middle-class] woman "for full individual expression in her economic activities and in her social relation" (257). Each person will have "one room at least" to ensure "progressive individuation" (258).

Gilman continues: "the home life of the human race should . . . promote—the highest development of personality" (260). As in her letters, she struggles with romanticizing both home and mother-hood: "the love of the mother for the child is at the base of all our higher love for one another" (260): "[w]hile the world lasts, we shall need not only the individual home, but the family home" (261). Gilman's thought about homes contains what, for me, is an uncomfortable degree of essentialism and classism: although she imagines women will develop grandly, she does not here imagine occupational innovation for both sexes—women in male positions, or men sharing the instrumental and expressive work of maintaining this home. One and one-half decades later, her *Forerunner* fiction somewhat more innovatively addresses issues of class and gender.

In a subsequent chapter, Gilman considers the duty of the individual to the community and reveals her Fabian (evolutionary, as opposed to revolutionary Marxist) socialism. She urges remembrance of the conditions required for nationhood as the basis for community: "the far-reaching, collective interests of every citizen, the common good . . . called for the willing sacrifice of every individual" (275). Individual labor must serve the world as a whole, labor serving oneself alone being the least valued (279).[48] And, although education has become a "social function," mothering has remained in the individual family home, unspecialized and untrained, maybe untalented and inexperienced as well: "[t]he individual mother can never be fit to take all the care of her children" (292). For the better service of the community, women and children need these changes.

Besides discussing home and mother, Gilman examines work. "We have," she notes, "differentiated our industries, our responsibilities, our very virtues, along sex lines" (41). And, as a result, we have "a dense prejudice in favor of the essential womanliness of home duties, as opposed to the essential manliness of every other kind of work" (225). *Herland* will reveal the inessential genderliness of any particular work—and it will show all citizens associating together outside of coupled relationships: "[a]s persons, we need more and more, in each generation, to associate with other persons. . . . for wider human relationship," which need not mean "wider sex-relationship" (304). Society needs "a natural, simple medium of social intercourse between men and women" (312). Gilman rhapsodizes, "[A]s the workshops of the world—women's sphere as well as men's—become homelike and beautiful under her influence; . . . we shall have new channels for the flow of human life" (313). History repeats itself: mid-twentieth-century feminist thinkers repeat a similar insight.[49]

The emotional bases of the social critique Gilman presented in *Women and Economics* lay in memory and experience: her mother as wife and mother, herself as that mother's child, her first traumatic marriage and its concurrent experience of new motherhood, her creativity fueled by Ho's acceptance of her remembering of this past. As Gayle Greene writes in "Feminist Fiction and the Uses of Memory," "the past must be remembered, but not entirely; it must be forgotten, but not entirely; it can kill though it can also heal, and it is most healing when remembered in response to another and when 'told' " (317).[50] Gilman remembered her past in her letters to Ho, her "morning prayers." After a decade of marriage to him, she established the *Forerunner,* locus of most of her fiction, again recasting the past—but this time projecting memory, substantially if not wholly healed and reformed, into the future. She was immensely aided in this venture by Ho, who handled the financial and legal details.

During the early 1890s, Gilman had published several stories in addition to "The Yellow Wallpaper." She placed these stories in the *Woman's Journal, Kate Field's Washington, Pacific Monthly,* and *Wasp.* Gilman's writing for the *Impress,* from October 1894 through February 1895, served as an apprenticeship in fiction writing. Gilman set herself the task of producing as puzzles for readers imitations of sundry fiction writers, including Mary E. Wilkins, Louisa May Alcott, George Eliot, and Olive Schreiner—women she liked—and Edward Everett Hale, Edward Bellamy, Hamlin Garlend, Kipling, Hawthorne, Poe, Dickens, James, Irving, and Twain—male utopists, reformers, and belletrists.[51] But she tired of the ardors of trying to place her writing: like Dorothy Bryant today, she decided to become her own publisher.[52]

In the 1910 *Forerunner,* as chapter 5 in a serial called "Our Androcentric World; or, The Man-Made World" (running concurrently with *What Diantha Did*), Gilman published a discussion of "Masculine Literature." In addition to explaining her belief that literature is "world-food" (21), she classified fiction into two main branches: the Story of Adventure, War, and Combat, and the Story of Love and Desire, a narrow array (19–20). Such a proliferation of stories demonstrates, Gilman claims, how "our one-sided culture has, in this art, most disproportionately overestimated the dominant instincts of the male—Love and War—an offense against art and truth, and an injury to life" (22). She found, however, that "the art of fiction is being re-born. . . . The humanizing of women itself opens five distinctly fresh fields of fiction":

> First the position of the young woman who is called upon to give up her career—her humanness—for marriage, and [Second] who, increasingly dislikes the middle-aged woman who at last discovers that her discontent is social starvation—that it is not more love that she wants, but more business in life; Third the inter-relation of women with women—a thing we could never write about before, because we never had it before, except in harems and convents; Fourth the inter-action between mothers and children; this not the eternal "mother and child," wherein the child is always a baby, but the long drama of personal relationship; the love and hope, the patience and power, the lasting joy and triumph, the slow eating disappointment which must never be owned to a living soul—here are grounds for novels that a million mothers and many million children would eagerly read; Fifth the new attitude of the full-grown woman, who faces the demands of love with the high standards of conscious motherhood (22).

The plots and subplots of Gilman's utopian *Forerunner* fiction —not the least of which is the woman-centered society of *Herland* —exemplify these, as well as other, new "fields."[53]

Gilman explored additional beliefs about literature in a chapter called "Effect of Literature Upon the Mind," from a 1912 *Forerunner* serial, "Our Brains and What Ails Them" (chap. 5). Like Sandra Gilbert and Susan Gubar in "Sexual Linguistics: Women's Sentence, Men's Sentencing," Gilman discussed the female origins of human language for both individual and species (*War*, 262–71). Both discussions subscribe to a "mother tongue" theory of prehistoric language innovation, transmission, and creativity, and consider the mother as the first teacher of language as the teller or reader of stories. Literature, Gilman believed, became "an external brain," "a vast secondary storage battery" (134). Thus authors are "true social servant[s]," and literature is "the brain of society": "all our individual brains are steadily remodified by it" (134, 136–37). Herein lies the "social use of fiction, its effect on the mind" (137).[54] Similar to Bakhtin, in "Art and Answerability," Gilman believed that ethics, "the science of conduct," inheres in fiction (138). And, like Bakhtin in "Discourse in the Novel," Gilman finds the novel "fluent," "less tradition-bound," "respond[ing] more healthfully to the needs of its age" than poetry (138).

In stories, and especially in the novel, Gilman found that, "when the mind specially sensitized to see and understand some part of life, began to use this fluent power to revisualize and interpret life to others, a great art was born" (138).[55] In her view, the art of fiction consists in writers' being able "to feel and see some vital phase of human life; to throw that feeling into such forms as to be easily assimilable to others (138). . . . As [fiction] rises, the mind rises" (139). The world of books is literally the outer form of our Social Brain, Gilman reiterated. That "vital phase of life" central to Gilman's concern is woman's place in society and man's ways toward her.

As if to demonstrate her belief in social change through fiction writing, Gilman wrote a 1914 *Forerunner* story with two endings, "With a Difference (Not Literature)." In the first ending, an innocent and ignorant young woman, seduced by a "modern mercantile villain," is thrust from home by her angry father (29). An alternative end shows the young woman's mother retrieving a sobbing daughter, accosting the father who has turned out his minor child, and vowing that her daughter will receive family support no matter what happens. Gilman provided an "old story" and then continued it beyond the expected ending of a young woman's victimization, to depict a mother standing with her daughter against a punitive and prideful father with sufficient force to change his mind and culminate in an innovative conclusion. The woman's father apologized to his daughter and took action against the man who had seduced her. The daughter "led a long, strong, useful life, happy in the large happiness of teaching and shielding young girls, and working for a permanent enlightenment of all of us, such as had miraculously fallen upon her family" (32). Gilman's closure refuses the death typically meted out to "fallen women" and insists upon this alternative model of finding happiness in working and living independently. Although the story reveals Gilman's restricted view of sexuality and possibilities for a nonvirginal woman, it does present behavioral options new for 1914. Long before the fashion for metafiction, Gilman self-consciously wrote a story about stories—about the possibilities for alternative outcomes, beyond the expectations of the genre.[56]

In the 1915 *Forerunner*, when *Herland* was three-quarters into print, Gilman presented her estimate of "Coming Changes in Literature": "it recognizes women as full citizens of the world, and treats of their relations to the world, both entirely new subjects" (230). Depiction of motherhood would be central, correcting previous male writers' "ignoring that great goddess of mother-love in whose service young Eros is but a running footman" (230). And she lists six new areas of subject matter for literature:

> 1. the mother-love story—"unlimited as life itself . . . never . . . content till all children upon earth are happy and well-reared" (listed fourth in 1910) (231);
> 2. the story of the common child—"the universal drama of personality, the young soul's entrance upon life," portrayed by the woman writer as artist, "voic[ing] for the world more clearly than ever before the story of its first twenty years" (232);
> 3. the story of the "effect of woman's new position upon industry and war . . . her new ambitions, new hopes, a new conscience" (233);
> 4. the story of "combination and adjustment" that marriage exacts of the new woman and her husband, when marriage is combined with careers for both, and leading to her happiness as well as his (listed first in 1910) (233);
> 5. the story of New Human Women, as mature "human creature[s] . . . married . . . ; remarried, demarried, or not married at all," with men "co-workers in a common sphere of action" (234); and finally
> 6. the story of the "man himself, in this new association . . . when mothered, sistered and wived by adequate normal women" (235).

Gilman surprisingly makes no separate mention of women's relationships to each other, as she had in 1910, but does focus upon the new man required by a new woman. With *Herland* nearly completed, and *With Her in Ourland* ahead, her concerns moved toward women and men together in the world. Such are the pursuits of Gilman's utopian fiction—some nine categories in all, two appearing on both 1910 and 1915 lists.[57]

Such fantasy, as in Gilman's utopian imaginings, is not, Clifford

Geertz has said in an epilogue to *The Anthropology of Experience,* "a simple turning of one's back on 'reality' but a way, however devious, strange, and explosive, of coming into contact with it; indeed, in part constructing it" (376). Either as a writer imagining or as a reader engrossed in a text of utopian fantasy, one enters a threshold state, which Victor Turner has named "liminality" and defines as "a fructile chaos, a storehouse of possibilities, not a random assemblage but a striving after new forms and structures, a gestation process, a fetation of modes appropriate to postliminal existence" (42). Liminal space permits us to "author ourselves" (373), as Gilman did in diaries, journals, letters, and published writing. Especially in the last, she "put her experience into circulation" for the benefit of historical cohorts and future readers (375).[58] And her texts become, in Kenneth Burke's words, "strategies for encompassing situations" (378) or "equipment for living"—for recognizing and reducing gaps between women's reality and women's desire.[59]

Gilman earns our applause for her fulfillment of social duty. Although a human not a perfect person, her relentless drive to accomplish, to do all she could to reform human society, leaves a student of her life with empowering awe. Perhaps additional analysis of her life can eventually enable us who follow to avoid her pitfalls and create in our lives more joy than she knew.

Because interpretation cannot be finalized, because readers will participate in additional unfinalizable readings of Gilman's writing, what ends this volume is not the expected conclusion, but rather a selection of documents upon which these chapters depend, thereby actively encouraging additional reading, the more closely to approach the subject of Charlotte Perkins Gilman's progress toward a world in which women and men, as equally responsible partners in the social construction of global villages, might engage in the realization of utopian values.

5

"Making Better People"
Experiencing Gilman's Legacy

AS CHAPTER 1 INDICATES, fourteen utopian fictions constitute the conclusion of this study. They provide readers with the opportunity to experience part of the utopian legacy that Charlotte Perkins Gilman has left to us. They permit readers, whether as students or scholars, to experience "an ultimate indeterminacy of meaning" as they peruse the following texts and find richness not yet suggested in the foregoing pages (Martin 1989, 384). And they encourage a developing community of readers, who gain "through an appreciation for the boundless capacity of language, which through storytelling, brings us together, despite great distances between cultures, despite great distances in time," as Leslie Silko explains (72). This view is seconded by Robert Coles in *The Call of Stories* (1989), who urges "respect for narrative as everyone's rock-bottom capacity, but also as a universal gift, to be shared with others" (30).

If we focus upon the selections' positive content, we find that they offer us possibilities, especially for gender alternatives, that are not yet widespread, including the elimination of androcentric arrangements. They permit no complacency regarding human existence and urge upon us experimentation. In her utopian selections, Gilman hypothetically urges, "Let's pretend that. . . ," and then proceeds to spin out webs of possibility for our perusal, possibilities that may, in fact, constitute realizable utopias.

How foolish are our practices; how broad alternative possibilities, Gilman's fiction suggests. Imaginative literature, more than factual books, can affect our minds. Gilman imagined tale after tale to show how changed minds might change behavior in the direction of social improvement. "A Strange Land," chapter 5 from *Her-*

115

land, and chapter 11 from *With Her in Ourland* attest to Gilman's belief regarding human purpose in life: "How to make the best kind of people and how to keep them at their best and growing better— surely that is what we are here for" (*Ourland*).

Dive now into the imaginative legacy of Charlotte Perkins Gilman: experience her utopian ways in the selections that follow.

Selection 1

"Aunt Mary's Pie Plant"
Woman's Home Companion 6 (June 1908): 14, 48–49

Discussed Chapter 3, 52–54

This Woman's Home Companion *short story, except for the never-completed "A Woman's Utopia" (1907), is the first self-conscious utopian fiction by Gilman to reach a wide audience, as the 1907 story did not. It fictionalized reforms suggested in* Women and Economics, *and it vindicated the social impact of women's club activites. The journalist-narrator models a new arrangement for young women, combining both public career and private relationship—a plot concerning the first (marriage versus career) and third ("inter-relation of women with women") of the "five distinctly fresh fields of fiction" that Gilman enumerated in 1910, as well as the fifth (woman "as a human creature"), and, though tentatively as yet, the sixth ("man himself, in this new association") from her 1915 discussion.*

This selection and the three following it exemplify Gilman's first stage of utopian imagining: family and neighborhood changes designed to adjust women and men to more equal status. Nearing the twenty-first century, feeling ourselves more informed than Gilman, we as readers may find criticizing her for what she does not imagine easier than appreciating the possible alternatives she does suggest, which have not even yet been sufficiently "realized" for us to judge their efficacy.

EDITORIAL NOTE [*Woman's Home Companion* 6 (June 1908)]:
Our readers have already been made acquainted with many of

Charlotte Perkins Gilman's ideas on subjects in which women are
interested. In "Aunt Mary's Pie Plant" Mrs. Gilman's characters
show in a convincing way how her beliefs and remedies would
work out in practise. It will be found a realistic miniature *Looking
Backward*.

MY EDITOR WANTED SOME STORIES of life in a small town, for his
Sunday edition. "Find a back number," he said. "An out-of-date, no-
account place, where they don't believe in evolution. Go and board
there a while, get acquainted with the families, work up a lot of
stuff about the little tragedies of the place—city people like it. Little
withered old ladies, you know—no men to speak of—town that's
dead, but doesn't know it." Then I bethought me of New Newton. It
was the first time I had ever considered the place as of any practical
value. That I was born there was no shame to me, for I was not
consulted, and no credit to the town, either—the product was certainly unexpected.

There were times when it seemed to be unappreciated—even
undesired—which is one reason I left so early. I recalled it well, a
rambling, disorderly little town, one of many strung along the railroad, a mere way station on connecting lines between great cities.
It was once the market center for a scattered farming community,
and had no particular industry of its own. It was narrow-minded. It
was quiet. It was poor. It was slow.

The principal excitement was caused by local quarrels, personal, or between the little struggling churches. The principal ambition of the young people was to grow up and get away. The old
people didn't seem to have any ambition.

Now, as I joggled along toward my old home, after twelve years'
absence, it all rose up clearly in my mind, as gray, monotonous and
uninviting as ever. I could see the rutted, unkept streets with a
string of dusty weeds along the sidewalks; gray picket fences that
were once white; gates whose creak and click aroused eager eyes
behind the blinds of the shut-up houses—several houses, as a matter of fact—what else had those women to think about but their
neighbors' affairs! The young men went away, of course, and the
smartest girls, but there were plenty of "unattached" women left,
and they attached themselves, for lack of other support, to the scant
affairs of their neighbors, like small vines among grasses.

Aunt Mary was very clear to my mind, because visiting her was
among my few pleasures as a child. She lived in a faded old house,
comfortable, but needing much repair, having a large front yard,

with roses and syringas, and a larger back yard, where were apple trees, currant bushes and rows on rows of pie plant [rhubarb].

Aunt Mary's pies were acknowledged perfect in a community where cooking was the only art studied, and pies the apex of that art. Of them all she held the rhubarb best, and assuredly I had never seen their equal. The crust melted deliciously upon the tongue, the glowing, transparent cubes, soft, but not mushy, shone like jewels in the clear pink sirup; and they tasted even better than they looked. A restless, somewhat querulous old lady was Aunt Mary, a widow, with a farm that rented for enough to keep her, and the house to furnish occupation all insufficient to her nervous energy.

For company, as well as to work in her garden, she had a "bound boy," Joe Westcott, a slow, quiet fellow. He was always nice to me when I was there—an eager, critical, greedy child; but I considered him a very inferior person indeed; and when he actually asked me to marry him!—well, that was another reason I left home at sixteen. No moldering, smothered life in a dead town for me! I was going to write! and—well, I have written.

First a year or two as a shop girl—no hope that way. Then a year in a kitchen, and two hundred and twenty-five dollars ahead— also some manuscript. Then a year or two of scrambling along as a reporter—much aided by the two hundred and twenty-five dollars. Now I had been fairly well established for some time, and got twenty-five dollars a week on an average—sometimes more when magazines took my stories. One can do a great deal of writing in twelve years and have very little to show for it.

My father died when I was little, and my mother died the year I went to Europe for the paper, so I couldn't even get back for the funeral. Mother and I never got on very well, so I had spent much time with Aunt Mary. She would make a fine type for my stories— she and old Miss Lathrop, who lived next door. There was a little gate in the fence between the places, and they used to exchange pies and layer cake (Miss Lathrop's layer cake was as famous in its way as Aunt Mary's pies), and gossip, of course.

Then there was the "Widder Hagan" in the little cottage down by the river; she used to do washing for the few people who didn't do it themselves—and how well she did her work! I sighed as I remembered my city laundry bills, and clothing that wasted from week to week under the nameless blight. The "Widder Hagan" would do for a type, too.

Then my girl friends popped up in my mind—Susy Mills, my

young schoolteacher of whom I was so fond, Jennie Gale and May Aldrich—what were they like now, I wondered. And then I thought of weary, discouraged-looking women from the country round, driving into town for a little necessary shopping, driving out again more tired than before, to take up the endless work of a small farm. I should find material in plenty.

"New Newton! New Newton!" shouted the brakeman, and I gathered up my belongings and descended.

A new station building was the first thing apparent. I had not dreamed this was my station, because it was so big, bright and bustling. Electric lights, electric cars, and—Why, there was Aunt Mary! Anywhere else I certainly shouldn't have known her! Why, I remembered her as old, though to be sure she wasn't fifty, with spectacles and a rusty little black lace cap, in a black calico gown mornings and a black alpaca afternoons. A thin, sad-looking, uneasy old lady she had been, bobbing back and forth in a wooden rocking chair with a red cushion, looking out "to see the passin'." Now behold her, looming larger to my unaccustomed eyes—at least she was plumper, wearing her gray hair in a wavy pompadour, gaily bonneted, and impressively well dressed. She seemed unaffectedly glad to see me; and I was so touched by an affection long unknown that it fairly brought tears to my eyes.

She took me home in a carriage, visibly not "the hack" that used to stand by the old station; and sat patting my hand, and asking how I was and where I'd been all these years, and why I hadn't come before, while I looked out on streets strangely unfamiliar, well kept, well lighted, lined with prosperous-looking places, until we reached the house.

The same big green yard with the honey-sweet syringas, but a new white fence enclosed it, the path was smoothly bricked, the grass trimmed close, and the house was as much changed as Aunt Mary. It was fresh with new paint, yellow and white, brightened with bay windows, broadened with a vine-shaded porch; and inside there was actually a bath room, electric light, steam heat, and such an air of comfort and modernity that I could hardly believe my eyes.

"What has happened to you, Aunt Mary?" I eagerly inquired. "Have I a new uncle and a rich one?"

"No, Maria Potter, and you never will," she replied a little severely. "If you want to know what has changed my circumstances, I can tell you in one word. Pies."

Pies. I remembered Aunt Mary's pies well, they were dreams of delight unquestionably, but how even the perfection of pie makery had been thus recognized and rewarded I did not perceive.

"Is it pies that have changed the town so?" I asked. "It doesn't look like the same place at all. What has happened to you here? This used to be the slowest, sleepiest old place—now the streets and houses look so different, the people have changed so—Do tell me about it."

"I'll tell you about it all in good time; but I want to show you about it first," said Aunt Mary. "Now you will want to rest a little, and change your dress before tea. If you're not too tired, I want you to go with me to the Woman's Club this evening."

"The Woman's Club! Aunt Mary in a Woman's Club! Pies! What has happened to this place!" I thought, as I enjoyed a hot bath in a porcelain tub.

Another surprise awaited me at supper—the three best friends of my girlhood, not only grown and changed as time might warrant, but also in ways I had not expected.

I was used to the movement and push of big cities, to current thought and comment of the freshest, and had expected this old home town of mine and its girlhood friends to be as I had left them. Of course, people would be older, that I had looked for, but to find them seeming actually younger was a surprise. I suppose Aunt Mary was only about forty-five when I left, but her hair was gray and she was a quiet, lonely woman. Now here she was with that gray hair so handsome and effective, and a sort of "up and coming" look that certainly was not there before. Then there was Miss Mills, my old teacher, very fond of the little children as I remembered her, and struggling somewhat ineffectually with the older ones. She looked younger, too, and happier.

Jennie and May were married, naturally enough—Mrs. Greenwood and Mrs. Fales—but here they were by themselves as gay as larks; and all four continued to excite and mystify me by allusions to the town and its doings, and to refuse any explanation.

"Time enough to tell you about it when you've seen something," said Aunt Mary; and presently I did see something, for they escorted me to a fine new building standing where Alison's store burned down—an ugly, vacant place I remembered well—and announced it as the Woman's Club House.

"How can you support such a club house in a town of this size?" I asked.

"It's a Country Club House," they said; "the country women

from all around use it. We have more country members than town ones."

"Country women—do you mean just farmers' wives?"

"The same women, but they are not 'just farmers' wives' any longer. Things have changed here, you see."

I refused to show any further curiosity, but sat in smothered astonishment, listening to short, but able papers read by the Women's Farm and Garden Club.

"These are all your 'farmers' wives,' " said Aunt Mary. "But they are in business for themselves now, you see."

One gave an account of her methods with asparagus—how much she raised, how much was sold fresh, and how much was canned and sold at a greater profit. Another had a bee farm, and made a fine income from it. Another raised celery; another lettuce; and several dealt in small fruits and their resultant jellies.

"And how do they find time to attend to all this work?" I inquired of Aunt Mary.

"Precisely by doing this work." she replied enigmatically.

They were all short papers; we had a little discussion, very lively and practical; then tea and cake, talk and laughter, a little music and a half-hour's dancing, and it was eleven and after before they all left.

"Farmers' wives!" I kept saying to myself. "Farmers' wives! And they don't look dull and tired. And they dress nicely. And they come in town and stay until eleven o'clock! Aunt Mary, how are the husbands persuaded to let them do this?"

"They are persuaded by a large addition to the family income," said Aunt Mary.

Next day she had a carriage, and proceeded to show me the town and some of the country round about.

"This," said she proudly, "is the New Newton Laundry," as we drove to the top of a grassy hill on the outskirts of the town. Its wide, exposed summit was certainly an ideal spot for drying clothes; they hung and fluttered there in full sunshine and fresh wind. "These are the workshops," she said; and here I found modern laundry machines, with steam driers for bad weather; rows of perfectly appointed tubs; clean, contented-looking men and women at work; and a clerical force keeping the necessarily elaborate accounts of a large laundry. At the head of it, all comely and competent, behold the Widow Hagan!

She was delighted to see me, expressed awed approval of my becoming "a great writer," said she had read "pieces" of mine, and cut them out; and I in turn congratulated her on her flourishing business.

" 'Tis a good business," she declared, smiling. "Sure, people must be clean, and that continuous. There's more money in washing than I would ever have supposed when I was doing it alone. The boys are with me here; Johnny is clerking, and Jimmy drives one of the wagons. We're doing fine."

I was quite bewildered, and asked Aunt Mary, as we left, "How do you get patronage enough to support such a big place?"

"A hundred families will support a small laundry," she answered. "We have five or six hundred in the town alone, to say nothing of the country."

"Do the country women patronize a laundry? How can they afford it?"

"They can't afford not to," said Aunt Mary.

She showed me the New Central School—a group of buildings in a sort of park; and here I found Miss Mills, the picture of contentment, in the midst of a large and flourishing kindergarten.

"This is my work," she said proudly; "I always loved it, and now I do nothing else. I teach these little ones, and train others to do it."

They showed me the great new schoolhouse, with its many grades and departments; and the children having a hot luncheon in a beautiful, well-arranged eating room. "Do they stay to luncheon? We didn't in my time. Why don't they go home?" I inquired.

"These are children from the outlying farms," I was told; "they haven't time to go home. It is easier to feed them here than to make four trips. We have a motor bus, and collect them for miles around."

Aunt Mary proudly exhibited the clean streets, the pretty yards, the well-kept trees, the many new and handsome houses and public buildings, and finally stopped with an air of complacent triumph before a pleasant-looking, businesslike place near the railroad station, bearing the sign M. GARDINER, PIES.

"Why, Aunt Mary!" I cried, "have you started a pie factory!"

"That is exactly what I've done," she calmly replied. "My pies are eaten from Maine to Illinois, and I don't know but farther—only they can't be so good then."

She showed me over the bright, airy place, with its rows of ovens; its beautiful, cold mixing rooms, with the shining glass slabs and glass rolling pins; the neatly dressed women at work, the brisk packers and busy manager. And here I was surprised again to find in this efficient person the object of my early scorn, Joe Westcott.

He was not so astonished, Aunt Mary having telephoned him of our visit, but seemed glad to see me, and very proud to exhibit and explain.

"We have had a fine, growing business now for ten years. Have all we can do and we're enlarging steadily."

"Yes," said Aunt Mary, "it's a beautiful business. I spend my mornings here—except when I have company."

"And you've made a fortune—out of pies!" I asked. "I wouldn't have believed it!"

"It's easy to figure," said Joe. "A good pie costs on the average, in a private family, ten cents for materials. It costs us about five, or eight, counting the plant and labor, because we get the materials so much more cheaply. We sell them to the trade at fifteen cents—they sell them at twenty cents—more sometimes. We clear five cents on a pie, and turn out from two to five hundred a day."

I never was quick at arithmetic, but I figured out that five cents a pie on even two hundred was one thousand cents—and that looked like ten dollars! Ten dollars a day was—why, it was three thousand dollars a year and over! Aunt Mary Gardiner making three thousand dollars a year, or four, or five, out of pies!

That evening I told her she'd simply got to tell me about it; and she was more than willing—it was what she'd been working up to all the time.

"My pies are only part of it," she said. "The changes you see in this town, pies and all, are due to the Rev. James Exeter Curtis. I'd haved introduced you to him at once, but he's away on a vacation. I don't know where to begin, but that man came here and began to tell us about the big institutional churches in New York and Boston and other places, and to show us how we could do things here if we would. He aroused our local pride—we didn't know we had any! You should see us bristle if any one says a word against New Newton!

"He got the charitable society interested in kindergartening—had a friend of his from St. Louis come and speak to them about it, got up a fund and sent Miss Mills off to study; we've had a fine one now for years, and a crêche, too. He stirred up the whole school system, got the women to vote on it—we could, you know, but had never realized the good we could do—and now we are the banner town of the state. He got the Woman's Club started—it used to be the Ladies' Literary, you know."

"But pies, Aunt Mary!" I interrupted. "I have a consuming hunger for the pies—in spite of that delicious one we had for supper."

"Oh, pies! Well, he took a personal interest in every one of his people, and he told me I was too able a woman to do nothing but wait on a house and attend church meetings. I had talked poor when they wanted money for that kindergarten, and he said, 'Why don't you make money, Mrs. Gardiner?' 'What could I do to make money?' I asked him. 'A woman of my age—I've no accomplishments.' It happened that I'd been baking that day, and I brought him a piece of mince pie—he liked them hot—some people do, you know.

" 'Did you make this pie, Mrs. Gardiner?' he asked. 'I did,' said I. 'Then you need no other accomplishment,' said he; 'to make a pie like that is Genius—simply Genius!'

"Well, he arranged for a place he knew in Buffalo to take a dozen of my mince pies every day; and the orders kept increasing. I had to get help soon, and a bigger outfit, and then he advised me regularly to open a shop—said it was a perfectly legitimate business —certainly a womanly one; and he arranged for me to borrow some money to build the shops—it was our lot, you know; I hated to borrow, but he said that was the way business was done, and now it's all cleared off, I own the place, I've fixed this house as you see— and—and now I can do things in the town when I want to!"

"That sounds easy, but, Aunt Mary, all these other women that I heard at the club, they don't all make pies, I'm sure. Tell me the whole thing."

"You see, it was like this," said she: "wealth is produced by the application of labor and intelligence to natural materials. All the materials we had about here was just land; and all the labor and intelligence we used was that of the farmers and a few shopkeepers. The women labored, but they didn't use intelligence. The minister showed us that agriculture was a grand profession and could be a paying one. And that women could labor intelligently as well as men. He got lecturers to come here, started a traveling library, and woke us all up to what he called our common gold mine. Then he got the women roused up, started them along in a small way, at bees and berries and one thing and another—we had a great 'Home Industry' show at the country fair—and he got an expert from a big grocery in New York to come up and sample our jellies, preserves and honey.

"He convinced the farmer that his wife's labor had a money value. Money talks, you know. When a man found that his wife could turn in fifty or a hundred dollars a season off a little patch of currants, he began to feel a new respect for her. The trade grew. I can see, now we look back, how that man did it, without seeming to try to. He'd place private orders, praise the women, get some shop to take them up—Why, you remember Miss Lathrop? She's made enough from layer cakes to clear the mortgage off her place. We're talking of going into partnership—'Gardiner & Lathrop, Pies and Cakes.' Some of them don't cook things; they raise high-grade asparagus or celery or some fancy vegetable. We being on the railroad, can send things easy; and there are plenty of big cities within a day's journey or so. The farms have increased in value, and the men have learned something, too. Tomatoes in glass bring twice or three times what the raw product does—and none is wasted."

"But, Aunt Mary, how do these women get the time—who does the housework?"

"Ah, that's the great triumph! Mr. Curtis has been working up to that all the time. You see, first the women learned to specialize, to do something perfectly, and earn money. Then the men learned that woman's labor had a money value. Here was a bunch of farms —say twenty—and twenty women on them working about fourteen hours a day to wait on that family—they couldn't 'afford' to hire a girl. Then comes Mr. Curtis and proves to them that their work was really worth a dollar and a half a day at the very lowest—that they were spending, or rather going without, nine dollars a week for housework!

"Nine dollars! Not counting Sundays. They'd never thought of that before—men or women. I never thought of it myself. He started the women to earning, and they liked it. A woman enjoys handling her own money, same as a man does, even if it isn't very much."

"But who does the housework?" I persisted.

"Don't you hurry me, Maria," said my respected aunt. "I'm coming to that. We don't, so to speak, do housework in New Newton any more."

I gasped and stared at the triumphant old lady. Was she going crazy? "Don't do housework? What do you do?"

"We do shop work," she answered proudly. "We do our work in shops, and come home when it's done. Of course, on farms they work outdoors or in the preserving rooms, but there are very few of us doing housework now."

"Do you all keep servants?"

"We did at first—but that is expensive, too. We do better than that."

"Oh, I know: co-operation!" I cried. I wish I could produce the lofty scorn with which Aunt Mary dismissed the word.

"Co-operation! No, thank goodness, it's not co-operation! There's no mixing up of families in New Newton, I can tell you. We have our separate homes, as we always did and always mean to; but we have those homes served by specialists. We buy our food cooked instead of raw, that's all."

"But how can you do it in the country on scattered farms?"

"We don't have cattle ranches here, Maria; you couldn't do it on them. But we've built up pretty thick around here lately, and where there are twenty farms within a radius of two miles, we can serve cooked food at the door, cheaper and a great deal better, than they can do it themselves. And hot, too. We have patent asbestos-lined food conveyors, we have a system of overhead carriers, like the parcel carriers in a shop—the simplest kind of wire and post arrangement—and they order by telephone. The thing stops at the door and rings a bell—all you have to do is to go out and bring it in."

"But, Aunt Mary, is it as good as what they cooked for themselves?"

She looked at me severely over her gold-rimmed glasses. "As good? Are my pies 'as good' as the average? Is Miss Lathrop's cake 'as good' as the average? I tell you, we have the best now—all of us. The best cooks do the cooking, and everybody gets the advantage of the best cooks. I don't want to bewilder you, Maria, nor to claim too much. This system is not established everywhere yet, even about here. But almost all the people in town use it; and numbers on farms. What we have done, thanks to the Reverend James Curtis, is to bring out all the productive energy of the place. The families earn more and spend less. The women are far happier, prouder, more ambitious and intelligent. The children get better advantages. The town is making a name as a center of pure-food industries. We are organizing—we have a Woman Preserving Company that does a big business; more are starting. You've seen how the place has waked up and improved. We have raised the standard of living in every way."

"How did you ever persuade the men to allow it?" I asked.

"By giving them happier wives, more money and better food." said Aunt Mary.

Once wound up, the good lady found it difficult to stop. She was filled to the brim with assorted information. She showed me books, rows of books, in her new bookcase, and suggested that I take a course of reading along these lines.

"You'd better stay right here and take hold, Maria. I can find a place for you—there's plenty to do—the town grows so fast. You're no hand at pies, I suppose?"

"No, Aunt Mary," said I sadly, "I never was good at pies. You are very kind, but—"

Aunt Mary had whisked out to open the door. She popped her head in again. "I thought it was business," she said, "and maybe it is—for you."

She popped out again, and in came Joe Westcott. Joe had certainly improved. He really was not bad looking—a big, solid, dependable sort of man. He was well informed, fully conscious of the town's improvement, and, as I began to see, an integral part of it. He made himself very agreeable then and after, and as he still boarded with Aunt Mary, I saw a good deal of him.

But my stay could not be long. As soon as the waves of bewilderment began to subside I remembered my errand. "A back number," the editor had said. "An out-of-date, no-account place. A town that's dead, but doesn't know it." And I had come to this prancing young Utopia!

I wrote to my editor suggesting articles on "Modern Progress in Country Towns," "What Our Country Women Are Doing," "The Domestic Miracles of New Newton," but he would have none of them. "The public won't stand for it," he replied. "They don't believe in that sort of thing. You'll have to find another place to work if you want this job."

So I said good-by to Aunt Mary. When Joe heard of it he came up town at once, and again asked me to marry him. "I wouldn't have hurried you so," he said, "but you're going away again and I've waited quite some time."

"I can't marry you, Joe," I said; but I said it without any scorn this time. "After all these years of preparation and practice I cannot give up my work. I must write."

"You dear child!" said Joe, looking down at me with his kind, steady eyes, "who wants you to give up your work? We have a mail service in this country—to say nothing of rural free delivery. Can't you sit and write in a cool, big, comfortable house in the country—laundry sent out, meals sent in, sweeping by the day, no trouble at all—as easy as you can sit and write in a hall bedroom?"

And after some consideration I concluded that I could.

Selection 2

"A Garden of Babies"
Success 12 (June 1909): 370–71, 410–11

Discussed Chapter 3, 51–52

"A Garden of Babies" answers "The Yellow Wallpaper" of 1892 in imagining what institutions are needed to make motherhood happy for both mothers and babies, a field of fiction prominent in both Gilman's 1910 and 1915 discussions of literature, in which it ranked fourth and first, respectively. The story articulates reasons and solutions for maternal exhaustion. It lays out the benefits to babies and mothers in providing for mothers' needs. A later story, the 1915 "Dr. Clair's Place" (Forerunner 6.6), depicts a rest home that restores exhausted women through a regimen wholly the opposite of what Dr. S. Weir Mitchell had extended to Gilman. But, unlike "Dr. Clair's Place," this story focuses upon the particular needs of women as mothers. Gilman neglects here to present men's capacity to nurture the young, although "Her Housekeeper" indicates that she did acknowledge this possibility.

IT WAS JESSIE'S LOSS, to begin with; a terrible loss, a loss so sweeping, so complete, that we feared for her reason. That's why I let her have the twins for a while, and that is how all the rest of it came about.

Of course, even then, I wouldn't have let her have them, but that she was my own sister, and she was in mother's big house, and mother was there. Father and my brother George were both doctors —it seemed providential. Then my health was completely broken

129

down—partly owing to the twins, and partly to worrying so over Jessie. Mother said it wouldn't do the babies any good for me to stay, nor Jessie, nor her; and my dear Huntley said they were right, and whisked me off to California for the winter, though I never knew how he afforded it.

This is what had happened, beginning with Jessie. There were three of us children, Jessie, George, and I, and we grew up in this fine, sunshiny, roomy old house, with wide lawns and gardens. Father, as I said, was a doctor, and I think mother would have been a doctor if she hadn't married one—she was a very wise woman.

So we grew up strong and jolly. I was perfectly contented if I could work in the garden—and Jessie was perfectly contented if she had babies to take care of. She was baby crazy—I never saw such a girl. All her dolls were babies—she dressed them as such, with a literalness which I used to tell her was fairly unpleasant; and she played with them long after she was old enough to know better. Only one thing would take her away from her dolls—that was a real baby. If she could beg, borrow, or steal a baby to take care of, she was absolutely happy.

And it was astonishing—how many women were willing to let her do it! Women talk so much about devotion to their children—I notice most of them are delighted to have the baby off their hands for a while.

Then we had a little sister, and Jessie gave her whole mind to her; mother was fairly jealous; and when she died—poor little May! (she had meningitis—nobody seems to be able to fight that yet!) —well, when she died, Jessie was so broken up that we were all frightened.

Then father had her take a regular course in nursing—baby nursing: he said if she *would* do it she might as well know how, and that more babies might distract her mind from little May. She was young then, of course; but she took to that hospital work like a duck to water—she didn't care where she was if she could play mother. Later she took up kindergartening—we didn't want her to be a regular nurse, of course.

Then she married—about the same time I did; and was so blissfully happy that it seemed almost wicked. I never saw anybody so happy! I was happy enough—I defy any reasonable woman to be happier than I was! But Jessie wasn't reasonable. She seemed to be walking in Paradise. She went around like one in a dream—a dream of heaven. To see those two together almost made me jealous. They were like poetry.

Then the baby came—Jessie's baby. I hadn't any, yet, and I was naturally proud of my nephew; but Jessie acted like—well as if that child was Buddha *at least*. And she—and he—and the baby together —it makes me cry to think of it.

After my twins came, I was as proud as she was—we were all happy together.

Then three dreadful things happened, one after the other—all in a week's time.

Her husband's property was in a big mill, up the valley; and there was a sudden flood and the whole plant was ruined—under-mined—washed away.

That they could have recovered from; but poor, dear Hal was there; was trying to save things, and he was killed. Jessie just took that baby in her arms and—well, we were afraid she hurt the poor child, just with her desperate, choking love and grief. But she had to have it, she would have it; and then, right on top of everything, it *died*—the baby—Jessie's baby!

It was awful. She wouldn't believe it. She was just as calm— and polite! She spoke softly and made no fuss. She said, "I know my husband is gone. Please don't disturb the baby." We couldn't get it away from her. Oh! it was terrible!

Then mother and father and George and my dear Huntley had a consultation. Father's gray head was suddenly much whiter; mother looked ten years older. The upshot of it was that they said I must go away, for a complete change—and Jessie must have the twins— simply must. I hated to leave them, but I was pretty much broken down, so that Huntley went with me himself.

It was the saving of Jessie. She wouldn't look at them at first, but mother laid them on the bed in her room and just left them there to cry. And Jessie had to get up and attend to them; she simply had to. Then, of course, they were so dear and sweet and lovely—it brought her out of that frozen stupor she was in.

She fussed over them so constantly that father went to some of his patients and borrowed a couple more, nice ones, where the mothers were sick or something. He said she must not concentrate too much.

We never expected it would turn out as it did. We thought it was only a temporary device; but it resulted in our home's becoming quite a permanent *crêche*. Not for working women, of course, but for women we all knew, and who knew us. The south wing was fitted up for babies. Sometimes there would be over a dozen, daytimes; and some of them stayed nights. Unless there were enough to keep

Jessie occupied she would mope and grieve. They kept her hands full for a year or two; and after that it became an institution.

I returned in the spring and settled down in our house next door; and I wasn't so jealous of the twins as I expected to be, because my other babies came along from time to time; and—well really it was a great convenience to have so nice a place for them.

With father's long-standing medical authority, and George's new knowledge; with mother's experience and Jessie's thorough training—to say nothing of her natural instinct—why the neighbors began to call it "The Babies University."

They did have the loveliest times, those little things! There was the big house, full of sunshine and fresh air, and then several acres around it for them to play and sleep out of doors. I kept up my fondness for gardening, and we made the whole place lovely for them. There was quite a stretch of lawn, good, solid, long-established turf, with plenty of sun and changing tree-shadows. That was kept as clean as a parlor; cleaner, for there was no dust on it; and we would let the blessed babies sprawl and tumble there, as happy as kittens.

There was a family on the other side, old friends and neighbors, who were very captious at first. "Won't they be crying all the time?" they asked.

But bless you! Those babies didn't cry. Why should they?

There was such a demand for us to take children a little older—two or three years—that after a while we opened a kindergarten, too, across the hall, with some of the teachers Jessie knew installed there. Our place got to be a regular institution—people came to see it; and pretty soon dear mother said she had rather teach on one day in the week than answer questions on six! So she had a mothers' class, and lots of women came. They had confidence in her because she was a grandmother, not what they called "a mere theorist."

George used to grin. He was full of theories, and had very little respect for mothers. A young doctor hasn't much respect for anything, seems to me—except science. He said if I knew as much about mothers as he did I wouldn't think so much of them. I told him he was only a man and never could be a mother, and not to talk about what he could not possibly understand.

Some people criticized us a good deal. They said we "came between mother and child"; and that we would "break up the home"! How absurd! As if leaving a baby in the care of my sister Jessie—with all her love of children and all her practical experience, and with my mother there to oversee, and two doctors within call—was going to do any harm!

Father and George established their office a few doors down the street. They said they wouldn't risk having patients come to that baby farm! Father will make fun of things, but he believes in it all. It has done Jessie all the good in the world. After a few years she came out strong again.

She said the nightmare horror was gone now; that her heart was shut completely on one side, but was wide open on another. "I lost everything—at once," she said, "but I never can again! Now I have dozens of babies to love—and dozens more are coming! I can have an endless procession of babies as long as I live; more than I ever could have had of my own! And I know I make them happy, and keep them healthy. Just look at them—the darlings!"

It was a pretty sight. There would be that sunshiny grass, the big trees, the roses and honeysuckle, and all the sweet, bright things about; still and clean and quiet, far back from the road. And there was Jessie, all in her soft white dress—she wore clean white always now—and these happy, sturdy, pink little creatures all around her.

The little helpless wiggly ones she liked best—the kind with limp fingers and Japanese dolly eyes. Little by little as they grew older she entrusted them more and more to the care of her assistants, and by the time they left the kindergarten for school they were just children. She liked children well enough, but she loved babies. Studying Jessie, I have come to the conclusion that I don't. I love my babies, of course—because they are mine, but I do not—to be honest—love to spend my whole time in their society. Neither do lots of women. We didn't even know this once, much less dare say it. We had nothing to compare with—no other love larger than ours, like Jessie's.

She isn't foolish about it. She doesn't treat a baby like a doll-idol—or a Teddy bear! She respects it. There is reverence in her love—and understanding. She seems to know just how a baby likes to lie, and whether there are any wrinkles under it—or if it is too warm, or anything. The little limp things just give a bubbly sigh of relief when she takes them; they blink and grope and snuggle down —she can put any baby to sleep. It's fairly hypnotic.

"Where are their mothers?" some people demand severely. "Where you are when your baby is out with a nursemaid," I answered. I've no patience with these women. They will hire any kind of an ignorant young thing—a low class foreigner—and deliver the baby into her clutches—without a qualm! Everybody knows what they do! Walk the streets and flirt, get together and gossip, take the babies, goodness knows where; but nobody blames the mother.

Now, in this case, the mother can wash and dress and do all she wants to for the youngster, and bring it herself to our place, and know that the child is absolutely secure and happy. If it's a nursing baby, she runs in and nurses it; they generally don't bring them before the three-hour period.

Then people ask all sorts of questions: What do we do if the mother lives at a distance? What do we do in stormy weather? What do we do with sick babies?—and so on. It's so foolish! If the distance is great they don't come, of course! We are not bringing up the whole town! If it's too stormy to bring a baby in a carriage, done up like a chrysalis, why they don't bring him that day, that's all. They are all the more ready to appreciate the opportunity when it is good weather. As to sick babies—we don't have any. Every baby is examined every day by my father—or George. No sickness is allowed—of course! We couldn't allow it, on account of the others. Back they go—we don't keep a hospital! It is quite an advantage to have competent medical inspection of your children every day. An ounce of prevention is worth a ton of cure.

What with our baby garden, father's lectures, and mother's classes, we are influencing the rate of infant mortality in the town. It's a new standard, you see. Lots of people never knew that babies could be so quietly happy. Girls come here, big-eyed, admiring, and Jessie talks to them—or mother—and they proceed to study up and fit themselves for their future responsibilities.

We have a constant procession of trained assistants, too; a waiting list. Jessie won't take one unless she honestly loves the work. They have to begin at the bottom—learn a lot of elementary physiology, hygiene, sanitation, all that sort of thing; and do the work, too; learn how to handle an infant. Some of our girls, enthusiasts when they see all that has to be studied, look discouraged. They say, "Dear me! I don't see why a mother need know all that!"

And then Jessie answers, "A mother must know all that, or be able to engage some one who does. The child needs competent care—he doesn't know who gives it. But a mother must know something of her business. She should be ashamed not to. Are you preparing for any other profession? she asks suddenly.

They giggle and say, "Oh, no—we don't have to!"

"Then why not prepare for this?" says Jessie. "What excuses you from preparation for your life-work? Every man must learn his trade—why do not you learn yours?"

They begin to talk about instinct—and then Jessie goes for them! She has facts and figures at her fingers' ends—things I never can remember—and just shows them how this "instinct" theory is accountable for thousands of little graves—thousands of blind, crippled, sick, imbecile, degenerate children. "You need knowledge," she says; "instinct is sufficient only for brutes."

We have not only affected the death-rate in our town, but the birth-rate as well! One of my girlhood friends confided to me once— as she brought her third baby to Jessie, and stood watching the contented little thing, among all the other contented little things— "I'm not afraid to have children now! I'm willing to have ever so many. It's not just having them women dread; it's the care, and awful responsibility; and their helplessness!"

Several have told us that. I guess it's so.

I know it makes a lot of difference to me. I have four now—and they are darlings—but if I have them all on my hands for many hours at a time, it exhausts me. Jessie never seems to be tired. "You don't tire of your hothouses and greenhouses and flower beds," she says; "that's your work—this is mine. I love flowers dearly, but not to work with all the time."

That seems reasonable. We all love our children, because they are ours, but Jessie loves them because they are children—and because it's her business!

It certainly is a great convenience for me. We are not at all rich, Huntley and I, and I find that I can keep splendidly well and earn quite a lot more money by my gardening. We have a big place, as I have said, and I feed the family on green corn, peas, salad, Japanese celery, and such things and sell a lot, besides; berries, fruit, and flowers, too. One or two other women are taking up intensive gardening, as a business—following my example.

I was talking with Mr. B. R. Green one day. He married a friend of mine, and they have three children; two of them are with Jessie.

"It has made all the difference in the world to our home," he said. "When our first baby came, Sue gave her whole mind to it— and made me give mine, also, when I was at home. I got tired of my own child—almost! She could not let the poor little duffer alone! He was sickly and nervous—she was sickly and nervous—same thing, I suppose; and I was about concluding that this home and family business was not all that it was cracked up to be. 'One's enough,' I said to myself. 'If we ever recover from this one, we'll be lucky.' Well now, look at it! Jack has survived, though he's not as sturdy as the others. But these two have come—and are growing up healthy and happy—without disorganizing our home at all. Sue is calm and gay and pretty, and I don't feel as if I'd swapped a satisfactory wife for an incompetent nursery governess. It's a great institution, this baby garden of yours!"

When the men came around that way—and lots of them have— we felt that there wouldn't be much more opposition. Men have a good deal of sense—business sense. They have never dared say much on the baby question, being promptly knocked down by the mother instinct theory; but now they are holding their heads up and beginning to criticize. There is a standard now you see—something they can compare with.

People write to us from other places, too. Several of Jessie's assistants have gone to other towns to start similar establishments; but it's not often you get such a splendid combination of advantages as we have here. Still they are making a beginning, and it's bound to grow.

Have we been written up? Yes, by one or two responsible persons, for magazines. But we won't let reporters in at all. Don't they misrepresent us? Of course they do. But they would anyway; they can't help it. And not being in a big city we are not such easy game you see. It's been good, just solid good, from the start.

Mother is well and happy; she has renewed her youth in this work. It has helped father and George in their business. It helps me. And it has made Jessie all over. She was like a dead woman or a crazy one. Now she is healthy and strong and calm; happy, too, in the big sense. She admits she's happy.

"I've lost my personal happiness," she says, "but I've got something bigger. It doesn't fill the same place, but it fills a larger place. I am not hungry—my heart is full and busy. I know that this is good work for all these babies, and for thousands more—babies and mothers, too."

I guess she is right.

Selection 3

Chapter 7: "Heresy and Schism" from
What Diantha Did, The Forerunner 1.7 (May 1910): 12–17

[Diantha's speech before the Orchardina Home and Culture Club]

Discussed Chapter 3, 54–58

Like "Aunt Mary's Pie Plant," this chapter from What Diantha Did
favorably presents women's-club activism and "re-presents" reforms
suggested in Women and Economics. *This novel touches the same*
array of fictional fields as the earlier story, with the addition of the
third from 1915—"effect of woman's new position upon industry [if
not] war," provided we construe industry *broadly to include a wide*
range of skilled employments.

Diantha's speech on "The True Nature of Domestic Service" re-
veals how close were Gilman's essays and fiction. The speech exists
in an earlier version as "Why Cooperative Housekeeping Fails"
(1907) and was later revised as "The Waste of Private Housekeeping"
(1913), each previously discussed. Diantha critiques housekeeping as
it is typically practiced and sets forth a new method for more efficient
household management that would free many women to fulfill non-
domestic social roles. Whether Gilman was writing fact or fiction, her
purpose was persuasive. (For historical cooked food experimentation,
see Dolores Hayden, The Grand Domestic Revolution: A History of
Feminist Designs for American Homes, Neighborhoods, and Cities,
especially chap. 10; app. A.1, A.2.)

> You may talk about religion with a free and open mind,
> For ten dollars you may criticize a judge;

You may discuss in politics the newest thing you find,
    And open scientific truth to all the deaf and blind,
But there's one place where the brain must never budge!

CHORUS

Oh, the Home is Utterly Perfect!
And all its works within!
    To say a word about it—
    To criticize or doubt it—
    To seek to mend or move it—
    To venture to improve it—
Is The Unpardonable Sin!
                —"Old Song."

MR. PORNE TOOK AN AFTERNOON OFF and came with his wife to
hear their former housemaid lecture. As many other men as were
able did the same. All the members not bedridden were present, and
nearly all the guests they had invited.

So many were the acceptances that a downtown hall had been
taken; the floor was more than filled, and in the gallery sat a block
of servant girls, more gorgeous in array than the ladies below, whispering excitedly among themselves. The platform recalled a "tour-
nament of roses," and, sternly important among all that fragrant
loveliness, sat Mrs. Dankshire in "the chair" flanked by Miss Torbus, the Recording Secretary, Miss Massing, the Treasurer, and
Mrs. Ree, tremulus [*sic*]with importance in her official position. All
these ladies wore an air of high emprise, even more intense than
that with which they usually essayed their public duties. They were
richly dressed, except Miss Torbus, who came as near it as she could.

At the side, and somewhat in the rear of the President, on a
chair quite different from "the chair," discreetly gowned and of a
bafflingly serene demeanor, sat Miss [Diantha] Bell. All eyes were
upon her—even some opera glasses.

"She's a good-looker anyhow," was one masculine opinion.

"She's a peach," was another. "Tell you—the chap that gets her
is well heeled!" said a third.

The ladies bent their hats toward one another and conferred in
flowing whispers; and in the gallery eager confidences were ex-
changed, with giggles.

On the small table before Mrs. Dankshire, shaded by a magnificent bunch of roses, lay that core and crux of all parliamentry dig-

nity, the gavel; an instrument no self-respecting chairwoman may be without; yet which she still approaches with respectful uncertainty.

In spite of its large size and high social standing, the Orchardina Home and Culture Club contained some elements of unrest, and when the yearly election of officers came round there was always need for careful work in practical politics to keep the reins of government in the hands of "the right people."

Mrs. Thaddler, conscious of her New York millions, and Madam Weatherstone, conscious of her Philadelphia lineage, with Mrs. Johnston A. Marrow ("one of the Boston Marrows!" was awesomely whispered of her), were the heads of what might be called "the conservative party" in this small parliament; while Miss Miranda L. Eagerson, describing herself as "a journalist," who held her place in local society largely by virtue of the tacit dread of what she might do if offended—led the more radical element.

Most of the members were quite content to follow the lead of the solidly established ladies of Orchard Avenue; especially as this leadership consisted mainly in the pursuance of a masterly inactivity. When wealth and aristocracy combine with that common inertia which we dignify as "conservatism" they exert a powerful influence in the great art of sitting still.

Nevertheless there were many alert and conscientious women in this large membership, and when Miss Eagerson held the floor, and urged upon the club some active assistance in the march of events, it needed all Mrs. Dankshire's generalship to keep them content with marking time.

On this auspicious occasion, however, both sides were agreed in interest and approval. Here was a subject appealing to every woman present, and every man but such few as merely "boarded"; even they had memories and hopes concerning this question.

Solemnly rose Mrs. Dankshire, her full silks rustling about her, and let one clear tap of the gavel fall into the sea of soft whispering and guttural murmurs.

In the silence that followed she uttered the momentous announcements: "The meeting will please come to order," "We will now hear the reading of the minutes of the last meeting," and so on most conscientiously through officer's reports and committees reports to "new business."

Perhaps it is their more frequent practice of religious rites, perhaps their devout acceptance of social rulings and the dictates of fashion, perhaps the lifelong reiterance of small duties at home, or all these things together, which makes women so seriously letter-perfect in parliamentary usage. But these stately ceremonies were ended in course of time, and Mrs. Dankshire rose again, even more solemn than before, and came forward majestically.

"Members—and guests," she said impressively, "this is an occasion which brings pride to the heart of every member of the Home and Culture Club. As our name implies, this Club is formed to serve the interests of The Home—those interests which stand first, I trust, in every human heart."

A telling pause, and the light patter of gloved hands.

"Its second purpose," pursued the speaker, with that measured delivery which showed that her custom, as one member put it, was to "first write and then commit," "is to promote the cause of Culture in this community. Our aim is Culture in the broadest sense, not only in the curricula of institutions of learning, not only in those spreading branches of study and research which tempts us on from height to height!"—("proof of arboreal ancestry, that," Miss Eagerson confided to a friend, whose choked giggle attracted condemning eyes)—"but in the more intimate fields of daily experience.

"Most of us, however widely interested in the higher education, are still—and find in this our highest honor—wives and mothers." These novel titles called forth another round of applause.

"As such," continued Mrs. Dankshire, "we all recognize the difficult—the well-nigh insuperable problems of the"—she glanced at the gallery, now paying awed attention—"domestic question.

"We know how on the one hand our homes yawn unattended" —("I yawn while I'm attending—eh?" one gentleman in the rear suggested to his neighbor)—"while on the other the ranks of mercenary labor are overcrowded. Why is it that while the peace and beauty, the security and comfort, of a good home, with easy labor and high pay, are open to every young woman, whose circumstances oblige her to toil for her living, she blindly refuses these true advantages and loses her health and too often what is far more precious! —in the din and tumult of the factory, or the dangerous exposure of the public counter."

Madam Weatherstone was much impressed at this point, and beat her black fan upon her black glove emphatically. Mrs. Thaddler also nodded; which meant a good deal from her. The applause was most gratifying to the speaker, who continued:

"Fortunately for the world there are some women yet who appreciate the true values of life." A faint blush crept slowly up the face of Diantha, but her expression was unchanged. Whoso had met and managed a roomful of merciless children can easily face a woman's club.

"We have with us on this occasion one, as we may say, our equal in birth and breeding,"—Madam Weatherstone here looked painfully shocked as also did the Boston Marrow; possibly Mrs. Dankshire, whose parents were Iowa farmers, was not unmindful of this, but she went on smoothly, "and whose first employment was the honored task of the teacher; who has deliberately cast her lot with the domestic worker, and brought her trained intelligence to bear upon the solution of this great question—The True Nature of Domestic Service. In the interests of this problem she has consented to address us—I take pleasure in introducing Miss Diantha Bell."

Diantha rose calmly, stepped forward, bowed to the President and officers, and to the audience. She stood quietly for a moment, regarding the faces before her, and produced a typewritten paper. It was clear, short, and to some minds convincing.

She set forth that the term "domestic industry" did not define certain kinds of labor, but a stage of labor; that all labor was originally domestic; but that most kinds had now become social, as with weaving and spinning, for instance, for centuries confined to the home and done by women only; now done in mills by men and women; that this process of socialization has now taken from the home almost all the manufactures—as of wine, beer, soap, candles, pickles and other specialties, and part of the laundry work; that the other processes of cleaning are also being socialized, as by the vacuum cleaners, the professional window-washers, rug cleaners, and similar professional workers; and that even in the preparation of food many kinds are now specialized, as by the baker and confectioner. That in service itself we were now able to hire by the hour or day skilled workers necessarily above the level of the "general."

A growing rustle of disapproval began to make itself felt, which increased as she went on to explain how the position of the housemaid is a survival of the ancient status of woman slavery, the family with the male head and the group of servile women.

"The keynote of all our difficulty in this relation is that we demand celibacy of our domestic servants," said Diantha.

A murmur arose at this statement, but she continued calmly:

"Since it is natural for women to marry, the result is that our domestic servants consist of a constantly changing series of young girls, apprentices, as it were; and, the complicated and important duties of the household cannot be fully mastered by such hands."

The audience disapproved somewhat of this, but more of what followed. She showed (Mrs. Porne nodding her head amusedly), that so far from being highly paid and easy labor, house service was exacting and responsible, involving a high degree of skill as well as moral character, and that it was paid less than ordinary unskilled labor, part of this payment being primitive barter.

Then, as whispers and sporadic little spurts of angry talk increased, the clear quiet voice went on to state that this last matter, the position of a strange young girl in our homes, was of itself a source of much of the difficulty of the situation.

"We speak of giving them the safety and shelter of the home," —here Diantha grew solemn; "So far from sharing our homes, she gives up her own, and has none of ours, but the poorest of our food and a cramped lodging; she has neither the freedom nor the privileges of a home; and as to shelter and safety—the domestic worker, owing to her peculiarly defenceless position, furnishes a terrible percentage of the unfortunate."

A shocked silence met this statement.

"In England shop-workers complain of the old custom of 'sleeping in'—their employers furnishing them with lodging as part payment; this also is a survival of the old apprentice method. With us, only the domestic servant is held to this antiquated position."

Regardless of the chill displeasure about her she cheerfully pursued:

"Let us now consider the economic side of the question. 'Domestic economy' is a favorite phrase. As a matter of fact our method of domestic service is inordinately wasteful. Even where the wife does all the housework, without pay, we still waste labor to an enormous extent, requiring one whole woman to wait upon each man. If the man hires one or more servants, the wastes increase. If one hundred men undertake some common business, they do not divide in two halves, each man having another man to serve him—fifty productive laborers, and fifty cooks. Two or three cooks could provide for the whole group; to use fifty is to waste 47 per cent. of the labor.

"But our waste of labor is as nothing to our waste of money. For, say twenty families, we have twenty kitchens with all their furnishings, twenty stoves with all their fuel; twenty cooks with all their wages; in cash and barter combined we pay about ten dollars a week for our cooks—$200 a week to pay for the cooking for twenty families, for about a hundred persons!

"Three expert cooks, one at $20 a week and two at $15 would save to those twenty families $150 a week and give them better food. The cost of kitchen furnishings and fuel, could be reduced by nine-tenths; and beyond all that comes our incredible waste in individual purchasing. What twenty families spend on individual patronage of small retailers, could be reduced by more than half if bought by competent persons in wholesale quantities. Moreover, our whole food supply would rise in quality as well as lower in price if it was bought by experts.

"To what does all this lead?" asked Diantha pleasantly.

Nobody said anything, but the visible attitude of the house seemed to say that it led straight to perdition.

"The solution for which so many are looking is no new scheme of any sort; and in particular it is not that oft repeated foredoomed failure called "co-operative housekeeping."

At this a wave of relief spread perceptibly. The irritation roused by those preposterous figures and accusations was somewhat allayed. Hope was relit in darkened countenances.

"The inefficiency of a dozen tottering households is not removed by combining them," said Diantha. This was of dubious import. "Why should we expect a group of families to 'keep house' expertly and economically together, when they are driven into companionship by the patent fact that none of them can do it alone."

Again an uncertain reception.

"Every family is a distinct unit," the girl continued. "Its needs are separate and should be met separately. The separate house and garden should belong to each family, the freedom and group privacy of the home. But the separate home may be served by a common water company, by a common milkman, by a common baker, by a common cooking and a common cleaning establishment. We are rapidly approaching an improved system of living in which the private home will no more want a cookshop on the premises than a blacksmith's shop or soap-factory. The necessary work of the kitchenless house will be done by the hour, with skilled labor; and we shall order our food cooked instead of raw. This will give to the employees a respectable well-paid profession, with their own homes and families; and to the employers a saving of about two-thirds of the expense of living, as well as an end of all our difficulties with the servant question. That is the way to elevate—to enoble [*sic*] domestic service. It must cease to be domestic service—and become world service."

Suddenly and quietly she sat down.

Miss Eagerson was on her feet. So were others.

"Madam President! Madam President!" resounded from several points at once. Madam Weatherstone—Mrs. Thaddler—no! yes—they really were both on their feet. Applause was going on—irregularly—soon dropped. Only from the group in the gallery it was whole-hearted and consistent.

Mrs. Dankshire, who had been growing red and redder as the paper advanced, who had conferred in alarmed whispers with Mrs. Ree, and Miss Massing, who had even been seen to extend her hand to the gavel and finger it threateningly, now rose, somewhat precipitately, and came forward.

"Order, please! You will please keep order. You have heard the —we will now—the meeting is now open for discussion, Mrs. Thaddler!" And she sat down. She meant to have said Madam Weatherstone, but Mrs. Thaddler was more aggressive.

"I wish to say," said that much beaded lady in a loud voice, "that I was against this—unfortunate experiment—from the first. And I trust it will never be repeated!" She sat down.

Two tight little dimples flickered for an instant about the corners of Diantha's mouth.

"Madam Weatherstone?" said the President, placatingly.

Madam Weatherstone arose, rather sulkily, and looked about her. An agitated assembly met her eye, buzzing universally each to each.

"Order!" said Mrs. Dankshire, "ORDER, please!" and rapped three times with the gavel.

"I have attended many meetings, in many clubs, in many states," said Madam Weatherstone, "and have heard much that was foolish, and some things that were dangerous. But I will say that never in the course of all my experience have I heard anything so foolish, and so dangerous, as this. I trust that the—doubtless well meant—attempt to throw light on this subject—from the wrong quarter—has been a lesson to us all. No club could survive more than one such lamentable mistake!" And she sat down, gathering her large satin wrap about her like a retiring Caesar.

"Madam President!" broke forth Miss Eagerson. "I was up first —and have been standing ever since—

"One moment, Miss Eagerson," said Mrs. Dankshire superbly, The Rev. Dr. Eltwood."

If Mrs. Dankshire supposed she was still further supporting the cause of condemnation she made a painful mistake. The cloth and the fine bearing of the young clergyman deceived her; and she forgot that he was said to be "advanced" and was new to the place.

"Will you come to the platform, Dr. Eltwood?"

Dr. Eltwood came to the platform with the easy air of one to whom platforms belonged by right.

"Ladies," he began in tones of cordial good will, "both employer and employed!—and gentlemen—whom I am delighted to see here to-day! I am grateful for the opportunity so graciously extended to me"—he bowed six feet of black broadcloth toward Mrs. Dankshire —"by your honored President.

"And I am grateful for the opportunity previously enjoyed, of listening to the most rational, practical, wise, true and hopeful words I have ever heard on this subject. I trust there will be enough open-minded women—and men—in Orchardina to make possible among us that higher business development of a great art which has been so convincingly laid before us. This club is deserving of all thanks from the community for extending to so many the privilege of listening to our valued fellow-citizen—Miss Bell."

He bowed again to Miss Bell—and to Mrs. Dankshire, and re-sumed his seat, Miss Eagerson taking advantage of the dazed pause to occupy the platform herself.

"Mr. Eltwood is right!" she said. "Miss Bell is right! This is the true presentation of the subject, 'by one who knows.' Miss Bell has pricked our pretty bubble so thoroughly that we don't know where we're standing—but she knows! Housework is a business—like any other business—I've always said so, and it's got to be done in a business way. Now I for one—" but Miss Eagerson was rapped down by the Presidential gavel, as Mrs. Thaddler, portentous and severe, stalked forward.

"It is not my habit to make public speeches," she began. "nor my desire; but this is a time when prompt and decisive action needs to be taken. This Club cannot afford to countenance any such far-rago of mischievous nonsense as we have heard to-day. I move you, Madam President, that a resolution of condemnation be passed at once; and the meeting then dismissed!"

She stalked back again, while Mrs. Marrow of Boston, in clear, cold tones seconded the motion.

But another voice was heard—for the first time in that assem-bly—Mrs. Weatherstone, the pretty, delicate widowed daughter-in-law of Madam Weatherstone, was on her feet with "Madam President! I wish to speak to this motion."

"Won't you come to the platform, Mrs. Weatherstone?" asked Mrs. Dankshire graciously, and the little lady came, visibly trembling, but holding her head high.

All sat silent, all expected—what was not forthcoming.

"I wish to protest, as a member of the Club, and as a woman, against the gross discourtesy which has been offered to the guest and speaker of the day. In answer to our invitation Miss Bell has given us a scholarly and interesting paper, and I move that we extend her a vote of thanks."

"I second the motion," came from all quarters.

"There is another motion before the house," from others.

Cries of "Madam President" arose everywhere, many speakers were on their feet. Mrs. Dankshire tapped frantically with the little gavel; Miss Eagerson, by sheer vocal power, took and held the floor.

"I move that we take a vote on this question," she cried in piercing tones. "Let every woman who knows enough to appreciate Miss Bell's paper—and has any sense of decency—stand up!"

Quite a large proportion of the audience stood up—very informally. Those who did not, did not mean to acknowledge lack of intelligence and sense of decency, but to express emphatic disapproval of Miss Eagerson, Miss Bell and their views.

"I move you, Madam President," cried Mrs. Thadder, at the top of her voice, "that every member who is guilty of such grossly unparliamentary conduct be hereby dropped from this Club!"

"We hereby resign!" cried Miss Eagerson. "*We* drop *you!* We'll have a New Woman's Club in Orchardina with some warmth in its heart and brains in its head—even if it hasn't as much money in its pocket!"

Amid stern rappings, hissings, cries of "Order—order," and frantic "Motions to adjourn" the meeting broke up; the club elements dissolving and reforming into two bodies as by some swift chemical reaction.

Great was the rejoicing of the daily press; some amusement was felt, though courteously suppressed by the men present, and by many not present, when they heard of it.

Some ladies were so shocked and grieved as to withdraw from club-life altogether. Others, in stern dignity, upheld the shaken standards of Home and Culture; while the most conspicuous outcome of it all was the immediate formation of the New Woman's Club of Orchardina.

Selection 4

"Her Housekeeper"
The Forerunner 1.4 (January 1910): 2–8

Discussed Chapter 3, 58–59

*Here Gilman devotes her imagination to "man himself, in this new
association" with woman, whereby he reciprocates the provision of
support by locating household help and even himself offering child
care. This story takes the form of argumentation, as Gilman's fiction
once again masquerades as rhetoric.*

*A comedic, satiric intent may also be here, as Gilman places a
man in the role of "housekeeper" in spite of contemporary efforts to
name women's duty to be consumers or "home managers." Dolores
Hayden, in* The Grand Domestic Revolution, *discusses "the key ideo-
logues of the antifeminist, pro-consumption, suburban home,"
namely Lillian M. Gilbreth (the efficiency-expert, Montclair [N.J.]
mother lauded in* Cheaper by the Dozen) *and Christine Frederick
(chap. 13; 348–49).*

ON THE TOP FLOOR of a New York boarding-house lived a particularly attractive woman who was an actress. She was also a widow,
not divorcee, but just plain widow; and she persisted in acting under
her real name, which was Mrs. Leland. The manager objected, but
her reputation was good enough to carry the point.

"It will cost you a great deal of money, Mrs. Leland," said the
manager.

"I make money enough," she answered.

"You will not attract so many—admirers," said the manager.

147

"I have admirers enough," she answered; which was visibly true.

She was well under thirty, even by daylight—and about eighteen on the stage; and as for admirers—they apparently thought Mrs. Leland was a carefully selected stage name.

Besides being a widow she was a mother, having a small boy of about five years; and this small boy did not look in the least like a "stage child," but was a brown-skinned, healthy little rascal of the ordinary sort.

With this boy, an excellent nursery governess, and a maid, Mrs. Leland occupied the top floor above mentioned, and enjoyed it. She had a big room in front, to receive in; and a small room with a skylight, to sleep in. The boy's room and the governess' room were at the back, with sunny south windows, and the maid slept on a couch in the parlor. She was a colored lady, named Alice, and did not seem to care where she slept, or if she slept at all.

"I never was so comfortable in my life," said Mrs. Leland to her friends. "I've been here three years and mean to stay. It is not like any boarding-house I ever saw, and it is not like any home I ever had. I have the privacy, the detachment, the carelessness of a boarding-house, and 'all the comforts of a home.' Up I go to my little top flat as private as you like. My Alice takes care of it—the housemaids only come in when I'm out. I can eat with the others downstairs if I please; but mostly I don't please; and up come my little meals on the dumbwaiter—hot and good."

"But—having to flock with a lot of promiscuous boarders!" said her friends.

"I don't flock, you see; that's just it. And besides, they are not promiscuous—there isn't a person in the house now who isn't some sort of a friend of mine. As fast as a room was vacated I'd suggest somebody—and here we all are. It's great."

"But do you *like* a skylight room?" Mrs. Leland's friends further inquired of her?

"By no means!" she promptly replied. "I hate it. I feel like a mouse in a pitcher!"

"Then why in the name of reason—?"

"Because I can sleep there! Sleep!—It's the only way to be quiet in New York, and I have to sleep late if I sleep at all. I've fixed the skylight so that I'm drenched with air—and not drenched with rain! —and there I am. Johnny is gagged and muffled as it were, and carried downstairs as early as possible. He gets his breakfast, and the unfortunate Miss Merton has to go out and play with him—in all weathers—except kindergarten time. Then Alice sits on the stairs and keeps everybody away till I ring."

Possibly it was owing to the stillness and the air and the sleep till near lunchtime that Mrs. Leland kept her engaging youth, her vivid uncertain beauty. At times you said of her, "She has a keen intelligent face, but she's not pretty." Which was true. She was not pretty. But at times again she overcame you with her sudden loveliness.

All of which was observed by her friend from the second floor who wanted to marry her. In this he was not alone; either as a friend, of whom she had many, or as lover, of whom she had more. His distinction lay first in his opportunities, as a co-resident, for which he was heartily hated by all the more and some of the many; and second in that he remained a friend in spite of being a lover, and remained a lover in spite of being flatly refused.

His name in the telephone book was given "Arthur Olmstead, real estate"; office this and residence that—she looked him up therein after their first meeting. He was rather a short man, heavily built, with a quiet kind face, and a somewhat quizzical smile. He seemed to make all the money he needed, occupied the two rooms and plentiful closet space of his floor in great contentment, and manifested most improper domesticity of taste by inviting friends to tea. "Just like a woman!" Mrs. Leland told him.

"And why not? Women have so many attractive ways—why not imitate them?" he asked her.

"A man doesn't want to be feminine, I'm sure," struck in a pallid, overdressed youth, with openwork socks on his slim feet, and perfumed handkerchief.

Mr. Olmstead smiled a broad friendly smile. He was standing near the young man, a little behind him, and at this point he put his hands just beneath the youth's arms, lifted and set him aside as if he were an umbrella-stand. "Excuse me, Mr. Masters," he said gravely, but you were standing on Mrs. Leland's gown."

Mr. Masters was too much absorbed in apologizing to the lady to take umbrage at the method of his removal; but she was not so oblivious. She tried doing it to her little boy afterwards, and found him very heavy.

When she came home from her walk or drive in the early winter dusk, this large quietly furnished room, the glowing fire, the excellent tea and delicate thin bread and butter were most restful. "It is two more stories up before I can get my own"; she would say—"I must stop a minute."

When he began to propose to her the first time she tried to stop him. "O please don't!" she cried. "*Please* don't! There are no end of reasons why I will not marry anybody again. Why can't some of you men be nice to me and not—that! Now I can't come in to tea any more!"

"I'd like to know why not," said he calmly. "You don't have to marry me if you don't want to; but that's no reason for cutting my acquaintance, is it?"

She gazed at him in amazement.

"I'm not threatening to kill myself, am I? I don't intend going to the devil. I'd like to be your husband, but if I can't—mayn't I be a brother to you?"

She was inclined to think he was making fun of her, but no—his proposal had had the real ring in it. "And you're not you're not going to—?" it seemed the baldest assumption to think that he was going to, he looked so strong and calm and friendly.

"Not going to annoy you? Not going to force an undesired affection on you and rob myself of a most agreeable friendship? Of course not. Your tea is cold, Mrs. Leland—let me give you another cup. And do you think Miss Rose is going to do well as 'Angelina'?"

So presently Mrs. Leland was quite relieved in her mind, and free to enjoy the exceeding comfortableness of this relation. Little Johnny was extremely fond of Mr. Olmstead; who always treated him with respect, and who could listen to his tales of strife and glory more intelligently than either mother or governess. Mr. Olmstead kept on hand a changing supply of interesting things; not toys—never, but real things not intended for little boys to play with. No little boy would want to play with dolls for instance; but what little boy would not be fascinated by a small wooden [c]lay figure, capable of unheard-of contortions. Tin soldiers were common, but the flags of all nations—real flags, and true stories about them, were interesting. Noah's arks were cheap and unreliable scientifically; but Barye lions, ivory elephants, and Japanese monkeys in didactic groups of three, had unfailing attraction. And the books this man had—great solid books that could be opened wide on the floor, and a little boy lie down to in peace and comfort!

Mrs. Leland stirred her tea and watched them until Johnny was taken upstairs.

"Why don't you smoke?" she asked suddenly. "Doctor's orders?"

"No—mine," he answered. "I never consulted a doctor in my life."

"Nor a dentist, I judge," said she.

"Nor a dentist."

"You'd better knock on wood!" she told him.

"And cry 'Uncle Reuben?' " he asked smilingly.

"You haven't told me why you don't smoke!" said she suddenly.

"Haven't I?" he said. "That was very rude of me. But look here. There's a thing I wanted to ask you. Now I'm not pressing any sort of inquiry as to myself; but as a brother, would you mind telling me some of those numerous reasons why you will not marry anybody?"

She eyed him suspiciously, but he was as solid and calm as usual, regarding her pleasantly and with no hint of ulterior purpose. "Why—I don't mind," she began slowly. "First—I have been married—and was very unhappy. That's reason enough."

He did not contradict her; but merely said, "That's one," and set it down in his notebook.

"Dear me, Mr. Olmstead! You're not a reporter, are you!"

"O no—" but I wanted to have them clear and think about them," he explained. "Do you mind?" And he made as if to shut his little book again.

"I don't know as I mind," she said slowly. "But it looks so— businesslike."

"This is a very serious business, Mrs. Leland, as you must know. Quite aside from any personal desire of my own, I am truly 'your sincere friend and wellwisher,' as the Complete Letter Writer has it; and there are so many men wanting to marry you."

This she knew full well, and gazed pensively at the toe of her small flexible slipper, poised on a stool before the fire.

Mr. Olmstead also gazed at the slipper toe with appreciation.

"What's the next one?" he said cheerfully.

"Do you know you are a real comfort," she told him suddenly. "I never knew a man before who could—well leave off being a man for a moment and just be a human creature."

"Thank you, Mrs. Leland," he said in tones of pleasant sincerity. I want to be a comfort to you if I can. Incidentally wouldn't you be more comfortable on this side of the fire—the light falls better— don't move." And before she realized what he was doing he picked her up, chair and all, and put her down softly on the other side, setting the footstool as before, and even daring to place her little feet upon it—but with so businesslike an air that she saw no opening for rebuke. It is a difficult matter to object to a man's doing things like that when he doesn't look as if he was doing them.

"That's better," said he cheerfully, taking the place where she had been. "Now, what's the next one?"

"The next one is my boy."

"Second—Boy," he said, putting it down. "But I should think he'd be a reason the other way. Excuse me—I wasn't going to criticize—yet! And the third?"

"Why should you criticize at all, Mr. Olmstead?"

"I shouldn't—on my own account. But there may come a man you love." He had a fine baritone voice. When she heard him sing Mrs. Leland always wished he were taller, handsomer, more distinguished looking; his voice sounded as if he were. "And I should hate to see these reasons standing in the way of your happiness," he continued.

"Perhaps they wouldn't," said she in a revery.

"Perhaps they wouldn't—and in that case it is no possible harm that you tell me the rest of them. I won't cast it up at you. Third?"

"Third, I won't give up my profession for any man alive."

"Any man alive would be a fool to want you to," said he setting down—"Third—Profession."

"Fourth—I like *Freedom!*" she said with sudden intensity. You don't know!—they kept me so tight!—so *tight!*—when I was a girl! Then—I was left alone, with a very little money, and I began to study for the stage—that was like heaven! And then—O what *idiots* women are!" She said the word not tragically, but with such hard-pointed intensity that it sounded like a gimlet. "Then I married, you see—I gave up all my new-won freedom to *marry!*—and he kept me tighter than ever." She shut her expressive mouth in level lines—stood up suddenly and stretched her arms wide and high. "I'm free again, free—I can do exactly as I please!" The words were individually relished. "I have the work I love. I can earn all I need—am saving something for the boy. I'm perfectly independent!"

"And perfectly happy!" he cordially endorsed her. "I don't blame you for not wanting to give it up."

"O well—happy!" she hestitated. "There are times, of course, when one isn't happy. But then—the other way I was unhappy all the time."

"He's dead unfortunately," mused Mr. Olmstead.

"Unfortunately?—Why?"

He looked at her with his straightforward, pleasant smile. "I'd have liked the pleasure of killing him," he said regretfully.

She was startled, and watched him with dawning alarm. But he was quite quiet—even cheerful. "Fourth—Freedom," he wrote. "Is that all?"

"No—there are two more. Neither of them will please you. You won't think so much of me any more. The worst one is this. I like—lovers! I'm very much ashamed of it, but I do! I try not to be unfair to them—some I really try to keep away from me—but honestly I like admiration and lots of it."

"What's the harm of that?" he asked, easily, setting down, "Fifth —Lovers.

"No harm, so long as I'm my own mistress," said she defiantly. "I take care of my boy, I take care of myself—let them take care of themselves! Don't blame me too much!"

"You're not a very good psychologist, I'm afraid," said he.

"What do you mean?" she asked rather nervously.

"You surely don't expect a man to blame you for being a woman, do you?"

"All women are not like that," she hastily asserted. "They are too conscientious. Lots of my friends blame me severely."

"Women friends," he ventured.

"Men, too. Some men have said very hard things of me."

"Because you turned 'em down. That's natural."

"You don't!"

"No, I don't. I'm different."

"How different?" she asked.

He looked at her steadily. His eyes were hazel, flecked with changing bits of color, deep, steady, with a sort of inner light that grew as she watched till presently she thought it well to consider her slipper again; and continued, "The sixth is as bad as the other almost. I hate—I'd like to write a dozen tragic plays to show how much I hate—Housekeeping! There! That's all!"

"Sixth—Housekeeping," he wrote down, quite unmoved. "But why should anyone blame you for that—it's not your business."

"No—thank goodness, it's not! And never will be! I'm *free*, I tell you and I stay free!—But look at the clock!" And she whisked away to dress for dinner.

He was not at table that night—not at home that night—not at home for some days—the landlady said he had gone out of town; and Mrs. Leland missed her afternoon tea.

She had it upstairs, of course, and people came in—both friends and lovers; but she missed the quiet and cosiness of the green and brown room downstairs.

Johnny missed his big friend still more. "Mama, where's Mr. Olmstead? Mama, why don't Mr. Olmstead come back? Mama! When is Mr. Olmstead coming back? Mama! Why don't you write to Mr. Olmstead and tell him to come back? Mama!—can't we go in there and play with his things?"

As if in answer to this last wish she got a little note from him saying simply, "Don't let Johnnie miss the lions and monkeys—he and Miss Merton and you, of course, are quite welcome to the whole floor. Go in at any time."

Just to keep the child quiet she took advantage of this offer, and Johnnie introduced her to all the ins and outs of the place. In a corner of the bedroom was a zinc-lined tray with clay in it, where Johnnie played rapturously at "making country." While he played his mother noted the quiet good taste and individuality of the place.

"It smells so clean!" she said to herself. "There! he hasn't told me yet why he doesn't smoke. I never told him I didn't like it."

Johnnie tugged at a bureau drawer. "He keeps the water in here!" he said, and before she could stop him he had out a little box with bits of looking-glass in it, which soon became lakes and rivers in his clay continent.

Mrs. Leland put them back afterward, admiring the fine quality and goodly number of garments in that drawer, and their perfect order. Her husband had been a man who made a chowder of his bureau drawers, and who expected her to find all his studs and put them in for him.

"A man like this would be no trouble at all," she thought for a moment—but then remembered other things and set her mouth hard. "Not for mine!" she said determinedly.

By and by he came back, serene as ever, friendly and unpresuming.

"Aren't you going to tell me why you don't smoke?" she suddenly demanded of him on another quiet dusky afternoon when tea was before them.

He seemed so impersonal, almost remote, though nicer than ever to Johnny; and Mrs. Leland rather preferred the personal note in conversation.

"Why of course I am," he replied cordially. "That's easy," and he fumbled in his inner pocket.

"Is that where you keep your reasons?" she mischievously inquired.

"It's where I keep yours," he promptly answered, producing the little notebook. "Now look here—I've got these all answered—you won't be able to hold to one of 'em after this. May I sit by you and explain?"

She made room for him on the sofa amiably enough, but defied him to convince her. "Go ahead," she said cheerfully.

"First," he read off, "Previous Marriage. This is not a sufficient objection. Because you have been married, you now know what to choose and what to avoid. A girl is comparatively helpless in this matter; you are armed. That your first marriage was unhappy is a reason for trying it again. It is not only that you are better able to choose, but that by the law of chances you stand to win next time. Do you admit the justice of this reasoning?"

"I don't admit anything," she said. "I'm waiting to ask you a question."

"Ask it now."

"No—I'll wait till you are all through. Do go on."

" 'Second—The Boy,' " he continued. Now Mrs. Leland, solely on the boy's account I should advise you to marry again. While he is a baby, a mother is enough; but the older he grows, the more he will need a father. Of course you should select a man the child could love—a man who could love the child."

"I begin to suspect you of deep double-dyed surreptitious designs, Mr. Olmstead. You know Johnnie loves you dearly. And you know I won't marry you," she hastily added.

"I'm not asking you to—now, Mrs. Leland. I did, in good faith, and I would again if I thought I had the shadow of a chance—but I'm not at present. Still, I'm quite willing to stand as an instance. Now, we might resume, on that basis. Objection one does not really hold against me—now does it?"

He looked at her cheerily, warmly, openly; and in his clean, solid strength and tactful kindness he was so unspeakably different from the dark, fascinating slender man who had become a nightmare to her youth, that she felt in her heart he was right—so far. "I won't admit a thing," she said sweetly. "But pray go on."

He went on, unabashed. " 'Second—Boy.' Now if you married me I should consider the boy as an added attraction. Indeed—if you do marry again—someone who doesn't want the boy—I wish you'd give him to me. I mean it. I think he loves me, and I think I could be of real service to the child."

He seemed almost to have forgotten her, and she watched him curiously.

"Now, to go on," he continued. " 'Third—Profession.' As to your profession," said he slowly, clasping his hands over one knee and gazing at the dark soft-colored rug, "if you married me, and gave up your profession I should find it a distinct loss. I should lose my favorite actress."

She gave a little start of surprise.

"Didn't you know how much I admire your work?" he said. I don't hang around the stage entrance—there are plenty of chappies to do that; and I don't always occupy a box and throw bouquets—I don't like a box anyhow. But I haven't missed seeing you in any part you've played yet—some of 'em I've seen a dozen times. And you're growing—you'll do better work still. It is sometimes a little weak in the love parts—seems as if you couldn't quite take it seriously— couldn't let yourself go—but you'll grow. You'll do better—I really think—after you're married."

She was rather impressed by this, but found it rather difficult to say anything; for he was not looking at her at all. He took up his notebook again with a smile.

"So—if you married me, you would be more than welcome to go on with your profession. I wouldn't stand in your way any more than I do now. 'Fourth—Freedom,' " he read slowly. "That is easy, in one way—hard in another. If you married me,"—She stirred resentfully at this constant reference to their marriage; but he seemed purely hypothetical in tone—"I wouldn't interfere with your freedom any. Not of my own will. But if you ever grew to love me— or if there were children—it would make some difference. Not much. There mightn't be any children, and it isn't likely you'd ever love me enough to have that stand in your way. Otherwise than that you'd have freedom,—as much as now. A little more; because if you wanted to take a foreign tour, or anything like that, I'd take care of Johnnie. 'Fifth—Lovers.' " Here he paused leaning forward with his chin in his hands, his eyes bent down. She could see the broad heavy shoulders, the smooth fit of the well-made coat, the spotless collar, and the fine, strong, clean-cut neck. As it happened she particularly disliked the neck of the average man—either the cordy, the beefy or the adipose, and particularly liked this kind, firm and round like a Roman's, with the hair coming to a clean-cut edge and stopping there.

"As to lovers," he went on—"I hesitate a little as to what to say about that. I'm afraid I shall shock you. Perhaps I'd better leave out that one."

"As insuperable?" she mischievously asked.

"No, as too easy," he answered.

"You'd better explain," she said.

"Well then—it's simply this: as a man—I myself admire you more because so many other men admire you. I don't sympathize with them, any!—Not for a minute. Of course, if you loved any one of them you wouldn't be my wife. But if you were my wife—"

"Well?" said she, a little breathlessly. "You're very irritating! What would you do? Kill 'em all? Come—If I were your wife?—"

"If you were my wife—" he turned and faced her squarely, his deep eyes blazing steadily into hers. "In the first place the more lovers you had that you didn't love, the better I'd be pleased."

"And if I did?" she dared him.

"If you were my wife," he purused with perfect quietness, "you would never love anyone else."

There was a throbbing silence.

" 'Sixth—Housekeeping,' " he read.

At this she rose to her feet as if released. "Sixth and last and all-sufficient!" she burst out, giving herself a little shake as if to waken. "Final and conclusive and admitting no reply!"—I will not keep house for any man. Never! Never!! Never!!!"

"Why should you?" he said, as he had said it before. "Why not board?"

"I wouldn't board on any account!"

"But you are boarding now. Aren't you comfortable here?"

"O yes, perfectly comfortable. But this is the only boarding-house I ever saw that was comfortable."

"Why not go on as we are—if you married me?"

She laughed shrilly. "With the other boarders round them and a whole floor laid between," she parodied gaily. "No, sir! *If* I ever married again—and I won't—I'd want a home of my own—a whole house—and have it run as smoothly and perfectly as this does. With no more care than I have now!"

"If I could give you a whole house, like this, and run it for you as smoothly and perfectly as this one—then would you marry me?" he asked.

"O, I dare say I would," she said mockingly.

"My dear," said he, "I have kept this house—for you—for three years.

"What do you mean?" she demanded, flushingly.

"I mean that it is my business," he answered serenely. "Some men run hotels and some restaurants: I keep a number of boarding-houses and make a handsome income from them. All the people are comfortable—I see to that. I planned to have you use these rooms, had the dumbwaiter run to the top so you could have meals comfortably there. You didn't much like the first housekeeper. I got one you liked better; cooks to please you, maids to please you. I have most seriously tried to make you comfortable. When you didn't like a boarder I got rid of him—or her—they are mostly all your friends now. Of course if we were married, we'd fire 'em all." His tone was perfectly calm and business like. "You should keep your special apartments on top; you should also have the floor above this, a larger bedroom, drawingroom, and bath, and private parlor for you; —I'd stay right here as I am now—and when you wanted me—I'd be here."

She stiffened a little at this rather tame ending. She was stirred, uneasy, dissatisfied. She felt as if something had been offered and withdrawn; something was lacking.

"It seems such a funny business—for a man," she said.

"Any funnier than Delmonico's?" he asked. "It's a business that takes some ability—witness the many failures. It is certainly useful. And it pays—amazingly."

"I thought it was real estate," she insisted.

"It is. I'm in a real estate office. I buy and sell houses—that's how I came to take this up!"

He rose up, calmly and methodically, walked over to the fire, and laid his notebook on it. "There wasn't any strength in any of those objections, my dear," said he. "Especially the first one. Previous marriage, indeed! You have never been married before. You are going to be—now."

It was some weeks after that marriage that she suddenly turned upon him—as suddenly as one can turn upon a person whose arms are about one—demanding.

"And why don't you smoke?—You never told me!"

"I shouldn't like to kiss you so well if you smoked !"—said he.

"I never had any idea," she ventured after a while, "that it could be—like this."

Selection 5

Chapter 9 from
Moving the Mountain, The Forerunner 2. 9–10

(September–October 1911): 247–52, 274–76
[John's examination of cultural changes in education]

Discussed Chapter 3, 59–63

This chapter on education, from Moving the Mountain—*a book-length depiction of a utopian society, a step toward* Herland *along with the next seven selections—returns to the concerns of "A Garden of Babies," the needs of children as "the most valuable people on earth." Gilman offers a new fictional field here, "the new attitude of the full-grown woman, . . . with the high standards of conscious motherhood." A new education for mothers and for children becomes the basis for the "manufacture" of "big sturdy blooming creatures." The imagery here anticipates that of selection 7, an allegory called "A Strange Land."*

Synopsis [Forerunner 2:247]: John Robertson, falling over a precipice in Tibet, loses all recollection for thirty years. He is found by his sister, recovers his memory, and returns home. On the way he learns of great changes in his native land, and is not pleased. Arriving, he cannot deny some improvements, but is still dissatisfied. New food and new housekeeping arrangements impress him; better buildings and great savings in money. As man to man, his new brother-in-law tells him of the change in women and its effect on men. He learns of steps taken to abolish poverty, and of rural

159

residence groups, of improved transit, orchard-roads, the passing of drunkenness, and a changed history.

I LEARNED TO UNDERSTAND the immense material prosperity of the country, much more easily than its social progress.

The exquisite agriculture which made millions of acres from raw farms and ranches into rich gardens; the forestry which had changed our straggling woodlands into great tree-farms, yielding their steady crops of cut boughs, thinned underbrush, and full-grown trunks; those endless orchard roads, with their processions of workers making continual excursions in their special cars, keeping roadway and bordering trees in perfect order—all this one could see.

There were, of course, far more of the wilder, narrower roads, perfect as to roadbed, but not parked, with all untrimmed nature to travel through.

The airships did make a difference. To look down on the flowing, outspread miles beneath gave a sense of the unity and continuous beauty of our country, quite different from the streak views we used to get. An airship is a moving mountain-top.

The cities were even more strikingly beautiful, in that the change was greater, the contrast sharper. I never tired of wandering about on foot along the streets of cities, and I visited several, finding, as Nellie said, that it took no longer to improve twenty than one; the people in each could do it as soon as they chose to.

But what made them choose? What had got into the people? That was what puzzled me most. It did show outside, like the country changes, and the rebuilt cities; the people did not look remarkable, though they were different, too. I watched and studied them, trying to analyze the changes that could be seen. Most visible was cleanliness, comfort, and beauty in dress.

I had never dreamed of the relief to the spectator in not seeing any poverty. We were used to it, of course; we had our excuses, religious and economic; we even found, or thought we found, artistic pleasure in this social disease. But now I realized what a nightmare it had been—the sights, the sounds, the smells of poverty—merely to an outside observer.

These people had good bodies, too. They were not equally beautiful, by any means; thirty years, of course, could not wholly return to the normal a race long stunted and overworked. But in the difference in the young generation I could see at a glance the world's best hope, that the "long inheritance" is far deeper than the short.

Those of about twenty and under, those who were born after some of these changes had been made, were like another race. Big, sturdy, blooming creatures, boys and girls alike, swift and graceful, eager, happy, courteous—I supposed at first that these were the children of exceptionally placed people; but soon found, with a heart-stirring sort of shock, that all the children were like that.

Some of the old folk still carried the scars of earlier conditions, but the children were new people.

Then of my own accord I demanded reasons. Nellie laughed sweetly.

"I'm so glad you've come to your appetite," she said. "I've been longing to talk to you about that, and you were always bored."

"It's a good deal of a dose, Nell; you'll admit that. And one hates to be forcibly fed. But now I do want to get an outline, a sort of general idea, of what you do with children. Can you condense a little recent history, and make it easy to an aged stranger?"

"Aged! You are growing younger every day, John. I believe that comparatively brainless life you led in Tibet was good for you. That was all new impression on the brain; the first part rested. Now you are beginning where you left off. I wish you would recognize that."

I shook my head. "Never mind me, I'm trying not to think of my chopped-off life; but tell me how you manufacture this kind of people."

My sister sat still, thinking, for a little. "I want to avoid repetition if possible—tell me just how much you have in mind already." But I refused to be catechised.

"You put it all together, straight; I want to get the whole of it— as well as I can."

"All right. On your head be it. Let me see—first—Oh, there isn't any first, John! We were doing ever so much for children before you left—before you and I were born! It is the vision of all the great child-lovers; that children are people, and the most valuable people on earth. The most important thing to a child is its mother. We made new mothers for them—I guess that is 'first.'

"Suppose we begin this way:

"a. Free, healthy, independent, intelligent mothers.

"b. Enough to live on—right conditions for child-raising.

"c. Specialized care.

"d. The new social consciousness, with its religion, its art, its science, its civics, its industry, its wealth, its brilliant efficiency. That's your outline."

I set down these points in my notebook.

"An excellent outline, Nellie. Now for details on 'a.' I will set my teeth till that's over."

My sister regarded me with amused tenderness. "How you do hate the new women, John—in the abstract! I haven't seen you averse to any of them in the concrete!"

At the time I refused to admit any importance to this remark, but I thought it over later—and to good purpose. It was true. I did hate the new kind of human being who loomed so large in every line of progress. She jarred on every age-old masculine prejudice—she was not what woman used to be. And yet—as Nellie said—the women I met I liked.

"Get on with the lesson, my dear," said I. "I am determined to learn and not to argue. What did your omnipresent new woman do to improve the human stock so fast?"

Then Nellie settled down in earnest and gave me all I wanted— possibly more.

"They wakened as if to a new idea, to their own natural duty as mothers: to the need of a high personal standard of health and character in both parents. That gave us a better start right away— clean-born, vigorous children, inheriting strength and purity.

"Then came the change in conditions, a change so great you've hardly glimpsed it yet. No more, never more again, please God, that brutal hunger and uncertainty, that black devil of want and fear. Everybody—everybody—sure of decent living! That one thing lifted the heaviest single shadow from the world, and from the children.

"Nobody is overworked now. Nobody is tired, unless they tire themselves unnecessarily. People live sanely, safely, easily. The difference to children, both in nature and nurture, is very great. They all have proper nourishment, and clothing, and environment—from birth.

"And with that, as advance in special conditions for child-culture, we build for babies now. We, as a community, provide suitably for our most important citizens."

At this point I opened my mouth to say something, but presently shut it again.

"Good boy!" said Nellie. "I'll show you later.

"The next is specialized care. That one thing is enough, almost, to account for it all. To think of all the ages when our poor babies had no benefit at all of the advance in human intelligence!

"We had the best and wisest specialists, we could train and hire in every other field of life—and the babies left utterly at the mercy of amateurs!

"Well, I mustn't stop to rage at past history. We do better now. John, guess the salary of the Head of the Baby Gardens in a city?"

"Oh, call it a million, and go on," I said cheerfully; which somewhat disconcerted her.

"It's as big a place as being head of Harvard College," she said, "and better paid than that used to be. Our very highest and finest people study for this work. Real geniuses, some of them. The babies, all the babies, mind you, get the benefit of the best wisdom we have. And it grows fast. We are learning by doing it. Every year we do better. 'Growing up' is an easier process than it used to be."

"I'll have to accept it for the sake of argument," I agreed. "It's the last point I care most for, I think. All those new consciousnesses you were so glib about. I guess you can't describe that so easily."

She grew thoughtful, rocking slowly to and fro for a few moments.

"No," she said at length, "it's not so easy. But I'll try. I wasn't very glib, really. I spoke of religion, art, civics, science, industry, wealth, and efficiency, didn't I? Now let's see how they apply to the children.

"This religion—Dear me, John! Am I to explain the greatest sunburst of truth that ever was—in two minutes?"

"Oh, no," I said loftily. "I'll give you five! You've got to try, anyway."

So she tried.

"In place of Revelation and Belief," she said slowly, "we now have Facts and Knowledge. We used to believe in God—variously, and teach the belief as a matter of duty. Now we know God, as much as we know anything else—more than we know anything else—it is The Fact of Life.

"This is the base of knowledge, underlying all other knowledge, simple and safe and sure—and we can teach it to children! The child mind, opening to this lovely world, is no longer filled with horrible or ridiculous old ideas—it learns to know the lovely truth of life."

She looked so serenely beautiful, and sat so still after she said this, that I felt a little awkward.

"I don't mean to jar on you, Nellie," I said. "I didn't know you were so—religious."

Then she laughed again merrily. "I'm not," she said. "No more than anybody is. We don't have 'religious' people any more, John.

It's not a separate thing; a 'body of doctrine' and set of observances —it is what all of us have at the bottom of everything else, the underlying basic fact of life. And it goes far, very far indeed, to make the strong good cheer you see in these children's faces.

"They have never been frightened, John. They have never been told any of those awful things we used to tell them. There is no struggle with church-going, no gagging over doctrines, no mysterious queer mess—only life. Life is now open to our children, clear, brilliant, satisfying, and yet stimulating.

"Of course, I don't mean that this applies equally to every last one. The material benefit does, that could be enforced by law where necessary; but this world-wave of new knowledge is irregular, of course. It has spread wider, and gone faster than any of the old religions ever did, but you can find people yet who believe things almost as dreadful as father did!

I well remembered my father's lingering Calvinism, and appreciated its horrors.

"Our educators have recognized a new duty to children," Nellie went on; "to stand between them and the past. We recognize that the child mind should lift and lead the world; and we feed it with our newest, not our oldest, ideas.

"Also we encourage it to wander on ahead, fearless and happy. I began to tell you the other day—and you snubbed me, John, you did really!—that we have a new literature for children, and have dropped the old."

At this piece of information I could no longer preserve the attitude of a patient listener. I sat back and stared at my sister, while the full awfulness of this condition slowly rolled over me.

"Do you mean," I said slowly, "that children are taught nothing of the past?"

"Oh, no, indeed; they are taught about the past from the earth's beginning. In the mind of every child is a clear view of how Life has grown on earth."

"And our own history?"

"Of course; from savagery to to-day—that is a simple story, endlessly interesting as they grow older."

"What do you mean, then, by cutting off the past?"

"I mean that their stories, poems, pictures, and the major part of their instruction deals with the present and future—especially the future. The whole teaching is dynamic—not static. We used to teach mostly facts—or what we thought were facts. Now we teach processes. You'll find out if you talk to children, anywhere."

This I mentally determined to do, and in due course did. I may as well say right here that I found children more delightful companions than they used to be. They were polite enough, even considerate; but so universally happy, so overflowing with purposes, so skillful in so many ways, so intelligent and efficient, that it astonished me. We used to have a sort of race-myth about "happy childhood," but none of us seemed to study the faces of the children we saw about us. Even among well-to-do families, the discontented, careworn, anxious, repressed, or rebellious faces of children ought to have routed our myth forever.

Timid, brow-beaten children, sulky children, darkly resentful; nervous, whining children; foolish, mischievous, hysterically giggling children; noisy, destructive, uneasy children—how well I remembered them.

These new ones had a strange air of being Persons; not subordinates and dependents, but Equals; their limitations frankly admitted, but not cast up at them, and their special powers fully respected. That was it!

I am wandering far ahead of that day's conversation, but it led to wide study among children, analysis, and some interesting conclusions. When I hit on this one I began to understand. Children were universally respected, and they liked it. In city or country, place was made for them; permanent, pleasant, properly appointed place; to use, enjoy, and grow up in. They had their homes and families as before, losing nothing; but they added to this background their own wide gardens and houses, where part of each day was spent.

From earliest infancy they absorbed the idea that home was a place to come out from and go back to; the sweetest, dearest place— for there was mother, and father, and one's own little room to sleep in; but the day hours were to go somewhere to learn and do, to work and play, to grow in.

I branched off from Nellie's startling me with her "new-literature-for-children" idea. She went on to explain it further.

"The greatest artists work for children now, John," she said. "In the child-gardens and child-homes they are surrounded with beauty. I do not mean that we hire painters and poets to manufacture beauty for them; but that painters and poets, architects and landscape artists, designers and decorators of all kinds, love and revere childhood, and delight to work for it.

"Remember that half of our artists are mothers now—a loving, serving, giving spirit has come into expression—a wider and more lasting expression than it was ever possible to put into doughnuts and embroidery! Wait till you see the beauty of our child-gardens!"

"Why don't you call them schools? Don't you have schools?"

"Some. We haven't wholly out-grown the old academic habit. But for the babies there was no precedent, and they do not 'go to school.' "

"You have a sort of central nursery?" I ventured.

"Not necessarily 'central,' John. And we have great numbers of them. How can I make it anyway clear to you? See here. Suppose you were a mother, and a very busy one, like the old woman in the shoe; and suppose you had twenty or thirty permanent babies to be provided for. And suppose you were wise and rich—able to do what you wanted to. Wouldn't you build an elaborate nursery for those children? Wouldn't you engage the very best nurses and teachers? Wouldn't you want the cleanest, quietest garden for them to play or sleep in? Of course you would.

"That is our attitude. We have at last recognized babies as a permanent class. They are always here, about a fifth of the population. And we, their mothers, have at last ensured to these, our babies, the best accommodation known to our time. It improves as we learn, of course."

"Mm!" I said. "I'll go and gaze upon these Infant Paradises later —at the sleeping hour, please! But how about that new literature you frightened me with?"

"O. Why, we have tried to treat their minds as we do their stomachs—putting in only what is good for them. I mean the very littlest, understand. As they grow older they have wider range; we have not expunged the world's past, my dear brother! But we do prepare with all the wisdom, love, and power we have, the mental food for little children. Simple, lovely music is about them always— you must have noticed how universally they sing?"

I had, and said so.

"The coloring and decoration of their rooms is beautiful—their clothes are beautiful—and simple—you've seen that, too?"

"Yes, dear girl. It's because I've seen—and heard—and noticed the surprisingness of the New Child that I sit here fairly guzzling information. Pray proceed to the literature!"

"Literature is the most useful of the arts—the most perfect medium for transfer of ideas. We wish to have the first impressions in our children's minds, above all things, true. All the witchery and loveliness possible in presentation—but the things presented are not senseless and unpleasant.

"We have plenty of 'true stories,' stories based on real events and on natural laws and Processes; but the viewpoint from which they are written has changed; you'll have to read some to see what I mean. But the major difference is in our stories of the future; our future here on earth. They are good stories, mind, the very best writers make them; good verses and pictures, too. And a diet like that, while it is just as varied and entertaining as the 'once upon a time' kind, leaves the child with a sense that things are going to happen—and he, or she, can help.

"You see, we don't consider anything as done. To you, as a new visitor, we 'point with pride,' but among ourselves we 'view with alarm.' We are just as full of Reformers and Propagandists as ever; and overflowing with plans for improvement.

"These are the main characteristics of the new child literature: Truth and Something Better Ahead."

"I don't like it!" I said firmly. "No wonder you dodged about so long. You've apparently made a sort of pap out of Gradgrind and Rollo, and feed it to these poor babies through a tube!"

This time my sister rebelled. She came firmly to my side and pulled my hair—precisely as she used to do forty years ago and more—the few little hairs at the crown which still troubled me in brushing—because of being pulled out straight so often.

"You shall have no more oral instruction, young man," said she. "You shall be taken about and shown things; you shall 'Stop! Look! Listen!' until you admit the advantages I have striven in vain to pump into your resisting intellect—you Product of Past Methods!"

"You're the product of the same methods yourself, my dear," I replied amiably; "but I'm quite willing to be shown—always was something of a Missourian."

No part of my re-education was pleasanter, and I'm sure none was more important, than the next few days. We visited place after place, in different cities, or in the country, and everywhere was the same high standard of health and beauty, of comfort, fun, and visible growth.

I saw babies and wee toddlers by the thousand, and hardly ever heard one cry! Out of that mass of experience some vivid pictures remain in my mind. One was "mother time" in a manufacturing village. There was a big group of mills with waterpower; each mill a beautiful, clean place, light, airy, rich in color; sweet with the flowers about it, where men and women worked their two-hours shifts.

The women took off their work-aprons and slipped into the

neighboring garden to nurse their babies. They were in no haste. They were pleasantly dressed and well fed and not tired.

They were known and welcomed by the women in charge of the child-garden; and each mother slipped into a comfortable rocker and took into her arms that little rosy piece of herself and the man she loved—it was a thing to bring one's heart into one's throat. The clean peace and quiet of it: time enough, the pleasant neighborliness, the atmosphere of contented motherhood, those healthy, drowsy little mites, so busy with their dinner.

Then they put them down, asleep for the most part, kissed them, and strolled back to the pleasant workroom for another two hours.

Specialization used to be a terror, when a whole human being was held down to one motion for ten hours. But specialization hurts nobody when it does not last too long.

In the afternoons some mothers took their babies home at once. Some nursed them and then went out together for exercise or pleasure. The homes were clean and quiet, too; no kitchen work, no laundry work, no self-made clutter and dirt. It looked so comfortable that I couldn't believe my eyes, yet it was just common, everyday life.

As the babies grew old enough to move about, their joys widened. They were kept in rooms of a suitable temperature, and wore practically no clothes. This in itself I was told was one main cause of their health and contentment. They rolled and tumbled on smooth mattresses; pulled themselves up and swung back and forth on large, soft horizontal ropes fastened within reach; delightful little bunches of rose-leaves and dimples, in perfect happiness.

Very early they had water to play in; clean, shallow pools, kept at a proper temperature, where they splashed and gurgled in rapture, and learned to swim before they learned to walk, sometimes.

As they grew larger and more competent, their playgrounds were more extensive and varied; but the underlying idea was always clear—safety and pleasure, full exercise and development of every power. There was no quarrelling over toys—whatever they had to play with they all had in abundance; and most of the time they did not have exchangeable objects, but these ropes, pools, sand, clay, and so on; materials common to all, and the main joy was in the use of their own little bodies, in as many ways as was possible.

At any time when they were not asleep a procession of crowing toddlers could be seen creeping up a slight incline, and sliding or rolling triumphantly down the other side. A sort of beautified cellar door, this. Strange that we always punished children for sliding down unsuitable things and never provided suitable ones. But then, of course, one could not have machinery like this in one brief family. Swings, see-saws, all manner of moving things they had; with building-blocks, of course, and balls. But as soon as it was easy to them they had tools and learned to use them; the major joy of their expanding lives was doing things. I speak of them in an unbroken line, for that was the way they lived. Each stage lapped over into the next, and that natural ambition to be with the older ones and do what they did was the main incentive in their progress.

To go on, to get farther, higher; to do something better and more interesting; this was in the atmosphere; growth, exercise, and joy. I watched and studied, and grew happy as I did so; which, I could see was a gratification to Nellie.

✧❦✧

Aren't they ever naughty?" I demanded one day.

"Why should they be?" she answered. "How could they be? What we used to call 'naughtiness' was only the misfit. The poor little things were in the wrong place—and nobody knew how to make them happy. Here there is nothing they can hurt, and nothing that can hurt them. They have earth, air, fire, and water to play with."

"Fire?" I interrupted.

"Yes, indeed. All children love fire, of course. As soon as they can move about they are taught fire."

"How many burn themselves up?"

"None. Never any more. Did you never hear 'a burnt child dreads the fire'? We said that, but we never had sense enough to use it. No proverb ever said 'a whipped child dreads the fire'! We never safeguarded them, and the poor little things were always getting burned to death in our barbarous 'homes'!"

"Do you arbitrarily burn them all?" I asked. "Have an annual 'branding'?"

"Oh, no; but we allow them to burn themselves—within reason. Come and see."

She showed me a set of youngsters learning Heat and Cold, with basins of water, a row of them; eagerly experimenting with cautious little fingers—very cold, cold, cool, tepid, warm, hot, very hot. They could hardly say the words plain, but learned them all, even when they all had to shut their eyes and the basins were changed about.

Straying from house to house, from garden to garden, I watched them grow and learn. On the long walls about them were painted an endless panorama of human progress. When they noticed and asked questions they were told, without emphasis, that people used to live that way; and grew to this—and this.

I found that as the children grew older they all had a year of travel; each human being knew his world. And when I questioned as to expense, as I always did, Nellie would flatten me with things like this:

"Remember that we used to spend 70% of our national income on the expenses of war, past and present. If we women had done no more than save that, it would have paid for all you see."

Or she would remind me again of the immense sums we used to spend on hospitals and prisons; or refer to the general change in economics, that inevitable socialization of industry, which had checked waste and increased productivity so much.

"We are a rich people, John," she repeated. "So are other nations, for that matter; the world's richer. We have increased our output and lowered our expenses at the same time. One of our big present problems is what to do with our surplus; we quarrel roundly over that. But meanwhile it is a very poor nation indeed that does not provide full education for its children."

I found that the differences in education were both subtle and profound. The babies' experience of group life, as well as the daily return to family life, gave a sure groundwork for the understanding of civics. Their first impressions included other babies; no child grew up with the intensified self-consciousness we used to almost force upon them.

In all the early year's learning was ceaseless and unconscious. They grew among such carefully chosen surroundings as made it impossible not to learn what was really necessary; and to learn it as squirrels learn the trees—by playing and working in them. They learned the simple beginnings of the world's great trades; led by natural interest and desire; gathering by imitation and asked instruction.

I saw nowhere the enforced task; everywhere the eager attention of real interest.

"Are they never taught to apply themselves? To concentrate?" I asked. And for answer she showed me the absorbed, breathless concentration of fresh young minds and busy hands.

"But they soon tire of these things and want to do something else, do they not?"

"Of course. That is natural to childhood. And there is always something else for them to do."

"But they are only doing what they like to do—that is no preparation for a life work surely."

"We find it an excellent preparation for life work. You see, we all work at what we like now. That is one reason we do so much better work."

I had talked on this line before with those who explained the working of industrial socialism.

"Still, as a matter of education," I urged, "is it not necessary for a child to learn to compel himself to work?"

"Oh, no," they told me; and, to say truth, convincingly showed me. "Children like to work. If anyone does not, we know he is sick."

And as I saw more and more of the child-gardens, and sat silently watching for well-spent hours, I found how true this was.

The children had around them the carefully planned stimuli of a genuinely educational environment. The work of the world was there, in words of one syllable, as it were; and among wise, courteous, pleasant people, themselves actually doing something, yet always ready to give information when asked.

First the natural appetite of the young brain, then every imaginable convenience for learning, then the cautiously used accessories to encourage further effort; and then these marvelous teachers —who seemed to like their work, too. The majority were women, and of them nearly all were mothers. It appeared that children had not lost their mothers, as at first one assumed, but that each child kept his own and gained others. And these teaching mothers were somehow more motherly than the average.

Nellie was so pleased when I noticed this. She liked to see me "going to school" so regularly. I was not alone in it, either. There seemed to be numbers of people who cared enough for children to enjoy watching them and playing with them. Nobody was worn out with child care. The parents were not—the nurses and teachers had short shifts—it seemed to be considered a pleasure and an honor to be allowed with the little ones.

And in all this widespread, costly, elaborate, and yet perfectly simple and lovely environment, these little New Persons grew and blossomed with that divine unconsciousness which belongs to children.

They did not know that the best intellects were devoted to their service, they never dreamed what thought and love and labor made these wide gardens, these bright playing-places, these endlessly interesting shops where they could learn to make things as soon as they were old enough. They took it all as life—just Life, as a child must take his first environment.

"And don't you think, John," Nellie said, when I spoke of this, "don't you really think this is a more normal environment for a young human soul than a kitchen? Or a parlor? Or even a nursery?"

I had to admit that it had its advantages.

As they grew older there was every chance for specialization. In the first years they gathered the rudiments of general knowledge, and of general activity, of both hand and brain; and from infancy each child was studied, and his growth—or hers—carefully recorded; not by adoring, intimately related love, but by that larger, wiser tenderness of these great child-lovers who had had hundreds of them to study.

They were observed intelligently. Notes were made; the mother and father contributed theirs; in freedom and unconsciousness the young nature developed; never realizing how its environment was altered to fit its special needs.

As the cool, spacious, flower-starred, fruitful forests of this time differed from the tangled underbrush, with crooked, crowded, imperfect trees struggling for growth, that I remembered as "woods"; or from clipped and twisted products of the forcing and pruning process; so did the new child-gardens differ from the old schools.

No wonder children wore so different an aspect. They had the fresh, insatiable thirst for knowledge which has been wisely slaked, but never given the water-torture. As I recalled my own youth, and thought of all those young minds set in rows, fixed open as with a stick between the teeth, and forced to drink, drink, drink till all desire was turned to loathing, I felt a sudden wish to be born again —now!—and begin over.

As an adult observer, I found this rearranged world jarring and displeasing in many ways; but as I sat among the children, played with them, talked with them, became somewhat acquainted with their views of things, I began to see that to them the new world was both natural and pleasant.

When they learned that I was a "left-over" from what to them seemed past ages, I became extremely popular. There was a rush to get near me, and eager requests to tell them about old times— checked somewhat by politeness, yet always eager.

But the cheerful pride with which I began to describe the world as I knew it was considerably dashed by their comments. What I had considered as necessary evils, or as no evils at all, to them appeared as silly and disgraceful as cannibalism; and there grew among them an attitude of chivalrous pity for my unfortunate up-bringing which was pretty to see.

"I see no child in glasses!" I suddenly remarked one day.

"Of course not," answered the teacher I stood by. "We use books very little, you see. Education no longer impairs our machinery."

I recalled the Boston school children and the myopic victims of Germany's archaic letter-press; and freely admitted that this was advance. Much of the instruction was oral—much, very much, came through games and exercises; books, I found, were regarded rather as things to consult, like a dictionary, or as instruments of high enjoyment.

"School books"—"text books"—scarcely existed, at least for children. The older ones, some of them, plunged into study with passion; but their eyes were good and their brains were strong; also their general health. There was no "breakdown from over study"; that slow, cruel, crippling injury—sometimes death, which we, wise and loving parents of past days, so frequently forced upon our helpless children.

Naturally happy, busy, self-respecting, these grew up; with a wide capacity for action, a breadth of general knowledge which was almost incredible, a high standard of courtesy, and vigorous, well-exercised minds. They were trained to think, I found; to question, discuss, decide; they could reason.

And they faced life with such loving enthusiasm! Such pride in the new accomplishments of the world! Such a noble, boundless ambition to do things, to make things, to help the world still further.

And from infancy to adolescence—all through these years of happy growing—there was nothing whatever to differentiate the boys from the girls! As a rule, they could not be distinguished.

Selection 6

"Her Memories"
The Forerunner 3.8 (August 1912): 197–201

Discussed Chapter 3, 64

A retrospective look at Home Court, one of the "beautiful blocks" of
Gilman's imagination, comes to us mediated through a male narra-
tor whose ignorance of such living conditions requires copious expla-
nation by his female companion. This "apartment house"–"pleasure
resort" accommodated residents from infancy to elderhood, much as
did the urban housing depicted in Moving the Mountain. *Gilman*
touched upon relations between parents and children, women and
men, work and leisure. But the past of this tale is not yet our present,
though it could become our future.

WE WERE DRIFTING ALONG THE HUDSON in a safe, broad-built
canoe. I was a man of over fifty; my companion a woman of about
the same age. She was looking steadily at one of the tall buildings
on Riverside Drive with an expression unusual to a city-dweller.

Her eyes were wet as she turned back to me:

"I was born there, you see; grew up there; I've lived there all
my life; it has always been 'home,'" she replied to my unspoken
question.

I looked up at the bannered towers of the great building high
over the Hudson, and wondered at her emotion. Home! An apartment house a "home"—such as to bring tears to the eyes! That
prodigious castle, occupying the four-square block up there near
Grant's Tomb; that twelve stories with towers above that—holding

some eight hundred persons at least—even with the luxurious room-space I knew they enjoyed—that a home!

"Which is your apartment?" I asked, trying to localize her feeling so that I could grasp it; as when a friend sends you a picture of the hotel with one of the thick-speckled windows marked with a cross—"this is my room."

She laughed sweetly at my lack of understanding: "My first was mother's, of course. It was on the south side—and not very high up —you can't see it from here. We moved to a bigger one when the family increased. Then when I was grown I took "two and a bath" up high there to the north. I loved that lone bleak stretch of country, and the wind!"

"Wasn't it cold?" I asked. I had lived on Riverside Drive myself, one year when I was a boy; after that I was willing to change "view" for comfort.

"It was cold outside, of course, but not inside, ever. Good building, wind-proof and sound-proof; a splendid heating apparatus— and my little golden fire if I wanted it—electric, you know. No, it was not cold. Those were beautiful years."

Her eyes dwelt lovingly on the north corner, way up.

"Worth had rooms up there, too," she said, "next to mine. When we married we didn't move—for ever so long."

"Didn't move?" I was frankly puzzled. "I thought when a girl married—or a man either—their first ambition was to have a home together."

"But we did," she repeated. "We were at home together—all the time—he was happy there, too. You don't understand about Home Court."

I admitted I didn't, but was willing to learn. "I'll try and tell you how it seemed to me, as I grew up." She looked far down the blue river, unseeing, a happy smile playing about her lips.

"Of course mother was there—back of always. Bless her—she's there yet, and just as happy! But I remember the Baby Rooms first, I think, the most vivid impressions. We spent most of our time there, you see, when we were awake. That was south and east—sun all day, our day; we went to bed when the sun did. It was the floor next the roof, and we were out on it in all weathers. Such a happy lot of roly-poly little things!

"I think the very first thing I can remember is rolling into the pool one day, and sitting up there, splashing, in the sun. Of all the lovliest things that pool shines out; warm, bright, clean, glittering, with big green growing things about—vines and shrubs and flowers. There were birds, too—free ones, I mean. They would stop in our roof-garden as they would in any garden. We never hurt them. I remember one day when a bluebird came and the first time I saw a scarlet tanager—"

"On a New York roof!" I said.

"Yes—why not? Roofs are the lovliest things on earth—in cities."

I remembered New York roofs in my boyhood—drear stretches of tar and tin and clothesline, black with drifts of cinders. Still I remembered the roof-garden idea, too. It was coming in before I left the country.

"The courts are beautiful, too—but the roofs are heavenly," she went on. "In the courts they have cool shade, and ferns and things that like it. Wonderful, high-growing vines, too. At our place the block is cut through cross-wise and has a sort of hexagonal opening in the middle. In Winter we close the north and west gates generally; sometimes the east, too. But in Summer they are all open, and it is cool down there as the cave of the winds.

"There's a beautiful fountain—a great, sleepy woman sitting back against a rock and letting a little spring trickle out over the lip of her pitcher. Ferns grow up all around her, and columbine. There's a big boxtree, and a wisteria vine rises there—older than I am, and it's up to the very roof now. I used to watch it, with the other children, and we'd prophecy [sic] how long it would take to get up top. We loved that court dearly."

"Did you play in it?"

"Oh, no; the court was for grown-ups. One had to keep still there, you know. Noise echoes so—inside. And the children need sunlight, too. But we used to look down from the windows and from the bridges—the four roofs joined that way—and wish we were grown up and could walk in those cool arcades—and sit on the carved benches and listen to the fountain."

"Always something wanting—isn't there?" I ventured.

"Oh, yes, of course. That adds interest to what one has. And I don't mean that we children were never allowed in the court—only we had to be quiet, and really we loved our sunny roof-garden better."

"How many children were there—for the roof?"

She tried to remember. "I don't know. They seemed to be countless then. There must have been—as I remember the number of families in the house, about forty babies of us—or fifty, and then over a hundred children.

"Wasn't it crowded? And a little mixed?"

"Crowded? Oh, no. You see the four roofs together made about 32,000 square feet; each one about 8,000. One was mostly gymnasium; one had a tennis court; one was for roof-suppers and dancing; and one the children's own—the baby-garden. Daytimes we divided them up, mostly. That allowed—I remember we used to boast of it to visitors—200 square feet per child. It seemed plenty, to us."

"Did your 'grown-ups' get any advantage of those roofs?" I asked rather curiously.

"Yes, indeed. Evenings they had it all—and they could come up daytimes and use some of it in school hours. We had most of our schooling outside, too, but then we took up less room." Her eyes grew brighter as the pleasant memories crowded up in her mind. "You see the top floor of the southeast building was the baby-house proper. There were day-nurseries and play-rooms and kindergartens and school-rooms—it was a kind of paradise. I've read of course of other children's lives; and see plenty of them still, in more backward places, but never any that seem to me so happy as ours."

I looked at her, puzzled and unconvinced.

"How could anything be better for a child than its own home—and its own mother?" I demanded.

"A larger home—and a larger motherhood," she answered promptly. "You see, my mother was a real child-lover. She was trained for it, too. She had the second nursery."

She saw that I was wondering at the distinction, and hastily added:

"I don't mean second-class, nor second—but second grade. The first was for the wee babies—red ones, you know. Mrs. Clara Mound was over that one. That woman loved babies world without end, so long as they were perfectly helpless. I remember when my youngest brother was born—we'd been looking forward to it for so long. What a heavenly marvel it was!" Her face was luminous with the love and wonder of childhood's first glimpse of life.

"Dear mother had him there as soon as she was with her children again, and she used to go in to nurse him. And we older ones would beg to come in—tip-toe—to see her. There were always some babies there, and happy young mothers nursing them, and the little reverent faces standing about—it was lovely."

It did make a pretty picture, I could see that, but it seemed to me dreadfully impersonal, and I said so.

"Impersonal? Yes—of course. We never mislaid our own little brothers and sisters; sometimes we thought them prettier and brighter than the others but not always. The facts were too strong for us. What we did see and love and learn from was babyhood and motherhood—the real thing."

"Didn't you love your own mother the best?"

"I did, but then my mother was more than my mother—she was *the* mother. All of us toddlers loved her."

"Better than their own?"

Some of them did. There were the Bates children—their mother was a teacher—a magnificent one—for half-grown minds. She taught in one of the big girls' schools downtown. I went there for a year or so—and *then* I loved her! She was simply great! But for babies and little children—she had no use for them—nor they for her. Those little Bateses used to cling to my mother's skirts when she came to herd them home. It hurt her feelings, I don't doubt—as I look back at it now. Then we just thought her cold and unattractive —if we thought at all. But Clorinda Bates was just my age, and we were together in her mother's classes later, and of all delicious things—to see that child fall in love with her mother! And her mother's dark, thin, sensitive face just shone with pride and plea-sure as she realized it!

"I can see now, of course, what was the matter. She was a very nervous woman, and keyed just right for her own work—a wonder at it. Little children made her nervous—and she made them ner-vous, I can tell you. But she had three nice ones. They grew up like sunbeams under my mother, and Miss Enderly in the next grade; and by and by they became adoring friends of their own mother— and stayed so."

"It seems to me that she lost a great deal," said I rather stiffly.

"She did—she was made that way. But she made up for it later. I love them little myself; fat and toddling, and learning the very first of things. But then she was a magnificent teacher—we couldn't spare her."

We were silent for a bit, drifting slowly up the broad river with the tide. I had seen mothers of that type, now that I came to think of it, wearing out their children, and themselves, with magnificent conscientiousness. She was thinking farther.

"As we grew along up it was so exciting," she began again.

"When we went down to the big dining-halls—or were taken to lectures or plays downstairs—or to the big basement pools."

"Look here!" said I. "What kind of a—Summer resort hotel is that place, anyhow?" And I looked up at Home Court, now sliding gently by us, with renewed interest.

"Oh, you don't know, do you?" she amiably allowed. "I keep forgetting about other people. You see when you grow up in a place, that's home—and you imagine other places are like it.

"It's like this," she went on in a business-like manner. "There are twelve stories, and the towers, and the basement. It's a good high basement—windows above ground, I mean. The machinery and so on is all in the cellar. They used to take classes of us down there—to show things about steam and electricity. About half the basement—that block is 200x200—is gymnasium, bowling-alley and swimming pools and baths. Kitchens and storerooms and so on are in the other half.

"The ground floor is our dining-room, with the public ones, and big entertainment rooms—for dances and lectures. Then there was a floor of small club-rooms, reading-rooms and the like. We used them, and people from the outside rented them—it paid well.

"Then nine stories of flats, all sizes, and the top floor; children in one building, the upstairs dancing-room, roof-kitchen in one, and all house employees."

"Why should they have the best floor?" I demanded.

"Why not?" she answered sweetly. "They liked it. They were an awfully nice set of people; good salaries, and homes of their own."

"It sounds more like a casino than a home," I growled.

"It was both." She watched my displeased face, trying to understand it. "Look here," she said at length. "Suppose you had a village of six or seven hundred people—living round in their separate homes—some richer, some poorer; doctor, lawyer, merchant, chief, you know; and there was a park where they all went, and a school, and places of amusement—you wouldn't call that mixed up, would you?"

"That is very different," I insisted.

"Oh, I know it is different—it's flat and there's more room. Ours was necessarily smaller and piled up on end. But a lot of people living together is no thicker one way than the other that I see."

"All this eating and dancing and swimming—weren't you herded together the whole time?"

"Why—in a way. In the theater people are herded together—or

in a church—or in a restaurant—or on the street. But you don't have to know them!"

"Oh, oh!" I admitted guardedly. "You didn't have to know them, then."

"Why should we—you've lived in apartment homes with people, haven't you? And gone solemnly up and down 'herded' in the same elevator without knowing them?"

I had, indeed. I remembered one rather cheap apartment house I had lived in once, with no elevator; and, going downstairs one day I saw crape on a door—and didn't even know who lived there. It came to me then as a shock—people died in an apartment house, it appeared. Coffins had to go down these stairs—or elevators.

"But this appears to be, not only an apartment house, but a— pleasure resort," I said.

"It was—it is, bless it!" she replied, gazing affectionately at the receding building. "Sweet, healthy pleasure, every day, from babyhood up! We had all our baby good times—all our little girl and boy good times; and then as we grew older—such *lovely* good times! As many of us as could stayed there from year to year. There were the roof-games and the basement sports, and the dances and the theatricals we got up—and the—"

"Courtships," I suggested, mischievously.

"Yes, courtships," she agreed with gay defiance. "Lots of them. Those cool alleys below there were fine on hot evenings, and the stone seats under the vines—they soon filled up, and drove a lot to the roof. There was plenty of space—and air—and the stars! There was music, too—good music—on one building—and we'd walk slowly around the running track on the farther corner—and hold hands!

"Worth came there when he was about ten—a nice, strong, earnest little boy. I was ten, too, and felt very superior. I remember showing him around. My mother got to know his mother, and they became great friends. We two would sit sometimes and hear them talk and wonder what it was all about."

"On the roof?"

"Oh, no—at home—evenings."

"Oh, you did go home, sometimes?"

She laughed contentedly. "Oh, yes. We were at home, all the time, but we went back to our own apartments, of course. The men and women came home from their work and the children came home from their play—we enjoyed our own family life as much as anybody."

"I don't see how you could—somehow," I persisted. "It sounds *so* like a big hotel."

"You'd get over that idea if you lived there," she explained patiently. "Now, see. You wake up—your own bed—your own room—your own mother and father and brothers and sisters in their rooms; you all get up and dress and flock together and the breakfast comes up—"

"Comes up?"

"Yes—of course—what's cooked comes up on the service elevator, and is set on your table."

"Hot?"

"Hot as anybody wants it. Besides we all had our little electric table heaters. Lots of people who had almost no breakfast, made it on the table—toast and coffee, you know. Well, so far that's home, isn't it—in spite of the 'up'? If I said the breakfast came 'in' from an adjoining kitchen—what's the difference?"

I agreed that so far it was home.

"Very well. Then the kids are kissed and sent to the nursery—kindergarten—school; mamma carries the baby and leaves her, rosy and gurgling, in the baby-garden. Mamma goes to her work and papa goes to his work—and home isn't home for the time being—eh? And by and by they all come back—mamma, papa and the baby —and then it's home again—isn't it? Well, then if they go out to the theatre, or a dance, or a club, home does not cease to be home, does it? We weren't any different from the people you remember, except that most of our pleasure was under the same roof—or on it—and the women had a far better time!"

I began to grasp the idea a little better, and said so.

"The loveliest of all," she went on, dreamily, looking back at the misty outlines of the city, "was when Worth and I decided to marry —and didn't have to move. I was born there—I was married there —my children were born there—I love every stone of the dear old place, for the whole twelve stories. It's home."

The next time I went by Home Court I regarded it with keen and special interest.

Selection 7

"A Strange Land"
The Forerunner 3.8 (August 1912): 207–8

Discussed Chapter 3, 67

What is "strange" about this land is its allegorical actualization of Democracy. Of its people, we are told, "They governed themselves." This land suggests the autarchy (self-rule or -power) discussed by Marilyn Ferguson in The Aquarian Conspiracy: Personal and Social Transformation in the 1980s, *a form of governance in which "social harmony springs ultimately from the character of individuals" (192). Such a social environment permits remarkable Beauty in its People —women, children, and men, who make of their land a Blooming Garden—a vision suggesting the* Herland *to come.*

THERE WAS A CERTAIN LAND wherein all the wealth and beauty, all the comfort and prosperity, all the growth and progress, were made by the people. It was not like other lands where the people are an expense, a burden, and a care; but possessed this remarkable distinction—its people were its wealth—and they knew it!

As a natural sequence of this amazing fact it presented for the first time on earth the spectacle of an entirely new form of government—a Democracy.

The people managed their own affairs; all the people, and all the affairs. They were not governed by a family or a clan or a sex; they governed themselves; and their idea of government was new and strange—they considered it merely as a means to facilitate business.

Also they had a new and strange idea of business; so new and so strange that to one from any civilized land to-day it would seem sheer idiocy or stupid benevolence, or both. This new, strange, and remarkable idea of business was this: they believed that coal was made to burn, corn to eat, water to drink and bathe in and to turn the wheels of mills; land to furnish food and living room, air to breathe; homes to dwell in; and all such foolish eccentricities as that. Work, they fondly imagined, was not only the means to produce these things; but the Chief Exercise and Basic Condition of Life.

Being obsessed with that Root Error about People—that people were after all the principal things to produce, maintain, and improve; because, as they childishly reasoned, if we do not make good people they cannot make good things, and the world will be unpleasant—they gave their minds to the problem of How to Make Better People, and continually studied it.

As the People Makers are principally Women; as women have especial love for maintaining and improving People, and especial power and skill at it, the Women stood high in the government, and worked continually at their task.

They had great galleries of pictures and statues wherein they studied the Beauty of People; and—this is what strikes the visitor as most absurd—their dress was such as to emphasize and develop The Beauty of People! Even the women themselves had learned the difference between Sex-Attraction and Beauty (being helped to this by a study of the alluring azure callosities of the Blue Mandrill); and between Fashion and Beauty; and between Conspicuous Waste and Beauty. In a word they had learned what Beauty was.

It was in truth a strange land. So that when one walked abroad one saw children as lovely as the cherubim, their grave, childish beauty was not stultified and made ridiculous by the garments of dolls; and women walking like the Graces, walking on real feet, feet that were beautiful and smooth and sound (not mere stunted shoe-trees, as it is our custom to admire!); and they were clothed in simple loveliness; in ease and comfort and freedom; in beauty of line and beauty of fabric and beauty of color and beauty of workmanship —so that one's heart sang for joy. In particular one saw and rejoiced in the beauty of the human head—a thing unknown to us for the most part.

Also the men were beautifully clothed, which proves the amazing strangeness of this land! (We, even upon the athletic field, where, if ever, beautiful strong bodies may be seen, carefully clothe the bodies in disfiguring and ridiculous short drawers; whereas any bathing suit can teach us better—a man's bathing suit, that is.)

The people of this land derived a ridiculous amount of satisfaction and pride from all this beauty. Little babies were taught to love it; children grew up surrounded with it, the schools explained it— and supplied it, being—of all eccentric things!—the most beautiful buildings they could make.

"This is where we worship God," said these peculiar people, "improving the image as fast as we can."

(Now we were told long since that man was made in the image of God, and some of us believed it, but it did not occur to us to consider if the images were a credit to the original or if we might not improve the copy.)

With this mad ambition to improve People, and with a base, degenerate fondness for enjoying life, the inhabitants of this land had got together and made a Blooming Garden of it. Trees grew everywhere, watched and tended, studied and cultivated, as if they were valuable. Birds sang in the trees; they had a theory that birds and trees were interdependent, and they preferred birds to caterpillars. Wide stretches of yellow cornland and green pastures were all bounded and broken by lines and groves of trees, and they protested it was not a waste, for the trees also bore fruit. They had another theory, that trees were as useful as the grains and grasses, if properly treated.

It was vainly preached to this people, by visitors from more rational countries, that there was more money to be made by bonanza farming; by great flat miles of wheat, with gang-plows and steam harvesters. They shook their stupid heads. "This is prettier to look at," they said, "and more comfortable and shady. We have plenty to eat."

And in truth they were all well-nourished.

But some of the younger, more inquisitive ones, listened to the visitors, seeking information.

"If you make more money by your system what do you do with it?" they demanded. "Are your people healthier and stronger, taller and handsomer than we? Is your garden more beautiful?" (They called their country their "garden"—an absurd people!)

The visitors were grieved at their stupidity and their idle questions. "It is no use to explain our system," they said. "You would not understand it."

But one young man remained with the visitors, and as he seemed intelligent, and useful, they brought him to their own more civilized land. Yet he was unable to benefit his people, for when he returned to them he was mad, and waved his arms and wept continually.

Selection 8

"Maidstone Comfort"
The Forerunner 3.9 (September 1912): 225–29

Discussed Chapter 3, 64–65

With its utopian institution founded upon capital largesse, "Maidstone Comfort" looks ahead to "Mrs. Hines' Money" and "Bee Wise." On a smaller scale than "Her Memories," "Maidstone Comfort" focuses upon mature women working together to realize a limited project. It recalls Diantha's establishment of innovative industry and anticipates the social reform fervor of "A Council of War." Like "A Garden of Babies," it treats women's need for recovery—though here from premature marriage.

WHY THAT LITTLE OWL-EYED DAUGHTER of the multi-millionaire was visiting Mrs. McAvelly in Pellettville this Summer, neither Mrs. McAvelly's friends nor the friends of Molly Bellew were able to fathom.

Pellettville was a dull little town near the shore—a shore of long, flat beaches, of much sand and curving inner bays. A few people owned "cottages" here and there; there was one hotel of modest pretensions with many elderly ladies rocking on one piazza and a few elderly gentlemen smoking on the other. It was rather a difficult place to get to, involving a tedious stage drive from a remote and desolate little station; and, apparently, a difficult place to get away from, for the little nucleus of "natives" clung to it like limpets, washed away, one by one, heavenwards—or at least in that general direction.

Mrs. McAvelly and I had one old friend there, Sarah Maidstone Pellett. Sarah had shown marked capacity in her schooldays, so that those of us who admired or those who envied, alike prophesied "a career" for her. She married, somewhat prematurely, a young medical student, in whom she had unlimited faith.

"He has such a splendid chin!" she boasted to us girls. "A man with a chin like that can do anything!" We used to joke her about it a good deal.

He of the splendid chin had slipped into her father's practice in Pellettville—the place was named after some great-grandfather whose farm had encompassed the original crossroads—and the grim energies predicted by the physiognomist were mainly used in sticking to his work against all suggestion or temptation to go elsewhere, and—for lack of other exercise—in opposing his wife.

As for Sarah, her strength of character, of which so much was predicted, was principally used in self-restraint. It takes as much power and patience to sit on a horse's head as to ride him—but one does not get anywhere in particular.

Benigna McAvelly told me how she was by mischance forced to take the "accommodation train" while on her way to visit in a town further on; how she had met and talked to our old friend on the cars; had watched her descend at that utterly unnoticeable little station ignored by all expresses, and drive away among the dusty fields and scattered woodlots of scrub oak; and how she had speculated for the rest of her slow and cindery trip on the dull, suppressed manner of that once brilliant girl.

I think it must have been to be near Sarah that the next summer she took a cottage in Pellettville. There Mrs. McAvelly proceeded to invite and to induce to come, a miscellaneous assortment of women, old and young, and various week-end men. Most of these were persons who did things. I was there on general principles, I guess, as an old friend; I don't write enough to be anybody.

But Molly Bellew seemed rather unaccounted for—unless you knew Mrs. McAvelly very well indeed. Her range of friendship was always a surprise to the widely varying types within that range; and why the temperament of Miss Bellew, which resembled at its best a distant thunder-storm that might "go by" and at its worst a combination of typhoon, sirocco and blizzard, should have appealed to her, was by no means visible to the ordinary observer.

"I'm sorry for that poor child." Benigna explained to me. "Her father is like that and worse. He killed her mother long since—oh,

quite legally, of course—and this young thing has grown up fighting. What do you suppose is her goal in life?—to be twenty-one."

"Twenty-one? What for? Does she come into property?"

"Yes, any quantity of it. She has enough now for any dozen girls,
but then she will have full control."

"And what does she propose to do with it?"

"I'm sure *I* don't know!" said Benigna. "And what's more, I don't
believe she's does herself. But she's really a nice child underneath."

The niceness underneath seemed to be more drawn out by this
quiet, adaptable, middle-aged woman, than it had ever been before.
She became quite confidential with me, too, after a while, and I
enjoyed studying her. I think Molly was middle-aged by nature. Her
childhood had been full of thwarted energy and burning rebellion.
She had despised her servants, distrusted her teachers, and lived in
a state of offensive and defensive warfare with her father. He had
never concealed from her his disappointment that she was not a
boy, and rigidly denied her the training she craved. Molly had no
particular chin, but she must have had something quite as good
somewhere, for she had managed in the very face of denial to train
herself in ways he steadily resisted. Mr. Bellew was opposed on
general principles to co-education—to much education of any sort
for girls, and to any kind of feminine independence.

I gathered a very clear picture of the girl's life. In the select
school to which he sent his daughter she found plenty to appreciate
her background of millions, but none to sympathize with her attitude of mind. Sullen and dumb she went through the necessary
tasks of such education as was given her, and "came out" in charge
of a domineering aunt, with the cheerful grace of a Christian enter-
ing the arena. A sort of nervous breakdown, attributed by the aunt
to mere bad temper, had necessitated quiet, and the aunt thought
Mrs. McAvelly a perfectly "safe" person to visit.

This smouldering firebrand of a girl felt herself unaccountably
soothed by the gentleness of handling she found here, and was interested by the various guests—they were different from what she was
used to, I imagine. Then, when she met Mrs. Pellett, when she heard
Mrs. McAvelly talking with her, and talking about her, in casual
friendly explanation, a new enthusiasm began within her.

We three sat chatting on the porch one day and Benigna told
her a lot about Sarah.

"Sarah always said she meant to keep her own name; she said

she meant to do something worth doing, and be proud of her name, as a man was. Poor thing! She never liked Pellett as well as Maidstone."

"I shouldn't think she would!" stormed Molly. "Pellett!" She fairly trod on the word: "I shouldn't think he could bear it himself."

"Oh, he's quite proud of it—and of the town having it. He's a Pellett of Pellettville, you see."

"Pellettville!" Molly was even more scornful. "What's Pellettville! It isn't anything and never was. And that old Pellett—he didn't found anything—he just happened to own the land—that's all!"

"That's all," Mrs. McAvelly admitted.

"Why didn't she do something in spite of him?" urged the girl. "I would have!" And she set her strong, white, little teeth like a vise. Molly's teeth were her best feature, but she did not display them as effectually as she might have.

"I think Sarah is discouraged. You see she loved him very much, and thought it was her duty to give in to him, I suppose. She expected him to do great things."

Molly meditated, her mouth very straight and hard. "What difference does that make? Suppose he did—why couldn't she, too?"

"Well, child, you see it's very hard when you are married to a man like that. He's good to her—they've never quarrelled that I know of. But the more she wants him to do things the more he won't. Sarah *is* a little dictatorial, you see. I think they are nearer to real friction now than they ever were before—on account of Sally. Her mother wants her to go to college—and her father thinks it's ridiculous—says so. And he won't put up the money."

"Does Sally want to go?"

"She's just crazy to go," I broke in. "She told me so herself. Sally's a bright girl—just like what her mother used to be. I think her mother feels her own ambition all over again, for Sally."

Molly pondered darkly. "I think it can be managed," she said in a determined voice.

But Benigna shook her head at her. "No, you don't, Molly," she said. "That's quite impossible. You can't 'help' Sarah Maidstone." And then she rambled on and told us a lot more about Dr. Pellett. "He's a good man," she said, "and very fond of Sarah. Thinks the world of her and of his children. But he certainly is opinionated. He thinks women have no business sense—should never be trusted with money. Whatever he can save he puts into real estate—in Pellettville. Says it's bound to rise some day—is a 'safe investment.' "

"As safe as a graveyard!" I remarked scornfully.

And Molly said: "I think he wants to own the town—like his miserable old great-grandfather."

"He'll never be rich enough for that," Benigna told her. "Sarah wanted him to 'improve' her property, but he wouldn't."

"Where is hers?" the girl asked.

Benigna waved her hand seawards. "It's beach land," she said. "Sand and marsh and more sand—with some hillocks—also sand. Her people came from about here too—that's how she came to know him, I guess. She thinks it could be made into a shore place—but he laughs at her.

"I think Sarah has a better business head than he has," I told them. "I'd give a good deal to see her prove it."

"Well, I don't know," said Benigna absently, "it's a good way from the trains, you see—an awfully poor road, and not developed at all. But I believe Sarah has more faith in her sand than in all Pellettville. And I have a good deal of faith in Sarah even yet!"

I guess it was five or six years before I visited Benigna again; I'd been abroad a good deal. She met me unexpectedly in the city and fairly carried me off to a place with a queer name, rather pretty —Maidstone Comfort. I asked her if it had anything to do with Sarah, and she said to wait and see.

"Wasn't this the Pellettville station once?" I asked when we got there. "It doesn't look in the least like it—but Pellettville used to be between Hogue and Penland.

"Yes, it's the same place," said Mrs. McAvelly, "but the traffic all goes over to Maidstone Comfort, and they offered to improve the road and run motor-buses if the railroad would change the name— and the railroad people were willing.

It was a charming station-house, built of concrete, roofed with red tiles, with vines and shrubs around it, and wide, smooth platforms, also of artificial stone.

"I hope you'll like Maidstone," continued my hostess, as we rolled smoothly and swiftly down the broad tree-lined road, the air growing salter and damper every moment. "This road will be pleasanter when the trees are grown—there'll be a triple arch, you see."

I gazed appreciatively at the careful planting. So many rural stations call for blind endurance; so many rural roads demand that sodden patience with unnecessary evils which distinguishes the American people; so may "summer resorts" find their chief attractiveness in contrast with the tediousness and difficulty of getting to them.

"That's Pellettville yonder, isn't it?" We made a curve and sped beachwards, leaving a straggling village to the right.

She nodded. "Yes, that's Pellettville—we can go through it if you want to."

I did not want to in the least, but asked: "What ever became of Sarah Pellett?"

"Oh, you'll see her while you're here," Benigna assured me. She said no more, just smiling comfortably; and we swept on, mounting a gentle rise of land, and caught the wide blue glitter all at once. The curve of the world sparkled before us across the golden stretch of sand, and the green land was joined to that wide beach by the spread embroidery of a rambling summer settlement.

But such a settlement I had never seen! Here were neither the colossal "cottages" monopolizing huge expanses of lawn and garden and regretfully leaving a riparian strip for common people; nor the clutter of cheap, tiny houses whose teeming inhabitants bring with them as many as possible of the disadvantages of city life—noises, smells and crowds.

I looked eagerly from side to side as we swung along. The hotel, where the bus stopped first, was not over large, but she assured me it was bigger than it looked, inside.

"It's mainly a sort of casino—most of us live in the cottages."

I felt a little premonitory shiver. Mrs. McAvelly I liked extremely, and am always glad of an invitation from her, but a seashore cottage, where one's facecloth and one's toothbrush sour instead of drying; one's shoes mould in the closet, one's underwear is dank and clammy in the morning, is not my idea of comfort. A good hotel, with all its noise and expense, is apt to be warmer. You can get hot water—at least by paying for it. However, I said nothing naturally.

We went more slowly along the curving streets. This was pleasant in itself; one missed the familiar gridiron angles gratefully. There was an astonishing variety in the houses, both in shape and color. They were all rather small and low; but here and there a graceful tower, vine-wreathed, rose over them. Each house spread out comfortably in its own garden; each garden had its wall; some low and broad, with young people in white flannels sitting on them; some higher, topped with nodding green, suggestive of hidden beauties beyond.

"Oh!" I cried suddenly. "It's the color—that's why it's so lovely!"

"Do you like it?" she questioned amiably. "I'm so glad."

Did I like it! I had never realized before how tired I was of ordinary house colors. These lay along the beach, each bedded in its green garden, as bright and varicolored as spilled beads. The whole village of them laughed and glowed—it was like coming on a big straggling flower-bed. There were flowers in plenty too; not the gardener's labored "beds," but vines and shrubs and trees and bushes, rose-vines nodding over porch and window, honeysuckle heaped along the walls, outbursts of rambling portulaca and soft wooly petunias—the houses were like big flowers surrounded by little ones, giving an effect of indescribable opulence and beauty.

I drew in my breath. "Isn't it almost too—hilarious?" I suggested, distrusting my own admiration.

"Some people think so," she agreed. "But most of us like it. I find I come here quite often nowadays. I hope you'll enjoy it."

Her cottage nestled like the others in its "garden close," with rather a high wall, a few vigorous young trees and high-trained vines.

"I like the shade and shut-in-ness," she said, "after the big shine outside."

It did look restful and pleasant. A smooth path of dull rock-red led to the wide, low-stepped porch—a deep porch with a wooden slatted seat all around it, wide enough to lie on if one chose. She showed me upstairs into a small rosy bed-chamber that smiled with blossoming cretonne, and breathed with fragrance from a window-box of mignonette.

"No hurry at all," she said. "Here's your bathroom, and dinner is any time you want it."

I thought "your bathroom" was a euphemism for a seashore cottage, but found it had but one door, and was really mine for the present.

A funny little bathroom with a tub solid with wall and floor, though smoothly enamelled inside; and a basin that jutted out from the wall like a shelf in a cave, also smooth and pearly within like a big seasbell.

"Must be one of those moulded houses," I thought, and turned the faucet marked "hot" with a forgiving smile. The water steamed.

Amazed and grateful I enjoyed a luxuriously hot bath, the one renovator after a day of travel, and descended to the promised dinner—of which I had so far gathered neither sound nor smell.

Benigna was waiting peacefully, and met me with her frank smile of welcome. I stood amazed at the size and height of the room.

"Why, it looks bigger than the whole house!" I said. "How on earth is it accomplished?"

She laughed happily. "Isn't it surprising? Ever so many of them are like this—but some people like a low ceiling—and more bedrooms. I have only this room, and mine, and three other bedrooms."

I looked around, a little questioningly perhaps.

"Don't be afraid—there'll be food. Perhaps you'd rather have it here—you must be tired."

While I admitted that I would, if perfectly convenient, she bent to the telephone at her elbow and said: "McAvelly—yes—dinner, please."

"That's a simple process," I admiringly observed. "Does it descend out of heaven—or come up through the floor?"

"Not quite so impressive, but still rather dramatic," she assured me. "This side of the house is on the lane, and this is the back door." She opened it, and showed a clean little passage between house and garden walls, down which presently rolled a brisk motor-wagon, and there was deposited beside our chairs a neat receptacle, so clean and shining that I felt as if it could hardly contain food.

But it did; food, excellent and varied; hot and cold as was suitable, with necessary dishes. We drew a light low table between us, and dined in ease and quiet, taking our time, and free to speak as intimately as we chose.

"We go out a great deal," she said. "It's very pleasant at the hotel. But of course—with special friends, it is nice to be just by ourselves."

I always did like Benigna. She never seems to do much of anything herself, but she has the knack of making people comfortable. Men like her, too.

I enjoyed the dinner hugely, and afterwards she put the dishes back and set the case on her tiny back step. Then we took a stroll, along smooth winding concrete walks, leaning on low walls and looking seaward, watching the wild glitter of the moon on the dancing ocean and the smooth silver sheet it made in the still bayous behind.

"You see it's mostly pretty flat," she showed me from the highest point we reached. "There used to be a lot of marshland, but it's all drained and dyked now, and in those shallow inlets the children play all day. There's room on the flats now for endless games. I never saw a place where there was so much fun—and so little trouble."

"How about servants?" I asked. "That's usually the main trouble in these places."

"We don't have any," she answered. "They have a lot of skilled employes who come in by the hour. One just takes comfort here."

"Maidstone Comfort!" I remarked. "Oh, how about Sarah Maidstone? This must be her land!"

"Yes, this is her land. It's a big paying property now. Sarah was right about that, after all."

"Where'd she get the money?"

"You remember that little Bellew girl? Why, she came of age that year we were there, and actually persuaded Sarah to let her invest in this place—got landscape architects and concrete constructors and sanitary engineers and all sorts of people to work on it. She got her money back, all right, and Sarah's quite rich. She manages the whole thing, most successfully."

Sarah's disappointed life was running through my mind. I was delighted to think she had made good after all.

"How does Mr. Pellett of Pellettville like it?" I asked, rather maliciously.

Benigna shook her head gently. "You mustn't make fun of Dr. Pellett! He's a very good friend of mine. They are far happier than they used to be, in spite of Sally's going to college. I think—" she gave her little, bright, friendly smile. "I think he thinks he advised it all."

Selection 9

"Forsythe & Forsythe"
The Forerunner 4.1 (January 1913): 1–5

Discussed Chapter 3, 65–66

In this story, as in "Her Housekeeper," new male possibilities appear —in both professional and personal life. This story's focus upon male needs concerns divorce and remarriage, but with clear inclusion of women's rights as well. Again the scope is limited, here to one firm and one residence—with no attention to child care in the families of professional couples. (Might Gilman tongue-in-cheek be writing against John Galsworthy's Forsyte family, whose solicitor-protagonist, Soames Forsyte, entered the literary scene in the 1906 The Man of Property, *the first volume of the 1922* The Forsyte Saga?)

THE BUSINESS OF MR. JAMES R. JACKSON took him to Northern Washington.

The health of Mrs. James R. Jackson took her to Southern California.

Both being on "the coast" their eastern friends casually assumed that they were together.

If Mrs. Jackson or Mr. Jackson regretted this temporary division, their New England breeding checked any outward sign of it. He continued to employ himself, as had been his custom, and she continued to enjoy herself, as had been her custom.

But when Mr. Jackson, standing for a moment on a doorstep to look up and down the broad, bustling street of the swift-growing city, saw the sign on an office window nearly opposite, "Forsythe &

Forsythe," he showed more emotion than any of his friends would
have expected of him. He started perceptibly, made a quick step
forward, and then drew back into the doorway, and stood looking at
the modest "Attorneys & Counsellors at Law" office windows as if
he saw something exciting.

He did, too. He saw a football field where he and George Forsythe had fought, bled, and almost died together; drowsy classrooms
electrified by some wicked joke of George's; their own chamber in old
Holworthy, with its pennants and trophies, its superfluous cushions,
gifts of admiring girlhood, and its crowding photographs from the
same source.

Most of all be saw one of these photographs, well-placed and
highly honored, much admired by all the boys—George's young sister Clare. A graceful, slender girl, with even more than her
brother's mischief in her sparkling dark eyes.

He had been engaged to her for six months . . . . . .

The quarrel was on a matter of principal—that they both stated.
A difference of views on things she desired and intended to do—
things he should never allow his wife to do—and an instant break
over the word "allow."

Young people are often intensely firm on matters of principle.
He maintained not only the righteousness of his position, but of
his necessary control over his wife. She maintained that she was
mercifully not his wife yet—and never would be while he retained
those opinions.

In another six months he had married little Sue Meredith, a
damsel of considerable beauty and no views of any sort.

Where Clare Forsythe had advocated Votes for Women even at
the point of the sword—if it ever came to that—Miss Susie thought
it unwomanly even to be an Anti. Jackson had money enough to
marry when it suited him, and marry he did, with all the pomp
and circumstance his happy bride could enlist to add luster to the
crowning event of her life.

That was eight years ago, eight years that were now scurrying
through his mind like a quickened cinematograph. Susie had no
ideals but for "the home," the largest, most elaborate homes (they
had changed more than once) his money could furnish her, the most
servants, the gayest dinners, the most lavish entertainments.

Mr. Jackson's home life had been expensive and laborious, but
somehow he had never felt that sense of restful attainment he expected. Susie's exquisite womanliness had so attracted him that he

was painfully shocked to find her absolutely opposed to bearing children. One had happened to them, a frail, unwelcome baby. Susie refused to nurse it; she said she had been kept in long enough, and that she did not wish to lose her figure. Her husband viewing with new eyes that closely corsetted, richly-gowned "figure," wondered what it was for.

The baby died—five years ago.

They had traveled, lived abroad, after that. He hardly felt at home in his own country now.

And here he stood thinking of the old days, remembering that George had studied law and gone out to join the firm of a western uncle, and wondering with a deep quickening of the heart what had become of Clare.

He crossed the street and entered the office of Forsythe & Forsythe.

His old friend was there, not a whit changed in appearance, the same quick, jovial eyes—

"Why, Jimmy-Jack! Of all things! Where did you drop from? I thought you were in Siam or Kamchatka or somewhere!"

"It's good to see you, George—I tell you, it's good to see you again!"

Mr. Jackson held his friend's hand as if it was something to tie to. Across the eager flood of reminiscence, the reviving of old affection, still warm and fresh, and with it a pleasant sense of youth's renewal—

"Where are you staying?" George suddenly demanded. "Is the Mrs. alongside—you'll come to us, of course!"

Mrs. Jackson's whereabouts and precarious health were explained with due care, Mr. Forsythe vaguely gathering that the subject was unwelcome.

"Well, well—you'll come to us anyhow, I'm sure."

Jackson's face fell a trifle as he noted the collective pronoun. "Why—I didn't know you were married!"

"Nothing criminal, is it? Most of us are sooner or later. Won't keep you away, will it?"

"Oh, of course not—but I think I'd better stay at the hotel. I can drop in here, you know. You'll come and lunch with me, perhaps—I don't wish to intrude."

George Forsythe tipped back in his swivel-chair and regarded his friend with a somewhat mixed expression. He was remembering his friend's opinions of years past, as rigidly conservative, even reactionary, also certain things he had heard hinted, in earlier years, as to his marriage. He studied the worn lines in his friend's face; perhaps, too, he was recalling circumstances in his own life of which he need not speak unless he chose.

"Now, I'll tell you what, old man," he said presently. "You needn't be thrown at Mrs. Forsythe's head. As a matter of fact, she is at present staying in her old home—you needn't meet her at all if you don't want to—I dare say you'd disagree on some points. But you are coming home with me—right now."

He closed his desk, went into another room and left some directions, and returned to his friend.

"Have you really seen the town?" he asked, and being unsatisfied with the answer, took a taxi, and rushed Mr. Jackson about for breathless miles of beauty, broad bay and nestling lakes, a wonderland of hills, trees like towers, whole parks and forests of them. "Most wonderful city on earth," he said, and boasted fervently.

Stopping at the hotel he insisted on taking Mr. Jackson's luggage at once, and before six o'clock he slipped in his latchkey, saying: "I tell you, it seems good, Jimmy, to be able to have you in my home!"

It was only an apartment, after all, to which not even years in European cities had reconciled Mr. Jackson. Still, it was undeniably comfortable. The room given him was large enough, warm, light and airy. George's, next to it, boasted a sleeping-porch, something of an innovation to the visitor.

The place was as perfectly appointed as a first-class club, yet bore the unmistakable stamp of personality. Deep, comfortable lounging-chairs—no rockers to lunge forward in the dark and smite unoffending ankles—shaded drop-lights that turned this way and that at a touch, but wore no petticoats of lace or beads; broad solid tables, rests for the feet, pictures well chosen, fascinating maps— yet something was lacking; it did not really strike the visitor as "home."

Suddenly it occurred to him that he saw no "traces of a woman's hand"—the place was pleasant, but undeniably bachelorish. Questions arose in his mind, but he asked none.

A most excellent dinner, perfect in all appointments, was served them by a noiseless, dextrous Japanese.

"You certainly have solved the servant question," he said, "as far as this part of it goes."

"Yes, we're very proud of our cuisine," the friend replied. "When

I'm alone, I mostly eat downstairs, but, of course, with an old friend it's pleasanter up here."

Jackson thought he detected a note of loneliness in the words, but said nothing as to that.

"You mean there is a sort of restaurant below? This is one of those 'apartment hotels,' then?"

"Yes, of a sort. This is for families and for singletons, too. Clare has rooms here, and—a cousin of ours."

Forsythe offered excellent cigars with: "I don't smoke myself, but I like to see the other fellow enjoy it." But Jackson declined; he smoked very little, he said, did not care for one that night, seemed a little restless. Forsythe watched him with the glimmer of a smile:

"Well, come along, we'll look up the girls."

It was only across the hall, opposite doors to adjoining apartments, similar in general arrangement, but refreshingly different in personal atmosphere. If Forsythe's rooms were the acme of masculine comfort, these spoke as vividly of a wholesome femininity. There was grace, beauty, an unerring good taste, a sweet sense of home, without that air of forced compromise which characterizes so many.

None of this did Mr. Jackson note that night. First, foremost and overwhelmingly he was impressed by Clare Forsythe, the girl to whom he had given his whole heart nine years ago. At first he felt a sort of wondering shock, by no means painful; she was so different from his memories. To be sure, seventeen is different from twenty-six, but this seemed something more than the flying of so many years of youth. She had grown taller—he was sure of it; fuller in outline, more vigorous. In place of the girlish sweetness and elfin charm there was poise, a gentle assurance, the air of a woman used to living. But the eyes were the same, sparkling now with the old mischief.

"Why so distraught, Mr. Jackson. I know I shall call you Jimmy presently, but I'll begin right. How do you like Seattle? Isn't it a glorious climate—when the sun's out? Those are the proper questions for newcomers."

He answered promptly enough; also when she inquired after his wife, but still watched her with covert surprise—she had so changed.

"You look as if you wanted to say: 'Why, how you've grown!' and 'Do you enjoy your lessons?' I have—and I do—I've learned a lot in these last ages."

"Tell me about it," he said. "The course has certainly agreed with you."

She told him, gaily and amusingly enough, but the more he heard the more his constitutional objection to her views rose up against his strong personal admiration and attraction for her.

She had been to college, a co-educational college; she had studied—of all unwomanly occupations—engineering.

"I'm a sanitary engineer!" she smilingly assured him. "I know more about plumbing than any plumber plus plumbers' assistant and three candle ends!" And she laughed outright at his effort to show polite approval.

"You never were a good dissembler, Jimmy. I can see the good American horror at a woman's earning her living behind all your recently gathered European graces. You have improved, though," she continued sweetly. "Your manners are far nicer—how did you ever get them through the custom house!"

"I suppose you are what they call a 'bachelor maid,'" he ventured. He hated the term, but fancied it might please her.

"Precisely—though I hold the phrase to be distinctly tautological. As well call a man 'a virgin bachelor.' I live here, you see, enjoying all the comforts of a home, with none of the cares, anxieties or difficulties."

"You do not live alone?" he inquired, and she replied:

"Why no indeed! There is a houseful of people—all ages and sizes. And then, here's dear old George next door, and—" she waved a competent hand, "here's Cousin Georgiana."

Jackson began to look closer at Cousin Georgiana, who was chatting earnestly with Forsythe at the far end of the two parlors, with occasional little giggles and exclamations of delight. They were certainly having an excellent, good time together. That worried look was gone, the air of forced cheerfulness—Forsythe was certainly at ease with his fair cousin.

She was fair, too; larger than Clare, and less sprightly; a calmer, more comforting type, hearty and restful. As Jackson watched them his vague doubts about his friend revolved themselves into real anxiety.

The evening left a mixed impression on his mind. No matter what had happened, it was a joy to see Clare again—that he did not conceal from himself at all. When he considered how much farther she had gone than her girlhood's firmly stated intentions, he said to himself: "I was right! It would have been a terrible mistake." But after he went to bed, and lay, sleepless, thinking over those pleasant hours, the touch of her firm, warm hand, the dancing light in her eyes, the gay voice that always stirred his heart, he said at last: "I wonder!" Also he wondered more than a little about Cousin Georgiana, with her sweet face, her soft shining coils of hair, and that delicious little gurgle of a laugh. There might be some reason, after all, for George's reversion to bachelorhood.

Ought he to stay there? That was the question he went to sleep with and woke up with. There seemed to be reasons many and good why he should not, if any were necessary beside his deep-rooted objection to a composite home of that sort. But George urged him almost pathetically to remain. "I tell you, it seems good!" he said, "to see anybody I used to know—let alone you, old boy! Why, Jimmy-Jack you're just the same old moss-back you always were— you're a relic of past ages, that's what you are. You stay here and get shaken up—it will do you good!"

He stayed. Possibly he had a vague idea that George wanted him to "stand by," that his presence was some sort of bulwark against temptation. If so, it failed of its purpose, for the longer Mr. Jackson stayed, the surer he grew that there was something more than kin between his friend and Cousin Georgiana.

If George had expressed his opinion he might have ventured to criticize his guest for dallying with temptation, for the attraction of sister Clare was evidently greater than the repulsion caused by her limitless progressive views. Mr. Jackson, urged by his friend, and apparently undeterred by his business affairs or whatever communications he may have received from his wife, lingered on and on, and spent much of his time in the society of the dark-eyed tormentor whose delight it was to rouse that expression of chill horror on his handsome features. He grew used to the smooth convenience of the apartment very rapidly, even tacitly approved of the steady excellence of the food and service, but one shock received on the second day of his visit, was so severe as almost to drive him forth at once.

Clare took him up to the roof "to set the kiddies." Two rosy youngsters out of the throng assailed her as "Auntie Clare" and asked "when Mama was coming."

"Pretty soon, dear, pretty soon. You be patient—she'll come by and by."

They were soon pacified. Indeed there seemed to be a perpetual children's party going on up there under the pleasantest of supervision, and with every sort of thing to slide and swing on, to paddle and dig in, to climb and race and play.

But Jackson's heart sank as he thought of his friend: "Poor old

George, if she's left him already, no wonder he takes comfort with that Cousin—she looks like a nice woman too. I don't believe she began it."

Meanwhile he never seemed to think that his continued attentions to Clare might lay her open to some criticism, but others thought of it, and George very reluctantly made up his mind to say "just a word"—if he could without hurting his friend.

Unfortunately for his good intentions he deferred them until something had happened which put Mr. Jackson in the position of mentor. Coming in late one night, he saw Cousin Georgiana enter her apartment, and let himself in the opposite door with a key George had long since given him. What was that? As he went quietly into his chamber he heard voices in George's room beyond— that little gurgling laugh—again. He made some hasty rattle of his toilet articles, heard a door shut with a sudden click. Ah, that door near the bed—he had always supposed it to be the closet.

George hailed him artlessly with: "Hello—Jimmy-Jack! Back already? Come in!"

He went in, deeply concerned, only to find George laughing irresistibly on his side of that door, while Georgiana laughed as helplessly on the other—and a corner of her flowing blue kimono latched in seemed the cause of this untimely mirth.

George opened the door and released the lady, who sprang to her feet, blushing but unashamed.

"Game's up!" he cried. "Have to own up now to save your face Jimmy, this is the other member of our firm—Forsythe & Forsythe —followed her father's footsteps, you see. Also my cousin, Georgiana Forsythe—as you know. Also my wife—Mrs. Forsythe— didn't have to change her name, either."

They had not the heart to say anything to him about Clare that night, and the next day it was too late, for he astonished that young lady by asking if he might show her the last news he had of Mrs. Jackson, and then putting in her hands a decree of divorce that lady had sent him.

"May I stay?" he asked. "May I begin again?"

"But—Jimmy—you hate my ideas, my principles, my business—"

"Ah," said he, "but I love you!"

Selection 10

"Mrs. Hines' Money"
The Forerunner 4.4 (April 1913): 85–89

Discussed Chapter 3, 65

Mrs. Hines is Gilman's prototypical woman who "increasingly dislikes the middle-aged woman" she has become and who "at last discovers that her discontent is social starvation—that it is not more love that she wants, but more business in life." Her widowhood, not at all a disaster, presents an opportunity. The plan she institutes will develop a multi-faceted cultural life for a neighborhood.

MRS. HINES LAY QUIETLY on her back, looking sideways out of the window. She was quite conscious of the dull ache in the splinted arms, the bandaged head, but with a strange, unusual sense of peace. Physically she was far from comfortable, but in her mind, in spite of some confusion and regret, was that queer increasing feeling that somehow things were going to be different now—and better.

They had broken it to her, gently and after due delay, that her husband had not survived the accident. She shut her eyes then, turned her head stiffly on the pillow, and they could see the slow salt tears forcing themselves from beneath closed lids, and the close-held lips quivering. Mrs. Hines had never complained of her husband. It was quite natural that she should cry. She "bore up" splendidly, they said. But they did not know why she cried nor what it was she bore up against.

As the lean, small woman with the patient face and iron-gray hair in its two thin little sick-bed braids lay there so still, none of her relatives and attendants knew the crossing currents of emotion that lifted her thin chest with an occasional shuddering sigh.

"Now, Eva, you must be brave!" said her sister Mrs. Arroway. "It is hard, I know, but you have always done your duty. You have nothing to blame yourself for."

Her brother, a heavy man with a determined mouth supplemented by an even more determined moustache, adds his words of cheer.

"You're left in comfortable circumstances, Eva," he said. "Very comfortable circumstances for a woman alone. Jason was better fixed than we knew. I won't worry you with details, but you'll be well taken care of. There's no executor or anything named—I suppose you'll want me to attend to things for you?"

To this she said nothing, but the tears welled afresh, and Mrs. Arroway said: "Now Frank Peterson, you wait. She's not strong enough to be troubled about anything yet. You go away."

So Frank went away, and presently, as Mrs. Hines seemed to be asleep, her sister went also. Then after awhile Mrs. Hines opened her eyes and looked at the drooping fir boughs by the window. Not far beyond them was a slate-colored wooden wall, the windowless side of the next house. She had looked out through those dark fir boughs at that wooden wall ever since she came to this house, a bride, thirty long years ago. Then she was eighteen. Now she was forty-eight.

When the doctor dropped in on his way home, just to see how she was getting along, she whispered that she wanted to see him alone. So he persuaded Mrs. Arroway, who sat, large and warm, in a creaky rocking-chair, fanning herself steadily, that a nap would do her good there and then, and sent her to take it.

"Your patient's doing beautifully now," he said, "and she'll sleep a bit, too, I think, if she's by herself."

The nurse was easily disposed of, and Dr. Osgood drew his chair closer and looked down, smiling in his wise friendly way on the pale little woman.

"You've known me near thirty years, haven't you, Doctor?"

"I certainly have," he agreed. "Sick and well—mostly well, I'm glad to say."

"And you've known—my family too."

"Knew your father and mother, and brother and sister, and several cousins—no doubt of it."

"Well—I'm not crazy—am I, Doctor?"

"Crazy! Certainly not. You've nothing but a few scalp wounds there, and a broken bone or two. You've no fever—you'll be up in no time."

"Your boy Charles is a real lawyer now, isn't he?" she pursued.

"What *are* you driving at? Yes, Charles is a lawyer all right, and going to be a good one—unless he's too honest."

"Well, I want to see him, Doctor. Frank tells me that I'm left— fairly well off—and he wants to manage the property—and I prefer to have it in my own hands—absolutely. Can't Charles take care of me?"

"He certainly can, and he'll be glad to. You gave my kids many a good time when they were little—and they're all fond of you. You can count on Charlie. I'll bring him around in the morning."

With the benefit of her attorney's inquiries and advice Mrs. Hines ascertained that she was absolute mistress of the place where she had lived so long, of two other houses and a centrally situated lot, and of some fifty thousand dollars in a reliable bank. He gave her all the details, and some wise advice.

"Is it my very own?" she said. "I can do just as I please with it all?"

"You can do exactly as you please with every cent of it," he told her. "You can sell all you have and give to the poor—but I don't advise it. You can give it all to me—but I won't charge that much."

Mr. Frank Peterson was offended and made that fact conspicuous. Mrs. Arroway was offended too, on general principles, that Eva should consult a lawyer when her own brother was one—it looked so bad—it was so inconsiderate.

To their criticisms and protests Mrs. Hines opposed no word, only the pale patient face, the set lines of the mouth. She was weak, she was silent under reproach, but she kept on quietly.

As soon as Mrs. Hines was up and about she consulted, further, her minister as well as her lawyer, and more than one real estate man. Her own place she sold at once, sold even at what seemed some sacrifice, showing what her sister called "real hard-heartedness" about it. The other two houses were left in Mr. Charles Osgood's hands to rent as before, and Mrs. Hines, taking the proceeds of her relinquished home in letters of credit and travelers' checks, summarily departed.

"I never saw anything so unnatural!" her sister protested. "She won't even say where she's going. She says her lawyer'll forward her letters. Her lawyer, indeed! And her own brother a lawyer all the time! I don't believe she knows what she's doing. I believe her mind's affected."

But here Dr. Osgood satisfied all inquiries. "Fiddlesticks," he said. "She's going off for change, travel, and a complete rest. I advised it. If she doesn't want to tell where she's going, why should she?"

Mrs. Hines, in truth, did not know where she was going. She had one settled determination; to make the price of that home which had held her prisoner so long, now carry her as far as it would hold out. Beyond that she had a longing deep and earnest for health— vigorous health—if it could be had at any price. And beyond that, still deeper and more earnest, was the desire to invest her money so that it should do the most good.

"This much I'll spend—just spend!" she told herself, "I can live easy enough on the rents of the other two, and then I'll put that fifty thousand to work for righteousness. But I've got to get well—*well*— strong, and clearheaded."

The very first thing she did was to take a "room and bath" in a New York hotel. She dined rather timidly in the big room with the music, flowers and lights, spent a riotous evening with three new magazines at once, then, with triumphant memories of the compromises and makeshifts of the large, inconvenient, old-fashioned house she had escaped from, she luxuriated in the shining, white-tiled bathroom, the gleaming porcelain tub, the swift, copious rush of the hot water.

"He *wouldn't* have the hot water connected," she thought. "He *wouldn't* have a porcelain tub—or even an enameled one. And he could have, just as well!"

Then Mrs. Hines crept into a wide smooth luxurious bed, and slept. She slept so deep and sound that on waking there was that sense of coming up from deep waters, of complete detachment.

"Where am I?" was the first thought, with the worried background of a fear that she would be late with Jason's breakfast.

Then she remembered.

She lay perfectly still for awhile, then stretched deliciously, as far as she could reach, to the uttermost corners of the wide bed. How fresh and empty the room smelled! How gently the curtain waved in a soft current of air! Mrs. Hines preferred the window open. Jason had preferred it shut.

She looked at her watch, smiled happily, and went to sleep again. Wakening at last an idea struck her—a daring, delightful idea. She would have her breakfast sent up!

For some weeks the little woman rested and freshened herself in unwonted idleness and freedom, and then, feeling strong enough to choose, spent a long Summer, half in the cool uplifting mountains, half by the cool refreshing sea.

How hot it used to be in that house—!

This Summer was divided into three equally pleasant processes: Rest, exercise and study. She had found out, in the big city, what she wanted to know, and all Summer she was filling her mind with new knowledge.

It came to her as a revelation, the things the world was doing to improve itself. With all her soft little heart she had grieved over the sorrows, the unnecessary sorrows, of humanity; with all her hard little head she had tried to think of ways of helping. But she had had little time or opportunity, and no money, and her ideas had been laughed at as womanish foolishness.

Now she found that men, hard-headed business men and statesmen, doctors and writers and scientific students, were thinking and working along these lines.

She had time now—all there was left. She had freedom. And she had fifty thousand dollars.

A year of travel followed. She was not going to be hasty. She could not afford to make mistakes. So she went methodically about from land to land, supplementing her recent study with more careful observation. *The Survey* and her collateral reading had filled her mind with stirring insight into conditions. The Bureau of Social Service in New York had given her definite lines of inquiry. Now she was learning fast.

"It mustn't be charity," she said to herself. "It must be business, good business. It must prove that it will pay."

When she came back to her home town she felt as if she had changed from a mouse to an elephant, so much stronger she felt, so much wider was her outlook upon life. So detached and upbuilt was she as to feel even a sort of affection for her brother who had always so rudely domineered over her as to check that natural feeling. Her sister, too, no longer seemed a dampener, a clog upon her spirit. That spirit was strong enough now to smile at their limitations and not mind them. Even the town looked pleasant to her—and to her pleased surprise the house by the big fir trees had become a grocery store.

She took two rooms at the best hotel.

Mrs. Arroway remonstrated continuously. "Look here, Julia," said Mrs. Hines at last. "I'm a woman of fifty, and ought to know my own mind. I prefer to live in this hotel for the present. Now suppose you just make up your mind to it." She was good-natured but firm, and peace ensued.

There was Charles Osgood and his father; there was the one live minister in town; there was out of many one woman's club with some real ambition to be useful, and the philanthropic associations of the place, such as they were; these were the assets. Ignorance, inertia, prejudice, conservatism and selfishness; these were the liabilities.

It was a large town, or rather, a small city, and small though it was, had many of the disadvantages of large ones, without their ameliorations.

Mrs. Hines blew no trumpet. She spent her first season in re-establishing herself in the place on a new basis, in affiliating with church, club and charity, making judicious contributions of money and service. People got to know her. Those who had known her liked her better than they had before.

The only thing she really did that season was to engineer the establishment of a lecture lyceum; the progressive church furnished the auditorium, and Mrs. Hines the funds. A number of carefully selected human dynamos were brought to the town, and the local mind was greatly stirred. Before the next Autumn there had risen on that conveniently situated lot of Mrs. Hines a building which she quietly announced was a memorial to her husband. It was called simply The Hines Building. Like other memorial buildings she had seen this contained many social conveniences.

The great airy basement was fitted with a swimming-pool and gymnasium; the roof had room for various games, and could be used as a tea-garden. There was an auditorium which could be used for sermon, lecture, mass meeting or theater, and the whole top floor was arranged for dancing or fairs and exhibitions, with a space reserved for the preparation and serving of refreshments.

There was the Hines Circulating Library, an excellent adjunct to the rather meager public one. A committee comprised of Mrs. Hines, Charles Osgood, the progressive minister and the extremely progressive librarian they employed, selected the books. If the selection comprised a wide range of sociological works, both in science and fiction, at least no one need read them who did not wish to.

Club rooms, large and small, filled the remaining space.

"There!" said Mrs. Hines, when it was done.

The place was opened by an invitation audience that filled the theater, addressed by a group of well-known ministers and philan-thropists, followed by a reception in the big ball-room, with refresh-ments. Everybody went over the building from roof to basement, interested and admiring, and all those interested in social better-ment held forth to congenial groups about the things they thought of preeminent importance to the world.

Then Mrs. Hines opened accommodations, free, to the two lead-ing philanthropic societies of the town, which offer was accepted promptly. She made the rent of her club rooms so reasonable that one after another the women's clubs grew to use them. "It was so central," they delightedly agreed. "And they could have tea and things when they wanted them—very reasonable, too.

The wealthy found that that big ball-room was a delightful place to give dances, high, cool, with the whole broad roof for stroll-ing couples between dances. Men's clubs, as well as women's, began to engage the rooms; girls' clubs and boys' clubs; classes of various descriptions; lectures, debates and private theatricals were held there.

The library was open evenings, all the evening, and many found it a pleasant place to rest and read, to meet friends, to change for the gymnasium, the dancing-room, the airy restaurant or the more airy roof, at will.

When that ball-room was not engaged by special patrons it was put to good use. Excellent dancing teachers were engaged, a man and wife, and good music furnished by a pianist more definite and regular than a pianola, and a muscular boy with a violin, who sup-ported a widowed mother by that tireless right arm and those quick, strong fingers. Then they had classes, friendly groups of different ages, one which admitted no one under forty, and had more fun than the youngest class of children.

The rents were low, but the patronage was continuous. It was astonishing how popular the place became. There was a club or class-ticket which enabled any regular patron of the building to use the women's parlor upstairs, or the men's lounging room in the basement, and the number of those who took advantage of them was surprising.

The superintendent and his wife, who had a little apartment on the premises, proved both useful and popular, especially in keeping up the interest of the boys' and girls' clubs. Some initiative, some direction, is always valuable.

Boy Scouts and Camp-Fire Girls met there; a "roque" court on the roof drew increasing memberships; classes in swimming and gymnastics followed one another swiftly. There are never enough places for water sports, and this pool was so big, so clean and fresh, and so enlivened with spring-boards, glistening chutes and all tile machinery for clean, natural fun.

From the busy class-rooms, the earnest club-rooms, the gay ball-rooms, the quiet reading rooms, to the shrieks of laughter from the jolly crowds in the basement, the whole space teemed with happy, social life, natural and developing.

Before the year was out Mrs. Hines had the pleasure of seeing that her memorial building was going to pay her ten per cent above all expenses, and besides a sinking fund which bade fair to replace her capital in ten years' time.

"Good!" said Mrs. Hines. "Jason wouldn't object to that anyway!"

Selection 11

"Bee Wise"
The Forerunner 4.7 (July 1913): 169–73

Discussed Chapter 3, 67–68

Gilman anticipated this title "Bee Wise" in her 1910 comment on the role of fiction in society: if fiction "truly re-presents" life, and is not falsely heroic or romantic, then "meeting life in reality we should be wise—and not be disappointed" (21). In this, her most ambitious utopian short story, a whole city—both urban and suburban regions —is delineated. Recalling the journalist-narrator of "Aunt Mary's Pie Plant," the female reporter-classmate discovers the "true nature of the sudden civic growth" financed by "a live man's gift" to a college-trained woman. In "Bee Wise," Gilman treated all of the "fresh fields of fiction" she had listed. The story fully anticipates Herland.

IT'S A QUEER NAME," said the man reporter.

"No queerer than the other," said the woman reporter. "There are two of them, you know—Beewise and Herways."

"It reminds me of something," he said, "some quotation—do you get it?"

"I think I do," she said. "But I won't tell. You have to consider for yourself." And she laughed quietly. But his education did not supply the phrase.

They were sent down, both of them, from different papers, to write up a pair of growing towns in California which had been built up so swiftly and yet so quietly that it was only now after they were well established and prosperous that the world had discovered something strange about them.

This seems improbable enough in the land of most unbridled and well-spurred reporters, but so it was.

One town was a little seaport, a tiny sheltered nook, rather cut off by the coast hills from previous adoption. The other lay up beyond those hills, in a delightful valley all its own with two most precious streams in it that used to tumble in roaring white during the rainy season down their steep little canyons to the sea, and trickled there, unseen, the rest of the year.

The man reporter wrote up the story in his best descriptive vein, adding embellishments where they seemed desirable, withholding such facts as appeared to contradict his treatment, and doing his best to cast over the whole a strong sex-interest and the glamor of vague suspicions.

The remarkable thing about the two towns was that their population consisted very largely of women and more largely of children, but there were men also, who seemed happy enough, and answered the questions of the reporters with good-will. They disclaimed, these men residents, anything peculiar or ultra-feminine in the settlements, and one hearty young Englishman assured them that the disproportion was no greater than in England. "Or in some of our New England towns," said another citizen, "where the men have all gone west or to the big cities, and there's a whole township of withering women-folks with a few ministers and hired men."

The woman reporter questioned more deeply perhaps, perhaps less offensively; at any rate she learned more than the other of the true nature of the sudden civic growth. After both of them had turned in their reports, after all the other papers had sent down representatives, and later magazine articles had been written with impressive pictures, after the accounts of permitted visitors and tourists had been given, there came to be a fuller knowledge than was possible at first, naturally, but no one got a clearer vision of it all than was given to the woman reporter that first day, when she discovered that the Mayor of Herways was an old college mate of hers.

The story was far better than the one she sent in, but she was a lady as well as a reporter, and respected confidence.

It appeared that the whole thing started in that college class, the year after the reporter had left it, being suddenly forced to drop education and take to earning a living. In the senior class was a group of girls of markedly different types, and yet so similar in their basic beliefs and ultimate purposes that they had grown through the four years of college life into a little "sorority" of their own. They called it "The Morning Club," which sounded innocent enough, and kept it secret among themselves. They were girls of strong character, all of them, each with a definite purpose as to her life work.

There was the one they all called "Mother," because her whole heart and brain were dominated by the love of children, the thought of children, the wish to care for children; and very close to her was the "Teacher," with a third, the "Nurse," forming a group within a group. These three had endless discussions among themselves, with big vague plans for future usefulness.

Then there was the "Minister," the "Doctor," and the far-seeing one they called the "Statesman." One sturdy, squarebrowed little girl was dubbed "Manager" for reasons frankly prominent, as with the "Artist" and the "Engineer." There were some dozen or twenty of them, all choosing various professions, but all alike in their determination to practice those professions, married or single, and in their vivid hope for better methods of living. "Advanced" in their ideas they were, even in an age of advancement, and held together in especial by the earnest words of the Minister, who was always urging upon them the power of solidarity.

Just before their graduation something happened. It happened to the Manager, and she called a special meeting to lay it before the club.

The Manager was a plain girl, strong and quiet. She was the one who always overflowed with plans and possessed the unusual faculty of carrying out the plans she made, a girl who had always looked forward to working hard for her own living of choice as well as necessity, and enjoyed the prospect.

"Girls!" said she, when they were all grouped and quiet. "I've news for you—splendid news! I wouldn't spring it on you like this, but we shall be all broken and scattered in a little while—it's just in time!" She looked around at their eager faces, enjoying the sensation created.

"Say—look here!" she suddenly interjected. "You aren't any of you engaged, are you?"

One hand was lifted, modestly.

"What does he *do?*" pursued the speaker. "I don't care who he is, and I know he's all right or you wouldn't look at him—but what does he *do?*"

"He isn't sure yet," meekly answered the Minister, "but he's to be a manufacturer, I think."

"No objection to your preaching, of course." This was hardly a question.

"He says he'll hear me every Sunday—if I'll let him off at home on week-days," the Minister replied with a little giggle.

They all smiled approval.

"He's all right," the Manager emphatically agreed. "Now then girls—to put you out of your misery at once—what has happened to me is ten million dollars."

There was a pause, and then a joyous clapping of hands.

"Bully for you!"

"Hurrah for Margery!"

"You deserve it!"

"Say, you'll treat, won't you?"

They were as pleased as if the huge and sudden fortune were common property.

"Long lost uncle—or what, Marge?"

"Great uncle—my grandmother's brother. Went to California with the 'forty-niners'—got lost, for reasons of his own, I suspect. Found some prodigious gold mine—solid veins and nuggets, and spent quiet years in piling it up and investing it."

"When did he die?" asked the Nurse softly.

"He's not dead—but I'm afraid he soon will be," answered the Manager slowly. "It appears he's hired people to look up the family and see what they were like—said he didn't propose to ruin any feeble-minded people with all that money. He was pleased to like my record. Said—" she chuckled, "said I was a man after his own heart! And he's come on here to get acquainted and to make this over before he's gone. He says no dead man's bequest would be as safe as a live man's gift."

"And he's *given* you all that!"

"Solid and safe as can be. Says he's quite enough left to end his days in peace. He's pretty old. . . . Now then, girls—" She was all animation. "Here's my plan. Part of this property is land, land and water, in California. An upland valley, a little port on the coast— an economic base, you see—and capital to develop it. I propose that we form a combination, go out there, settle, build, manage—make a sample town—set a new example to the world—a place of woman's work and world-work too. . . . What do you say??"

They said nothing for the moment. This was a large proposition.

The Manager went on eagerly: "I'm not binding you to anything; this is a plain business offer. What I propose to do is to develop that little port, open a few industries and so on, build a reservoir up above and regulate the water supply—use it for power—have great gardens and vineyards. Oh, girls—it's California! We can make a little Eden! And as to Motherhood—" she looked around with a slow, tender smile, "there's no place better for babies!"

The Mother, the Nurse, and the Teacher all agreed to this.

"I've only got it roughly sketched out in my mind," pursued the speaker eagerly. "It will take time and care to work it all out right. But there's capital enough to tide us over first difficulties, and then it shall be just as solid and simple as any other place, a practical paying proposition, a perfectly natural little town, planned, built, and managed—" her voice grew solemn, "by women—for women— and *children!* A place that will be of real help to humanity.—Oh girls, it's such a chance!"

That was the beginning.

The woman reporter was profoundly interested. "I wish I could have stayed that year," she said soberly.

"I wish you had, Jean! But never mind—you can stay now. We need the right kind of work on our little local paper—not just reporting—you can do more than that, can't you?"

"I should hope so!" Jean answered heartily. "I spent six months on a little country paper—ran the whole thing nearly, except editorials and setting up. If there's room here for me I can tell you I'm coming—day before yesterday!" So the Woman Reporter came to Herways to work, and went up, o'nights, to Beewise to live, whereby she gradually learned in completeness what this bunch of women had done, and was able to prepare vivid little pamphlets of detailed explanations which paved the way for so many other regenerated towns.

And this is what they did:

The economic base was a large tract of land from the seacoast hills back to the high rich valley beyond. Two spring-fed brooks ran from the opposite ends of the valley and fell steeply to the beach below through narrow cañons.

The first cash outlay of the Manager, after starting the cable line from beach to hill which made the whole growth possible, was to build a reservoir at either end, one of which furnished drinking water and irrigation in the long summer, the other a swimming pool and steady stream of power. The powerhouse in the cañon was supplemented by wind-mills on the heights and tide-mill on the beach, and among them they furnished light, heat, and power— clean, economical electric energy. Later they set up a solar engine which furnished additional force, to minimize labor and add to their producing capacity.

For supporting industries, to link them with the world, they had these: First a modest export of preserved fruits, exquisitely prepared, packed in the new fibre cartons which are more sanitary than tin and lighter than glass. In the hills they raised Angora goats, and from their wool supplied a little mill with high-grade down-soft yarn, and sent out fluffy blankets, flannels and knitted garments. Cotton too they raised, magnificent cotton, and silk of the best, and their own mill supplied their principal needs. Small mills, pretty and healthful, with bright-clad women singing at their looms for the short working hours. From these materials the designers and craftswomen, helped by the Artist, made garments, beautiful, comfortable, easy and lasting, and from year to year the demand for "Beewise" gowns and coats increased.

In a windy corner, far from their homes, they set up a tannery, and from the well-prepared hides of their goats they made various leather goods, gloves and shoes, "Beewise" shoes, that came to be known at last through the length and breadth of the land—a shoe that fitted the human foot, allowed for free action, and was pleasant to the eye. Many of the townspeople wore sandals and they were also made for merchandise.

Their wooded heights they treasured carefully. A forestry service was started, the whole area studied, and the best rate of planting and cutting established. Their gardens were rich and beautiful; they sold honey, and distilled perfumes.

"This place is to grow in value, not deteriorate," said the Manager, and she planted for the future.

At first they made a tent city, the tents dyed with rich colors, dry-floored and warm. Later, the Artist and the Architect and the Engineer to the fore, they built houses of stone and wood and heavy sheathing paper, making their concrete of the dead palm leaves and the loose bark of swift-growing eucalyptus, which was planted everywhere and rose over night almost, like the Beanstalk—houses beautiful, comfortable, sea-shell clean.

Steadily the Manager held forth to her associates on what she called "the business end" of their enterprise. "The whole thing must pay," she said, "else it cannot stand—it will not be imitated. We want to show what a bunch of women can do successfully. Men can help, but this time we will manage.

Among their first enterprises was a guest house, planned and arranged mainly for women and children. In connection with this was a pleasure garden for all manner of games, gymnastics and dancing, with wide courts and fields and roofed places for use in the rainy season.

There was a sanitarium, where the Doctor and the Nurse gathered helpers about them, attended to casual illness, to the needs of child-birth, and to such visitors who came to them as needed care.

Further there was a baby-garden that grew to a kindergarten, and that to a school, and in time the fame of their educational work spread far and wide, and there was a constantly increasing list of applicants, for "Beewise" was a Residence club; no one could live there without being admitted by the others.

The beach town, Herways, teemed with industry. At the little pier their small coast steamer landed, bringing such supplies as they did not make, leaving and taking passengers. Where the beach was level and safe they bathed and swam, having a water-pavilion for shelter and refreshment. From beach to hill-top ran a shuttle service of light cars; "Jacob's Ladder," they called it.

The broad plan of the Manager was this: with her initial capital to develop a working plant that would then run itself at a profit, and she was surprised to find how soon that profit appeared, and how considerable it was.

Then came in sufficient numbers, friends, relatives, curious strangers. These women had no objection to marrying on their own terms. And when a man is sufficiently in love he sees no serious objection to living in an earthly paradise and doing his share in building up a new community. But the men were carefully selected. They must prove clean health—for a high grade of motherhood was the continuing ideal of the group.

Visitors came, increasing in numbers as accommodations increased. But as the accommodations, even to land for tenting, must be applied for beforehand, there was no horde of gaping tourists to vulgarize the place.

As for working people—there were no other. Everyone in Herways and Beewise worked, especially the women—that was the prime condition of admission; every citizen must be clean physically and morally as far as could be ascertained, but no amount of negative virtues availed them if they were not valuable in social service. So they had eager applications from professional women as fast as the place was known, and some they made room for—in proportion. Of doctors they could maintain but a few; a dentist or two, a handful of nurses, more teachers, several artists of the more practical sort who made beauty for the use of their neighbors, and a few far-reaching world servants, who might live here, at least part of the time, and send their work broadcast, such as poets, writers and composers.

But most of the people were the more immediately necessary workers, the men who built and dug and ran the engines, the women who spun and wove and worked among the flowers, or vice versa if they chose, and those who attended to the daily wants of the community.

There were no servants in the old sense. The dainty houses had no kitchens, only the small electric outfit where those who would might prepare coffee and the like. Food was prepared in clean wide laboratories, attended by a few skilled experts, highly paid, who knew their business, and great progress was made in the study of nutrition, and in the keeping of all the people well. Nevertheless the food cost less than if prepared by many unskilled, ill-paid cooks in imperfect kitchens.

The great art of child-culture grew apace among them with the best methods now known. Froebelian and Montessorian ideas and systems were honored and well used, and with the growing knowledge accumulated by years of observation and experience the right development of childhood at last became not merely an ideal, but a commonplace. Well-born children grew there like the roses they played among, raced and swam and swung, and knew only health, happiness and the joy of unconscious learning.

The two towns filled to their normal limits.

"Here we must stop," said the Manager in twenty years' time. "If we have more people here we shall develop the diseases of cities. But look at our financial standing—every cent laid out is now returned, the place is absolutely self-supporting and will grow richer as years pass. Now we'll swarm like the bees and start another— what do you say?"

And they did, beginning another rational paradise in another beautiful valley, safer and surer for the experience behind them.

But far wider than their own immediate increase was the spread of their ideas, of the proven truth of their idea, that a group of human beings could live together in such wise as to decrease the hours of labor, increase the value of the product, ensure health, peace and prosperity, and multiply human happiness beyond measure.

In every part of the world the thing was possible; wherever people could live at all they could live to better advantage. The economic base might vary widely, but wherever there were a few hundred women banded together their combined labor could produce wealth, and their combined motherhood ensure order, comfort, happiness, and the improvement of humanity.

"Go to the ant, thou sluggard, consider her ways and be wise."

Selection 12

"A Council of War"
The Forerunner 4.8 (August 1913): 197–201

Discussed Chapter 3, 68–69

*"A Council of War" develops three themes from Gilman's two listings:
the "inter-relation of women with women" (listed third in 1910); the
"effect of woman's new position upon industry and war" (listed third
in 1915); and the mature woman "as a human creature"—"married . . . , remarried, demarried, or not married at all" (listed fifth in
1915). Published the month after "Bee Wise," it presents the possibility of finding strategies for realizing such utopian changes as those
depicted the previous month. Gilman shows a group of women in the
process of implementing the societal changes they believe necessary.
The story recalls "A Cabinet Meeting" (Impress, 5 Jan. 1895: 4–5),
an imitation of Edward Bellamy, wherein a woman as President of
the United States asks for suggestions regarding the "problem before
us," namely "how to improve the people" (4), and it anticipates
"World Rousers" (Forerunner 6.5, May 1915: 131–32—concurrent
with Herland)—a one-page essay aiming to wake people up "to a
recognition of the real conditions now about them and their own
real powers" to reform these conditions (131). The story both models
possibilities and exhorts readers "to a recognition of the real conditions now about them and their own real powers" (131). World rousers [such as Gilman herself, readers must surmise] are to wake
people up and move us to action: "we cannot sleep as we used . . .
[given] the whirling changes of our times. We can do this and that;
not you or I, but We" (132). Gilman's 1915 call to action is fictionalized in this earlier 1913 short story.*

THERE WAS AN INFORMAL MEETING of women in a London drawing room, a meeting not over large, between twenty and thirty, perhaps, but of a deadly earnestness. Picked women were these, true and tried, many wearing the broad arrow pin, that badge of shame now turned to honor by sheer heroism. Some would qualify this as "blind" heroism or "senseless" heroism. But then, heroes have never been distinguished by a cautious farsightedness or a canny common sense.

No one, not even a one-ideaed physician, could call these women hysterical or morbid. On the contrary they wore a look of calm, uncompromising determination, and were vigorous and healthy enough, save indeed those who had been in prison, and one rather weazened working woman from the north. Still, no one had ever criticized the appearance of the working women, or called them hysterical, as long as they merely worked.

They had been recounting the measures taken in the last seven years, with their results, and though there was no sign of weakening in any face, neither was there any lively hope.

"It is the only way," said one, a slender pretty woman of over forty, who looked like a girl. "We've just got to keep it up, that's all."

"I'm willing enough," said one who wore the arrow badge, speaking with slow determination. Her courage was proved, and her endurance. "I'm *willing*—but we've got to be dead certain that it's really the best way."

"It's the only way"—protested Lady Horditch, a tall gentle earnest woman, with a pink face and quiet voice.

"They'll ruin us all—they're after the money now." This from a woman who had none of her own.

"They'll simply kill our leaders—one after another." One of the working women said that with a break in her voice. She could not lead, but she could follow—to the very end.

"One thing we have done, anyhow—we've forced their hand," suggested Mrs. Shortham, a pleasant matronly woman who had been most happily married, the mother of a large and fine family, now all grown and established—"we've made the men say what they really think of us—what they've really thought all the time— only they hid it—owing to chivalry."

Another thing is that we've brought out the real men—the best ones—we know our friends from our enemies, now," said a clear-eyed girl.

"It begins to look like war—in this country, at least," Lady Horwich remarked.

Little Mrs. Wedge suggested:

"It's a sort of strike, *I* think—begging your Ladyship's pardon. They're willing to have us—and use us—on their own terms. But we're on strike now—that's what we are! We're striking for shorter hours,"—she laughed a grim little laugh, intelligent smiles agreed with her, "and for higher wages, and for" there was a catch in her breath as she looked around at them—"for the Union!"

"Ah!"—and a deep breath all around, a warm handclasp from Lady Horditch who sat next to her, "Hear Hear!" from several.

Miss Waltress, a sturdy attractive blonde woman of about thirty, well-known for her highly popular love stories, had been sitting quite silent so far, listening to every word. Now she lifted her head.

"When men began to strike they were in small groups—fiercely earnest, but small and therefore weak. They were frequently violent. They were usually beaten on legal grounds, because of their violence; they were supplemented by others who took their places, or they were starved out—because of their poverty. Why do they so frequently succeed now?"

She looked at Mrs. Wedge from Lancashire, and Mrs. Wedge looked back at her with a kindling eye.

"Because there's so many of 'em now—and they hang together so well, and they keep on the safe side of the law, and they've got the brass."

Miss Waltress nodded. "Exactly," said she. "Now, friends, I've got something to suggest to you, something very earnest. Mrs. Shortham and I have been talking about it for days—she has something to say first."

"I think it comes with as good grace from me as from anybody," that lady began quietly. "All of you know how absolutely happy I was with one of the best men God ever made. That shows I'm not prejudiced. And it can't hurt his feelings, now. As to his 'memory'— he put me up to most of this, and urged me to publish it—but I—I just *couldn't* while he was alive."

Most of them had known Hugh Shortham, a tall deep-chested jovial man, always one of the most ardent advocates of the enlargement of women. His big manliness, his efficiency and success, had always made him a tower of strength against those who still talk of "short-haired women and long-haired men" as the sole supporters of this cause.

What Mrs. Shortham now read was a brief but terrible indictment of what the title called "The Human Error." It recounted the evil results of male rule, as affecting the health, beauty, intelligence, prosperity, progress and happiness of humanity, in such clear and terrible terms, with such an accumulating pile of injuries, that faces grew white and lips set in hard steely lines as they listened.

"All this does not in the least militate against the beauty and use of true manhood in right relation to women, nor does it contradict the present superior development of men in all lines of social progress. It does, however, in some sort make out the case against man. There follows the natural corollary that we, the women of to-day, seeing these things, must with all speed possible set ourselves to remove this devastating error in relation, and to establish a free and conscious womanhood for the right service of the world."

There was a hot silence, with little murmurs of horror at some of the charges she had made, and a stir of new determination. Not all of them, keen as they were for the ballot, deeply as they felt the unnecessary sorrows of women, had ever had the historic panorama of injustice and its deadly consequences so vividly set before them.

"I knew it was bad enough," broke forth little Mrs. Wedge, "but I never knew it was as bad as *that*. Look at the consequences."

"That's exactly it, Mrs. Wedge! It's the consequences we are looking at. We are tired of these consequences. We want some new ones!" and Miss Waltress looked around the room, from face to face.

"I'm ready!" said a pale thin woman with an arrow pin.

They were, every one of them. Then Miss Waltress began.

"What I have to suggest, is a wider, deeper, longer, stronger strike."

Mrs. Wedge, her eyes fixed on the calm earnest face, drew in her breath with a big intake.

"Even if we get the ballot in a year—the work is only begun. Men have had that weapon for a good while now, and they have not accomplished everything—even for themselves. And if we do not get it in a year—or five—or ten—are we to do nothing in all that time save repeat what we have done before? I know the ballot is the best weapon, but—there are others. There are enough of us to keep up our previous tactics as long as we hold it necessary. I say nothing whatever against it. But there are also enough of us to be doing other things too.

"Here is my suggestion. We need a government within a government; an organization of women, growing and strengthening against the time when it may come forward in full equality with that of men; a training school for world-politics. This may become a world-group, holding international meetings and influencing the largest issues. I speak here only of a definite, practical beginning in this country.

"Let us form a committee, called, perhaps, 'Advisory Committee on Special Measures,' or simpler still, we might call it 'Extension Committee'—that tells nothing, and has no limitations.

"The measures I propose are these:—

"That we begin a series of business undertakings, plain ordinary, every day businesses—farms, market gardens, greenhouses, small fruits, preserves, confections, bakeries, eating-houses, boarding and lodging houses, hotels, milliners and dressmakers' shops, laundries, schools, kindergartens, nurseries—any and every business which women can enter.

"Yes, I know that women are in these things now—but they are not united, not organized. This is a great spreading league of interconnected businesses, with the economic advantages of such large union."

"Like a trust," said Mrs. Shortham.

"A woman's trust."

"Or a Co-operative Society—or a Friendly," breathed little Mrs. Wedge, her cheeks flushing.

"Yes, all this and more. This is no haphazard solitary struggle of isolated women, competing with men, this is a body of women that can grow to an unlimited extent, and be stronger and richer as it grows. But it can be as small as you please, and without any noise whatever.

"Now see here—you all know how women are sweated and exploited; how they overwork us and underpay us, and how they try to keep us out of trades and professions just as the Americans try to keep out Chinese labor—because they are afraid of being driven out of the market by a lower standard of living.

"Very well. Suppose we take them on their own terms. *Because* we can live on nothing a week and find ourselves—therefore we can cut the ground out from under their feet!"

The bitter intensity of her tones made a little shiver run around the circle, but they all shared her feeling.

"Don't imagine I mean to take over the business of the world by no means. But I mean to initiate a movement which means on the surface, in immediate results, only some women going into business —that's no novelty! Underneath it means a great growing association with steady increase of power."

"To what end—as a war measure, I mean?" Lady Horwich inquired.

"To several ends. The most patent, perhaps, is to accumulate the sinews of war. The next is to become owners of halls to speak in, of printing and publishing offices, of paper mills perhaps, of more and more of the necessary machinery needed for our campaign. The third is to train more and more women in economic organization, in the simple daily practice of modern business methods, and to guarantee to more and more of them that foundation stone of all other progress, economic independence. The fourth is to establish in all these businesses as we take them up, *right conditions*—proper hours, proper wages, everything as it should be."

"Employing women, only?"

"As far as possible, Mrs. Wedge. And when men are needed, employing the right kind."

There was a thoughtful silence.

"It's an ENORMOUS undertaking," murmured the Honorable Miss Erwood, a rather grim faced spinster of middle age. "How can you get 'em to do it?"

Miss Waltress met her cheerfully.

"It is enormous, but natural. It does not require a million women to start at once you see; or any unusual undertaking. The advisory central committee will keep books and make plans. Each business, little or big, starts wherever it happens to be needed. The connection is not visible. That connection involves in the first place definite help and patronage in starting, or in increasing the custom of one already started; second, an advantage in buying—which will increase as the allied businesses increase; and then the paying to the central committee of a small annual fee. As the membership increases, all these advantages increase—in arithmetical progression."

"Is the patronage in your plan confined to our society? or to sympathizers?" pursued Miss Erwood.

"By no means. The very essence of the scheme is to meet general demands to prove the advantage of clean honest efficiency.

"Now, for instance—" Miss Waltress turned over a few notes she held in a neat package—"here is—let us say—the necktie trade. Now neckties are not laborious to make—as a matter of fact women do make them to-day. Neckties are not difficult to sell. As a matter of fact women frequently sell them. Silk itself was first made use of by a woman, and the whole silk industry might be largely in their hands. Designing, spinning, weaving, dyeing, we might do it all.

But in the mere matters of making and selling the present day necktie of mankind, there is absolutely nothing to prevent our stretching out a slow soft hand, and gathering in the business. We might begin in the usual spectacular 'feminine' way. A dainty shop in a good street, some fine girls, level-headed ones, who are working for the cause, to sell neckties, or—here is an advertising suggestion—we might call it 'The Widows' Shop' and employ only widows. There are always enough of the poor things needing employment.

"Anyhow we establish a trade in neckties, fine neckties, good taste, excellent materials, reliable workmanship. When it is sufficiently prosperous, it branches—both in town and in the provinces—little by little we could build up such a reputation that 'Widow Shop Neckties' would have a definite market value the world over. Meanwhile we could have our own workrooms, regular show places—patrons could see the neckties made, short hours, good wages, low prices."

She was a little breathless, but very eager. "Now I know you are asking how we are going to make all these things *pay,* for they must, if we are to succeed. You see, in ordinary business each one preys on the others. We propose to have an interconnected group that will help one another—that is where the profit comes. This was only a single instance, just one industry, but now I'll outline a group. Suppose we have a bit of land in some part of the country that is good for small fruit raising, and we study and develop that industry to its best. For the product we open a special shop in town, or at first, perhaps getting patronage by circularizing among our present membership, but winning our market by the goodness of the product and the reasonable price. Then we have a clean, pretty, scientific preserving room, and every bit of the unsold fruit is promptly turned into jam or jelly or syrup, right in sight of the patrons. They can see it done—and take it home, 'hot' if they wish to, or mark the jars and have them sent. That would be a legitimate beginning of a business that has practically no limits—and if it isn't a woman's business, I don't know what is!

"Now this could get a big backing of steady orders from boarding houses and hotels managed by women, and gradually more and more of these would be run by our own members. Then we could begin to effect a combination with Summer lodgings—think what missionary work it would be to establish a perfect chain of Summer boarding houses which should be as near perfect as is humanly possible, and all play into one another's hands and into our small market garden local ventures.

"On such a chain of hotels we could found a growing laundry business. In connection with the service required, we could open an Employment Agency; in connection with that a Training School for Modern Employees—not 'slaveys,' to be 'exploited' by the average household, but swift, accurate, efficient, self-respecting young women, unionized and working for our own patrons. That would lead to clubhouses for these girls—and for other working girls; and step by step, as the circles widened, we should command a market for our own produce that would be a tremendous business asset."

She paused, looking about her, eager and flushed. Mrs. Shortham took up the tale in her calm, sweet voice.

"You see how it opens," she said. "Beginning with simple practical local affairs—a little laundry here, a little bakeshop there; a fruit garden—honey, vegetables—what you like; with dressmakers and milliners and the rest. It carries certain definite advantages from the start; good conditions, wages, hours; and its range of possible growth is quite beyond our calculations. And it requires practically no capital. We have simply to plan, to create, to arrange, and the pledged patronage of say a thousand women of those now interested would mean backing enough to start any modest business.

"There are women among us who have money enough to make several beginnings," Lady Horwich suggested.

"There'll be no trouble about that—we have to be sure of the working plan, that's all," Miss Erwood agreed.

"There's a-plenty of us workers that could put it through—with good will!" Mrs. Wedge confidently asserted. "We're doing most of this work you speak of now, with cruel hours and a dog's wages. This offers a job to a woman with everything better than she had before—you'll have no trouble with the workers."

"But how about the funds?—there might be a great deal of money in time," suggested Mrs. Doughton-Highbridge. "Who would handle it?"

"There would have to be a financial committee of our very best —names we all know and trust; and then the whole thing should be kept open and above board, as far as possible.

"There should be certain small return benefits—that would attract many; a steady increase in the business, and a 'war chest'— the reserve power to meet emergencies."

"I don't quite see how it would help us to get the ballot," one earnest young listener now remarked, and quiet Mrs. Shortham answered out of a full heart.

"Oh, my dear! Don't you see? In the mere matter of funds and membership it will help. In the very practical question of public opinion it will help; success in a work of this sort carries conviction with it. It will help as an immense machine for propaganda—all the growing numbers of our employees and fellow-members, all these shops and their spreading patronage. It will help directly as soon as we can own some sort of hall to speak in, in all large towns, and our own publishing house and printing shop. And while we are waiting and working and fighting for the ballot, this would be improving life for more and more women all the time."

"And it would carry the proof that the good things we want done are practical and *can* be done—it would promote all good legislation," Miss Waltress added.

"I see; it's all a practical good thing from the start," said Miss Erwood, rather argumentatively. "To begin with, it's just plain good work. Furnishes employment and improves conditions. And from that up, there is no top to it—it's education and organization, widening good fellowship and increasing power—I'm for it definitely."

"It would be a world within a world—ready to come out full-grown a woman's world, clean and kind and safe and serviceable," Lady Horwich murmured, as if to herself. "Ladies, I move that a committee be appointed forthwith, consisting of Mrs. Shortham, Mrs. Wedge and Miss Waltress, with power to consult as widely as they see fit, and to report further as to this proposition at our next meeting."

The motion was promptly seconded, as promptly carried, and the women looked at one another with the light of a new hope in their eyes.

Selection 13

Chapter 5: "A Unique History" from
Herland, The Forerunner 6.5 (May 1915): 123–29

Discussed Chapter 3, 69–76

*"If," Gilman wrote in her 1910 discussion of "Masculine Literature,"
"the beehive produced literature, the bee's fiction would be rich and
broad; full of the complex tasks of comb-building and filling; the care
and feeding of the young, the guardian-service of the queen. It would
treat of the vast fecundity of motherhood, the educative and selective
processes of the group-mothers; and the passion of loyalty, of social
service, which holds the hive together" (21). Such are the subjects of*
Herland, *an account of an imagined society surpassing in its fictional
power the hortatory vigor of Gilman's* Women and Economics. *Like
Diantha's speech, this chapter of historical exposition demonstrates
Gilman's blending of genres, a fictional possibility for which Bakhtin
extols the novel in his "Discourse in the Novel" (1981, 410–14).*

*Interesting as an indication of a changed evaluation is the fact
that, in 1915, when she was in the process of writing* Herland, *Gilman listed the "mother-love story" first, whereas in 1910 she had
thought it fourth place. A not-surprising second place is "the story of
the child"—children being "the most valuable people on earth" for
the residents in* Moving the Mountain. *In* Herland, *Gilman develops
each of the new fictional fields that she finds "the humanizing of
woman" to have opened up.*

*In particular this chapter, "A Unique History," provides parallels
to chapter 11 from* With Her in Ourland, *but, more important, in
providing* Herland's *historical development, it makes clear what Herlanders value. This chapter harks back to earlier presentations of*

education and religion. And Herland *as a whole restores to fiction
what Gilman, in 1915, denounced as literary oversight—namely, "ignoring that great goddess of mother-love in whose service young Eros
["the god of man's desire"] is but a running footman" (18). Twice in
the following chapter Gilman alludes to a Mother Goddess, to a religion that is a "sort of Maternal Pantheism."*

*Readers would do well to consider these references a survival
(revival?) of interest in a goddess thealogy* [sic.]. *In 1861, Johann
Jakob Bachofen's* Das Mutterrecht *(Motherright) appeared. From
this book, along with other contemporary studies, "an all but world-
wide distribution" of a "prepatriarchal order of communal life" was
recognized, according to Joseph Campbell (Gimbutas, xiii). A characteristic of such an order is worship of a goddess-mother creator,
whose divine body is the universe itself, including all its living
things. Recently Riane Eisler, Elinor Gadon, and Marija Gimbutas,
among others, have again argued this claim. Gilman's* Herland
*stands as a historical marker partaking of a religous tradition of
goddess-worship, a gynaecocentric as opposed to androcentric religion; however, I must add the cautionary note that, in comparison to
current goddess thealogy, Gilman's view does not embrace human
diversity (see Culpepper 1987).*

Synopsis [Forerunner 6: 123]: Three young men discover an unknown country in which there are only women, by whom they are
presently captured. They escape, but are recaptured.

IT IS NO USE for me to try to piece out this account with adventures.
If the people who read it are not interested in these amazing women
and their history, they will not be interested at all.

As for us—three young men to a whole landful of women—what
could we do? We did get away, as described, and were peacefully
brought back again without, as Terry complained, even the satisfaction of hitting anybody.

There were no adventures because there was nothing to fight.
There were no wild beasts in the country and very few tame ones.
Of these I might as well stop to describe the one common pet of the
country. Cats, of course. But such cats!

What do you suppose these lady Burbanks had done with their
cats? By the most prolonged and careful selection and exclusion
they had developed a race of cats that did not sing! That's a fact.

The most those poor dumb brutes could do was to make a kind of squeak when they were hungry or wanted the door open; and, of course, to purr, and make the various mother-noises to their kittens.

Moreover they had ceased to kill birds. They were rigorously bred to destroy mice and moles and all such enemies of the food supply; but the birds were numerous and safe.

While we were discussing birds, Terry asked them if they used feathers for their hats, and they seemed amused at the idea. He made a few sketches of our women's hats, with plumes and quills and those various tickling things that stick out so far; and they were eagerly interested, as at everything about our women.

As for them, they said they only wore hats for shade when working in the sun; and those were big light straw hats, something like those used in China and Japan. In cold weather they wore caps or hoods.

"But for decorative purposes—don't you think they would be becoming?" pursued Terry, making a picture as he could of a lady with a plumed straw hat.

They by no means agreed to that, asking quite simply if the men wore the same kind. We hastened to assure her that they did not—and drew for them our kind of headgear.

"And do no men wear feathers in their hats?"

"Only Indians," Jeff explained, "savages, you know." And he sketched a war-bonnet to show them.

"And soldiers," I added, drawing a military hat with plumes.

They never expressed horror or disapproval, nor indeed much surprise—just a keen interest. And the notes they made!—miles of them!

But to return to our pussy-cats. We were a good deal impressed by this achievement in breeding, and when they questioned us—I can tell you we were well pumped for information—we told of what had been done for dogs and horses and cattle, but that there was no effort applied to cats, except for show purposes.

I wish I could represent the kind, quiet, steady, ingenious way they questioned us. It was not just curiosity—they weren't a bit more curious about us than we were about them, if as much. But they were bent on understanding our kind of civilization and their lines of interrogation would gradually surround us and drive us in till we found ourselves up against some admissions we did not want to make.

"Are all these breeds of dogs you have made useful?" they asked.

"Oh—useful! Why, the hunting dogs and watch-dogs and sheep-dogs are useful—and sled-dogs of course!—and ratters, I suppose, but we don't keep dogs for their *usefulness*. The dog is 'the friend of man,' we say—we love them."

That they understood. "We love our cats that way. They surely are our friends, and helpers too. You can see how intelligent and affectionate they are."

It was a fact. I'd never seen such cats, except in a few rare instances. Big, handsome silky things, friendly with everyone and devotedly attached to their special owners.

"You must have a heartbreaking time drowning kittens," we suggested.

But they said: "Oh, no! You see we care for them as you do for your valuable cattle. The fathers are few compared to the mothers, just a few very fine ones in each town; they live quite happily in walled gardens and the houses of their friends. But they only have a mating season once a year."

"Rather hard on Thomas, isn't it?" suggested Terry.

"Oh, no—truly! You see it is many centuries that we have been breeding the kind of cats we wanted. They are healthy and happy and friendly, as you see. How do you manage with your dogs? Do you keep them in pairs, or segregate the fathers, or what?"

Then we explained that—well, that it wasn't a question of fathers exactly; that nobody wanted a—a mother dog; that, well, that practically all our dogs were males—there was only a very small percentage of females allowed to live.

Then Zava, observing Terry with her grave sweet smile, quoted back at him: "Rather hard on Thomas, isn't it? Do they enjoy it—living without mates? Are your dogs as uniformly healthy and sweet-tempered as our cats?"

Jeff laughed, eyeing Terry mischievously. As a matter of fact we began to feel Jeff something of a traitor—he so often flopped over and took their side of things; also his medical knowledge gave him a different point of view somehow.

"I'm sorry to admit," he told them, "that the dog, with us, is the most diseased of any animal—next to man. And as to temper—there are always some dogs who bite people especially children."

That was pure malice. You see children were the—the *raison d'être* in this country. All our interlocutors sat up straight at once. They were still gentle, still restrained, but there was a note of deep amazement in their voices.

"Do we understand that you keep an animal—an unmated male animal—that bites children? About how many are there of them, please?"

"Thousands—in a large city," said Jeff, "and nearly every family has one in the country."

Terry broke in at this. "You must not imagine they are all dangerous—it's not one in a hundred that ever bites anybody. Why, they are the best friends of the children—a boy doesn't have half a chance that hasn't a dog to play with!"

"And the girls?" asked Somel.

"Oh—girls—why they like them too," he said, but his voice flatted a little. They always noticed little things like that, we found later.

Little by little they wrung from us the fact that the friend of man, in the city, was a prisoner; was taken out for his meager exercise on a leash; was liable not only to many diseases, but to the one destroying horror of rabies, and, in many cases, for the safety of the citizens, he had to go muzzled. Jeff maliciously added vivid instances he had known or read of injury and death from mad dogs.

They did not scold or fuss about it. Calm as judges, those women were. But they made notes; Moadine read them to us.

"Please tell me if I have the facts correct," she said. "In your country—and in others too?"

"Yes," we admitted, "in most civilized countries."

"In most civilized countries a kind of animal is kept which is no longer useful—"

"They are a protection," Terry insisted. "They bark if burglars try to get in."

Then she made notes of "burglars" and went on: "because of the love which people bear to this animal."

Zava interupted here. "Is it the men or the women who love this animal so much?"

"Both!" insisted Terry.

"Equally?" she inquired.

And Jeff said: "Nonsense, Terry—you know men like dogs better than women do—as a whole."

"Because they love it so much—especially men. This animal is kept shut up, or chained."

"Why?" suddenly asked Somel. "We keep our father cats shut up because we do not want too much fathering; but they are not chained—they have large grounds to run in."

"A valuable dog would be stolen if he was let loose," I said. "We put collars on them, with the owner's name, in case they do stray. Besides, they get into fights—a valuable dog might easily be killed by a bigger one."

"I see," she said. "They fight when they meet—is that common?" We admitted that it was.

"They are kept shut up, or chained." She paused again, and asked, "Is not a dog fond of running? Are they not built for speed?" That we admitted too, and Jeff, still malicious, enlightened them farther.

"I've always thought it was a pathetic sight, both ways—to see a man or a woman taking a dog to walk—at the end of a string."

"Have you bred them to be as neat in their habits as cats are?" was the next question. And when Jeff told them of the effect of dogs on sidewalk merchandise and the streets generally, they found it hard to believe.

You see their country was as neat as a Dutch kitchen, and as to sanitation—but I might as well start in now with as much as I can remember of the history of this amazing country before further description.

And I'll summarize here a bit as to our opportunities for learning it. I will not try to repeat the careful, detailed account I lost; I'll just say that we were kept in that fortress a good six months all told; and after that, three in a pleasant enough city where—to Terry's infinite disgust—there were only "Colonels" and little children—no young women whatever. Then we were under surveillance for three more—always with a tutor or a guard or both. But those months were pleasant because we were really getting acquainted with the girls. That was a chapter!—or will be—I will try to do justice to it.

We learned their language pretty thoroughly—had to; and they learned ours much more quickly and used it to hasten our own studies.

Jeff, who was never without reading matter of some sort, had two little books with him, a novel, and a little anthology of verse; and I had one of those pocket encyclopedias—a fat little thing, bursting with facts. These were used in our education—and theirs. Then as soon as we were up to it, they furnished us with plenty of their own books, and I went in for the history part—I wanted to understand the genesis of this miracle of theirs.

And this is what happened, according to their records:

As to geography—at about the time of the Christian era this land had a free passage to the sea. I'm not saying where, for good reasons. But there was a fairly easy pass through that wall of mountains behind us, and there is no doubt in my mind that these people were of Aryan stock, and were once in contact with the best civilization of the old world. They were "white," but somewhat darker than our northern races because of their constant exposure to sun and air.

The country was far larger then, including much land beyond the pass, and a strip of coast. They had ships, commerce, an army, a king—for at that time they were what they so calmly called us—a bi-sexual [two-sexed] race.

What happened to them first was merely a succession of historic misfortunes such as have befallen other nations often enough. They were decimated by war, driven up from their coast line till finally the reduced population with many of the men killed in battle, occupied this hinterland, and defended it for years, in the mountain passes. Where it was open to any possible attack from below they strengthened the natural defences so that it became unscalably secure, as we found it.

They were a polygamous people, and a slave-holding people, like all of their time; and during the generation or two of this struggle to defend their mountain home they built the fortresses, such as the one we were held in, and other of their oldest buildings, some still in use. Nothing but earthquakes could destroy such architecture— huge solid blocks, holding by their own weight. They must have had efficient workmen and enough of them in those days.

They made a brave fight for their existence, but no nation can stand up against what the steamship companies call "an act of God." While the whole fighting force was doing its best to defend their mountain pathway, there occurred a volcanic outburst, with some local tremors, and the result was the complete filling up of the pass —their only outlet. Instead of a passage, a new ridge, sheer and high, stood between them and the sea; they were walled in, and beneath that wall lay their whole little army. Very few men were left alive, save the slaves; and these now seized their opportunity, rose in revolt, killed their remaining masters even to the youngest boy, killed the old women too, and the mothers, intending to take possession of the country with the remaining young women and girls.

But this succession of misfortunes was too much for those infuriated virgins. There were many of them, and but few of these would-be masters, so the young women, instead of submitting, rose in sheer desperation, and slew their brutal conquerors.

This sounds like Titus Andronicus, I know, but that is their account. I suppose they were about crazy—can you blame them?

There was literally no one left on this beautiful high garden land but a bunch of hysterical girls and some older slave women.

That was about two thousand years ago.

At first there was a period of sheer despair. The mountains towered between them and their old enemies, but also between them and escape. There was no way up or down or out—they simply had to stay there. Some were for suicide, but not the majority. They must have been a plucky lot, as a whole, and they decided to live—as long as they did live. Of course they had hope, as youth must, that something would happen to change their fate.

So they set to work, to bury the dead, to plow and sow, to care for one another.

Speaking of burying the dead, I will set down while I think of it, that they had adopted cremation about the thirteenth century, for the same reason that they had left off raising cattle—they could not spare the room. They were much surprised to learn that we were still burying—asked our reasons for it, and were much dissatisfied with what we gave. We told them of the belief in the resurrection of the body, and they asked if our God was not as well able to resurrect from ashes as from long corruption. We told them of how people thought it repugnant to have their loved ones burn, and they asked if it was less repugnant to have them decay. They were inconveniently reasonable, those women.

Well—that original bunch of girls set to work to clean up the place and make their livings as best they could. Some of the remaining slave women rendered invaluable service, teaching such trades as they knew. They had such records as were then kept, all the tools and implements of the time, and a most fertile land to work in.

There were a handful of the younger matrons who had escaped slaughter, and a few babies were born after the cataclysm—but only two boys and they both died.

For five or ten years they worked together, growing stronger and wiser and more and more mutually attached, and then the miracle happened—one of these young women bore a child. Of course they all thought there must be a man somewhere, but none was found. Then they decided it must be a direct gift from the gods, and placed the proud mother in the Temple of Maaia—their Goddess of Motherhood—under strict watch. And there, as years passed, this wonder-woman bore child after child, five of them—all girls.

I did my best, keenly interested as I have always been in sociology and social psychology, to reconstruct in my mind the real position of these ancient women. There were some five or six hundred of them, and they were harem-bred; yet for the few preceding generations they had been reared in the atmosphere of such heroic struggle that the stock must have been toughened somewhat. Left alone in that terrific orphanhood, they had clung together, supporting one another and their little sisters, and developing unknown powers in the stress of new necessity. To this pain-hardened and work-strengthened group, who had lost not only the love and care of parents, but the hope of ever having children of their own, there now dawned the new hope.

Here at last was Motherhood, and though it was not for all of them personally, it might—if the Power was inherited—found here a new race.

It may be imagined how those five Daughters of Maaia, Children of the Temple, Mothers of the Future—they had all the titles that love and hope and reverence could give—were reared. The whole little nation of women surrounded them with loving service, and waited, between a boundless hope and an as boundless despair, to see if they too would be Mothers.

And they were! As fast as they reached the age of twenty-five they began bearing. Each of them, like her mother, bore five daughters. Presently there were twenty-five New Women, Mothers in their own right, and the whole spirit of the country changed from mourning and mere courageous resignation, to proud joy. The older women, those who remembered men, died off; the youngest of all the first lot of course died too, after a while, and by that time there were left one hundred and fifty-five parthenogenetic women, founding a new race.

They inherited all that the devoted care of that declining band of original ones could leave them. Their little country was quite safe. Their farms and gardens were all in full production. Such industries as they had were in careful order. The records of their past were all preserved, and for years the older women had spent their time in the best teaching they were capable of, that they might leave to the little group of sisters and mothers all they possessed of skill and knowledge.

There you have the start of Herland! One family, all descended from one mother! She lived to be a hundred years old; lived to see her hundred and twenty-five great-granddaughters born; lived as Queen-Priestess-Mother of them all; and died with a nobler pride and a fuller joy than perhaps any human soul has ever known—she alone had founded a new race!

The first five daughters had grown up in an atmosphere of holy calm, of awed watchful waiting, of breathless prayer. To them the longed-for Motherhood was not only a personal joy, but a nation's hope. Their twenty-five daughters in turn, with a stronger hope, a richer, wider outlook, with the devoted love and care of all the surviving population, grew up as a holy sisterhood, their whole ardent youth looking forward to their great office. And at last they were left alone; the white-haired First Mother was gone, and this one family, five sisters, twenty-five first cousins, and a hundred and twenty-five second cousins, began a new race.

Here you have human beings, unquestionably, but what we were slow in understanding was how these ultra-women, inheriting only from women, had eliminated not only certain masculine characteristics, which of course we did not look for; but so much of what we had always thought essentially feminine.

The tradition of men as guardians and protectors had quite died out. These stalwart virgins had no men to fear and therefore no need of protection. As to wild beasts—there were none in their sheltered land.

The power of mother-love, that maternal instinct we so highly laud, was theirs of course, raised to its highest power; and a sister-love which, even while recognizing the actual relationship, we found it hard to credit.

Terry, incredulous, even contemptuous, when we were alone, refused to believe the story. "A lot of traditions as old as Herodotus —and about as trustworthy!" he said. "It's likely women—just a pack of women—would have hung together like that! We all know women can't organize—that they scrap like anything—are frightfully jealous.

"But these New Ladies didn't have anyone to be jealous of, remember," drawled Jeff.

"That's a likely story," Terry sneered.

"Why don't you invent a likelier one?" I asked him. "Here *are* the women—nothing but women, and you admit yourself there's no trace of a man in the country." This was after we had been about a good deal.

"I'll admit that," he growled. "And it's a big miss, too. There's not only no fun without 'em—no real sport—no competition; but these women aren't *womanly*. You know they aren't."

That kind of talk always set Jeff going; and I gradually grew to side with him. "Then you don't call a breed of women whose one concern is Motherhood—womanly?" he asked.

"Indeed I don't," snapped Terry. "What does a man care for motherhood—when he hasn't a ghost of a chance at fatherhood? And besides—what's the good of talking sentiment when we are just men together? What a man wants of women is a good deal more than all this 'motherhood'!"

We were as patient as possible with Terry. He had lived about nine months among the Colonels when he made that outburst; and with no chance at any more strenuous excitement than our gymnastics gave us—save for our escape fiasco. I don't suppose Terry had ever lived so long with neither Love, Combat, nor Danger to employ his superabundant energies, and he was irritable. Neither Jeff nor I found it so wearing. I was so much interested intellectually that our confinement did not wear on me; and as for Jeff, bless his heart! —he enjoyed the society of that tutor of his almost as much as if she had been a girl—I don't know but more.

As to Terry's criticism, it was true. These women, whose essential distinction of Motherhood was the dominant note of their whole culture, were strikingly deficient in what we call "femininity." This led me very promptly to the conviction that those "feminine charms" we are so fond of are not feminine at all, but mere reflected masculinity—developed to please us because they had to please us—and in no way essential to the real fulfillment of their great process. But Terry came to no such conclusion.

"Just you wait till I get out!" he muttered.

Then we both cautioned him. "Look here, Terry, my boy! You be careful! They've been mighty good to us—but do you remember the anaesthesia? If you do any mischief in this virgin land, beware of the vengeance of the Maiden Aunts! Come, be a man! It won't be forever."

To return to the history:

They began at once to plan and build for their children, all the strength and intelligence of the whole of them devoted to that one thing. Each girl, of course, was reared in full knowledge of her Crowning Office, and they had, even then, very high ideas of the moulding powers of the mother, as well as those of education.

Such high ideals as they had! Beauty, Health, Strength, Intellect, Goodness—for these they prayed and worked.

They had no enemies; they themselves were all sisters and friends; the land was fair before them, and a great Future began to form itself in their minds.

The religion they had to begin with was much like that of old Greece—a number of gods and goddesses; but they lost all interest in deities of war and plunder, and gradually centered on their Mother Goddess altogether. Then, as they grew more intelligent, this had turned into a sort of Maternal Pantheism.

Here was Mother Earth, bearing fruit. All that they ate was fruit of motherhood, from seed or egg or their product. By motherhood they were born and by motherhood they lived—life was, to them, just the long cycle of motherhood.

But very early they recognized the need of improvement as well as of mere repetition, and devoted their combined intelligence to that problem—how to make the best kind of people. First this was merely the hope of bearing better ones, and then they recognized that however the children differed at birth, the real growth lay later —through education.

Then things began to hum.

As I learned more and more to appreciate what these women had accomplished, the less proud I was of what we, with all our manhood, had done.

You see, they had had no wars. They had had no kings, and no priests, and no aristocracies. They were sisters, and as they grew, they grew together; not by competition, but by united action.

We tried to put in a good word for competition, and they were keenly interested. Indeed we soon found, from their earnest questions of us, that they were prepared to believe our world must be better than theirs. They were not sure; they wanted to know; but there was no such arrogance about them as might have been expected.

We rather spread ourselves, telling of the advantages of competition; how it developed fine qualities; that without it there would be "no stimulus to industry." Terry was very strong on that point.

"No stimulus to industry," they repeated, with that puzzled look we had learned to know so well. *"Stimulus? To Industry? But don't you *like* to work?"*

"No man would work unless he had to," Terry declared.

"Oh, no *man!* You mean that is one of your sex distinctions?"

"No, indeed!" he said hastily. "No one, I mean, man or woman, would work without incentive. Competition is the—the motor power, you see."

"It is not with us," they explained gently, "so it is hard for us to understand. Do you mean, for instance, that with you no mother would work for her children without the stimulus of competition?"

No, he admitted that he did not mean that. Mothers, he supposed, would of course work for their children in the home; but the world's work was different—that had to be done by men, and required the competitive element.

All our teachers were eagerly interested.

"We want so much to know—you have the whole world to tell us of, and we have only our little land! And there are two of you—the two sexes—to love and help one another. It must be a rich and wonderful world. Tell us—what is the work of the world, that men do—which we have not here?"

"Oh, everything," Terry said, grandly. "The men do everything, with us." He squared bis broad shoulders and lifted his chest. "We do not allow our women to work. Women are loved—idolized—honored—kept in the home to care for the children."

"What is 'the home'?" asked Somel a little wistfully.

But Zava begged: "Tell me first, do no women work, really?"

"Why, yes," Terry admitted. "Some have to, of the poorer sort."

"About how many—in your country?"

"About seven or eight million," said Jeff, as mischievous as ever.

Selection 14

Chapter 11 from
With Her in Ourland, The Forerunner 7.11
(November 1916): 291–97

[Van and Ellador's discussion of feminist issues]

Discussed Chapter 3, 76–78

In contrast to the history of Herland, this chapter presents the 1920s history of women in Ourland and ends with a plea regarding "what we are here for"—this "we" implicating you and me, Gilman's readers.

What is striking in this chapter—a conversation reported by Van between himself and his wife, Ellador—is Gilman's stressing, through the voice of Ellador, our current understanding of social change and of utopian realization as changes of mind. Sociology of symbolic interaction, as in Erving Goffman's Frame Analysis *(1974), and feminist standpoint theory (ably developed by Iris Young, Donna Haraway, Sandra Harding, and especially Nancy Hartsock 1983), as well as critiques of ideology, place viewpoint at the center of behavior. Utopian scholar Lee Cullen Khanna has argued that, in recent feminist utopias, "the reader finds utopia in the process of experiencing a convincing fiction, and finds it—not 'out there' in another place or time—but within the self" (1981, 59). In Ellador, Gilman recognizes this utopian possibility of a changed mind, the result Gilman expected for readers of her fiction.*

Utopia then begins to be realized as changed minds lead to changed behaviors. As the visitor in "A Strange Land" states, "People were after all the principal things to produce, maintain, and improve.

. . . They gave their minds to the problem of How to Make Better People, and continually studied it." The end of the following chapter repeats this point. Charlotte Perkins Gilman, again through Ellador, surmises that three generations will be needed to effect changed people, the very span Elizabeth Stuart Phelps had surmised to be required for the creation of a new woman (The Story of Avis, *1877, repr. 1988, 246–47). The rest is now up to us.*

IT WAS INEVITABLE that my wife should take a large interest in Feminism. With that sweeping swiftness of hers she read a dozen or so of the leading—and misleading—books on the subject; spent some time in library work looking over files of papers and talked with all manner of people we met who had views on the matter. Furthermore, she thought about it.

As I grew more and more accustomed to seeing Ellador think, or at least to seeing the results of that process, I was sharply struck with the lack of thinking among people in general. She smiled sociably when I mentioned it.

"Why, yes, dear, that is largely what is the matter. You do not train your children to think—you train them not to. Your men think hard in narrow lines, just little pushing lines of their special work, or how to get richer, and your women—"

"Oh, come, let's have it !" I cried despairingly. "Whatever else you say or don't say you are always thinking about the women; I can fairly hear your brain click. And I'll tell you honestly, my dear, that I don't believe you can hurt me now, no matter how hard you hit them or the men. It certainly has been a liberal education to live with you. Also I've had my time in Herland to show me the difference. I confess that as I now see this life of ours the women shock me, in some ways, more than the men. And I've been doing some reading as well as you, even some thinking. I suppose one thing that has made you so reticent about this is that you can't criticize the women without blaming the men. Perhaps it will encourage you if I begin to do the blaming."

She mildly said that perhaps it would seem more magnanimous, so I started in and found the case worse when stated at length than I had seen it in glimpses.

"Of course, there is no getting around Lester Ward," I began slowly. "No one can study biology and sociology much and not see that on the first physiological lines the female is the whole show, so to speak, or at least most of it. And all the way up she holds her own, even into early savagery, till Mr. Man gets into the saddle. How he came to do it is a mystery that I don't believe even you can explain."

"No," she agreed, "I can't. I call it 'The Great Divergence.' There is no other such catastrophic change in all nature—as far as I've been able to gather."

What Ellador had "gathered" in two years was perhaps not equal in detailed knowledge to the learning of great specialists, but she had a marvellous gift for selecting the really important facts and for arranging them. That was the trick—she did something with what she knew—not merely stored it.

"Well, he did take the reins, somehow," I resumed, "and we began our historic period, which is somewhat too large to be covered in an hour—by me. But in all this time, as far as I can make out, he has never been even fair to women, and has for the most part treated her with such an assortment of cruelty and injustice as makes me blush for my sex."

"What made you think so, Van? What first?"

"Why Herland first," I answered promptly. "Seeing women who were People and that they were People *because* they were women, not in spite of it. Seeing that what we had called "womanliness" was a mere excess of sex, not the essential part of it at all. When I came back here and compared our women with yours—well, it was a blow. Besides, if I'd had no other evidence *You* would have shown me—just living with you, my Wonder Darling."

She looked at me with shining eyes, that look that was more than wife, more than mother; the illimitable loving Human look.

"What I have learned from you, Dearest; from our companionship without the physical intimacy of sex, is this; that Persons, two Persons who love each other, have a bigger range of happiness than even two lovers. I mean than two lovers who are not such companions, of course. I do not deny that it has been hard, very hard, sometimes. I've been disagreeable to live with—" "Never!" she interpolated, "but somehow the more I loved you the less it troubled me. Now I feel that when we do reach that union, with all our love, with all the great mother purpose that is in your heart and the beginning of a sense of father purpose in mine, I'm sure that it will be only an incident in our love, our happiness, not the main thing."

She gave a long soft sigh of full content, still listening.

"All this makes me see the—limitations of our women," I continued, "and when I look for a reason there is only the conduct of men toward them. Cruelty? Why, my dear, it is not the physical cruelty to their tender bodies; it is not the shame and grief and denial that they have had to bear; those are like the 'atrocities' in warfare—it is the war itself which is wrong. The petted women, the contented women, the 'happy' women—these are perhaps the worst result."

"It's wonderful how clearly you see it," she said.

"Pretty plain to see," I went on. "We men, having all human power in our hands, have used it to warp and check the growth of women. We, by choice and selection, by law and religion, by enforced ignorance, by heavy overcultivation of sex, have made the kind of woman we so made by nature, that that is what it was to be a woman. Then we heaped our scornful abuse upon her, ages and ages of it, the majority of men in all nations still looking down on women. And then, as if that was not enough—really, my dear, I'm not joking, I'm ashamed, as if I'd done it myself—we, in our superior freedom, in our monopoly of education, with the law in our hands, both to make and execute, with every conceivable advantage—we have blamed women for the sins of the world!"

She interrupted here, eagerly—"Not *all* of you, Van dear! That was only a sort of legend with some people. It was only in the Jewish religion you think so much of that the contemptible lie was actually stated as a holy truth—and even God made to establish that unspeakable injustice."

"Yes, that's true, but nobody objected. We all accepted it gladly —and treated her accordingly. Well, sister—have I owned up enough? I guess you can't hurt my feelings any with anything you say about men. Of course, I'm not going into details, that would take forever, but just in general I can see what ails the women—and who's to blame for it."

"Don't be too hard on Mr. Man," she urged gently. "What you say is true enough, but so are other things. What puzzles me most is not at all that background of explanation, but what ails the women *now*. Here, even here in America, *now*. They have had some education for several generations, numbers of them have time to think, some few have money—I cannot be reconciled to the women, Van!"

She was so unusually fierce about it that I was quite surprised at her. I had supposed that her hardest feeling would be about men. She saw my astonishment and explained.

"Put yourself in my place for a moment, Van. Suppose in Herland we had a lot of—subject men. Blame us all you want to for doing it, but look at the men. Little creatures, undersized and generally feeble. Cowardly and not ashamed of it. Kept for sex purposes only or as servants; or both, usually both. I confess I'm asking something difficult of your imagination, but try to think of Herland women, each with a soft man she kept to cook for her, to wait upon her and to—'love' when she pleased. Ignorant men mostly. Poor men, almost all, having to ask their owners for money and tell what they wanted it for. Some of them utterly degraded creatures, kept in houses for common use—as women are kept here. Some of them quite gay and happy—pet men, with pet names and presents showered upon them. Most of them contented, piously accepting kitchen work as their duty, living by the religion and laws and customs the women made. Some of them left out and made fun of for being left—not owned at all—and envying those who were! Allow for a surprising percentage of mutual love and happiness, even under these conditions; but also for ghastly depths of misery and a general low level of mere submission to the inevitable. Then in this state of degradation fancy these men for the most part quite content to make monkeys of themselves by wearing the most ridiculous clothes. Fancy them, men, with men's bodies, though enfeebled, wearing open-work lace underclothing, with little ribbons all strung through it; wearing dresses never twice alike and almost always foolish; wearing hats—" she fixed me with a steady eye in which a growing laughter twinkled—"wearing such hats as your women wear!"

At this I threw up my hands. "I can't!" I said. "It's all off. I followed you with increasing difficulty, even through the lace and baby ribbon, but I stop there. Men wear such hats! Men! I tell you it is unthinkable!"

"Unthinkable for such men?"

"Such men are unthinkable, really; contemptible, skulking, cowardly spaniels! They would deserve all they got."

"Why aren't you blaming the women of Herland for treating them so, Van?"

"Oh!" said I, and "Yes," said I, "I begin to see, my dear Herlander, why you're down on the women."

"Good," she agreed. "It's all true, what you say about the men, nothing could be blacker than that story. But the women, Van, the women! They are not dead! They are here, and in your country they have plenty of chance to grow. How can they bear their position,

Van; how can they stand it another day? Don't they know they are *Women?*"

"No," said I slowly. "They think they are—women."

We both laughed rather sadly.

Presently she said, "We have to take the facts as we find them. Emotion does not help us any. It's no use being horrified at a— hermit crab—that's the way he is. This is the woman man made— how is she going to get over it?"

"You don't forget the ones who have gotten over it, do you? And all the splendid work they are doing?"

"I'm afraid I did for a moment," she admitted. "Besides—so much of their effort is along side lines, and some of it in precisely the wrong direction."

"What would you have them do?"

"What would you have those inconceivable men of Herland do?" she countered. "What would you say to them—to rouse them?"

"I'd try to make them realize that they were *men*," I said. "That's the first thing."

"Exactly. And if the smooth, plump, crazily dressed creatures answered 'A true man is always glad to be supported by the woman he loves' what would you say to that?"

"I should try to make him realize what the world really was," I answered slowly, "and to see what was a man's place in it."

"And if he answered you—a hundred million strong—'A man's place is in the home!'—what would you say then?"

"It would be pretty hard to say anything—if men were like that."

"Yes, and it is pretty hard to say anything when women are like that—it doesn't reach them."

"But there is the whole women's movement—surely they are changing, improving."

She shook off her mood of transient bitterness. "My ignorance makes me hard, I suppose. I'm not familiar enough with your past history, recent past history, I mean, to note the changes as clearly as you do. I come suddenly to see them as they are, not knowing how much worse it has been. For instance, I suppose women used to dress more foolishly than they do now. Can that be possible?"

I ran over in my mind some of the eccentricities of fashion in earlier periods and was about to say that it was possible when I chanced to look out of the window. It was a hot day, most oppressively hot, with a fiercely glaring sun. A woman stood just across the street talking to a man. I picked up my opera glass and studied her for a moment. I had read that "the small waist is coming in again." Hers had come. She stood awkwardly in extremely high-heeled slippers, in which the sole of the foot leaned on a steep slant from heel to ball, and her toes, poor things, were driven into the narrow-pointed toe of the slipper by the whole sliding weight of the body above. The thin silk hose showed the insteps puffing up like a pincushion from the binding grip of that short vamp.

Her skirts were short as a child's, most voluminous and varied in outline, hanging in bunches on the hips and in various fluctuating points and corners below. The bodice was a parti-colored composition, of indiscreet exposures, more suitable for a ballroom than for the street.

But what struck me most was that she wore about her neck a dead fox or the whole outside of one.

No, she was not a lunatic. No, that man was not her keeper. No, it was not a punishment, not an initiation penalty, not an election bet.

That woman, of her own free will and at considerable expense, wore heavy furs in the hottest summer weather.

I laid down the glass and turned to Ellador. "No, my dear," said I gloomily. "It is not possible that women ever could have been more idiotic in dress than that."

We were silent for a little, watching that pitiful object with her complacent smile as she stood there on those distorted feet, sweating under her load of fur, perfectly contented and pleased with herself.

"Some way," said Ellador slowly, "it makes me almost discouraged about the woman's movement. I'm not, of course, not really. I do know enough to see that they are far better off than a hundred years ago. And the laws of life are on their side, solid irresistible laws. They are women after all, and women are people—are *the* people, really, up to a certain point. I must make more allowances, must learn to see the gain in some ways even where there is none in others. Now that—that tottering little image may be earning her own living or doing something useful. . . . What's worst of all, perhaps, is the strange missing of purpose in those who are most actively engaged in 'advancing.' They seem like flies behind a window, they bump and buzz, pushing their heads against whatever is in front of them, and never seem really to plan a way out. . . . No, there's one thing worse than that—much worse. I wouldn't have believed it possible—I can hardly believe it now.

"What's this horror?" I asked. "Prostitution? White slavery?"

"Oh, no," she said, "those things are awful, but a sort of natural awfulness, if I may say so; what a scientific observer would expect of the evil conditions carried to excess. No—this thing is—*unnatural!* I mean—the Antis."

"Oh—the Anti-Suffragists?"

"Yes. Think of the men again—those poor degraded men I was imagining. And then think of some of them struggling for freedom, struggling long and hard, with pathetically slow progress, doing no harm in the meantime, just talking, arguing, pleading, petitioning, using what small money they could scrape together to promote their splendid cause, their cause that meant not only their own advantage, but more freedom and swifter progress for all the world. And then think of some other of those pet men, not only misunderstanding the whole thing, too dull or too perverse even to see such basic truth as that, but actually banding together to oppose it—!

"Van, if you want one all-sufficient and world-convincing proof of the degradation of women, you have it in the antisuffragist!"

"The men are backing them, remember," I suggested.

"Of course they are. You expect the men to oppose the freeing of women, they naturally would. But the women, Van—the women themselves—it's un-natural."

With a sick shudder she buried her face in her hands for a moment, then straightened up bravely again, giving that patient little sigh of dismissal to the subject. I was silent and watched her as she sat, so strong, so graceful, so beautiful, with that balanced connection in line and movement we usually see only in savages. Her robe was simple in form, lovely in color, comfortable and becoming. I looked at her with unfailing pleasure always, never having to make excuses and reservations. All of her was beautiful and strong.

And I thought of her sisters, that fair land of full grown women, all of whom, with room for wide personal distinction, were beautiful and strong. There were differences enough. A group of thoroughbred race horses might vary widely in color, size, shape, marking and individual expression; yet all be fine horses. There would be no need of scrubs and cripples to make variety. And I looked again out of our window, at the city street, with its dim dirtiness, its brutal noise and the unsatisfied, unsatisfying people going so hurriedly about after their food, crowding, pushing, hurrying like hungry rats; the sordid eagerness of the men, the shallow folly of the women. And all at once there swept over me a great wave of homesickness for Herland.

Ellador was never satisfied merely to criticize; she must needs plan some way out, some improvement. So, laying aside her discouragement, she plunged into this woman question with new determination and before long came to me in loving triumph.

"I was wrong, Van, to be so harsh with them; it was just my Herland background. Now I have been deliberately putting myself in the woman's place and measuring the rate of progress—as of a glacier. And it's wonderful, really wonderful. There was the bottom limit—not so very far back—some savages still keeping to it— merely to live long enough to bear a daughter. Then there's the gain, this way in one land and that way in another, but always a gain. Then this great modern awakening which is now stirring them all over the world. By keeping my own previous knowledge of women entirely out of my mind and by measuring your really progressive ones to-day against their own grandmothers—that movement I was so scornful about now seems to me a sunburst of blazing improvement. Of course they 'bump and buzz' in every direction, that is mere resilience—haven't they been kept down in every direction? They'll get over that as they grow accustomed to real liberty.

"It would be inconceivable that they should have been so unutterably degraded for so long and not show the results of it, the limitations. Instead of blaming them I should have been rejoicing at the wonderful speed with which they have surged forward as fast as any door was opened, even a crack. I have been looking at what might be called the unconscious as apart from the conscious woman's movement, and it comforts me much."

"Just what do you mean?"

"I mean the women's clubs, here in this country especially; and largest of all the economic changes; the immense numbers who are at work."

"Didn't they always work? The poor ones, that is?"

"Oh, yes, at home. I mean human work."

"Wage earning?"

"That, incidentally, as a descriptive term; but it would be [a] different grade of work, even without that."

"So I've heard people say, some people. But what is there superior in doing some fractional monotonous little job like bookkeeping, for instance, as compared with the management and performance of all the intimate tasks in a household?"

I was so solemn about this that she took me seriously, at least for a moment.

"It isn't the difference between a bookkeeper and a housekeeper that must be considered; it is the difference between an organized business world that needs bookkeeping and an unorganized world of separate families with no higher work than to eat, sleep and keep alive."

Then she saw me grin and begged pardon, cheerfully. "I might have known you were wiser than that, Van. But, oh, the people I've been talking to! The questions they ask and the comments they make! Fortunately we do not have to wait for universal conviction before moving onward."

"If you could have your way with the women of this country and the others what would you make them do?" I asked.

She set her chin in her hand and meditated a little. "What they are doing, only more of it, for one thing," she answered presently, "but, oh, so much more! Of course they have to be taught differently, they need new standards, new hopes, new ideals, new purposes. That's the real field of work, you see, Van, in the mind. That is what was so confusing to me at first. You see the difference in looks between your women and our women is as one to a thousand compared to the differences between their mental content.

"Your conditions are so good, the real ones, I mean, the supplies, the materials, the abilities you have, that at first I underrated the difficulties. Inside you are not as advanced as outside, men or women. You have such antique minds! I never get used to it. You see we, ever so long ago, caught up with our conditions; and now we are always planning better ones. Our minds are ahead of our conditions—and yet we live pretty comfortably."

"And how are our women going to catch up?"

"They have to make a long jump, from the patriarchal status to the democratic, from the narrowest personal ties to the widest social relation, from first hand labor, mere private service of bodily needs, to the specialized, organized social service of the whole community. At present this is going on, in actual fact, without their realizing it, without their understanding and accepting it. It is the mind that needs changing."

"I suppose it seems a trifling matter to you to change the working machinery of twenty million homes—that's what it amounts to —doesn't it?"

"How long does it take to do up twenty million women's hair?" she inquired. "No longer than it does one—if they all do it at once. Numbers don't complicate a question like this. What could be done in one tiny village could be done all over the country in the same time. I suppose I do underestimate the practical difficulties here on account of our having settled all those little problems. The idea of your still not being properly fed!—I can't get used to it."

Then I remembered the uniform excellence of food in Herland; not only all that we ourselves had enjoyed, but that I never saw in any shop or market any wilted, withered, stale or in any way inferior supplies.

"How did you manage that?" I asked her. "Did you confiscate all the damaged things? Was there a penalty for selling them?"

"Does one of your housekeepers confiscate her damaged food? Is there any penalty for feeding her family with it?"

"Oh, I see. You only provided enough to keep fresh."

"Exactly. I tell you numbers don't make any difference. A million people do not eat any more—apiece—than a dozen at one table. We feed our people as carefully and as competently as you try to feed your families. You can't do as well because of the inferiority of materials."

This I found somewhat offensive, but I knew it was true.

"It's so simple!" she said wearily. "A child could see it. Food is to *eat,* and if it is not good to eat it is not food. Here you people use food as a thing to play with, to buy and sell, to store up, to throw away, with no more regard for its real purpose than—"

"Than the swine with pearls before him," I suggested. "But you know those economic laws come in—"

She laughed outright.

"Van, dear, there is nothing in all your pitiful tangled life more absurd than what you so solemnly call 'economics.' Good economics in regard to food is surely this: to produce the best quality, in sufficient quantity, with the least expenditure of labor, and to distribute it the most rapidly and freshly to the people who need it.

"The management of food in your world is perhaps the most inexplicably foolish of anything you do. I've been up and down the streets in your cities observing. I've been in the hotels and restaurants far and wide and in ever so many homes. And I confess, Van, with some mortification, that there is no one thing I'm more homesick for than food."

"I am getting discouraged, if you are not, Ellador. As compared with a rational country like yours, this is rather a mess. And it looks so hopeless. I suppose it will take a thousand years to catch up."

"You could do it in three generations," she calmly replied.

"Three generations! That's barely a century."

"I know it. The whole outside part of it you could do inside of twenty years; it is the people who will take three generations to remake. You could improve this stock, say, 5 per cent. in one, 15 in two and 80 per cent. in three. Perhaps faster."

"Are not you rather sanguine, my dear girl?"

"I don't think so," she answered gravely. "People are not *bad* now; they are only weighed down with all this falsehood and foolishness in their heads. There is always the big lifting force of life to push you on as fast as you will let it. There is the wide surrounding help of conditions, such conditions as you even now know how to arrange. And there is the power of education—which you have hardly tried. With these all together and with proper care in breeding you could fill the world with glorious people—soon. Oh, I wish you'd do it! I *wish* you'd do it!"

It was hard on her. Harder even than I had foreseen. Not only the war horrors, not only the miseries of more backward nations and of our painful past, but even in my America where I had fondly thought she would be happy, the common arrangements of our lives to which we are so patiently accustomed, were to her a constant annoyance and distress.

Through her eyes I saw it newly and instead of the breezy pride I used to feel in my young nation I now began to get an unceasing sense of what she had called "an idiot child."

It was so simply true, what she said about food. Food is to eat. All its transporting and preserving and storing and selling—if it interferes with the eating value of the food—is foolishness. I began to see the man who stores eggs until they are reduced to the grade called "rots and spots" as an idiot and a malicious idiot at that. Vivid and clear rose in my mind the garden-circled cities of Herland, where for each group of inhabitants all fresh fruits and vegetables were raised so near that they could be eaten the day they were picked. It did not cost any more. It cost less, saving transportation. Supplies that would keep they kept—enough from season to season, with some emergency reserves; but not one person, young or old, ever had to eat such things as we pay extortionately for in every city.

Nothing but women, only mothers, but they had worked out to smooth perfection what now began to seem to me to be the basic problem in human life.

How to make the best kind of people and how to keep them at their best and growing better—surely that is what we are here for.

Notes
Bibliography
Index

Notes

1. Utopian Writing as "Cultural Work"

1. Catharine R. Stimpson claims that Gertrude Stein was a "prophet of television's dominant method of conveying ideas—through having a figure embody them" (1989, 377). And as early was Gilman. This practice is not new, of course: we need only recall the morality plays, altar triptychs, and stained glass windows of medieval European churches, or the oral traditions of folk cultures all over the globe.

2. See Valerie Walkerdine, "Some Day My Prince Will Come: Young Girls and the Preparation for Adolescent Sexuality," in *Gender and Generation,* ed. A. McRobbie and M. Nava (New York: Macmillan, 1984).

3. Philosopher Linda Alcoff concurs in observing that "you must have a positive alternative, a vision of a better future that can motivate people to sacrifice their time and energy toward its realization" (419).

4. In this article, Zagarell cites Stowe's *The Pearl of Orr's Island* (1861) as part of this tradition of community (510n. 6), although, according to her most recent thinking, neither this novel nor *Oldtown Folks* (1869) embraces the heterogeneity she has come to locate in the "narrative of community" (letter to the author, 10 September 1991). Gilman is ideologically closer to Isabella Beecher Hooker and heterogeneity than to Stowe's understanding of community as more homogeneous: see *The Limits of Sisterhood: The Beecher Sisters on Women's Rights and Woman's Sphere* (1988), ed. Jeanne Boydston, Mary Kelley, and Anne Margolis.

5. Unpublished paper delivered at the American Literature Association Conference, Washington, D.C., May 1991, entitled "Narrative of Community: Speculating on Nineteenth-Century American Writers." Quoted with permission.

6. For a complete development of Goffman's theory, see *Frame Analysis: An Essay on the Organization of Experience* (1974).

7. I allude here to Bakhtin's notion of interpretative "unfinalizability." Bakhtin's concepts—"prosaics," dialogism, unfinalizability—are remarkably in tune with current feminist utopian thought, with the major flaw that Bakhtin failed to note the applicability of his concepts to women's living and writing. We need not be hindered by his lack of vision, given our own today: Dale Bauer, Joanne Frye, and Patricia Yeager, among other feminist literary theorists, are engaged in extending Bakhtin's vision to include feminism. I acknowledge the study *Mikhail Bakhtin: Creation of a Prosaics,* by Gary Saul Morson and Caryl Emerson (1990), for its

explication of a "prosaics," though this study, following Bakhtin, does not discuss his relevance to feminist thought. Another shortcoming of the *Prosaics* is its restrictive definition of Bakhtin's carnivalesque, an undermining of the trope's "utopian . . . implications": see Gardiner 44.

8. For more extended discussions, see Elise Boulding, *Building a Global Civic Culture* (1988); Fritjof Capra, *The Turning Point: Science, Society, and the Rising Culture* (1982); Marilyn Ferguson, *The Aquarian Conspiracy: Personal and Social Transformation in the 1980s* (1980); James Gleick, *Chaos: Making a New Science* (1987); Paul Hawken and others, *Seven Tomorrows* (1982); and David Loye and Riane Eisler, "Chaos and Transformation: Implications of Nonequilibrium Theory for Social Science and Society" (1987).

9. Compare the words of Susan K. Harris regarding Elizabeth Stuart Phelps' *The Silent Partner* (1871): Phelps "examine[s] the effectiveness of women's voices in the political world, the world of [heretofore] undiminished, absolute, male power" and "shows just how difficult both access and alternatives to that world would be" (196).

10. Mary Armfield Hill has selected and edited this voluminous correspondence for publication. See discussion in the third section of chapter 4. And see Carolyn Heilbrun on *The Living of Charlotte Perkins Gilman* in *Writing a Woman's Life* (24–25).

11. Nancy K. Miller accurately claims that "the historical truth of a woman writer's life lies in the reader's grasp of her intratext: the body of her writing" (1988, 61).

12. I owe to Lee Cullen Khanna the insight to apply Jane Tompkins' concept of "cultural work" to feminist utopian fiction: see her March 1988 paper, "Feminist Quest for Utopia," delivered at the Popular Culture Convention in New Orleans. For Tompkins, see *Sensational Designs: The Cultural Work of American Fiction 1790–1860* (1985), especially the concluding chapter, "But Is It Any Good? The Institutionalization of Literary Value," 186–201.

13. Readers wishing a more detailed discussion regarding this process in the context of such fantasy as utopia and realism can consult chap. 1 of Kathryn Hume's, *Fantasy and Mimesis: Responses to Reality in Western Literature* (1984).

14. See Janice A. Radway, who, in an analysis of her study of romance reading, "Identifying Ideological Seams," advocates an "ethnographic investigation of the activity of reading as a social process" (104).

15. Jean Wyatt, in *Reconstructing Desire: The Role of the Unconscious in Women's Reading and Writing* (Chapel Hill: Univ. North Carolina Press, 1990) answers in some detail the question "Can Reading Change the Reader?" (7–13). She later discusses the social function of fantasy (215–18). Patricia Waugh also discusses these issues in *Feminine Fictions: Revisiting the Postmodern* (London: Routledge, 1989), especially chap. 2. One example of an eloquent reader's response to feminist scholarship is Jane Tompkins' "Me and My Shadow," an exposition of where reading in the widest sense can lead.

16. Twice in the *Forerunner,* Gilman discussed at length her beliefs about fictional plots—first as "Masculine Literature," chapter 5 of "Our Androcentric Culture; or, the Man-Made World" (1910; published as *The Man-Made World* in 1911), and second as "Coming Changes in Literature" (1915). In between these two longer discussions, Gilman also wrote in the *Forerunner* "Effect of Literature Upon the Mind" (chapter 5 of "Our Brains and What Ails Them," 1912), and "With a Differ-

ence (Not Literature)" (1914), a story having two alternative endings, a piece illustrating Gilman's belief in the need for new plots with different endings. See the discussion in chapter 4, the fourth section.

17. Remember, however, that Bakhtin missed recognizing the applicability of his insight to boundaries marking gender, a locale of social change that was engaging ever more interest as he began his career. See note 7 above.

18. Additional terms discriminating utopian subtypes exist. For instance, *anti-utopia* or *parodic/satiric utopia* undermines and ridicules the very concept of utopia, as in Hawthorne's "Celestial Railroad." Tom Moylan's term "critical utopia," from *Demand the Impossible: Science Fiction and the Utopian Imagination* (1986), defines utopia not as blueprint but as dream, a dream of a world improving upon (i.e., critical of) the author's world, and generating through the responses of readers a "critical mass" of social reformers of that society. This is not greatly different from what Gilman believed she was accomplishing through her writing, although her literary practice, save for "The Yellow Wallpaper," did not include the narrative innovation that might have touched readers more convincingly than her didacticism. Frances Bartkowski, in *Feminist Utopias* (1989), sees Gilman's *Herland* as a "static utopia," in the mode of late nineteenth-century generic conventions, in contrast to the current feminist "dynamic utopia," initiated by Monique Wittig's *Les Guérillères* (1973). I think *Herland* offers more innovation in the context of 1915 than our hindsight from the late twentieth century suggests: Chapter 3 presents Gilman's innovation in plot, theme, and characterization, rather than in narrative structure.

Peter Ruppert, in *Reader in a Strange Land: The Activity of Reading Literary Utopias* (1986), believes that "utopias are better understood as open-ended interrogations of social reality that are themselves contradictory and inconsistent" (xii). They are "works of the imagination," designed "to serve as thought-provoking catalysts whose value is in their shock effect on readers" (xiii). He concludes that utopias imply "a 'thorough-going restructuration' [Fredric Jameson's words]—and readers who are willing to entertain its possibilities" (xiv). Ruppert discusses cognitive, therapeutic, and anticipatory effects of utopias in his first two chapters. See Ruth Levitas, *The Concept of Utopia* (1990), for further discussion.

19. See *The Chalice and the Blade: Our History, Our Future* (1988), and also her "Pragmatopia: Women's Utopias and Scenarios for a Possible Future," a paper delivered at the 1986 Conference of the Society for Utopian Studies at Asilomar (198, 239 n. 65). Eisler's study suggests an updated version of Gilman's 1898 *Women and Economics*, now including recent archeological discoveries and evolutionary theory. For further information on this recent research, see the works cited by Elinor W. Gadon, Marija Gimbutas, Buffie Johnson, and Lucy R. Lippard for art and archeology, and by Stephen Jay Gould for evolution.

The concept of "pragmatopia" calls to mind that of the "not yet" from Ernst Bloch's *The Principle of Hope* (1959; trans. 1986), but I prefer such positive nomenclature as "achievable" or "realizable," with its emphasis upon "what could be" rather than upon "what is not yet." For further discussion of Bloch and of his influence upon Marcuse's concept of "realizability-in-principle," see Ruth Levitas, chaps. 4 and 6, respectively; see also the special issue featuring Ernst Bloch, *Utopian Studies* 1.2 (1990): 1–95.

20. As a name for the partnership principle of social organization that Eisler advocates, she posits *gylany*, a term she coined from Greek antecedents meaning "a social system in which women [gy] are linked with or re/solved or set free [l] from

men |an|" (105). The original Greek antecedents are *gy* from *gyne* for "woman"; *l* from English *linking,* and Greek *lyein* or *lyo* which has a "double meaning: to solve or resolve (as in ana*l*ysis) and to dissolve or set free (as in cata*l*ysis)"; *an* from *andros* for "man" (105).

21. Eisler also provides an extensive listing of feminist theorists of power (193).

22. Anne Cranny-Francis, in her recent study *Feminist Fiction: Feminist Uses of Generic Fiction* (1990), discussing Marge Piercy's *Woman on the Edge of Time* (1976), writes, "three intersecting narratives—realist, utopian, dystopian—construct a complex text in which Piercy deconstructs dominant ideological discourses, examines the interpellation of the individual in ideology and[,] one of the principal means by which ideology is naturalized into the lives of individuals, the realist narrative (137)." See chap. 4, "Feminist Utopias," 107–142.

23. In an earlier discussion of Gilman's story "Bee Wise," I discussed the relationship between utopian and realistic writing. I suggested that fictional solutions can be called utopian to the extent that they are not yet widely practiced; they can also be called "realistic" to the extent that they are possible. Acknowledging that ideology shapes and limits expectations, that reality is always socially constructed within the parameters of ideology, I would here define literary realism as a rationally constructed version of what could be expected to happen in a currently existing society, hence "realistic."

24. A similar point is made by Molly Hite, in *The Other Side of the Story* (1989), as she concludes her introduction:

> there exist a number of works by female authors, works that might well be regarded as experimental if it were possible to discount the reviews and criticism that, with ingenuity and even sympathy, translate experimentalism into flawed realism (for example, faulting a utopian romance for being insufficiently plausible) or into hyperbolic mimesis (for example, presuming that a disjointed narrative reflects the state of mind of a flaky or insane heroine). My own enterprise here might be to indicate an "other side" to these critical accounts, specifically to indicate ways in which works by Rhys, Lessing, Walker, and Atwood have eluded or overflowed certain established modes of reading and ways in which we might learn to read—as they write—other-wise (17–18).

See also Nancy K. Miller, who observes, "The attack on female plots and plausibilities assumes that women writers cannot or will not obey the rules of fiction. It also assumes that the truth devolving from *veri*similitude is male" (1981, 46). Making another but equally relevant point, Amy Kaplan, in *The Social Construction of American Realism* (1988), claims, "Realistic novels have utopian moments that imagine resolutions to contemporary social conflicts by reconstructing society as it might be" (12). And Mary D. Garrard, in *Artemisia Gentileschi* (1989), comments that Italian Baroque painting can also be "understood as *realization*—giving concrete form to important spiritual or philosophical concepts" (9), an observation equally relevant to Gilman's use of realism.

25. For a discussion of the concept of voluntary history, see Paul Hawken, James Ogilvy, and Peter Schwartz, *Seven Tomorrows: Toward a Voluntary History* (1982), especially chap. 2, "Constructing Scenarios of the Future," and the conclusion. See also Boulding's "Building Utopias in History" (1987). With coauthor David Loye,

Eisler has provided us with a how-to text for becoming increasingly conscious about the behavioral choices that we make, namely, *The Partnership Way: New Tools for Living and Learning, Healing Our Families, Our Communities and Our World* (1990). Another comparably useful, somewhat more radical, how-to text is Starhawk [Miriam Simos], *Truth or Dare: Encounters with Power, Authority, and Mystery* (1987).

26. Jane Marcus reminds us that "theory is necessary and useful but is not superior to other literary practice or immune to historical forces" (87): we must be especially wary to resist theorists' constriction of the world of readers and writers to a limited elite. Deborah L. Rhode warns: "[I]t is possible to remain skeptical about Theory while recognizing the need for theories, for multiple accounts from multiple disciplines at multiple levels that avoid privileging any single framework. In place of metanarratives that claim universal application, this volume argues for contextual, situational analysis" (1990, 8). And my volume tries to practice such a methodology.

27. Mary Hill generously made her work available to me in manuscript form. I wish to acknowledge my substantial thanks and appreciation. She has edited and interpreted for publication selected letters from the 1897–1900 courtship correspondence between Charlotte Perkins Gilman and George Houghton Gilman, to appear under the tentative title "Journey from Within: The Private Letters of Charlotte Perkins Gilman." I have read the typescript. Since the book is not yet published, I have cited references to the letters as located in SLR. Chapter 4 provides a detailed discussion of these letters as background for Gilman's utopian writing. Mary Hill's sharing and expertise regarding Gilman have influenced my own understanding of the importance of this correspondence.

I find that Hill's historical acumen and my scholarly base in feminist utopian and literary studies have been interactive. Her generosity with her manuscript has permitted me to build far more quickly than would have been possible if I had, like her, transcribed the whole correspondence of more than twelve hundred items. Her excellent selection and mapping of this correspondence have permitted me to go forward by building upon her foundation to show how this correspondence provides the base for the utopian fiction of the next decades in Gilman's life. I suggest that this near-collaboration represents the best in feminist scholarship, a division of labor and a sharing of foundations that permits the house of scholarly interpretations to rise more quickly than a purely individualistic and egocentric hoarding of research would permit. I am grateful to Hill for this pre-publication gift of her years of studying these very complex and seemingly contradictory letters.

28. Discussions of her once-lost utopia *Herland* constitute parts of two important recent books: for examples, see Frances Bartkowski, who devotes half of the first chapter in *Feminist Utopias* (1989) to *Herland,* and Sandra Gilbert and Susan Gubar, who discuss *Herland* in the last third of the second chapter of *No Man's Land: The Place of the Woman Writer in the Twentieth Century,* Vol. 2: *Sexchanges* (1989). Recent publications on Gilman include the following: Lynne Sharon Schwartz, ed., *The Yellow Wallpaper and Other Writings* (1989); Ann J. Lane, *To 'Herland' and Beyond: The Life and Works of Charlotte Perkins Gilman* (New York: Pantheon, 1990), and a new Introduction for *The Living of Charlotte Perkins Gilman* (1990); Larry Ceplair, ed., *Charlotte Perkins Gilman: A Nonfiction Reader* (1991); Catherine Golden, ed., *The Captive Imagination: A Casebook on "The Yellow Wallpaper"* (1992); Joanne Karpinski, ed., *Critical Essays on Charlotte Perkins Gilman* (1992); Barbara H. Solomon, ed., *'Herland' and Selected Stories by Charlotte Perkins Gilman* (1992);

Connie L. White and Thomas L. Erskine, eds., *"The Yellow Wallpaper,"* Women Writers: Text and Context series (Fall 1993); and Mary Armfield Hill, ed., *Journey From Within: The Private Letters of Charlotte Perkins Gilman* (forthcoming).

2. Making Herself: A Biographical Exploration

1. A Swedish translation exists.

2. A listing of the holdings for the Charlotte Perkins Gilman Collection, the principal primary resource for the study of her life and work, is published in *The Arthur and Elizabeth Schlesinger Library on the History of Women in America: The Manuscript Inventories and the Catalogs of the Manuscripts, Books, and Periodicals,* 2nd revised and enlarged edition (Boston: G. K. Hall, 1984). Researchers wishing additional information may request from the Schlesinger Library at Radcliffe College a detailed listing of manuscript materials compiled by Eva Moseley, "Charlotte Perkins Gilman Papers, 1846–1961." "SLR" followed by a folder or volume citation will identify in the text sources contained in this collection.

3. Scholars attribute to Gilman intellectual leadership in the United States women's movement at the turn of the century. Examples include Carl Degler (1966, xiii), Alice Rossi (1973, 568), and Dale Spender (1982, 373).

4. I have resolved the dilemma of referring to Gilman as follows. When using a surname would confuse her with husbands Stetson or Gilman in text concerning these couples, I use "Charlotte." Otherwise, I use "Gilman" for consistency even when "Stetson" would be historically more accurate, as during the late 1880s and throughout the 1890s after she separated from Stetson and before her second marriage to Gilman. Since she herself used "Gilman" publicly and privately as her own surname, I believe my practice accurately represents her.

5. For discussion and documentation of the relationship among the Beecher sisters, see *The Limits of Sisterhood: The Beecher Sisters on Women's Rights and Woman's Sphere,* by Jeanne Boydston, Mary Kelley, and Anne Margolis (1988), especially 8, 340–41, 357, on Mary Beecher Perkins as an "ideal woman." In addition, Mary was an ardent antisuffragist: in 1874, she refused to have sister Isabella Beecher Hooker in her home unless she ended "all intercourse with Mrs. [Elizabeth Cady] Stanton and Miss [Susan B.] Anthony and all that set" (quoted 298).

6. Hale also wrote other utopian works, including *The Brick Moon* (1869–1870).

7. Mary A. Hill (1980, 56–57) and Ann J. Lane (1990, 62–63) explain that Hale introduced Charlotte to both the Bucklin and the Hazard families: each had daughters about Charlotte's age.

8. Henry Ward Beecher was accused of having an affair with his Brooklyn parishioner, Elizabeth Tilton, wife of Theodore Tilton, reform editor of the *Independent.* The "affair" and Tilton's suit against Beecher were reported widely, from the *Boston Investigator* to *Woodhull and Claflin's Weekly* (Nov. 1871). The outcome of the trial was a hung jury.

9. Psychological and personal explanations are possible. The adult Gilman carried the ravages of an intrusive parent in her anxiety regarding possible intrusions of her personal boundary, exhibited in her dislike of cooperative ventures, where personal boundaries must be somewhat subject to one's peer cooperators. Additionally, Gilman described in her autobiography a very unpleasant experience of her mother's insisting she apologize for an act she insists she did not commit (*Living,* 33–34). For further discussion, see *Living,* chap. 3; Lane 1990, 51–56.

10. See *Woman's Fiction: A Guide to Novels by and about Women in America, 1820–1870* for a discussion of form and ideology, chap. 2. Also relevant are *Private Woman, Public Stage: Literary Domesticity in Nineteenth-Century America*, by Mary Kelley, which stresses women writers' experience of role conflict, and *Sensational Designs: The Cultural Work of American Fiction, 1790–1860*, by Jane Tompkins, especially chap. 5 on *Uncle Tom's Cabin* by Harriet Beecher Stowe, who deliberately designed the novel to change cultural values in the direction of elevating motherhood. Stowe's example of using writing as social action provided for Gilman a model from her own family of womanhood as positive and powerful. In addition, *Reading the Romance: Women, Patriarchy, and Popular Literature*, by Janice A. Radway, argues that such novels can provide the nurturance that women's lives in patriarchy frequently lack.

11. See Kenneth Burke's essay, "Literature as Equipment for Living," in *The Philosophy of Literary Form: Studies in Symbolic Action*, where he argues that novels achieving great popularity or longevity do so because they "name" a previously unnamed human condition.

12. See Shirley Nelson Garner, in "Constructing the Mother: Contemporary Psychoanalytic Theorists and Women Autobiographers": she urges that mothers' as well as children's stories be told and receive attention. Gilman is one who tells a mother's story in her autobiography and in her fiction.

13. Gilman's 1878 diary entry for 17 May notes: "Pleasing epistle from father stating that he can't send us any more money for some months. 'This is too redikelous [sic].' Verily I must toil and moil" (SLR Volume 28). Her journal for 1879 contains a class card for the Rhode Island School of Design for 1878–1879: these financial arrangements clearly were honored (SLR Volume 15), but her diary entries attest to unreliable financial support over time from her father. One undated letter from him, the contents suggesting 1878, is decidedly capricious with its qualification, "*if I can*" (SLR, Folder 26, undated).

14. The dates for the Lanes appear thanks to Todd S. Gernes, doctoral candidate, American Civilization, Brown University.

15. In the 1911 *Forerunner*, reviewing Schreiner's *Woman and Labor* (1911), Gilman observed that two books were essential to her during the years when her "domicile was a trunk"—Whitman's poetry and Schreiner's *Dreams* (2:197). For discussions of the relationship between the thought of Olive Schreiner and Gilman, see Barbara Scott Winkler, "Victorian Daughters: The Lives and Feminism of Charlotte Perkins Gilman and Olive Schreiner," *Michigan Occasional Paper* No. 13 (1980), and Sandra M. Gilbert and Susan Gubar, *No Man's Land*, Vol. 2: *Sexchanges* (1989), chap. 2, "Home Rule: The Colonies of the New Woman."

16. Compare, for example, the viewpoint of Elizabeth Stuart Phelps [Ward] (1844–1911) in *The Story of Avis* (Boston: James R. Osgood & Company, 1877): introduction, xiii-xxvi (repr. 1988). The heroine, a promising young artist, whose husband had assured her that he did not marry her so that she might become his housekeeper, finds him to hold the opposite opinion once married (153). This relationship is strikingly similar to that of Stetson and Perkins Gilman: compare the diarist's sentiments and behavior in *Endure: The Diaries of Charles Walter Stetson* with those of the husband depicted in *Avis*.

17. SLR Folder 21 includes 1889 copyrights for two plays, "A Pretty Idiot: A Comedy in Three Acts" (summer 1888, SLR Folders 21, copyright; 214, manuscript) and "Noblesse Oblige." SLR does not appear to hold a play manuscript having the latter title, nor do Hill (*Making*), Scharnhorst (1985), or Lane (*Life*) discuss a play by

this title. This might be one of the plays about which Charlotte wrote to Martha Luther Lane, 13 March 1886 (Rhode Island Historical Society; Hill 1980, 134). Or it might also have been written in Bristol, as Lane claims true for "A Pretty Idiot" (1990, 139), or be another name for "Changing Hands" (c. 1890, SLR Folder 215), written about the same time as "A Pretty Idiot."

18. For a discussion of Gilman's Nationalist activities, see Gary Scharnhorst, "Making Her Fame: Charlotte Perkins Gilman in California," *California History* 64: 192–201 (Summer 1985).

19. For a discussion of Howells' interactions with Gilman, see Joanne B. Karpinski, "When the Marriage of True Minds Admits Impediments: Charlotte Perkins Gilman and William Dean Howells," in *Patrons and Protégées: Gender, Friendship, and Writing in Nineteenth-Century America,* ed. Shirley Marchalonis. Karpinski notes that Howells' name does not appear among Gilman's list of "good friends among editors." The article demonstrates Howells' reluctant support, in meeting the letter though not the spirit of mentorship.

20. William Dean Howells, *Great Modern American Stories: An Anthology* (1920), vii; quoted in C. Shumaker in Meyering 65–66.

21. For a discussion of the publication history of "The Yellow Wallpaper," see *Living,* 119–121; Conrad Shumaker, " 'Too Terribly Good to Be Printed': Charlotte Perkins Gilman's 'The Yellow Wallpaper,' " *American Literature* 57 (December 1985): 588–99, repr. Sheryl L. Meyering, ed., *Charlotte Perkins Gilman: The Woman and Her Work.*

22. Gilman wrote "The Yellow Wallpaper" in August 1890; it was first published in *The New England Magazine* 5: 647–56 (Jan. 1892), and then reprinted in Boston by Small, Maynard & Company in 1899. In 1973, the Feminist Press reprinted it with an afterword by Elaine R. Hedges. This is the edition cited in this text. Subsequent reprinting includes Ann J. Lane, ed., *The Charlotte Perkins Gilman Reader: "The Yellow Wallpaper" and Other Fiction,* 1980, (includes an introduction, "The Fictional World of Charlotte Perkins Gilman," 11 stories, and excerpts from 7 novels); Lynne Sharon Schwartz, ed., *The Yellow Wallpaper and Other Writings,* 1989 (8 stories and excerpts from *Herland, Women and Economics,* and *The Man-Made World*); Barbara H. Solomon, ed., *'Herland' and Selected Stories by Charlotte Perkins Gilman,* 1992, ("The Yellow Wallpaper" plus 19 *Forerunner* stories).

23. For an essential survey of critical responses to this story, see Elaine Hedges, " 'Out at Last?': Critics Read 'The Yellow Wallpaper,' " in *The Captive Imagination: A Casebook on 'The Yellow Wallpaper,'* a collection of primary and critical selections, edited by Catherine Golden (1992), 319–33. A second forthcoming collection is Connie L. White and Thomas L. Erskine, eds., *"The Yellow Wallpaper,"* Women Writers: Text and Context series (fall 1993). And see Wai-Chee Dimock, "Feminism, New Historicism, and the Reader" for a discussion using Gilman's "The Yellow Wallpaper" to exemplify her argument.

24. In 1894, Knapp wrote a brief utopian essay, "One Thousand Dollars a Day: A Financial Experiment," in which she fantasized economic change. She imagined that income from the Golconda mines daily distributed for eighteen years to "every man and every woman" erased wealth inequity. The strategy could succeed only if a San Francisco man innovated a labor exchange to provide needed services.

25. Susan Ware, "Charlotte Perkins Gilman: The Early Lectures, 1890–1893," unpublished paper, May 29, 1973, cited by Ann J. Lane, *To 'Herland' and Beyond:*

The Life and Works of Charlotte Perkins Gilman (New York: Pantheon, 1990, 4, 162, 365.)

26. Earlier, smaller editions preceded the third and final 1898 edition published in Boston by Small, Maynard & Company: first, this 1893 edition in Oakland, California: McComb & Vaughan, 1893; then followed San Francisco: J. H. Barry and J. H. Marble, 1895; and London: T. Fisher Unwin, 1895.

Although Gilman never published a second book of verse, individual poems appear frequently in *The Forerunner,* and she planned a collection of poetry about women to be called "Of Her," that never reached completion (SLR Folders 161, 195, 209).

27. Gilman's report of the event is "Married in Providence/Quiet Wedding of Artist Stetson and Miss Channing," San Francisco *Call,* 8: (19 June 1894), 5.

28. At least three of Campbell's novels for adults suggest heroines who will inhabit Gilman's later *Forerunner* stories. See Chapter 3 for discussion.

29. One of Gilman's "Studies in Style" imitations followed Edward Bellamy: "A Cabinet Meeting," *Impress* (5 Jan. 1895), 4–5, features a woman as President of the United States, thereby offering a corrective to Bellamy's neglect of women's rights and utopian needs. The selection also anticipates Gilman's 1913 story, "A Council of War," and the 1915 utopian novel, *Herland.*

30. In the 1910 *Forerunner,* Gilman reviewed *Pure Sociology* (1893), by Lester Frank Ward, who then held the chair of sociology at Brown University.

31. Mann later married John Martin. In 1932, she published a utopian, economic reform tract, *Prohibiting Poverty: Suggestions for a Method of Obtaining Economic Security.* This satiric critique of masculine finance assumes that making a living is society's goal. To this end, it suggests a national livelihood plan to organize youth of both sexes between the ages of 18 and 26 for industrial production. The plan would provide all society's needed goods without buying or selling.

32. For Gilman's contributions to the *American Fabian,* see SLR Folder 55 and Volume 3; also Scharnhorst 1985, 99–103. *The American Fabian,* the organ of Fabian Socialism in the United States, was based in New York City. Additional contributing editors included Edward Bellamy, Helen Campbell, Henry Demarest Lloyd, and Prestonia Mann, as well as Gilman, then still Stetson.

33. A number of newspaper reports of Gilman's speeches appear in scrapbooks (SLR Folders 286–94, Volume 3). The speeches themselves for the most part have not survived (but see SLR Oversized Folder 2). Gilman spoke from notes. She developed a topic, then varied it extemporaneously to suit her audience. For one eyewitness report of her as a speaker, see James L. Hughes, "World Leaders I Have Known," *The Canadian Magazine* 61 (August 1923): 335–338.

34. SLR Folder 137: Addams to Gilman, 19 July 1898; Kelley to Gilman, 26 July 1898.

35. During 1898, two articles by Gilman (at this time Stetson) and one mention of her in the *Woman's Journal* concerned themes of *Women and Economics.* See the articles entitled "The Economic Basis of the Woman Question" and "Causes and Uses of the Subjection of Women," as well as the report of Gilman's Parker House speech before the New England Woman's Press Association (NEWPA), "The Business Woman's Home."

36. In addition to the influence of Lester F. Ward, in "Our Better Selves" (1888), and of Prof. Patrick Geddes and J. Arthur Thomson, *The Evolution of Sex* (1890) (*Living,* 259), in an 1897 letter to George Houghton Gilman, Charlotte privately

acknowledged as influences upon *Women and Economics* Edward Bellamy, *Looking Backward: 2000–1887* (1888); Ignatius Donnelly [pseudonym for Edmund Boisgilbert], *Caesar's Column: A Story of the Twentieth Century* (1890); along with reports of peasant uprisings, and essays by Fabian socialists, among whom she counted herself (SLR Folder 41, 11 May 1897). The biology text by Geddes and Thomson was intended for the general reader as well as the biology student (preface). The volume surveys the existence of sex differentiation across phyla and species. It discusses various theories explaining the differences, including evolution. Although unacknowledged in either *Women and Economics* or *The Living of Charlotte Perkins Gilman*, another influence was American economist Thorstein Veblen (1857–1929), so many of whose concerns paralleled her own. For example, see his "The Economic Theory of Women's Dress" (1894) and *The Theory of Leisure Class: An Economic Study of Institutions* (1899), works appearing even as she was herself formulating her ideas on similar subjects.

37. The total correspondence of more than 1200 individual items, sometimes more than one per date, is held by SLR in Boxes III, IV, V, VI, and VII, Folders 40–86. References cite the SLR locations.

38. Gilman noted in her autobiography that they had here a "home without a kitchen" (*Living*, 283). I believe that by "kitchen" she intended to convey "keeping a kitchen as an ongoing activity": this she does not do. Gary Scharnhorst has kindly reminded me that her diaries do indicate a room being designated as a kitchen in this apartment, since she does record cleaning a kitchen (SLR Volume 42, 13 October 1900, and Volume 43, 19 September 1901).

39. At least one critic, Ann Palmeri, ranks this, along with *Women and Economics*, as one of Gilman's "two major books" (106).

40. For a listing of articles published in the *Woman's Journal* during this period, see Gary Scharnhorst's 1985 *Bibliography*, 108–119. *Woman's Journal* articles for 1905 had appeared previously elsewhere, as for example "Housing for the Poor," first appearing in the New York *Evening Post* for 18 Nov 1905, a discussion pointing toward such forthcoming utopian fiction as the 1907 "A Woman's Utopia." My thanks to Elaine Hedges for bringing this article to my attention.

41. See Scharnhorst's bibliography of Gilman for duplications: works are listed by first known publication.

42. *The Forerunner* 1–7 (New York: Charlton Company, 1909–1916) is currently available as part of the series Radical Periodicals in the United States, 1890–1960, reprinted with an introduction by Madeleine B. Stern (1968). For each of the 14 issues of vol. 1, contents appear on the issue's title page; indices for vols. 2–7 appear at the end of each volume. For additional bibliographic information, see the essential Gilman research tool by Gary Scharnhorst, *Charlotte Perkins Gilman: A Bibliography*. For Gilman's description of the *Forerunner*, see *Living*, 304–10.

43. When she published this work in book form, Gilman reversed the title and subtitle from the *Forerunner* version: the book title is named here.

44. The titles alluded to are "Three Hundred Years Hence," in *Camperdown* by Mary Griffith, and *Mizora* by Mary E. Bradley Lane. The most up-to-date bibliography is Carol Farley Kessler, "Bibliography of Utopian Fiction by United States Women 1836–1988," *Utopian Studies* 1, no. 2 (1990): 1–58. For a historical survey through 1980, see Carol Farley Kessler, introduction to *Daring to Dream: Utopian Stories by United States Women 1836–1919* (1984). A revised edition is forthcoming

in the Utopianism and Communitarianism Series published by Syracuse University Press.

45. For Lester Ward, see note 30 above. In this *Forerunner* book review of *Pure Sociology* (1893, 1903), Gilman also cites his two-volume *Dynamic Sociology* (1883) and *Psychic Factors in Civilization* (1893).

46. Gilman writes, "One third of the inhabitants of New York now are Jews, and we know of the hundreds of Italians, Germans, and others. . . . The petty minority of Americans in New York receive small respect from their supplanters. Why should they? What must any people think of another people who voluntarily give up their country—not conquered—not forced out—simply outnumbered and swallowed up without a struggle" (*Living*, 316). Later she noted, "The people I meet [in Norwich], and mostly those I see in the neighborhood, are of native stock" (324).

47. For documentation, see correspondence between Gilman and her daughter, Kate, and between Gilman and the Bruères (SLR).

48. Manuscript Division, Library of Congress: Benjamin Huebsch Papers, Container 10, 1 March 1932, Gilman to Huebsch, including three-page circular, with photograph, announcing her lectures. The course of lectures entitled "The Larger Feminism" included talks on "The Biological Base," "The Economic Relation," " 'Love,' Love and Marriage," "The Home—Past, Present and Future," "Motherhood—Personal and Social," and "The Normal Woman and the Coming World." She also offered six different lectures on "The Woman Question." See also SLR Volume 7, Oversize Folders 2 and 3.

49. Jill Kerr Conway finds that Gilman, among others, wrote letters revealing "the self-aware interesting person with a great variety of moods, lots of strong managerial and intellectual drives," but an autobiography saying comparatively little of "emotional and personal growth" (1983, 6, 7). Carolyn G. Heilbrun observes that "these women had no models on which to form their lives, nor could they themselves become mentors since they did not tell the truth about their lives": in particular, Heilbrun continues, "The expression of anger has always been a terrible hurdle in women's personal progress" ("Non-Autobiographies" 71).

3. "This Prancing Young Utopia"

1. I would like to acknowledge the instructive article by Christopher P. Wilson, "Steady Burghers: The Terrain of *Herland*," which led me to Gilman's literary criticism.

2. A version of this statement appeared during the mid-1980s in a brochure for posters and other political items benefiting the Syracuse Cultural Workers. Reference librarians and I have searched fruitlessly to locate the source of this statement. If any reader knows, please send me the information care of the Syracuse University Press. Thank you.

3. Bakhtin, in "Discourse in the Novel" (1930s), observes that "the novel, and artistic prose in general, has the closest genetic, family relationship to rhetorical forms" (269): he insists upon the closeness—short of the collapse of novel into rhetoric —of this relationship. His is an early statement of the collapsing of traditional boundaries typical of much postmodernist feminist critical theory.

4. Alexander Black, in "The Woman Who Saw It First" (1923), quoted Gilman as saying about "The Yellow Wallpaper," "I wrote it to preach. If it is literature, that

just happened" (39). I would caution against too glibly accepting Gilman's offhand denial of literary skill.

5. This essay was flanked by two related to it: "Domestic Economy" (16 June 1904: 1359–63) and "Housing for Children" (25 August 1904: 434–38), both appearing in the *Independent*.

6. In February 1914, Gilman would give a talk on "The Right to Specialize in Home Industries" as part of a "Second Feminist Mass Meeting" at Cooper Union in New York City. See reproduced handbill, Nancy F. Cott, *The Grounding of Modern Feminism*, p. 10.

7. Illuminating criticism of Gilman's racism appears in Susan S. Lanser, "Feminist Criticism, 'The Yellow Wallpaper,' and the Politics of Color in America" (1989), and Elizabeth Ammons, *Conflicting Stories: American Women Writers at the Turn into the Twentieth Century* (1991), chap. 3: 34–43. Hazel V. Carby, in *Reconstructing Womanhood: The Emergence of the Afro-American Woman Novelist* (1987), demonstrates widespread racism against African-Americans as revealed in fiction of this era, and Jeanne Madeleine Weimann, in *The Fair Women: The Story of the Woman's Building, World's Columbian Exposition, Chicago 1893* (1981), delineates a case study of racism manifest in the women's committees associated with the 1893 fair (chap. 6: 103–24).

8. My thanks to Madelyn Gutwirth for suggesting this insightful interpretation of Gilman's racism. We must recall the racism of the women's suffrage movement and of the eugenics movement, both of which interested Gilman. Her thinking was, therefore, part of social reforms condoning racism.

9. Gilman explains in her autobiography, *The Living of Charlotte Perkins Gilman*, why this never reached completion: "One enthusiast, starting a new magazine, engaged me to write a serial novel for him, but was punished for his rashness by the prompt failure of his venture" (303). Only three installments appeared, while a fourth exists as page proofs: see Bibliography.

10. Subtitled "An Outline of Practical Co-operative Individualism." Henry Olerich, who wrote numerous utopias, had published in 1893 the story of a visit from a Martian to the United States. Martian society was communal, with parks and farms, residences, and workplaces interspersed. The nuclear family did not exist. People lived in complexes of one thousand, each with a private room.

11. For a discussion of racism in the suffrage movement, see Angela Y. Davis, *Women, Race & Class* (1981). Emma Lazarus (1849–1887), a Sephardic Jewish poet living in New York City, wrote the sonnet "The New Colossus" (1883), lines from which are reproduced upon a plaque attached to the base of the Statue of Liberty. She was inspired by "huddled masses yearning to breathe free," who were then escaping from Russian pogroms of the 1880s. From Emma Lazarus, "The New Colossus" (1883), in *Poems of Emma Lazarus*, vol. 1: 202 (1889).

12. Is Gilman failing here to acknowledge the Whitebergs as possibly-Jewish Weissbergs? Might this lack exemplify another bias, a veiled anti-Semitism that cannot come to grips with the degree of anguish experienced by this particular group?

13. Thanks to Madelyn Gutwirth for noting Gilman's tendency to level here.

14. "Dr. Clair's Place" reverses "The Yellow Wallpaper" by demonstrating what *should be done* for exhausted women, instead of exposing the gross error of Gilman's treatment. Dr. Willy Clair, a southerner by birth and a specialist in psychopathy, established a sanitorium in Southern California called "The Hills." As her patient here, Octavia Welch recovers genuine happiness. The story outlines Dr. Clair's proce-

dure for accomplishing a "cure." See *Forerunner* (June 1915). Also of interest is Gilman's "The 'Nervous Breakdown' of Women" in the *Forerunner* (August 1916), in which she discusses its widespread prevalence and finds long-established sex-prejudice exacting this "heavy price to pay for progress" (206).

15. *The Reproduction of Mothering: Psychoanalysis and the Sociology of Gender* (1978); for a critical discussion of the theory, see also *Signs* 6 (1981): 482–514 for critiques. A brief discussion appears in "Being and Doing: A Cross-Cultural Examination of the Socialization of Males and Females" (1971) in *Woman in Sexist Society*, ed. by Vivian Gornick and Barbara K. Moran. Subsequent research suggests why imagining children positively in fictional marriages presents so large a challenge to writers, during Gilman's era as now. Lynn K. White, Alan Booth, and John N. Edwards, in "Children and Marital Happiness: Why the Negative Correlation?" (1986), enumerate the ways in which the presence of children adds stress to a marriage—(1) by reducing the quality of the relationship with respect to interaction, finances, and division of labor, and (2) by braking the move to divorce so that difficult relationships go on longer than they otherwise might.

16. See Gilman's books *Concerning Children* (1900) and *Human Work* (1904) for expanded discussion of her thinking on these issues.

17. See chap. 1 and Gary Scharnhorst, "Making Her Fame: Charlotte Perkins Gilman in California" (Summer 1985).

18. Gilman considered the women's club movement "one of the most important sociological phenomena of the century" (*Living,* 164–66). More recently Nancy F. Cott, in *The Grounding of Modern Feminism* (1987), argues that the experience of participating in women's clubs at the turn of the century gave women the confidence to make demands for suffrage and in some cases for a more general emancipation, comparable to the experience of members of consciousness-raising groups of the 1960s and 1970s.

19. Gilman might here be honoring her uncle, utopist Edward Everett Hale.

20. Dolores Hayden, in *The Grand Domestic Revolution: A History of Feminist Designs for American Homes, Neighborhoods, and Cities* (1981), argues that Gilman, though a self-proclaimed socialist, in fact supported highly individualistic social solutions based upon a "benevolent" capitalistic economy (197). If we are to classify Gilman's economic views according to her recommendations rather than her abstract preferences, then we must recognize that she advocated capitalism, albeit a grassroots version defiant of corporate hegemony. And, as Hayden notes, Gilman did not disturb the hierarchy of class structure.

21. See, for example, Rachel Blau DuPlessis, in *Writing Beyond the Ending: Narrative Strategies of Twentieth-Century Women Writers* (1985); the issue receives further discussion in Chap. 4.

22. See Gilman's poem, "Two Callings," published in *The Home: Its Work and Influence* (1903), ending with the line, "Home was the World—the World was Home to me!" (vii–xi).

23. Carol Kolmerten suggests a possible precedent for Gilman's *Diantha* in the intentional community called the Woman's Commonwealth (1866–1918) of Belton, Texas; they actually provided domestic service as a means of communal livelihood. They are cited by Hayden (49), and one article in Rohrlich and Baruch discusses them (86–96). For more detailed information, see Sally Kitch, *Chaste Liberation: Celibacy and Female Cultural Status* (1989).

24. Compare the "noiseless, dextrous Japanese" servant in "Forsythe & For-

sythe" (3). Less explicit ethnocentrism occurs as well: an "atmosphere of contented pride" is attributed to the kitchens of such northern Europeans as the "Dutch, German, and French," in contrast to unspecified others lacking this (chap. 2). See Susan S. Lanser, previously cited; on bias against Asians, see Edward W. Said, *Orientalism* (1978).

25. See Dolores Hayden, *The Grand Domestic Revolution: A History of Feminist Designs for American Homes, Neighborhoods, and Cities* (1981), for a history and analysis of such experimentation. Part V, "Charlotte Perkins Gilman and Her Influence," discusses in detail Gilman's thought and writing on the subject.

26. For additional commentary on Gilman's utopian fiction, see Polly Wynn Allen in *Building Domestic Liberty: Charlotte Perkins Gilman's Architectural Feminism* (1988), chap. 4, "Gilman's Utopian Portrait of Nonsexist Landscapes" (81–102) and chap. 7, "The Power of Gilman's Storytelling Voice" (143–64).

27. In the 1912 *Forerunner,* Gilman serialized an uninspired tale called "Mag-Marjorie," exploring another unwed mother's pluckiness and a loving man's desire to join with her professionally, maritally, and parentally—though in this case the child is a girl, daughter Dolly. Parental behavior, especially of the male parent, does not receive detailed exploration. Research reported by Lynn K. White, Alan Booth, and John N. Edwards in 1986 indicates a negative correlation between children and marital happiness: might this very stressful, complex relation account for Gilman's and others' difficulty in imagining detailed alternative models? See note 16 above.

28. She explains, "There's the German Gate, and the Spanish Gate, the English Gate, the Italian Gate—and so on. . . . They have to come up to a certain standard before they are graduated" (80). All gates are western Anglo-European; the process of judging these standards remains disturbingly unexplained.

29. For example, as Hayden explains, utopian author Marie Howland (chap. 5), home economist and social scientist Ellen Swallow Richards, and social reformer Jane Addams of Hull House (chap. 8), like Gilman (chap. 11), and somewhat later, academic philosopher turned domestic reformer Ethel Puffer Howes (chap. 12), all advocated community kitchens and day care for children. Howland (1836–1921) wrote *Papa's Own Girl; A Novel* (1874), reprinted as *The Familistere; A Novel* (1918). An engagingly readable communitarian romance, this feminist novel makes equitable relations between women and men basic to the improved conduct of society in probably Lowell, Massachusetts, where a European count finances a Social Palace. Hayden documents the influence of Howland's description of the Social Palace in Guise, France, upon Gilman, citing *Women and Economics* and *The Home* (195, 332).

30. Maydston (Maidstone) was the original name of East Hampton, Long Island, where during the 1890s Gilman enjoyed summer vacations with her daughter Kate.

31. Benigna McAvelly (listen to the pun on Machiavelli) also appears in the novel serialization "Benigna McAvelly" in the *Forerunner* 5 (1914).

32. Gilman's good friend, Martha S. Bensley Bruère, wrote for the *Survey,* and in 1919 published in the *Ladies' Home Journal* a serialization of a utopian novel, *Mildred Carver, U.S.A.*—an updated, gender-equal version of the universal service to one's country imagined by Edward Bellamy in *Looking Backward.*

33. Marilyn Ferguson, in *The Aquarian Conspiracy,* discusses autarchy, government by the self, as a basis for effective social functioning (192).

34. See Charlene Spretnak, *The Spiritual Dimension of Green Politics* (1986); and Charlene Spretnak and Fritjof Capra, *Green Politics: The Global Promise* (1984).

35. From the *King James' Bible*, Proverbs 6.6–11:

> 6 Go to the ant, thou sluggard; consider her ways, and
>   be wise:
> 7 Which having no guide, overseer, or ruler,
> 8 Provideth her meat in the summer, and gathereth her
>   food in the harvest.
> 9 How long wilt thou sleep, O sluggard? when wilt thou
>   arise out of thy sleep?
> 10 Yet a little sleep, a little slumber, a little folding of
>   the hands to sleep:
> 11 So shall thy poverty come as one that travelleth, and
>   thy want as an armed man.

36. Then-contemporary feminist interest in eugenics seeps into Gilman's text here. Eugenics interested middle-class women for reasons of population control, especially to be practiced by classes less fortunate than themselves. The concern, hardly fully altruistic, provides yet another instance of xenophobia and racism on the part of white feminists. For more detailed discussion, see Germaine Greer, *Sex and Destiny* (1984).

37. In the January 1913 *Forerunner,* Gilman had written "A Platform for Women," in which she claimed that women needed "not a 'Woman's Party,' but certainly a Woman's Platform" (6), much as this council is enumerating. Her 1895 *Impress* imitation of Edward Bellamy, called "A Cabinet Meeting," had demonstrated women leading public reform, although then in the company of men. See earlier note 29, chap. 2.

38. For discussion of the relationship between women's rising expectations and the coming World War I, see chapter 7: "Soldier's Heart," from Sandra M. Gilbert and Susan Gubar, *No Man's Land: The Place of the Woman Writer in the Twentieth Century,* Vol. 2: *Sexchanges* (1989).

39. Elise Boulding, in "Building Utopias in History" (1987), cites *Herland* to illustrate a feminist utopian tradition attuned to "structures and processes of the natural order which enable individual actors and social groups to work with the potentials in any organic entity without doing violence to those potentials" (216). Boulding places *Herland* within a context of worldwide utopian practice.

40. *Herland* is not the first all-female or gender role–reversal utopia written by a woman in the United States. In 1870, Annie Denton Cridge collected in *Man's Rights; or, How Would You Like It?* five dreams from the nine published in *Woodhull and Claflin's Weekly.* These satiric role reversals make ludicrous the nineteenth-century "cult of true womanhood" when it is practiced by men. In 1881, Mary E. Bradley Lane published *Mizora: A Prophecy* in *The Cincinnati Commercial,* where it appeared between November 1880 and February 1881 (repr. New York: G. W. Dillingham, 1889; New York: Gregg, 1975). An all-female society in which education is the highest concern, Mizora is reached through an entrance at the North Pole. Though nonviolent, it is hierarchical and white racist. The tradition of women's utopias in the United States is overviewed in the introduction to Carol Farley Kessler, ed., *Daring to Dream: Utopian Stories by United States Women, 1836–1919* (Boston and London: Pandora/Routledge & Kegan Paul, 1984), to be reissued in

an expanded edition by Syracuse University Press as part of its Utopianism and Communitarianism Series.

41. In the May 1915 *Forerunner,* Gilman would write "World Rousers": here she proclaimed the need for "the rousing of people to a recognition of the real conditions now about them and their own real powers" (131), an awakening to "the main idea—WE! *We* can do this and that; not you or I, but We" (132).

42. Feminist evolutionists—Frances Dahlberg in *Woman the Gatherer* (1981) and Nancy Tanner in *On Becoming Human* (1981)—find early foraging societies likely to have been gender-egalitarian, though not matriarchal. Recall the introductory discussion by Riane Eisler in *The Chalice and the Blade,* who, in reviewing recent archeological research, demonstrates that early civilizations in Crete and Sumer were Goddess-centered in religion and gender-equal in social practice. Not rule of men through domination (what she labels "androcracy"), but a practice of partnership between the sexes prevailed in the management of society (a condition she names "gylany"). The former mode of rule leads to domination hierarchies based upon force, while the latter creates actualization hierarchies whose subsequent levels indicate increased complexity (105–6). In addition, Eisler cites research by psychologist David McClelland indicating that gylanic eras stress creation over destruction, and typically are periods of great cultural creativity (145–46). For additional background, see Jessie Bernard, *The Female World* (1981); Elise Boulding, *The Underside of History: A View of Women Through Time* (1976; rev. 2-vol. edition, 1992); Marilyn French, *Beyond Power: On Women, Men, and Morals* (1985); and Gerda Lerner, *The Creation of Patriarchy* (1986).

43. Theoretical background for this paragraph comes from Victor Turner's expansion of Arnold van Gennep's concept of a three-phased *rite de passage* or transition from one state to another (1960)—(1) separation from a previous state, (2) existence on a margin or *limen* (Latin for "threshold") between old and new states, and (3) aggregation with a new state (94–95). Turner, in "Liminality and Communitas," stresses this second phase (1969, 94–130). Bakhtin's dialogic mindset or double-voiced discourse can be seen as a version of liminality. And liminality is the estranged, everyday state of marginalized individuals or peoples, who live with feet figuratively planted on either side of a margin or border. It is also the state of readers, who are in fact cognitive visitors, as they peruse utopias. They can undergo a cultural conversion from the mind-set they hold as they begin reading to a new frame of reference by the time they finish. Such cultural change, or conversion, is discussed in Hans Toch, *The Social Psychology of Social Movements* (1965), and Anthony N. B. Wallace, "Revitalization Movements" (1956).

44. Living in California at the time, Gilman was nonetheless aware of the World's Columbian Exposition in Chicago in 1893, with its Woman's Building designed, managed, and exhibited "not for herself, but for humanity," the building's motto. It provided clear, material evidence of the *"civilized"* competence attainable by the world's women and was widely reported in contemporary newspapers. The fame of this World's Fair and its Woman's Building also emerged in fiction of the time: for examples, see the juvenile *Two Little Pilgrims' Progress: A Story of the City Beautiful* (1895), by Frances Hodgson Burnett, or the adult satiric *Samantha at the World's Fair* (1893), by Marietta Holley. A recent study is *The Fair Women: The Story of the Woman's Building, World's Columbian Exposition, Chicago 1893* (1981), by Jeanne Madeleine Weimann. This event is among the cultural antecedents of *Herland.* At least some of Gilman's audience, as a result of this event, would have

been more amenable to imagining a women's civilization. Racism, however, was rampant during the planning of this White City and was a blight on its success. See Weimann, chap. 6, already cited, on prejudice against African Americans, and Robert W. Rydell, "The World's Columbian Exposition of 1893: Racist Underpinnings of a Utopian Artifact" (1978), which treats racism with respect to Japanese, Chinese, and American Indians as well as African Americans. These references supply an overview of the widespread racism practiced during this era. Nor did Gilman escape being implicated. Considerable irony thus rests in Gilman herself writing "What 'World Expositions' Mean" for the *Stockton Mail* in 1893 and explaining that such expositions "prove the one great tendency of the times: that international unity, that oneness of race, which is growing upon us so fast" (4). In chapter 9, "The Effects of the Position of Women on the Race Mind" of a 1912 *Forerunner* serialization, "Our Brains and What Ails Them," Gilman discussed what she would imagine in *Herland* as the possibilities of women: "After a few centuries of full human usefulness on the part of women, we shall have not only new achievements to measure but new standards of measurement" (249). The experience and responsibility that she found to be lacking in many women of her time (250), she would provide imaginatively in *Herland*.

45. Gilman may well have known of J. J. Bachofen's 1854 study *Mutterrecht* [Motherright/power], which argued for the ancient historical precedence of matriarchy over patriarchy. Most contemporary archeologists do not accept this theory, but believe that, although several earlier Western societies were far more egalitarian than is our own with regard to the sexes, in none did women have power over men as men have had over women. Rather what existed was worship of a female as the supreme being—worship of a Great Goddess. The Goddess's existence has amazingly survived millennia of concerted effort to eradicate her religion, called "pagan," a word originally meaning "rural," "countrified"—hence the religion of country people, who of necessity live close to seasonal cycles. See note 39 above for evolutionary theories; for a contemporary evaluation of Bachofen, see Hildebrandt. Emily Erwin Culpepper, in a "Sympathetic Critique" of thealogy, urges: "Pluralism is more likely to help us recognize our differences as positive and to explore what Mirtha Quintanales has called 'our different primary emergencies' " (68). For further background on Goddess thealogies, among a great critical outpouring, see the following chronological selection: Merlin Stone, *When God Was a Woman* (New York: Schocken, 1976); *Heresies: A Feminist Publication on Art and Politics* 5 (1978; rev. 1982), special issue, "The Great Goddess"; Charlene Spretnak, ed., *The Politics of Women's Spirituality* (New York: Doubleday, 1982); Pamela C. Berger, *The Goddess Obscured, Transformation of the Grain Protectress from Goddess to Saint* (Boston: Beacon, 1985); Carl Olson, ed., *The Book of the Goddess Past and Present: An Introduction to Her Religion.* (New York: Crossroad, 1985); Emily Erwin Culpepper, "Contemporary Goddess Thealogy: A Sympathetic Critique," in *Shaping New Vision: Gender and Values in American Culture,* ed. by Clarissa W. Atkinson, Constance H. Buchanan, and Margaret R. Miles (Ann Arbor, Mich.: UMI, 1987), 51–71; Buffie Johnson, *Lady of the Beasts: Her Ancient Images of the Goddess and Her Sacred Animals* (San Francisco: Harper and Row, 1988); Elinor W. Gadon, *The Once and Future Goddess: A Symbol for Our Time* (San Francisco: Harper and Row, 1989); Marija Gimbutas, *The Language of the Goddess: Unearthing the Hidden Symbols of Western Civilization* (San Francisco: Harper and Row, 1989); Judith Plaskow and Carol Christ, eds., *Weaving the Visions: New Patterns in Feminist Spirituality* (New York: HarperCollins, 1989);

Gloria Feman Orenstein, *The Reflowering of the Goddess* (Elmsford, N.Y., Pergamon, 1990); Marija Gimbutas, *The Civilization of the Goddess: The World of Old Europe* (New York: HarperCollins, 1991).

46. See note 35 above, providing complete Biblical citation of Proverbs 6.6, quoted fully in connection with the short story "Bee Wise."

47. For instance, in her 1898 *Women and Economics,* she notes that "the hideous injustice of Christianity to the Jew attracted no attention through many centuries" (78), and again in a 1913 *Forerunner* article called "Race Pride," states "that we have cheated the Indian, oppressed the African, robbed the Mexican and childishly wasted our great resources, is ground for shame" (90). But by 1935, widowed and threatened by incurable cancer, she was far less generous and loosed a tirade against immigrants in New York City, where but 7% could claim a birthright: "One third of [its] inhabitants . . . now are Jews, and we know of the hundreds of thousands of Italians, Germans, and others" (*Living,* 316). She did not recognize the cosmopolitan strength of New York as a center for the "world rousing" she *advocated* (*Forerunner* 6: 131–32).

48. Elizabeth Spelman, in *Inessential Woman: Problems of Exclusion in Feminist Thought* (1988), argues eloquently not for the difference of women as a sex, but for the differences that a great diversity of women represent (chap. 6). She stresses that the similarities that women share exist within a context of differences, which influence how much power one group of women has with respect to another. Frequently Gilman ignored the power of these differences and failed to recognize the basic and contributing strength of diversity in a heterogeneous democratic society.

49. In 1975, Joanna Russ published *The Female Man* (New York: Bantam), a novel in which the utopia Whileaway provides similar conditions for children. The whole Whileawayan society is home: "you cannot fall out of the kinship web and become sexual prey for strangers, for there is no prey and there are no strangers—the web is world-wide" (repr. 1978, 81). Russ had no knowledge of Gilman's *Herland* when she wrote this novel (letter to the author, 1 August 1992).

50. Jane Roland Martin, in chapter 6: "Gilman's Mothers" of *Reclaiming a Conversation: The Ideal of the Educated Woman* (1985), because she did not connect her interpretation to Gilman's biography, fails to distinguish between Gilman's projection of emotional restraint toward children, such as her mother practiced, and Gilman's insistence that childrearing, like every other social role, can be a specialization (168–69).

51. For a brief introduction to several of the issues concerning women and religion, see Casey Miller and Kate Swift, *Words and Women: New Language in New Times,* chap. 5. Sandra M. Gilbert and Susan Gubar extend the foregoing discussion of language power in *No Man's Land: The Place of the Woman Writer in the Twentieth Century,* Vol. 1: *The War of the Words,* chap. 5. Important for Gilman was *The Woman's Bible* edited in 1895 by Elizabeth Cady Stanton (repr. 1974): Gilman was present for the National American Woman Suffrage Association (NAWSA) Convention debate, chaired by Susan B. Anthony, that concluded in the rejection of Stanton's work as too radical, as irreligious. Gilman, much taken with Stanton's ideas, was appalled at this outcome. Recall that in 1923, eight years after *Herland,* Gilman wrote *His Religion and Hers: A Study of the Faith of Our Fathers and the Work of Our Mothers.*

52. "The relation," Gilman's code word for sexual intercourse, appeared also in a letter to her friend Grace Channing Stetson, reassuring Grace of her own capacity

to enjoy sexual intercourse in a second marriage, even though she had not in her first.

53. An early *Forerunner* story, "Martha's Mother" (April 1910), demonstrates the importance of a mother to her daughter and her daughter's peers by running a boarding house for young working women. Stenographer and typist in a real estate office, Martha Joyce thus has good lodging and food, and also a mother to keep off men she does not want to see, a place to have fun with those she enjoys. Only women board, but men, too, are "mealers." This story is an early all-woman, mother-centered community, prefiguring *Herland*.

54. Gilman disapproves of such capitalist greed at the same time that she finds inheritance of capital useful in establishing fictional utopias. She seems not to have recognized conceptual inconsistency.

55. Running concurrently with *Herland* in the *Forerunner* was Gilman's serialization of "The Dress of Women" (1915). She believed that women's clothes would become more sensible when women's lives changed. Her ideas show the influence of Thorstein Veblen's "The Economic Theory of Women's Dress" (1894) and *The Theory of Leisure Class: An Economic Study of Institutions* (1899).

56. For an incisive discussion of birth imagery, see Susan Stanford Friedman, "Creativity and the Childbirth Metaphor: Gender Difference in Literary Discourse" (1989).

57. Catharine R. Stimpson, in a 1981 keynote address before the Society for Utopian Studies, noted that Gilman imagines *Herland* "as if neither gender roles nor eros existed" (4). Gilman erases differences rather than celebrating them, as is more typical of recent feminist utopias, such as Marge Piercy's *Woman on the Edge of Time* (1976). But Gilman's cultural context differed from Piercy's: nineteenth-century stereotypes still thrived.

58. For a recent collection of articles, see Rachel T. Hare-Mustin and Jeanne Maracek, eds., *Making a Difference: Psychology and the Construction of Gender* (1990).

59. For a popular discussion, see David D. Burns, M.D., *Feeling Good: The New Mood Therapy* (1981), a self-help book presenting a sequence of cognitive exercises to retrain a reader's mind in avoiding thought patterns causing depression.

60. The epithet is Elaine Hedges' used in remarks about "Gilman's Pragmatopias: Nine Stories, 1908–1913," delivered by Carol Farley Kessler at the May 1991 American Literature Association Conference in Washington, D.C. and later revised and published as "Consider Her Ways: The Cultural Work of Charlotte Perkins Gilman's Pragmatopian Stories, 1908–1913," in *Utopian and Science Fiction by Women: Worlds of Difference,"* ed. Jane Donawerth and Carol A. Kolmerten (Syracuse: Syracuse Univ. Press, 1994).

61. For references providing more extended theoretical discussions, see Chap. 1, n. 8.

62. Again from Hedges' remarks at the 1991 American Literature Association Conference, in response to my discussion of nine Gilman short stories written between 1908 and 1913 (note 60 above).

4. Writing to Empower Living

1. Quoted by Susan Stanford Friedman, from Lucille Clifton's Kali sequence, *An Ordinary Woman*, New York: Random, 1974, 50. The context for Friedman's

quotation is her discussion of the poet's being "her own mother as well as mother to squalling babies and poems. She is both word and flesh, by divine and poetic authority" (93).

2. Concepts of "prosaics," "unfinalizability," and "dialogic," central to the cultural criticism of Bakhtin (1895–1975), receive detailed discussion in the recent study by Gary Saul Morson and Caryl Emerson, *Mikhail Bakhtin: Creation of a Prosaics* (1990); see especially chap. 1. For a discussion of "unfinalizability" in particular, see Morson and Emerson, 36–49; chap. 5 on the psychology of the self. Bakhtin posited an open (33–36), chaotic (36–38) universe in which closure will not occur and meaning is immanent (38–40). Bakhtin first developed this concept in the 1929 *Problems of Dostoevsky's Creative Art*. He insisted upon the existence of surprise and the unexpected, even to the upending of reason and law: compare his concept of the "carnivalesque," developed in 1940 and expanded into *Rabelais and his World* (1965). The very element of "unfinalizability" makes possible human creativity and human freedom. And it requires of us responsibility, in Bakhtin's word "answerability," for our actions (38).

3. He lived from 1895 to 1975, overlapping the last forty years of Gilman's life. During the 1920s, he was working on a treatise about the nature of moral responsiblity and aesthetics, a relationship that had also concerned Gilman during the previous two decades. See chap. 1 for a discussion of Gilman's 1910 literary views: fiction is "world-food" that prepares readers so that "meeting life in reality we should be wise—and not be disappointed" (*Forerunner* 1.5: 21).

4. This is one of several discrepancies between the autobiography and other extant documents. Recall that one of Gilman's purposes in writing *Living* was to inspire young women. Since she never lost an insatiable need for approval, she thus downplayed factors detracting from her personal heroism in overcoming difficulties.

5. One unfinished tale, "The Story of a Bad Boy," concerns a good girl and a bad boy. In an early "attempt" at writing an autobiography, Gilman noted the ceaseless childhood teasing of her brother, a possible explanation for her nearly unremitting preference for bad boys (SLR Folder 234, "Autobiography," chap. 2).

6. In her essay "Mother-Daughter Relationships: Psychodynamics, Politics, and Philosophy," Jane Flax comments, "There seems to be an endless chain of women tied ambivalently to their mothers, who replicate this relation with their daughters" (37). Kate would see her mother, Charlotte, with even greater ambivalence and less understanding as an adult. See Lane 1990, chap. 12.

7. Of course, we are aware of Sigmund Freud's belief in the polymorphous sexuality of human infants and of the learned nature of human sexuality. In addition, Carroll Smith-Rosenberg, in her 1975 *Signs* article, "The Female World of Love and Ritual: Relations Between Women in Nineteenth-Century America," presents correspondence between women indicating the strongly emotional nature of these relationships and its acceptance as normal conduct. These letters indicate that women frequently shared beds as suggested in this story: we cannot, however, draw definitive conclusions about the erotic nature of this behavior.

8. In a letter to George Houghton Gilman dated 18 May 1897, Gilman would write, "I am well used to giving up what I like—thoroughly well trained in it" (SLR Folder 41).

9. Young girls frequently experience their fathers as romantic strangers, so that Gilman's characterization of a father and daughter here is a typical one. When Charlotte was 14 or 15, she began a second version of "A Fairy Story" (SLR Volume

14, 32–36), this time with brother and sister protagonists named Gabriel and Ara-phenia, in place of the 1870 "only child," and an unnamed fairy princess, who func-tions as the fairy-savior "Elmondine" of the 1870 version. This gender change from two female protagonists of 1870 to male/female siblings saved by a female fairy reflects an adolescent writer's increased awareness of heterosocial relations, as her concurrent journals indicate.

10. *Forerunner* stories concerning mothers and daughters include "Martha's Mother" (1.6), "What Occupation?" (2.8), "My Poor Aunt" (4.12), "With a Difference (Not Literature)" (5.2), "Joan's Defender" (7.6), and "The Unnatural Mother" (7.11). Gilman also depicts mothers- and daughters-in-law as in "Old Mrs. Crosley" (2.11), "Making a Change" (2.12), and "A Strange Influence" (3.5). Her *Concerning Children* (1900) questions many nineteenth-century truisms of child rearing. For instance, she doubts the value of exacting absolute obedience from children in a chapter called "The Effect of Minding on the Mind": instead of benefits, Gilman finds that this practice develops docility, subservience, and quick surrender of purpose. And she stresses the importance of nurturance for all of a society's children, not just one's own—what she calls "social," as opposed to individual, parenting.

11. Mary A. Hill also discusses "A Fairy Story" in *Charlotte Perkins Gilman: The Making of a Radical Feminist,* calling it " A Fairy Tale" (33).

12. The exception, "Prince Cherry" (3 pp.), concludes with Cherry, too, finally turning bad, although he manages well for a while, guided by his "best friend," Fairy Candide, who of course is female. "The Story of a Bad Boy" (2 pp.) and "The story of a good girl and a bad boy" (one-paragraph fragment) relentlessly imagine various naughty behaviors perpetrated by boys.

13. Her viewpoint is substantiated by R. Gordon Kelly, in his *Mother Was a Lady: Self and Society in Selected American Childrens' Periodicals, 1865–1890* (1974). Kelly demonstrates how such writing inculcates a culture's values and shared meanings, and how such a body of writing reveals exactly what a culture's values are. Because the writing is for the learner, the uninitiated, assumptions are articu-lated with a clarity not present in writing for adults.

14. Three titles by Campbell suggest solutions appearing in Gilman's *Forerun-ner* fiction. *Mrs. Herndon's Income* (1885) shows the use of inheritance to relieve individual stress: Margaret Herndon is a member of a group called the Ultimates, who help others and avoid strife. *Miss Melinda's Opportunity* (1886) presents a one-year experiment in group living: a private duplex houses a group of working women, who live cheaply and well while escaping the excessive restrictiveness that was then typically placed upon "working girls" living in public boarding homes. *Some Passages in the Practice of Dr. Martha Scarborough* (1893) depicts the education and profes-sional success of an intelligent young woman, who will marry another physician.

15. Henry James, in "The Art of Fiction" (1888), implies that the "moral" brav-ery of a novelist consists in being able "to face the difficulties with which on every side the treatment of reality bristles"; that the "essence of moral energy is to survey the whole field"—"be as complete as possible"; the novelist's "only condition" is to "be sincere." The novel does not, in his view, directly concern "questions of morality." William Dean Howells, in "Novel-Writing and Novel-Reading" (1899), notes, "It is [the novelist's] function to help you to be kinder to your fellows, juster to yourself, truer to all"—a credo of effects approaching Gilman's own. (Both essays are included in Nina Baym et al., eds., *Norton Anthology of American Literature,* Vol. 2, 3rd ed., 1989.)

16. For background on Jane Addams, see Allen F. Davis, *American Heroine: The Life and Legend of Jane Addams* (1973); on women and Hull House, see Kathryn Kish Sklar, "Hull House in the 1890s: A Community of Women Reformers" (1985); on Hull House programs, see Rivka Shpak Lissak, *Pluralism and Progressives: Hull House and the New Immigrants, 1890–1919* (1989); for Hull House residents, see photos by resident Wallace Kirkland published as *The Many Faces of Hull-House*, ed. Mary Ann Johnson (1989); for the experience of one Hull House woman, see Hilda Satt Polacheck, *I Came a Stranger: The Story of a Hull-House Girl* (1989). I thank Priscilla Ferguson Clement for reminding me about the article by Kathryn Kish Sklar.

17. See also Chap. 2, n. 10.

18. This ambivalence emerges again in letters to George Houghton Gilman. During the month of August 1897, Gilman visited two intentional communities, Prestonia Mann's Summer Brook Farm in New York's Adirondacks and Greenacres in Eliot near Maine's coast. Of Summer Brook Farm, she wrote Ho, "A community life is evidently well suited to my style of beauty; and presently when I am wooed to enter lots of them, I can flit agreeably from point to point and maintain my equanimity without difficulty!" (SLR Folder 44, 8 August 1897). She was less enthusiastic regarding Greenacres. Two years later in February 1899, visiting Ruskin [Tennessee] Co-operative Colony, Gilman informed Ho, "All kinds of people are here, but mostly inferior and queer. I am more convinced than ever of the hopelessness of colony life—of any attempt to establish little separate organisms within one great inescapable social organism" (SLR Folder 64, 1 February 1899). She emphasized her belief that all domestic work should be professionalized, not cooperative.

19. For additional background, see Hill 1980, 228–37, 255–57, 272–82; Lane 1990, chap. 11.

20. The theories of Karen Horney (1885–1952), as studied by Marcia Westkott in *The Feminist Legacy of Karen Horney,* offer additional insight into the mother-daughter relationship. Westkott discusses the development of female altruism ("the characterological need to care for others") in the context of mother-daughter relationships (134–40). Horney hypothesizes that an ideal self is constructed to meet external demands at the expense of a real self, which is then submerged. Mothers in patriarchy typically require the development of ideal selves in their daughters, selves that negate authentic feeling in favor of accepted responses, frequently serving the needs of others—the aforementioned altruism. Westkott then explains how Alice Miller extends the thought of Karen Horney on female altruism. Miller notes that the (usually parental) sheer cruelty of refusing to permit children to express their true feelings, save at the risk of losing parental love and approval, is a form of parental use of a child to meet the parent's needs, this use damaging a child's emotional development. Mothers raised with such affective deficits—the submerging of any negative emotion, the expression of positive emotion, with the fear of otherwise losing affection—must then depend upon daughters for support (the altruism already defined), mothers' needs perpetuating emotional deficit in the next generation. The healed female hero, who finds or remakes her real self, according to Westkott's explication of Horney, "experiences, finally, the extraordinary power of her ordinary real self" (214). No study of motherhood can omit Rich's *Of Woman Born* (1976). And see a recent sociological study by Lucy Rose Fischer, *Linked Lives: Adult Daughters and Their Mothers,* and a recent psychological study by Paula J. Caplan, *Don't Blame Mother: Mending the Mother-Daughter Relationship,* especially chaps. 4 and 5 on

myths. For further background, see Marcia Westkott's study of Karen Horney (1986), especially chap. 5; Karen Horney, *Neurosis and Human Growth: The Struggle Toward Self-Realization* (1950) and *Feminine Psychology* (1967); Alice Miller, *The Drama of the Gifted Child: How Narcissistic Parents Form and Deform the Emotional Lives of Their Talented Children* (1979); and *For Your Own Good: Hidden Cruelty in Child-Rearing and the Roots of Violence* (1983).

21. Judith Fryer quotes Edith Cobb's understanding of the childhood bases of adult creativity: see Cobb's "The Ecology of Imagination in Childhood" 159.

22. I agree with Mary A. Hill's conclusion regarding the impact upon Charlotte of her renewed connection with her cousin Ho. Hill states: "It was almost as though he helped her to reconnect with energies of childhood, with a youthful sense of wholeness, with the possibility of integrating a rich variety of needs—for work and travel, for love and intimacy, for professional development as well as for affirmation of her private life" ("Journey" chap. 1). In examining Gilman's letters to her daughter, I find precisely this exuberance and I find it also appearing in *Herland*. I quote from Hill's commentary as additional evidence to support the utopian spirit I find emerging in the childhood fantasies, these letters to Kate, and in the utopian fiction, especially *Herland*.

23. The correspondence provides one account of "an active female desire of the other," in the words of Christine Holmlund examining Luce Irigaray's central female figures (294). In discussing Irigaray's figure of the "heterosexual female lover" (292–295) from the third phase of her work, Holmlund actually cites four texts: *Amante marine de Friedrich Nietzsche* (1980), *Passions élémentaires* (1982), *L'Ethique de la différence sexuelle* (1984), and *Sexes et parentés* (1987). Earlier in the article, she names three additional titles that are part of this third, recent phase of Irigaray's work: *L'Oubli de l'air* (1983), *La Croyance même* (1983), and *Parler n'est jamais neutre* (1985) (286). See 304, n. 1 for existing English translations.

24. I acknowledge the perceptive observation of my colleague, historian Priscilla Ferguson Clement, that Gilman's destroying these letters constitutes "the ultimate act of possession."

25. Showalter defines a "muted group" as one "the boundaries of whose culture and reality overlap, but are not wholly contained by, the *dominant (male) group*" (261). The "wild zone" then contains those facets of culture or reality "outside the dominant boundary" (262). From a male viewpoint, the "wild zone" is "imaginary," a "projection of the unconscious." Additional attention to differences between women and men reading appears in Jane Marcus' sensitive explication of the Ramsays as readers in Virginia Woolf's *To the Lighthouse:* see "Still Practice, A/Wrested Alphabet: Toward a Feminist Aesthetic" in *Art and Anger: Reading Like a Woman.*

26. We must, of course, remember that, because children have impossible expectations for mothers, children's accounts may be inaccurate. Both Charlotte and daughter Kate found their mothers inadequate. For background regarding this phenomenon, see Rachel T. Hare-Mustin and Patricia Broderick, "The Myth of Motherhood: A Study of Attitudes Toward Motherhood," and Nancy Chodorow and Susan Contratto, "The Fantasy of the Perfect Mother."

27. Marianne Hirsch, in her 1981 *Signs* review essay, "Mothers and Daughters," reports a consensus that "women, like men, need the nurturance that will allow them to become creative, productive adults, and as long as mothers carry the burden of child rearing alone, they will not be able to nurture and support their daughters in their struggle for self-realization: the maternal role creates too much

ambivalence about their own and their daughters' female identity" (208). (Mary Perkins, Charlotte Perkins [Stetson] Gilman, and Kate Stetson Chamberlin are all implicated in this statement.) The consensus Hirsch reports includes works by Benjamin, Bernard, Chodorow, Dinnerstein, Flax, and J. B. Miller. Included, too, in the review essay is a pertinent quotation from Judith Arcana, *Our Mothers' Daughters* (1979), which I expand to the original paragraph: "All that our mothers teach us is what they have learned in the crucible of sexism. They cannot give us a sense of self-esteem which they do not possess. We must learn to interpret anew the experience our mothers have passed on to us, to see these lives in terms of struggle, often unconscious, to find and maintain some peace, beauty and respect for themselves as women" (70). Gilman, in her *The Living of Charlotte Perkins Gilman,* makes this effort. Hirsch also discusses Adrienne Rich, "Compulsory Heterosexuality and Lesbian Experience" (1980). She quotes Rich: "If we consider the possibility that all women . . . exist on a lesbian continuum, we can see ourselves as moving in and out of this continuum, whether we identify ourselves as lesbian or not" (quoted 221–22). Hirsch observes that this may be one among other ways to envision ourselves "outside patriarchal conceptions" (222). Given the centrality and continuity of women in Gilman's life, Rich's concept may be helpful for exploring and evaluating this dimension of her experience. See *Signs* 7.1 (1981) for four responses to Rich's article. The same *Signs* issue includes Luce Irigaray on mother-daughter symbiosis, a deficiency of individuated selves, "And the One Doesn't Stir without the Other," trans. with introd. Hélène Vivienne Wenzel, 56–67.

28. But see Hill for a discussion of Gilman's glossing over the stress that lower- and middle-class mothers experience, since Gilman perceives this maternal stress as her individual disability, rather than as a function of female subordination ("Journey" chap. 6).

29. See relevant pages and chapters in the Hill and Lane biographies, as well as *The Living of Charlotte Perkins Gilman,* the correspondence with Martha Luther Lane as discussed by Juliet A. Langley in " 'Audacious Fancies': A Collection of Letters from Charlotte Perkins Gilman to Martha Luther," and especially the letters to Ho dated 7 Mar. 1899 and 9 May 1900.

30. See the discussion regarding Horney's views in n. 20 above.

31. Lane shows, while Hill acknowledges but places less emphasis upon, this tendency (Lane 1990, chap. 8; Hill "Journey" chap. 9).

32. The letters show that an "enemy within" included such traditional gender-stereotyping as this set of harsh statements she sent to Ho:

> It is a woman's business to wait, not a man's.
> It is for a woman to be patient and still—not a man.
> If you are truly lover and husband—show it.
> If not—God bless you and Good bye
> (SLR Folder 62, 25 Jan. 1899).

This passage shows Charlotte demanding that Houghton be a traditional man or depart her company—not at all what she in fact wanted. She would also state, "A marriage that dreads children is *WRONG*" (SLR Folder 66, 15 Mar. 1899). The letters also show that the "enemy within" included Charlotte's fears of losing herself in another, of erasing the boundaries of self. Charlotte fears connection, writes Ho that she "cannot rest till I have torn loose again and am stammering—'no—I'm not tied

—I can get away—I can get away—I *can* get along without him—I *can!'* " (SLR Folder 55, 21 Sept. 1898). She clearly communicates in these lines an experience that resonates with that of many women—her terror of erasure, of engulfment. And see chap. 2, n. 3, for references on Gilman's prominence in the women's movement.

33. And see also the letter to Ho dated 18 Dec. 1898 for Charlotte's jovial good humor regarding her relationship to Ho (SLR Folder 61).

34. See Floyd Dell, *Women as World Builders* (1913), for a discussion of Gilman, as well as of other women, who exemplify this role.

35. In Flax's words, "What seems to be repressed . . . is the possibility of autonomous, internally motivated sexuality . . . the possibility that woman *qua* embodied sexual female can also be a thinking/autonomous being" ("Re-Membering" 101).

36. Compare with "Class and Gender: The Divided Voices of *Twenty Years at Hull House*," chapter 6 of *The Politics of Voice: Liberalism and Social Criticism from Franklin to Kingston*, by Malini Johar Schueller. I acknowledge conversation with Mildred Mortimer for helping to solidify my thinking about this dilemma.

37. About a year later, Gilman worriedly reconsiders the work/love balance: "Work first—love next . . . the burden of our common womanhood . . . weighing on me so. To give up neither. To be both, to do both, to prove that it can be done. . . . And if you love me well enough I think it can be done" (SLR Folder 71, 26 July 1899). She reaffirms the wisdom of marriage even as she does her goal of proving that a married woman can also perform world service (recall SLR Folder 55, 16 Sept. 1898).

38. In "Re-Membering the Selves: Is the Repressed Gendered?" (1987), Jane Flax (and Irigaray, among others) find yet missing or "forbidden" to women as an assumption of this culture: the "incorporation" of women as embodied and desiring, concrete and differentiated beings *within* culture and language, ruling or thinking *on our own terms*—not as man's "other," "object of desire," or linguistic construct (104, my paraphrase, her italics). Flax, discussing Irigaray's views, states, "Men want the 'excess' [namely, women's body/capacity for pleasure, seen as 'excess' because outside culture] accessible to *them*, but then they must keep it in control and inaccessible to/for women themselves. . . . He still does not want her to speak for herself, or as Irigaray points out ('Commodities') among her/our selves, without him" (104).

39. Jessica Benjamin, in a 1986 article, "A Desire of One's Own: Psychoanalytic Feminism and Intersubjective Space," explains the need for "intersubjectivity" as a new psychoanalytic construct. By this she means "what happens between individuals, and within the individual-with-others, rather than within the individual psyche" (92). She continues, "The intersubjective mode assumes the possibility of a context with others in which desire is constituted for the self. It thus assumes the paradox that in being with the other, I may experience the most profound sense of self" (92). Such intersubjectivity may permit to women independent desire, acceptance of autonomy, the experience of genuine partnership, in the sense of utopian women's writing. Benjamin explains that the intersubjective mode (1) refers to the self which each individual brings from infancy and which "requires response and recognition," as well as (2) acknowledges the existence and the importance of another person in the present moment (93). Benjamin concludes, "Receptivity, knowing or taking in the other, becomes a mode of activity in its own right. My point is that this set of experiences—experiences of recognition—is not adequately represented by the concepts and symbols we have used" (93). Benjamin provides at the microinteraction level a description of how a partnership mode of social organization would function.

Her view of a mature self is not the autonomous, discontinuous self of masculinist theory, but rather a connected, empathic self, able to accept others as individuals in their own right, even as she does herself.

40. For another discussion of Eliot's essay in the context of her relationship to Lewes, see Phyllis Rose, *Parallel Lives: Five Victorian Marriages* (1984), 208–12. She concludes her discussion: "By turning their backs on the search for happiness in their daily lives, by committing themselves to each other, to their work, and to Duty, the Leweses managed to be as happy together for the twenty-four years they lived together as any two people I have heard of outside fantasy literature" (226). And for a discussion of the "sympathetic and discerning listener," the facilitator of another's creativity, as depicted in then-contemporary United States fiction, see Elaine Sargent Apthorp, "Re-Visioning Creativity: Cather, Chopin, Jewett" (15). Compare, also, Sharon O'Brien's analysis of Willa Cather's "emerging voice" as an "intersection among the loss of the mother, the desire to regain her, the child's imaginative development, and adult creativity" (211ff). Both Wyatt and O'Brien extrapolate theories of creative development from D. W. Winnicott.

41. I would join Ruth Perry, in her introduction to *Mothering the Mind: Twelve Studies of Writers and Their Silent Partners*, by adding George Houghton Gilman's support for Charlotte Perkins Gilman to her claim that "necessary others have never been credited properly for the role that they played . . . , and yet to a greater or lesser extent the . . . achievements were shaped by their presences" (5). Perry adds, "Men can also mother. . . . [T]he way to solve the problem of women's overdeveloped sense of responsibility for others . . . [is] to extend it as an available mode to men" (11). Of course, Tillie Olsen led the way in beginning to recognize enablers' contributions: Perry calls attention to "Wives, Mothers, Enablers" in *Silences* (218–23). Olsen states, "We are only beginning to understand the process of discouragings, of silencings, of the making of enabled and of enablers" (232, n.2).

In addition, Mary G. Mason, in "The Other Voice: Autobiographies of Women Writers," notes that, unlike most men in autobiographical writing, women "record and dramatize self-realization and self-transcendence through the recognition of another" (44), much as Gilman does in these letters.

42. For background, see Karen Horney, *Neurosis and Human Growth* (1950): she stands apart from Freud, but is as well indebted to him. Likewise, Clara Thompson, in *On Women* (1976), agrees with and extends Horney's humanistic views, especially with respect to women.

43. Current research finds two bases for postpartum depression: one, chemical imbalance of hormones following birth, and two, the great burden of fatigue, unrealistic expectations, and reversion to stereotypic gender roles that frequently occurs with the birth of a child. For background on the changes in a couple's life that the arrival of a child brings, see Lynn K. White, Alan Booth, and John N. Edwards, "Children and Marital Happiness: Why the Negative Correlation?" I am grateful to Rachel Hare-Mustin for discussing postpartum research with me and suggesting this article. See also Rachel T. Hare-Mustin and Jeanne Maracek, "A Short History of the Future: Feminism and Clinical Psychology" (1991).

44. Horney's self-inflated pride system interprets the "way of the hero," who requires external affirmation, given the lack of established internal supports in the immature; Sara Ruddick's "maternal thinking" or Carol Gilligan's "different voice" exemplify the "way of the mother," who finds satisfaction within the act of doing itself. Gilligan's work has generated much discussion; see for instance "On *In a Different Voice:* An Interdisciplinary Forum," *Signs* 11.2 (1986).

45. "Self-creation," Rank continues in "Creative Urge," "is one of the essential components of artistic creation" (29):

> Creativeness lies equally at the root of artistic production and of life experience. That is to say, lived experience can only be understood as the expression of volitional creative impulse, and in this the two spheres of artistic production and actual experience meet and overlap. . . . [P]ersonality . . . produces art-work and experience in the same way ("Life and Creation," 38).

In "Life and Creation," Rank clearly takes issue with Freud regarding sexual sublimation:

> "[T]he psychological factor *par excellence,* the individual will, . . . manifests itself both negatively as a controlling element, and positively as the urge to create. This creator-impulse is not, therefore, sexuality, as Freud assumed, but expresses the antisexual tendency in human beings, which we may describe as the deliberate control of the impulsive life. To put it more precisely, I see the creator-impulse as the life impulse made to serve the individual will" (39).

Rank concludes *Art and Artists* by hypothesizing a new type of creative person and a new society:

> The new type of humanity . . . must grow out of those artists themselves who have achieved a renunciant attitude towards artistic production. A [wo]man with creative power who can give up artistic expression in favour of the formation of personality—since [s]he can no longer use art as an expression of an already developed personality—will remould the self-creative type and will be able to put h[er] creative impulse *directly* in the service of h[er] own personality. . . . The condition of this is the conquest of the fear of life, for that fear has led to the substitution of artistic production for life, to the eternalization of the all-too-mortal ego in a work of art. . . . The creative type who . . . can devote h[er] whole creative force to life and the formation of life will be the first representative of the new human type, and in return for this renunciation will enjoy, in personality-creation and expression, a greater happiness ("Deprivation and Renunciation" 430–31).

46. Locations of these short stories are as follows: "The Giant Wistaria," *New England Magazine* NS 4:480–85 (June 1891), reprint *Legacy: A Journal of Nineteenth-Century American Women Writers* 5, no. 2 (1988): 39–43; "The Rocking Chair," *Worthington's Illustrated* 1: 453–59 (May 1893), reprint *Boston Budget* (25 June 1893), 10 and also SLR Folder 260.

47. For background, see Floyd Dell, *Women as World Builders* and Gilman's "World Rousers."

48. In a letter to George Houghton Gilman, Gilman railed against what she considered the ridiculousness of an hourly wage for labor (SLR Folder 44, 27 Aug. 1897). Neither the Exchange theory of labor for wages nor the Supply and Demand theory of labor receiving more or less in return depending upon its scarcity suited her. Both missed the point in her view. Producing creative people, better human

beings, should be the goal of a society, not the largest possible gross national product, which derived from a price-wage accounting. See "A Strange Land," selection 7.

49. In the context of a resurgent women's movement, Adrienne Rich, writing *Of Woman Born* (1976), suggests that "many women are *even now* thinking in ways which traditional intellection denies, decries, or is unable to grasp" (283–84). For a recent statement of the impact of such woman-centered thought and culture, see Sara Ruddick, *Maternal Thinking: Toward a Politics of Peace* (1989). She describes and defines a "maternal practice" that involves commitment to meeting the needs of a child for preservation, nurturance, and training in social acceptability (17–23); "maternal thinking" is the discipline of evaluating strategies for accomplishing the maternal work of preservation, nurturance, and training in social acceptability, a discipline exemplified by the discourse of "mothers" (they can be male), comparing and contrasting these differing strategies (23–27).

50. See also Carol Christ, in *Diving Deep and Surfacing* (1980), on the centrality of stories, a form of memory. Without them, a woman cannot articulate her experience and misses the expression of her spiritual quest. Women need stories of "free and independent womanhood" (1). Gilman has provided many of these. And consider Leslie Marmon Silko's observation in *Storyteller:* "As I tell the story/ it will begin to happen" (133)—a keen awareness of the self-fulfilling nature of fiction or of visualization. Gilman also noted this phenomenon: sociologists label it self-fulfilling prophecy.

51. See Gary Scharnhorst, *Charlotte Perkins Gilman: A Bibliography*, pp. 59–62, for citations to Gilman's fiction from 1890–1895.

52. Dorothy [M. Calvetti Ungaretti] Bryant, author of the utopia *The Kin of Ata Are Waiting for You* (1971), describes her experience of publishing her own writing in "My Publisher/Myself" (1978), reprinted in *Myths to Lie By* (1984).

53. See also her "The Only Hero," *Forerunner* (1911), concerning a figure whom she relegates to the museum with other obsolete "specimens" (210).

54. Contemporary feminist literary analysts hold similar views regarding the power of literature to change lives. For several examples among many, see Joanne S. Frye, *Living Stories, Telling Lives: Women and the Novel in Contemporary Experience* (1986); Patricia Yeager, *Honey-Mad Women: Emancipatory Strategies in Women's Writing* (1988); or Gayle Greene, *Changing the Story: Feminist Fiction and the Tradition* (1991).

55. In "Expiation," a story Edith Wharton collected in *The Descent of Man* (1904), a character sermonizes:

> 'And of all forms of literature, fiction is doubtless that which has exercised the greatest sway, for good or ill, over the passions and imagination of the masses. . . . No sermon . . . has ever inflamed the heart and imagination like a novel—a simple novel. . . . The novelist's hand can pour balm on countless sufferings, or inoculate mankind with the festering poison of a corrupt imagination.'

56. Patricia Waugh, especially in chap. 1 of in her study *Metafiction: The Theory and Practice of Self-Conscious Fiction* (1984), explains the concern of metafiction with the conventions of realism, the difficulties of representation. Its focus ranges from "fictionality as a theme" to fantasy with its rejection of realism. And, in so doing, observes Waugh, "metafiction helps us to understand how the reality we live day by day is similarly constructed, similarly 'written' " (18).

57. Recent discussions of plots possible for women writers include Joanna Russ, "What Can a Heroine Do? or Why Women Can't Write," and Ursula K. Le Guin, "The Carrier Bag Theory of Fiction" and "Heroes," both collected in *Dancing on the Edge of the World.*

58. Judith Fryer, speaking of Willa Cather in *Felicitous Space,* describes as well Gilman's process: projecting imaginative structures is a "fundamentally radical utopian mode—as if there were another possibility in response to the double bind of muteness, on the one hand, and the restricted language of the dominant culture, on the other, as if there were a possiblity of transcendence, of re-creation, from memory and desire, of living forms that retain all their primary ecstasy" (1986, 342). And Fryer stresses the community of writer and reader which has infinite continuity (224): "in uniting teller, tale and listener, the story—which creates culture by discovering and reinforcing tales to be told not only twice, but continuously—is a *process*" (227). Gilman exemplifies these possibilities.

59. Janice A. Radway makes a similar point in "On the Uses of 'Serious' Fiction," where, in discussing Book-of-the-Month Club (BOMC) practices, she notes the utilitarian function of reading for the Club's membership (534). Like BOMC members, Gilman's readers can find "self-help" in fiction that is "readily applicable to [their] own life, problems, and concerns" (535), "continuity between art and life" (536). Radway continues, "The value of 'serious fiction,' in fact, is a function of its capacity to be used as a map which is, despite its status as a representation, a tool for enabling its reader to move about more effectively in the world to which it refers" (537). And see Radway's *Reading the Romance* for more on utopian effects of reading fiction (1984).

Bibliography

Manuscript Collections

The Arthur and Elizabeth Schlesinger Library (SLR) on the History of Women in America, Radcliffe College, Cambridge, Mass. Charlotte Perkins Gilman Collection: major depository. Also Grace Channing Stetson. See *The Arthur and Elizabeth Schlesinger Library on the History of Women in America: The Manuscript Inventories and the Catalogs of the Manuscripts, Books, and Periodicals*. 2nd rev. and enlarged ed. Boston: G. K. Hall, 1984.

Library of Congress (DLC), Manuscripts Division, Washington, D.C. Benjamin Huebsch Papers; Women's movement correspondence.

Stowe-Day Foundation, Hartford, Conn. Two typescripts; miscellaneous family correspondence.

Works by Charlotte Perkins (Stetson) Gilman

"Applepieville." *Independent* 103 (25 Sept. 1920): 365, 393–95.

"Aunt Mary's Pie Plant." *Woman's Home Companion* 6 (June 1908): 14, 48–49.

"The Beauty of the Block." *Independent* 57 (14 July 1904): 67–72.

"Bee Wise." *Forerunner* 4.7 (July 1913): 169–73.

"Benigna McAvelly." *Forerunner* 5.1–12 (1914).

"A Cabinet Meeting" [imitation of Edward Bellamy]. Studies in Style series. *Impress* (5 Jan 1895): 4–5.

"Causes and Uses of the Subjection of Women." *Woman's Journal* (24 Dec. 1898): 410.

"Coming Changes in Literature." *Forerunner* 6.9 (1915): 230–36.

"Comment and Review." *Forerunner* 1.12 (1910): 26.

Concerning Children. Boston: Small, Maynard, 1900.

"A Council of War." *Forerunner* 4.8 (1913): 197–201.

The Crux. Forerunner 2.1–12 (1911). New York: Charlton, 1911.

"Dr. Clair's Place." *Forerunner* 6.6 (June 1915): 141–45.
"Domestic Economy." *Independent* 56 (16 June 1904): 1359–63.
"The Dress and the Body." *Pacific Rural Press* (4 July 1891): 6.
"The Dress of Women." *Forerunner* 6.1–12 (1915).
"The Economic Basis of the Woman Question." *Woman's Journal* (1 Oct. 1898): 313–14.
The Forerunner. New York: Charlton, 1909–1916. Reprint, introduction by Madeleine B. Stern. Radical Periodicals in the United States, 1890–1960. New York: Greenwood, 1968.
"Forsythe & Forsythe." *Forerunner* 4.1 (Jan. 1913): 1–5.
"A Garden of Babies." *Success* 12 (June 1909): 370–71, 410–11.
"The Giant Wistaria." *New England Magazine* NS4 (June 1891): 480–85. Reprint, *Legacy: A Journal of Nineteenth-Century American Women Writers* 5.2 (1988): 39–44.
"Growth and Combat." *Forerunner* 7.1–12 (1916).
"Her Housekeeper." *Forerunner* 1.4 (Jan. 1910): 2–8.
"Her Memories." *Forerunner* 3.8 (Aug. 1912): 197–201.
Herland. Forerunner 6.1–12 (1915). *Herland: A Lost Feminist Utopian Novel.* Introduction by Ann J. Lane. New York: Pantheon Books, 1979. Reprint, *"Herland" and Selected Stories by Charlotte Perkins Gilman.* Introduction by Barbara H. Solomon. New York: Penguin, 1992.
His Religion and Hers: A Study of the Faith of Our Fathers and the Work of Our Mothers. New York: Century, 1923. Reprint, Pioneers of the Woman's Movement series. Westport, Conn.: Hyperion Press, 1976.
The Home: Its Work and Influence. New York: McClure, Phillips, 1903. Reprint. New York: Source Book Press, 1970. Reprint, introduction by William L. O'Neill. Urbana: Univ. of Illinois Press, 1972.
"Housing for Children." *Independent* 57 (25 Aug. 1904): 434–38.
"How Home Conditions React upon the Family." *American Journal of Sociology* 14 (March 1909): 592–605.
Human Work. New York: McClure, Phillips, 1904.
In This Our World. 3rd ed. Boston: Small, Maynard, 1898.
The Living of Charlotte Perkins Gilman: An Autobiography. 1935. Reprint, introduction by Ann J. Lane. Madison: Univ. Wisconsin Press, 1990.
'Mag-Marjorie." *Forerunner* 3.1–12 (1912).
"Maidstone Comfort." *Forerunner* 3.9 (1912): 225–29.
"Making Towns Fit to Live In." *Century* 102 (July 1921): 361–66.
The Man-Made World, or Our Androcentric Culture. Forerunner 1.1–14 (1909–1910). New York: Charlton, 1911.
"Married in Providence/Quiet Wedding of Artist Stetson and Miss Channing." [San Francisco] *Call* 8 (19 June 1894): 5.
"Martha's Mother." *Forerunner* 1.6 (1910): 1–6.
"Masculine Literature," chap. 5 of "Our Androcentric Culture; or, The Man-Made World." *Forerunner* 1.5: 18–22. Reprint, *The Yellow Wallpaper*

and Other Writings, edited by Lynne Sharon Schwartz, 216–23. New York: Bantam, 1989.

Moving the Mountain. Forerunner 2.1–12 (1911). New York: Charlton, 1911. Reprint, Radical Periodicals in the United States, 1890–1960. Westport, Conn.: Greenwood, 1968.

"Mrs. Hines' Money." *Forerunner* 4.4 (1913): 85–89.

"The 'Nervous Breakdown' of Women." *Forerunner* 7.8 (1916): 202–6.

"The Only Hero." *Forerunner* 2 (1911): 209–10.

"Our Brains and What Ails Them." *Forerunner* 3.1–12 (1912). No. 5, chap. 5: "Effect of Literature Upon the Mind" 133–39. No. 9, chap. 9: "The Effects of the Position of Women on the Race Mind" 245–51.

"The Passing of the Home in Great American Cities." *Cosmopolitan* 38 (December 1904): 137–147.

"A Personal Motive." *Forerunner* 4.5 (1913): 114–18.

"A Platform for Women." *Forerunner* 4.1 (1913): 6–7.

"A Proclamation of Interdependence." [Sept. 1928]. The Arthur and Elizabeth Schlesinger Library on the History of Women in America, Radcliffe College, Collection 177, Charlotte Perkins Gilman Papers (1860–1935): Folder 184.

"Race Pride." *Forerunner* 4 (1913): 89–90.

"The Rocking Chair." *Worthington's Illustrated* 1: (May 1893) 453–59. *Boston Budget* (25 June 1893): 10. SLR Folder 260, Gilman Papers, Radcliffe College.

"Standardizing Towns." *Forerunner* 6.2 (1915): 52–54.

"A Strange Land." *Forerunner* 3.8 (Aug. 1912): 207–8.

"A Suggestion on the Negro Problem." *American Journal of Sociology* 14 (July 1908): 78–85.

"Unpunished." Unpublished typescript. 1929. SLR Folder 231, Gilman Papers, Radcliffe College.

"The Waste of Private Housekeeping." *American Academy of Political and Social Science Annals* 48 (July 1913): 91–95.

What Diantha Did. Forerunner 1.1–14 (1909–1910). New York: Charlton, 1910. Radical Periodicals in the United States, 1890–1960. Westport, Conn.: Greenwood, 1968.

"What 'World Expositions' Mean." *Stockton* [CA Evening] Mail 9 (Aug. 1893): 4, col. 3.

"Why Cooperative Housekeeping Fails." *Harper's Bazar* 41 (July 1907): 625–29.

"Why I Wrote the Yellow Wallpaper?" *Forerunner* 4.10 (1913): 271.

"With a Difference (Not Literature)." *Forerunner* 5 (1914): 29–32.

With Her in Ourland. Forerunner 7.1–12 (1916). Radical Periodicals in the United States, 1890–1960. Westport, Conn.: Greenwood Press, 1968.

"A Woman's Utopia." Chaps.I–IV, *The Times Magazine* 1 (Jan.–Mar. 1907): 215–20, 369–76, 498–504; chap. V [page proofs], SLR Box 21, Folder 260.

Women and Economics: A Study of the Economic Relation Between Men and Women as a Factor in Social Evolution. Boston: Small, Maynard, 1898. Reprint, edited and with an introduction by Carl N. Degler. New York: Harper, 1966.

"Working Love." *American Fabian* [Organ of Fabian Socialism in the United States] 3 (12 Dec. 1897): 1–2.

"World Rousers." *Forerunner* 6 (1915): 131–32.

"The Yellow Wallpaper." *New England Magazine* NS 5 (Jan. 1892): 647–56. Reprint, Boston: Small, Maynard, 1899. Reprint, Afterword by Elaine R. Hedges. New York: Feminist Press, 1973. Reprint, *The Charlotte Perkins Gilman Reader: "The Yellow Wallpaper" and Other Fiction,* edited Ann J. Lane. New York: Pantheon, 1980. Reprint, *The Yellow Wallpaper and Other Writings.* edited by Lynne Sharon Schwartz. New York: Bantam, 1989.

Secondary Sources

Alcoff, Linda. "Cultural Feminism versus Poststructuralism: The Identity Crisis in Feminist Theory." *Signs* (1988): 405–36.

Allen, Polly Wynn. *Building Domestic Liberty: Charlotte Perkins Gilman's Architectural Feminism.* Amherst: Univ. of Massachusetts Press, 1988.

Ammons, Elizabeth. *Conflicting Stories: American Women Writers at the Turn into the Twentieth Century.* New York: Oxford Univ. Press, 1991.

Aptheker, Bettina. *Tapestries of Life: Women's Work, Women's Consciousness, and the Meaning of Daily Experience.* Amherst: Univ. of Massachusetts Press, 1989.

Apthorp, Elaine Sargent. "Re-Visioning Creativity: Cather, Chopin, Jewett." *Legacy: A Journal of American Women Writers* 9.1 (1992): 1–22.

Arcana, Judith. *Our Mothers' Daughters.* Berkeley: Shameless Hussy, 1979.

Bakhtin, M[ikhail] M[ikhailovitch]. *Art and Answerability,* translated by Vadim Liapunov and edited by Michael Holquist and Vadim Liapunov. Austin: Univ. of Texas Press, 1990.

———. "Response to a Question from *Novy Mir.*" 1970. Reprint, *Speech Genres and Other Late Essays,* translated by Vern W. McGee and edited by Caryl Emerson and Michael Holquist. Austin: Univ. of Texas Press, 1986.

———. "Discourse in the Novel." *The Dialogic Imagination: Four Essays,* translated by Caryl Emerson and Michael Holquist and edited by Michael Holquist, 259–421. Austin: Univ. of Texas Press, 1981.

Bartkowski, Frances. *Feminist Utopias.* Lincoln: Univ. of Nebraska Press, 1989.

Bauer, Dale M. *Feminist Dialogics: A Theory of Failed Community.* Albany: State Univ. of New York Press, 1988.

Baym, Nina. *Woman's Fiction: A Guide to Novels by and about Women in America, 1820–1870.* Ithaca, N.Y.: Cornell Univ. Press, 1978.

Baym, Nina, et al., eds. *The Norton Anthology of American Literature.* 3rd ed. Vol. 2. New York: Norton, 1989.

Beecher, Catharine. *Treatise on Domestic Economy, For the Use of Young Ladies at Home and at School.* Boston: T. H. Webb, 1843.

Beecher, Catharine, and Harriet Beecher Stowe. *The American Woman's Home, or Principles of Domestic Science.* New York: J. B. Ford & Co., 1869.

Bellamy, Edward. *Looking Backward, 2000–1887.* 1888. Reprint, edited by John L. Thomas. Cambridge, Mass.: Harvard Univ. Press, 1967.

Benjamin, Jessica. "A Desire of One's Own: Psychoanalytic Feminism and Intersubjective Space." In *Feminist Studies/Critical Studies,* edited by Teresa de Lauretis, 78–101. Bloomington: Indiana Univ. Press, 1986.

Berger, Pamela C. *The Goddess Obscured, Transformation of the Grain Protectress from Goddess to Saint.* Boston: Beacon Press, 1985.

Berkin, Carol Ruth. "Private Woman, Public Woman: The Contradictions of Charlotte Perkins Gilman." In *Women in America: A History,* edited by C. R. Berkin and Mary Beth Norton. Boston: Houghton, 1979.

Bernard, Jessie. *The Female World.* New York: Free, 1981.

———. *The Future of Motherhood.* New York: Dial, 1974.

Black, Alexander. "The Woman Who Saw It First." *Century* 107 (Nov. 1923): 33–42.

Bloch, Ernst. *The Principle of Hope.* 1959. Reprint, translated by Neville Plaice, Stephen Plaice, and Paul Knight. 3 vols. Cambridge, Mass.: MIT Press, 1986.

———. Special issue. *Utopian Studies* 1.2 (1990): 1–95.

Boulding, Elise. *Building a Global Civic Culture: Education for an Interdependent World.* New York: Teachers College, 1988.

———. "Building Utopias in History." In *Towards a Just World Peace,* edited by R. B. J. Walker and Saul H. Mendlovitz, 213–34. Guilford, Eng.: Butterworths, 1987.

———. *The Underside of History: A View of Women Through Time.* 1976. Rev. 2-vol. ed. Newberry Park, Calif.: Sage, 1992.

Boydston, Jeanne, Mary Kelley, and Anne Margolis. *The Limits of Sisterhood: The Beecher Sisters on Women's Rights and Woman's Sphere.* Chapel Hill: Univ. of North Carolina Press, 1988.

Brodski, Bella, and Celeste Schenck, eds. *Life/Lines: Theorizing Women's Autobiography.* Ithaca, N.Y.: Cornell Univ. Press, 1988.

Bruère, Martha S. Bensley. *Mildred Carver, U.S.A.* New York: Macmillan, 1919.

Bryant, Dorothy [M. Calvetti Ungaretti]. *Myths to Lie By.* Berkeley, Calif.: Ata, 1984.

Burke, Kenneth. "Literature as Equipment for Living." In *The Philosophy of Literary Form: Studies in Symbolic Action.* N.p.: 1941. Reprint, Berkeley: Univ. of California Press, 1973. 293–304.

Burns, David D., M.D. *Feeling Good: The New Mood Therapy*. New York: Signet-NAL, 1980.

Campbell, Helen Stuart. *The Ainslee Stories*. New York: Hurd and Houghton, 1868.

———. *Miss Melinda's Opportunity*. Boston: Roberts, 1886.

———. *Mrs. Herndon's Income*. Boston: Roberts, 1885.

———. *Prisoners of Poverty: Women Wage-Workers, Their Trades and Their Lives*. Boston: Roberts, 1887.

———. *Some Passages in the Practice of Dr. Martha Scarborough*. Boston: Roberts, 1893.

Caplan, Paula J. *Don't Blame Mother: Mending the Mother-Daughter Relationship*. New York: Harper, 1989.

Capra, Fritjof. *The Turning Point: Science, Society, and the Rising Culture*. New York: Simon and Schuster, 1982.

Carby, Hazel V. *Reconstructing Womanhood: The Emergence of the Afro-American Woman Novelist*. New York: Oxford Univ. Press, 1987.

Ceplair, Larry, ed. *Charlotte Perkins Gilman: A Nonfiction Reader*. New York: Columbia Univ. Press, 1991.

Chesler, Phyllis. "The Amazon Legacy." 1972. In *The Politics of Women's Spirituality: Essays on the Rise of Spiritual Power within the Feminist Movement*, edited by Charlene Spretnak, 97–113. Garden City, N.Y.: Doubleday, 1982.

Chodorow, Nancy. "Being and Doing: A Cross-Cultural Examination of the Socialization of Males and Females." In *Woman in Sexist Society: Studies in Power and Powerlessness*, edited by Vivian Gornick and Barbara K. Moran, 259–91. New York: Basic, 1971.

———. *The Reproduction of Mothering: Psychoanalysis and the Sociology of Gender*. Berkeley: Univ. of California Press, 1978. Critiqued *Signs* 6 (1981): 482–514.

Chodorow, Nancy, and Susan Contratto. "The Fantasy of the Perfect Mother." In *Rethinking the Family: Some Feminist Questions*, edited by Barrie Thorne with Marilyn Yalom, 54–75. New York: Longman, 1982.

Christ, Carol. *Diving Deep and Surfacing: Women Writers on Spiritual Quest*. Boston: Beacon, 1980.

Cobb, Edith. "The Ecology of Imagination in Childhood." *Daedalus* 88.3 (Summer 1959): 537–48.

Coles, Robert. *The Call of Stories: Teaching and the Moral Imagination*. Boston: Houghton, 1989.

Conway, Jill Kerr. "Convention vs. Self-Revelation: Women's Autobiography in the Progressive Era." Project on Women and Social Change, Smith College, Northampton, Mass., 13 June 1983.

———. "Women Reformers and American Culture, 1870–1930." *Journal of Social History* 5: 164–77 (Winter 1971–1972).

Cott, Nancy F. *The Grounding of Modern Feminism*. New Haven: Yale Univ. Press, 1987.

Cranny-Francis, Anne. *Feminist Fiction: Feminist Uses of Generic Fiction.* New York: St. Martin's, 1990.

Crawford, Mary, and Roger Chaffin. "The Reader's Construction of Meaning: Cognitive Research on Gender and Comprehension." In *Gender and Reading: Essays on Readers, Texts, and Contexts,* edited by Elizabeth A. Flynn and Patrocinio P. Schweickart. Baltimore: Johns Hopkins Univ. Press, 1986.

Cridge, Annie Denton. *Man's Rights; or, How Would You Like It?* Boston: William Denton, 1870.

Culpepper, Emily Erwin. "Contemporary Goddess Thealogy: A Sympathetic Critique." In *Shaping New Vision: Gender and Values in American Culture,* edited by Clarissa W. Atkinson, Constance H. Buchanan, and Margaret R. Miles, 51–71. Ann Arbor: Univ. of Michigan, 1987.

Dahlberg, Frances, ed. *Woman the Gatherer.* New Haven: Yale Univ. Press, 1981.

Davidson, Cathy N. *Revolution and the Word: The Rise of the Novel in America.* New York: Oxford Univ. Press, 1986.

Davis, Allen F. *American Heroine: The Life and Legend of Jane Addams.* New York: Oxford Univ. Press, 1973.

Davis, Angela Y. *Women, Race & Class.* New York: Random, 1981.

Degler, Carl N. Introduction. In *Women and Economics: A Study of the Economic Relations Between Men and Women as a Factor in Social Evolution,* by Charlotte Perkins Gilman, 1898. Reprint, edited by Carl N. Degler. New York: Harper, 1966.

———. "What Ought to Be and What Was: Women's Sexuality in the Nineteenth Century." *American Historical Review* 58 (Dec. 1974): 1467–90.

Dell, Floyd. *Women as World Builders.* Chicago: Forbes, 1913.

Dimock, Wai-Chee. "Feminism, New Historicism, and the Reader." *American Literature* 63 (1991): 601–22.

Dinnerstein, Dorothy. *The Mermaid and the Minotaur: Sexual Arrangements and Human Malaise.* New York: Harper, 1976.

Donnelly, Ignatius [Edmund Boisgilbert]. *Caesar's Column: A Story of the Twentieth Century.* Chicago: F. J. Schulte, 1890.

DuPlessis, Rachel Blau. *Writing Beyond the Ending: Narrative Strategies of Twentieth-Century Women Writers.* Bloomington: Indiana Univ. Press, 1985.

Eisler, Riane. *The Chalice and the Blade: Our History, Our Future.* San Francisco: Harper, 1988.

———. "Pragmatopia: Women's Utopias and Scenarios for a Possible Future." Conference of the Society for Utopian Studies, Asilomar, 1986.

———, and David Loye. *The Partnership Way: New Tools for Living and Learning, Healing Our Families, Our Communities and Our World.* San Francisco: HarperCollins, 1990.

Eliot, George. "How I Came to Write Fiction." In *The George Eliot Letters,* edited by Gordon S. Haight. Vol. 2, 406–10. New Haven: Yale Univ. Press, 1954.

Ferguson, Marilyn. *The Aquarian Conspiracy: Personal and Social Transformation in the 1980s.* Los Angeles: J. P. Tarcher, 1980.

Fischer, Lucy Rose. *Linked Lives: Adult Daughters and Their Mothers.* New York: Harper, 1986.

Flax, Jane. "Mother-Daughter Relationships: Psychodynamics, Politics, and Philosophy." In *The Future of Difference,* edited by Hester Eisenstein and Alice Jardine. New Brunswick, N.J.: Rutgers Univ. Press, 1985.

———. "Re-Membering the Selves: Is the Repressed Gendered?" *Michigan Quarterly Review* 26 (1987): 92–110.

French, Marilyn. *Beyond Power: On Women, Men, and Morals.* New York: Summit, 1985.

Friedman, Susan Stanford. "Creativity and the Childbirth Metaphor: Gender Difference in Literary Discourse." In *Speaking of Gender,* edited by Elaine Showalter, 73–100. New York: Routledge, 1989.

Frye, Joanne S. *Living Stories, Telling Lives: Women and the Novel in Contemporary Experience.* Women and Culture Series. Ann Arbor: Univ. of Michigan Press, 1984.

Fryer, Judith. "From White City to *Herland.*" *Felicitous Space: The Imaginative Structures of Edith Wharton and Willa Cather,* 5–51. Chapel Hill: Univ. of North Carolina Press, 1986.

Fuller [Ossoli], Margaret. *Woman in the Nineteenth Century.* 1845. Reprint, edited by Bernard Rosenthal. New York: Norton, 1971.

Gadon, Elinor W. *The Once and Future Goddess: A Symbol for Our Time.* San Francisco: Harper, 1989.

Gale, Zona. "Charlotte Perkins Gilman." *Nation* 141 (25 Sept. 1935): 350–51.

Gardiner, Mike. "Penultimate Words." *Radical Philosophy* 60 (1992): 43–46.

Garner, Shirley Nelson. "Constructing the Mother: Contemporary Psychoanalytic Theorists and Women Autobiographers." In *Narrating Mothers: Theorizing Maternal Subjectivities,* edited by Brenda O. Daly and Maureen T. Reddy, 76–93. Knoxville: Univ. of Tennessee Press, 1991.

Garrard, Mary D. *Artemisia Gentileschi: The Image of the Female Hero in Italian Baroque Art.* Princeton: Princeton Univ. Press, 1989.

Geddes, Sir Patrick, and J. Arthur Thomson. *The Evolution of Sex.* 1889. New York: Scribner and Welford, 1890.

Geertz, Clifford. *The Interpretation of Cultures.* New York: Basic, 1973.

———. "Making Experiences, Authoring Selves." In *The Anthropology of Experience,* edited by Victor W. Turner and Edward M. Bruner. Urbana: Univ. of Illinois Press, 1986.

Gilbert, Sandra, and Susan Gubar. *No Man's Land: The Place of the Woman Writer in the Twentieth Century.* Vol. 1, *The War of the Words* and Vol. 2, *Sexchanges.* New Haven: Yale Univ. Press, 1987, 1989.

Gilligan, Carol. *In a Different Voice: Psychological Theory and Women's Development.* Cambridge, Mass.: Harvard Univ. Press, 1982.

Gimbutas, Marija. *The Civilization of the Goddess: The World of Old Europe*. New York: HarperCollins, 1991.

———. *The Language of the Goddess: Unearthing the Hidden Symbols of Western Civilization*. San Francisco: Harper, 1989.

Gleick, James. *Chaos: Making a New Science*. New York: Viking Penguin, 1987.

Goffman, Erving. *Frame Analysis: An Essay on the Organization of Experience*. New York: Harper, 1974.

Golden, Catherine, ed. *The Captive Imagination: A Casebook on "The Yellow Wallpaper"*. New York: Feminist, 1992.

Gould, Stephen Jay. *The Mismeasure of Man*. New York: Norton, 1981.

Greene, Gayle. *Changing the Story: Feminist Fiction and the Tradition*. Bloomington: Univ. of Indiana Press, 1991.

———. "Feminist Fiction and the Uses of Memory." *Signs* 16 (1991): 290–31.

Greer, Germaine. *Sex and Destiny*. New York: Harper, 1984.

Hale, Edward Everett. *The Brick Moon. Atlantic Monthly* 1869–1870. Barre, Mass.: Imprint Society, 1971.

———. *Sybaris and Other Homes*. Boston: Fields, Osgood, & Co., 1869. Utopian Literature series, ed. Arthur Orcutt Lewis, Jr. New York: Arno, 1971.

Hare-Mustin, Rachel T., and Patricia Broderick. "The Myth of Motherhood: A Study of Attitudes Toward Motherhood. *Psychology of Women Quarterly* 4 (1979): 114–28.

Hare-Mustin, Rachel T., and Jeanne Maracek, eds. *Making a Difference· Psychology and the Construction of Gender*. New Haven: Yale Univ. Press, 1990.

———. "A Short History of the Future: Feminism and Clinical Psychology." *Psychology of Women Quarterly* 15.4 [Centennial Issue] (Dec. 1991): 521–536.

Harris, Susan K. *Nineteenth-Century American Women's Novels: Interpretive Strategies*. Cambridge: Cambridge Univ. Press, 1990.

Hartsock, Nancy. "The Feminist Standpoint: Developing the Ground for a Specifically Feminist Historical Materialism." In *Discovering Reality: Feminist Perspectives on Epistemology, Metaphysics, Methodology, and Philosophy of Science,* edited by Sandra Harding and Merrill B. Hintikka, 283–310. Boston: D. Reidel, 1983.

Hawken, Paul, James Ogilvy, and Peter Schwartz. *Seven Tomorrows: Toward a Voluntary History*. New York: Bantam, 1982.

Hayden, Dolores. "Charlotte Perkins Gilman and Her Influence." Part 5 of *The Grand Domestic Revolution: A History of Feminist Designs for American Homes, Neighborhoods, and Cities,* 182–277 Cambridge, Mass.: MIT Press, 1981.

Hedges, Elaine. " 'Out at Last?': Critics Read 'The Yellow Wallpaper.' " In *The Captive Imagination: A Casebook on 'The Yellow Wallpaper',* edited by Catherine Golden, 319–33. New York: Feminist, 1991.

Heilbrun, Carolyn G. "Non-Autobiographies of 'Privileged' Women: England and America." In *Life/Lines Theorizing Women's Autobiography*, edited by Bella Brodski and Celeste Schenck, 62–76. Ithaca: Cornell Univ. Press, 1988.

———. *Writing a Woman's Life*. New York: Norton, 1988.

Heresies: A Feminist Publication on Art & Politics 5 (1978). Rev. 1982. Special issue: "The Great Goddess."

Hildebrandt, Hans-Juergen. *Johann Jakob Bachofen: The Primary and Secondary Literature*. Aachen, Ger.: Herodot, 1988.

Hill, Mary A[rmfield]. *Charlotte Perkins Gilman: The Making of a Radical Feminist, 1860–1896*. American Civilization Series. Philadelphia: Temple Univ. Press, 1980.

Hill, Mary Armfield, ed. *Endure: The Diaries of Charles Walter Stetson*. Philadelphia: Temple Univ. Press, 1985.

———, ed. *Journey From Within: The Private Letters of Charlotte Perkins Gilman*. Forthcoming.

Hirsch, Marianne. "Mothers and Daughters." Review Essay. *Signs* 7 (1981): 200–22.

Hite, Molly. *The Other Side of the Story: Structures and Strategies of Contemporary Feminist Narrative*. Ithaca, N.Y.: Cornell Univ. Press, 1989.

Holmlund, Christine. "The Lesbian, the Mother, the Heterosexual Lover: Irigaray's Recodings of Difference." *Feminist Studies* 17 (1991): 283–308.

Horney, Karen. *Feminine Psychology*. Ed. Harold Kelman. New York: Norton, 1967.

———. *Neurosis and Human Growth: The Struggle Toward Self-Realization*. New York: Norton, 1950.

Howe, Harriet. "Charlotte Perkins Gilman—As I Knew Her." *Equal Rights* 5 (5 Sept. 1936): 211–216 .

Howells, William Dean. *The Great Modern American Short Stories: An Anthology*. New York: Boni and Liveright, 1920.

———. "The New Poetry." *North American Review* 68 (May 1899): 581–92.

Howland, Marie [Stevens Case]. *Papa's Own Girl; A Novel*. New York: Jewett, 1874. Microf. *American Fiction, 1851–1875*. Ed. Lyle H. Wright. Vol. 2, 1290. New Haven: Research Publications, 1971. Reprint, *The Familistere; A Novel*. Boston: Christopher, 1918. Reprint, Philadelphia: Porcupine, 1975.

Hughes, James L. "World Leaders I Have Known." *Canadian Magazine* 61 (August 1923): 335–38.

Hume, Kathryn. *Fantasy and Mimesis: Responses to Reality in Western Literature*. London: Methuen, 1984.

Irigaray, Luce. "And the One Doesn't Stir without the Other." Trans. and introd. Hélène Vivienne Wenzel. *Signs* 7 (1981): 56–67.

Johnson, Buffie. *Lady of the Beasts: Her Ancient Images of the Goddess and Her Sacred Animals*. San Francisco: Harper, 1988.

Jones, Libby Falk and Sarah Webster Goodwin, eds. *Feminism, Utopia, and Narrative.* Tennessee Studies in Literature 32. Knoxville: Univ. of Tennessee Press, 1990.

Kaplan, Amy. *The Social Construction of American Realism.* Chicago: Univ. of Chicago Press, 1988.

Karpinski, Joanne B. "When the Marriage of True Minds Admits Impediments: Charlotte Perkins Gilman and William Dean Howells." In *Patrons and Protégées: Gender, Friendship, and Writing in Nineteenth-Century America,* edited by Shirley Marchalonis, 212–34. New Brunswick, N.J.: Rutgers Univ. Press, 1988.

Kelley, Mary. *Private Woman, Public Stage: Literary Domesticity in Nineteenth-Century America.* New York: Oxford Univ. Press, 1984.

Kelly, R. Gordon. *Mother Was a Lady: Self and Society in Selected American Children's Periodicals, 1865–1890.* Westport, Conn.: Greenwood, 1974.

Kerber, Linda K., et al. "On *In a Different Voice:* An Interdisciplinary Forum." *Signs* 11:2 (1986): 304–33.

Kessler, Carol Farley. "Bibliography of Utopian Fiction by United States Women 1836–1988." *Utopian Studies* 1:2 (1990): 1–58.

——. "Charlotte Perkins Gilman, 1860–1935." In *Modern American Women Writers,* edited by Elaine Showalter with Lea Baechler and A. Walton Litz, New York: Scribner's, 1991.

——. "Consider Her Ways: The Cultural Work of Charlotte Perkins Gilman's Pragmatopian Stories, 1908–1913." In *Utopian and Science Fiction by Women: Worlds of Difference,* edited by Jane Donawerth and Carol A. Kolmerten. Syracuse: Syracuse Univ. Press, 1994.

——, ed. *Daring to Dream: Utopian Stories by United States Women 1836–1919.* Boston and London: Pandora-Routledge & Kegan Paul, 1984.

Khanna, Lee Cullen. "Feminist Quest for Utopia." Popular Culture Convention, New Orleans, March 1988.

——. "Women's Utopias: New Worlds, New Texts." In *Feminism, Utopias and Narrative,* edited by Libby Falk Jones and Sarah Webster Goodwin, 130–40. Tennessee Studies in Literature 32. Knoxville: Univ. of Tennessee Press, 1990.

——. "Women's Worlds: New Directions in Utopian Fiction." *Alternative Futures: The Journal of Utopian Studies* 4, nos. 2–3 (1981): 47–60.

[Kirkland, Wallace, resident/photographer]. *The Many Faces of Hull-House.* Edited by Mary Ann Johnson. Urbana: Univ. of Illinois Press, 1989.

Kitch, Sally. *Chaste Liberation: Celibacy and Female Cultural Status.* Urbana: Univ. of Illinois Press, 1989.

Knapp, Adeline. "One Thousand Dollars a Day: A Financial Experiment." In *One Thousand Dollars a Day: Studies in Economics.* Boston: Arena, 1894.

Kramarae, Cheris. *Women and Men Speaking*. Rowley, Mass.: Newbury House, 1981.

Lane, Ann J. Introduction. In *The Charlotte Perkins Gilman Reader: "The Yellow Wallpaper" and Other Fiction*. New York: Pantheon, 1980.

———. *To 'Herland' and Beyond: The Life and Works of Charlotte Perkins Gilman*. New York: Pantheon, 1990.

[Lane, Mary E. Bradley]. *Mizora: A Prophecy. The Cincinnati Commercial* (Nov. 1880-Feb. 1881). New York: G. W. Dillingham, 1889. Microf. *American Fiction, 1876–1900*. Ed. Lyle H. Wright. Vol. 3, 3203. New Haven: Research Publications, 1971. Reprint, New York: Gregg, 1975.

Langley, Juliet A. " 'Audacious Fancies': A Collection of Letters from Charlotte Perkins Gilman to Martha Luther." *Trivia* 6 (Winter 1985): 52–69.

Lanser, Susan S. "Feminist Criticism, 'The Yellow Wallpaper,' and the Politics of Color in America." *Feminist Studies* 15 (1989): 415–89.

Lazarus, Emma. *Poems of Emma Lazarus*. 2 vols. Boston: Houghton, 1889.

Le Guin, Ursula K. "The Carrier Bag Theory of Fiction" and "Heroes." In *Dancing on the Edge of the World*. New York: Grove, 1989.

Lerner, Gerda. *The Creation of Patriarchy*. New York: Oxford Univ. Press, 1986.

Levitas, Ruth. *The Concept of Utopia*. Syracuse: Syracuse Univ. Press, 1990.

Lippard, Lucy R. "Feminism and Prehistory." In *Overlay: Contemporary Art and the Art of Prehistory*, 41–75. New York: Pantheon, 1983.

Lissak, Rivka Shpak. *Pluralism and Progressives: Hull House and the New Immigrants, 1890–1919*. Chicago: Univ. of Chicago Press, 1989.

Loye, David, and Riane Eisler. "Chaos and Transformation: Implications of Nonequilibrium Theory for Social Science and Society." *Behavioral Science* 32 (1987): 53–65.

Martin, Bruce K. "Teaching Literature as Experience." *College English* 51 (1989): 377–85.

Martin, Jane Roland. "Gilman's Mothers." *Reclaiming a Conversation: The Ideal of the Educated Woman*, 139–70. New Haven: Yale Univ. Press, 1985.

Martin, Prestonia Mann. *Prohibiting Poverty: Suggestions for a Method of Obtaining Economic Security*. New York: Farrar & Rinehart, 1932.

Marcus, Jane. "Still Practice, A/Wrested Alphabet: Toward a Feminist Aesthetic" (1984). In *Feminist Issues in Literary Scholarship*, edited by Shari Benstock. Bloomington: Indiana Univ. Press, 1987.

Mason, Mary G. "The Other Voice: Autobiographies of Women Writers." In *Life/Lines: Theorizing Women's Autobiography*, edited by Bella Brodski and Celeste Schenck, 19–44. Ithaca, N.Y.: Cornell Univ. Press, 1988.

Meyering, Sheryl L., ed. *Charlotte Perkins Gilman: The Woman and Her Work*. Foreword by Cathy N. Davidson. Ann Arbor: Univ. of Michigan, 1989.

Miller, Alice. *For Your Own Good: Hidden Cruelty in Child-Rearing and the Roots of Violence*. New York: Farrar, Straus, Giroux, 1983.

————. *The Drama of the Gifted Child: How Narcissistic Parents Form and Deform the Emotional Lives of Their Talented Children.* 1979. Reprint, New York: Basic, 1981.

Miller, Casey, and Kate Swift. *Words and Women: New Language in New Times.* New York: Doubleday, 1977.

Miller, Jean Baker. *Toward a New Psychology of Women.* Boston: Beacon, 1976.

Miller, Nancy K. "Emphasis Added: Plots and Plausibilities in Women's Fiction." *PMLA* 96 (1981): 36–48.

————. "Writing Fictions: Women's Autobiography in France." In *Life/Lines: Theorizing Women's Autobiography,* edited by Bella Brodski and Celeste Schenck, 45–61. Ithaca, N.Y.: Cornell Univ. Press, 1988.

Montagu, Ashley. *The Natural Superiority of Women.* New York: Macmillan, 1952.

Morson, Gary Saul, and Caryl Emerson. *Mikhail Bakhtin: Creation of a Prosaics.* Stanford, Calif.: Stanford Univ. Press, 1990.

Moylan, Tom. *Demand the Impossible: Science Fiction and the Utopian Imagination.* New York: Methuen, 1986.

"N[ew] E[ngland] W[oman's] P[ress] A[ssociation]. "The Business Woman's Home." *Woman's Journal* (22 Oct. 1898): 340.

O'Brien, Sharon. *Willa Cather: The Emerging Voice.* New York: Oxford Univ. Press, 1987.

Olerich, Henry. *A Cityless and Countryless World: An Outline of Practical Co-Operative Individualism.* Holstein, Iowa: Gilmore and Olerich, 1893.

Olsen, Tillie. *Silences.* New York: Delacorte, 1978.

Olson, Carl, ed. *The Book of the Goddess Past and Present: An Introduction to Her Religion.* New York: Crossroad, 1985.

Orenstein, Gloria Feman. *The Reflowering of the Goddess.* Elmsford, NY: Pergamon, 1990.

Palmeri, Ann. "Charlotte Perkins Gilman: Forerunner of a Feminist Social Science." In *Discovering Reality: Feminist Perpsectives on Epistemology, Metaphysics, Methodology, and Philosophy of Science,* edited by Sandra Harding and Merill B. Hintikka. Boston: D. Reidel, 1983.

Perry, Ruth. Introduction. In *Mothering the Mind: Twelve Studies of Writers and Their Silent Partners,* edited by Ruth Perry and Martine Watson Brownley. New York: Holmes and Meier, 1984.

Phelps [Ward], Elizabeth Stuart. *The Story of Avis.* 1877. Reprint, edited by Carol Farley Kessler. New Brunswick: Rutgers Univ. Press, 1988.

————. *Doctor Zay.* 1882. Reprint, edited by Michael Sartisky. New York: Feminist, 1987.

Piercy, Marge. *Woman on the Edge of Time.* New York: Knopf, 1976.

Plaskow, Judith and Carol Christ, eds. *Weaving the Visions: New Patterns in Feminist Spirituality.* New York: HarperCollins, 1989.

Polacheck, Hilda Satt. *I Came a Stranger: The Story of a Hull-House Girl.* Urbana: Univ. of Illinois Press, 1989.

Rabuzzi, Kathryn Allen. *Motherself: A Mythic Analysis of Motherhood.* Bloomington: Indiana Univ. Press, 1988.

Radway, Janice A. "The Book-of-the-Month Club and the General Reader: On the Uses of 'Serious' Fiction." *Critical Inquiry* 14 (1988): 516–38.

———. "Identifying Ideological Seams: Mass Culture, Analytical Method, and Political Practice." *Communications* 9 (1986): 93–123.

———. *Reading the Romance: Women, Patriarchy, and Popluar Literature.* Chapel Hill: Univ. of North Carolina Press, 1984.

Rank, Otto. "Creative Urge and Personality Development." In *Art and Artist: Creative Urge and Personality Development,* translated by Charles Francis Atkinson, 3–33. New York: Knopf, 1932.

———. "Deprivation and Renunciation." In *Art and Artist: Creative Urge and Personality Development,* translated by Charles Francis Atkinson, 415–31. New York: Knopf, 1932.

———. "Life and Creation." In *Art and Artist: Creative Urge and Personality Development,* translated by Charles Francis Atkinson, 37–65. New York: Knopf, 1932.

Rich, Adrienne. "Compulsory Heterosexuality and Lesbian Experience." *Signs* 5 (1980): 631–60. Reprint, *Blood, Bread, and Poetry.* New York: Norton, 1986.

———. *Of Woman Born: Motherhood as Experience and Institution.* New York: Norton, 1976.

Rhode, Deborah L., ed. *Theoretical Perspectives on Sexual Difference.* New Haven: Yale Univ. Press, 1990.

Rose, Phyllis. *Parallel Lives: Five Victorian Marriages.* New York: Knopf, 1984.

Rossi, Alice, ed. *The Feminist Papers: From Adams to de Beauvoir.* 1973. Reprint, New York: Bantam, 1974.

Ruddick, Sara. *Maternal Thinking: Toward a Politics of Peace.* Boston: Beacon, 1989.

Ruppert, Peter. *Reader in a Strange Land: The Activity of Reading Literary Utopias.* Athens: Univ. of Georgia Press, 1986.

Russ, Joanna. *The Female Man.* New York: Bantam, 1975. Reprint, Boston: Gregg-G. K. Hall, 1977.

———. "What Can a Heroine Do? or Why Women Can't Write?" In *Images of Women in Fiction: Feminist Perspectives,* edited by Susan Koppelman Cornillon, 3–20. Bowling Green: Bowling Green Univ. Popular Press, 1973.

Rydell, Robert W. "The World's Columbian Exposition of 1893: Racist Underpinnings of a Utopian Artifact." *Journal of American Culture* 1 (1978): 253–75.

Said, Edward W. *Orientalism.* New York: Pantheon, 1978.

Scharnhorst, Gary. *Charlotte Perkins Gilman.* Twayne's United States Authors Series 482. Boston: Twayne Publishers, 1985.

———. *Charlotte Perkins Gilman: A Bibliography.* Scarecrow Author Bibliographies 71. Metuchen, N.J.: Scarecrow, 1985.

————. "Making Her Fame: Charlotte Perkins Gilman in California." *California History* 64 (Summer 1985): 192–201.

Schueller, Malini Johar. *The Politics of Voice: Liberalism and Social Criticism from Franklin to Kingston.* Albany: State Univ. of New York Press, 1992.

Showalter, Elaine. "Feminist Criticism in the Wilderness." In *The New Feminist Criticism: Essays on Women, Literature, and Theory,* New York: Pantheon, 1985.

Shumaker, Conrad. " 'Too Terribly Good to Be Printed': Charlotte Perkins Gilman's 'The Yellow Wallpaper.' " In *Charlotte Perkins Gilman: The Woman and Her Work,* edited by Sheryl L. Meyering. Ann Arbor: Univ. of Michigan Research Press, 1989.

Silko, Leslie Marmon. "Language and Literature from a Pueblo Indian Perspective." In *English Literature: Opening Up the Canon,* edited by Leslie A. Fiedler and Houston A. Baker, Jr., 54–72. Selected Papers from the English Institute, 1979. Baltimore: Johns Hopkins Univ. Press, 1981.

————. *Storyteller.* New York: Seaver, 1981.

Sklar, Kathryn Kish. *Catharine Beecher: A Study in American Domesticity.* New Haven: Yale Univ. Press, 1973.

————. "Hull House in the 1890s: A Community of Women Reformers." *Signs* 10 (1985): 658–77.

Smith-Rosenberg, Carroll. "The Female World of Love and Ritual: Relations Between Women in Nineteenth-Century America." *Signs* 1 (1975): 1–30. Reprint, *Disorderly Conduct: Visions of Gender in Victorian America.* New York: Oxford Univ. Press, 1985.

Spelman, Elizabeth V. *Inessential Woman: Problems of Exclusion in Feminist Thought.* Boston: Beacon, 1988.

Spender, Dale. *Women of Ideas and What Men Have Done to Them: From Aphra Behn to Adrienne Rich.* London: Routledge, 1982.

Spretnak, Charlene. *The Spiritual Dimension of Green Politics.* Santa Fe, N. Mex.: Bear, 1986.

————, ed. *The Politics of Women's Spirituality: Essays on the Rise of Spiritual Power within the Feminist Movement.* New York: Doubleday, 1982.

Spretnak, Charlene, and Fritjof Capra. *Green Politics: The Global Promise.* New York: Dutton, 1984.

Stanton, Elizabeth Cady. *The Woman's Bible.* 1895–1898. New York: Arno, 1972.

Starhawk [Miriam Simos]. *Truth or Dare: Encounters with Power, Authority, and Mystery.* San Francisco: Harper, 1987.

Stetson, Charles Walter. In *Endure: The Diaries of Charles Walter Stetson,* edited by Mary Armfield Hill. Philadelphia: Temple Univ. Press, 1985.

Stimpson, Catharine R. "Are the Differences Spreading: Feminist Criticism and Postmodernism." *English Studies in Canada* 15:4 (1989): 364–82.

————. "Feminisms and Utopia." Keynote Address. *Utopian Studies III,* edited by Michael S. Cummings, and Nicholas D. Smith, 1–5. Lanham, Md.: Univ. Press of America, 1991.

Stone, Merlin. *When God Was a Woman*. New York: Schocken, 1976.

Stowe, Harriet Beecher. *Lady Byron Vindicated*. Boston: Fields, Osgood, 1870.

———. *Uncle Tom's Cabin; or, Life among the Lowly*. Boston: John P. Jewett, 1852.

Tanner, Nancy Makepeace. *On Becoming Human*. Cambridge: Cambridge Univ. Press, 1981.

Thompson, Clara. *On Women*. New York: New American Library, 1967.

Toch, Hans. *The Social Psychology of Social Movements*. New York: Bobbs-Merrill, 1965.

Tompkins, Jane. "Me and My Shadow." In *Gender and Theory: Dialogues on Feminist Criticism*, edited by Linda Kauffman, 121–39. London: Basil Blackwell, 1989.

———. *Sensational Designs: The Cultural Work of American Fiction 1790–1860*. New York: Oxford Univ. Press, 1985.

Turner, Victor. "Liminality and Communitas." In *The Ritual Process: Structure and Anti-Structure*, 94–130. Chicago: Aldine, 1969.

van Gennep, Arnold. *The Rites of Passage*. 1908. Reprint, Chicago: Univ. of Chicago Press, 1960.

Veblen, Thorstein. "The Economic Theory of Women's Dress." *Popular Science Monthly* 56 (Nov. 1894): 198–205.

———. "Dress as an Expression of the Pecuniary Culture." In *The Theory of Leisure Class: An Economic Study of Institutions*, Chap. 12. New York: Macmillan, 1899.

Walkerdine, Valerie. "Some Day My Prince Will Come: Young Girls and the Preparation for Adolescent Sexuality." In *Gender and Generation*, edited by A. McRobbie and M. Nava. New York: Macmillan, 1984.

Wallace, Anthony N. B. "Revitalization Movements." *American Anthropologist* 58 (1956): 264–81.

Ward, Lester Frank. *Dynamic Sociology*. New York: Appleton, 1883.

———. "Our Better Halves." *Forum* 6 (Nov. 1888): 266–75.

———. "The Past and Future of the Sexes." *Independent* 60 (Mar. 1906): 541–45.

———. *Pure Sociology*. 1893. New York: Macmillan, 1903.

———. *Psychic Factors in Civilization*. Boston: Ginn, 1893.

Watson, Barbara Bellow. "On Power and the Literary Text." *Signs* 1 (1975): 111–18.

Waugh, Patricia. *Feminine Fictions: Revisiting the Postmodern*. London: Routledge, 1989.

———. *Metafiction: The Theory and Practice of Self-Conscious Fiction*. London: Methuen, 1984.

Weimann, Jeanne Madeleine. *The Fair Women: The Story of the Woman's Building, World's Columbian Exposition, Chicago 1893*. Chicago: Academy, 1981.

Westkott, Marcia. *The Feminist Legacy of Karen Horney*. New York: Oxford Univ. Press, 1986.

Wharton, Edith. "Expiation." *The Descent of Man*. New York: Scribner's, 1904.

White, Connie L. and Thomas L. Erskine, eds. *"The Yellow Wallpaper"*. Women Writers: Text and Context series. New Brunswick, N.J.: Rutgers Univ. Press, Fall 1993.

White, Lynn K., Alan Booth, and John N. Edwards. "Children and Marital Happiness: Why the Negative Correlation?" *Journal of Family Issues* 7 (1986): 131–47.

Wilson, Christopher P. "Charlotte Perkins Gilman's Steady Burghers: The Terrain of *Herland*." In *Charlotte Perkins Gilman: The Woman and Her Work*, edited by Sheryl L. Meyering, 173–90. Ann Arbor: Univ. of Michigan Research Press, 1989.

Winkler, Barbara Scott. "Victorian Daughters: The Lives and Feminism of Charlotte Perkins Gilman and Olive Schreiner." [Univ. of] *Michigan Occasional Paper* 13. Ann Arbor: American Culture Program, 1980.

Wyatt, Jean. *Reconstructing Desire: The Role of the Unconscious in Women's Reading and Writing*. Chapel Hill: Univ. of North Carolina Press, 1990.

Yeager, Patricia. *Honey-Mad Women: Emancipatory Strategies in Women's Writing*. Gender and Culture Series. New York: Columbia Univ. Press, 1988.

Young-Eisendrath, Polly. *Hags and Heroines: A Feminist Approach to Jungian Psychotherapy with Couples*. Toronto: Inner City, 1984.

Zagarell, Sandra A. "Narrative of Community: The Identification of a Genre." *Signs* 13 (1988): 498–527.

———. "Narrative of Community: Speculating on Nineteenth-Century American Writers." American Literature Association Conference, Washington, D.C., May 1991.

Index

99, 110; mental health of, 14, 18, 20, 22, 24, 29–30, 39, 100–101, 105; as a mother, 9, 19, 22, 25–27, 33, 46, 52, 88, 90, 93–95, 99, 107; as a novelist, 42; paternal relationship, 9, 16–17, 18, 19, 25, 30, 86, 88, 89, 95; peer relationships of, 17, 19–20, 22–23, 25, 27–29, 88, 95, 100; and personal freedom, 90, 92–93, 104, 109; personal life critics of, 26–28, 40; public persona of, 22, 39, 105, 106–14; as public speaker, 13–14, 22, 23, 25–30, 33–38, 53, 54, 96, 98; as a racist, 39, 45, 47–48, 50–52, 56, 68, 73, 74, 76–77; and reading, 89; and self-denial, 18, 20, 22, 39, 106; and self-denigration, 14, 39, 98, 100–101, 105; as social activist, 4–7, 10–14, 18, 20–22, 27–30, 34–41, 54, 58, 80–83, 89, 91, 102–8, 111–16, 220

Gilman, Charlotte Perkins—Major Life Events and Stages: birth, 14, 16; birth of daughter, 22, 39, 107, 110; childhood, 16–19, 26, 52, 84–88, 93, 94–95, 102, 106, 108; depression, 14, 18, 22, 29–30, 39, 53, 98, 101, 129; divorce, 9, 26, 28; first marriage, 9, 20–25, 54, 57, 104, 110; marital separation, 22; parents' divorce, 16–17; pregnancy, 21–22; retirement, 39, 42–43; second marriage, 9, 11–12, 21–22, 25, 33, 49, 53, 64, 92, 93, 99, 106, 108, 110; suicide, 13, 40–41, 82; surrender of daughter, 26–27, 29, 93–94

Gilman, Charlotte Perkins—Works:
—Books: Books are listed as separate index entries
—Drama: *Changing Hands,* 22; *A Pretty Idiot,* 22; "Interrupted," 37
—Essays: "Applepieville," 78, 79; "The Beauty of the Block," 9, 45, 64; "The Dress and the Body," 35–36; "Everyday Ethical Problems," 28; "How Home Conditions React upon the Family," 45, 46–47;

"Making Towns Fit to Live In," 78, 79–80; "The Passing of the Home in Great American Cities," 45–46; "Progress Through Birth Control," 39; "Sex and Race Progress," 39; "Standardizing Towns," 78–79, 80; "Studies in Style," 28; "A Suggestion on the Negro Problem," 45, 47–48, 50; "The Waste of Private Housekeeping," 55, 59, 63, 66, 79, 137; "Why Cooperative Housekeeping Fails," 45, 46–47, 55, 137; "Working Love," 30, 72; "World Rousers," 220
—Lectures: "The Falsity of Freud," 38; "Home: Past, Present and Future," 30; "The Larger Feminism," 13, 38; "The New Motherhood," 30; "Our Brains and What Ails Them," 30; "Studies in Masculism," 38; "Women and Politics," 30
—Poems: "Nature's Answer," 22; "Similar Cases," 23; "Six Hours a Day," 26, 47; "Two Callings," 13
—Serialization: "The Dress of Women," 35; "Growth and Combat," 36; "Humanness," 35; "Our Brains and What Ails Them," 35, 66, 70, 111; "Social Ethics," 35
—Short stories: Short stories are listed as separate index entries
—Unpublished: "The Balsam Fir," 37; "A Dream," 85; "A Fairy Tale," 17, 85–88, 94; "The Literary and Artistic Vurks of the Princess Charlotte," 10, 17, 82, 84, 88, 94, 95; "Prince Cherry," 88; "A Proclamation of Interdependence," 80; "The Story of Mr. and Mrs. Rabbit," 88; "Unpunished," 40

Gilman, Charlotte Perkins—Writing in General: criticism of, 23–24, 26, 31–32, 35, 42, 47, 117; detective, 40; dramatic, 13, 22; effects of, 1–7, 10–11, 13–14, 24–25, 35, 41, 42, 57–58; emotions